The Economics of Flexible Exchange Rates

Proceedings of a Conference at the Institute for Advanced Studies, Vienna, March 29-31, 1978

Beihefte zu Kredit und Kapital

Heft 6

The Economics of Flexible Exchange Rates

Proceedings of a Conference at the Institute for Advanced Studies, Vienna, March 29-31, 1978

Edited by

Helmut Frisch
Technical University of Vienna

Gerhard Schwödiauer
University of Bielefeld

DUNCKER & HUMBLOT / BERLIN

Gedruckt 1980 bei Fotokop Wilhelm Weihert, Darmstadt 1
Printed in Germany
ISBN 3 428 04644 7

CONTENTS

PREFACE

We are pleased to present the outcome of a conference held at the Vienna Institute for Advanced Studies from March 29th to 31st, 1978. It reflects the theoretical discussion and empirical findings on the role of flexible exchange rates since the Stockholm conference in 1975. Special emphasis has been given to the problem of small open economies.

The volume opens with a paper by Martin Bronfenbrenner analyzing the advantages partial indexation schemes offer in particular for small countries open to both internal and external shocks. It is followed by a group of theoretical contributions by Staffan Viotti, Masanao Aoki, Alfred Steinherr (in cooperation with Paul De Grauwe and Giorgio Basevi), Jacob Frenkel, Dale Henderson, and Harmen Lehment which deal with the dynamics implied by a regime of flexible exchange rates, the demand for international reserves, and the efficacy of exchange market interventions and monetary policy. A variety of empirical research results are presented in the papers by William Dewald, Martin Fase and A. Huijser, Peter Bernholz and Peter Kugler, Werner Gaab, Karl Socher, Heinz Handler, Fritz Schebeck, Hannes Suppanz and Gunther Tichy. The volume closes with an empirical study on the impact of financial policies on the volatility of exchange rates in the industrialized countries by Paul De Grauwe.

This is certainly a somewhat heterogenous collection of stimulating pieces of research whose diversity indicates, however, the broadness of analytical and empirical questions posed by the institution of flexible exchange rates as well as the liveliness of the debate at the Vienna conference. It is the editors' hope that this publication may be an encouragement to further research into the problems of economic policy under flexible exchange rates.

The conference has been made possible by a grant from the Austrian Ministry of Finance. The editors wish to thank the Austrian Vice Chancellor and Minister of Finance, Dr. Hannes Androsch, for this generous support. They also acknowledge gratefully the organizational help provided by the Institute for Advanced Studies in Vienna and its staff.

Helmut Frisch Gerhard Schwödiauer

A PARTIAL INDEXATION SCHEME

Martin Bronfenbrenner

"Half a loaf is better than no bread". (Anglo-American Proverb)

RATIONALE

There is no need to review before a group of economists with relatively fixed nominal incomes the rationale of indexation schemes in inflationary environments, as applied to at least the progressive taxes, to at least the lower public-sector salaries and pensions, to relief and allied social security payments in cash, and to the nominal value of at least the non-marketable public debt.[1)] If a rationale is needed, it is for making such schemes only partial.[2)]

Two major difficulties appear to have arisen under (nearly) full indexation plans, causing their abandonment or modification. One of these problems is positive and the other normative. Both are more severe, and hence more important, in small countries open to both internal and external shocks than in large countries more capable of fending off the external ones.

---

1) The current (1977) Chairman of the U.S. Council of Economic Advisers, Dr. Charles Schultze, has suggested in public discussion that, after inflation has raised nominal interest rates on public securities, recipients of the increased interest income are less entitled than others to claim additional benefits of indexing their tax payments. I am not convinced by Schultze's arguments, but in any case, if the nominal value of such securities were indexed (and the subsequent fictitious "capital gains" exempted from income taxation) the nominal rates on the securities would be largely insensitive to inflation rates, so that Schultze's problem would be a non-problem.

2) This partial character is proposed to apply only to governmental indexations. Private firms may, in an incompletely socialized economy, retain the option of more complete indexation than the public sector, but at their own risk.

The positive difficulty is the danger of accelerating the inflation rate as the result of Acts of God or other random disturbances unconnected with any errors in macroeconomic policy which the country may have made. (Such disturbances may result from the weather, OPEC, Peruvian anchovies, Japanese trading companies, foreigners' macroeconomic blunders, or what have you.) The difficulty is accentuated when the indexation scheme includes an extra modicum of compensation - called in America a "kicker" - for the inevitable lag in the periodic indexational adjustments behind the actual rise of the price indexes. Indexational adjustments must be financed, and the financing process normally involves currency and credit expansion - a rightward shift in the LM side of the standard Hicksian cross. In addition, the indexational payments are included in government spending and set off additional consumption and possibly also investment expenditures, shifting the Hicksian IS curve to the right as well, augmented by the Keynesian multiplier.[3)]

The normative difficulty has arisen most starkly, I believe, in Israel in connection with war and defense inflation during and after 1973.[4)] Suppose an economy to suffer damage in real terms from a war, a crop failure, a sharp increase in pressure-group militance, or some other shock external or internal. Had this damage or loss been reflected or acknowledged in higher nominal taxes or in lower nominal social expenditures, fixed-income receivers would have suffered along with everyone else. If, for whatever reason right or wrong, the government decides upon an

---

3) If the axes of the Hicksian cross diagram are in real terms, as they should be for reasonable stability, the analysis of the last two sentences requires some recasting. Under these definitions, the IS and LM functions need not indeed move outward at all. Rather, the inward movement is prevented, which might otherwise have reduced the Keynesian "inflationary gap" had it been permitted to work itself out.

4) See Ephraim Kleiman, "Monetary Correction and Indexation; The Brazilian and Israeli Experience", in NBER, Explorations in Economic Research (Winter 1977), pp.144-153.

inflation tax instead, there is no better reason to exempt fixed-income receivers as full indexation would do.

A PARTIAL INDEXATION FORMULA

What is needed for successful partial indexation is a plausible "quick-and-dirty" formula for separating the effects of shocks from those of public monetary and fiscal operations. The task of this section is to supply such a formula.

Let the trended income growth rate of the economy be G_y, and the current growth rate of a broadly-defined money stock[5)] G_m. Let the trended change in velocity be G_v,[6)] the current growth rate of "autonomous expenditures" G_a,[7)] and the current growth rate of public receipts (less transfers) G_r.

We can now define a normal (un-shocked) inflation rate $\overline{G}_p$ for any year as

$$\overline{G}_p = G_o + h(G_m + G_v - G_y) + kG_a - jG_r$$

---

5) In American notation, the money stock involved should perhaps be M_2, M_3, or M_5. (It should include savings deposits in commercial banks, in savings banks, savings and loan shares, and-or large certificates of deposit.)

6) The velocity concept should of course be consistent with the money stock concept used.

7) A crude "autonomous expenditures" concept, which ignores both exogenous elements in consumption and endogenous elements in other expenditure components, is the sum of (1) gross private domestic investment I, (2) public expenditure (exclusive of transfers) G, and (3) the foreign trade balance B, or exports (X) less imports (M). (The last two terms may of course be negative.) This crude concept I derive from the Friedman-Meiselman tests of the Keynesian system and the equation of exchange for the U.S. in the early 196os, except that F-M use the public deficit as a single term. (Milton Friedman and David Meiselman, "The Relative Stability of the Velocity of Circulation and the Investment Multiplier," in Commission on Money and Credit, Stabilization Policies (1963)).

where (G_o, h, k, j) are parameters fitted by ordinary least squares over the last n periods, with G_v and G_y averaged over all the observations, and with G_m, G_a, G_t varying from period to period.[8)]

An attractive feature of this form is its neutrality in the ongoing monetarist-fiscalist debate. If "Chicago-type" monetarism applies in the country with which we are dealing, we should expect h (or Σh_α in the more complex form of Note 8) to approach unity, while $G_o{}^k$ and j (or Σk_β and Σj_β) would be close to zero. If, on the other hand, the country's macroeconomic structure were more fiscalist, k and-or j might well exceed h. If "structural" cost-pushes, profit-stretches, and-or wage-price spirals were in operation, they would be reflected in a large positive G_o. In a developing country with its monetary sector encroaching upon its subsistence or barter sector, one might likewise expect a large and positive G_o.

Given an estimate of the normal or shock-free inflation rate $\overline{G}_p$ which will ordinarily differ from the actual rate G_p, how may a partial-indexation rule be applied? The answer, in my view, is to assume that the residual or differential inflation rate $G_p - \overline{G}_p$ represents the negative or positive effect of favorable or unfavorable shocks, and to use whichever figure is lower as the basis for indexation. (The deflator will be, say, $(1 + \overline{G}_p)$ rather than $\overline{G}_p$ itself.)

---

8) A considerably more complex form for which allows for lags on both the monetary and the fiscal sides may be written:

$$\overline{G}_p = G_o + \sum_{\alpha=0}^{n} h_\alpha (G_{m,t-\alpha} + G_v - G_y) + \sum_{\beta=0}^{m} k_\beta G_{a,t-\beta} - \sum_{\beta=0}^{m} j_\beta G_{r,t-\beta}$$

Unless both α and β are small, or unless the h_α terms are related artifically by some formula (and likewise the k_β) this complex form involves the loss of large numbers of degrees of freedom - a definite disadvantage in empirical work.

Also, as a further buffer against acceleration of inflation, the prices from which G_p and indirectly also $\overline{G}_p$, are computed should be taken net of sales taxes, excises, and import duties. In addition, direct taxes should in no way be treated as commodities in computing price levels. The contrary practices, which I believe to be embedded in the Italian scala mobile formulae, render anti-inflationary fiscal policies themselves indirect engines of inflation on the tax side.

THREE IRRITATING QUESTIONS

Three additional irritating questions enter our discussion at this stage:

1. How, in summary, do external shocks affect our proposed indexation pattern?
2. Does not our system harbor a certain built-in bias against its ostensible beneficiaries, by always using the lower of our two indexation bases, i.e., always taking Min (G_p, $\overline{G}_p$)? And if so, how can such a bias be justified?
3. How is our system affected by the country's foreign-exchange system?

Ad (1): Let us make our discussion temporarily less abstract, by recalling the events of 1973-74 in our representative small country. OPEC has taken measures which suddenly and unexpectedly increase the price of crude oil. The rise in petroleum prices has quickly permeated, in input-output fashion, the cost structure of our country's economy, sometimes directly and sometimes via imports. How would our partial indexation system respond?

The answer is: it depends. What does it depend upon? The extent to which our government makes a fiscal and-or monetary accommodation to the higher oil prices. Let us take two extreme cases, which I shall call Alpha and Beta. In practice, all the Western governments (and Japan), so far as I know, have followed long-term policies closer to Beta than to Alpha.

Policy Alpha makes no accommodation whatever to the higher oil prices. If our country has been following a Friedman-type monetary rule, it does not alter its monetary growth rate in any way. Rather than generalizing the rise in oil prices to the entire economy, this policy confines it to the domain of relative prices. If petroleum-intensive commodity prices rise, the rise is to be balanced by eventual declines in other prices, including profit margins and wage rates. The eventual movement of the general price level may be in either direction, depending upon computational vagaries, but will be small in the long run. In the short run, of course, such a stiff-necked non-accommodating policy runs a high risk of triggering a recession, unemployment, open or covert strikes or production slow-downs, and adverse popular votes at the next election - adverse, that is, to the non-accommodating government. But to return to indexation: this policy, right or wrong, noble or foolhardy, would have resulted in the OPEC-dominated climate of 1973-74 in complete insulation of the indexation percentage from the "oil shock". For however long $\overline{G}_p$ remained zero there would be no indexation whatever, regardless of the movement of G_p.

Policy Beta permits the higher oil prices to be absorbed without pressure on employment, real wages, or real profit margins in any sector of the economy. This policy can involve monetary and-or fiscal expansion, at the expense of a substantial degree of inflation and a minimal shift in the country's relative-price structure, as all prices rise more or less <u>pari passu</u> with those of oil and oil-intensive commodities. Because of these expansive macroeconomic policies, right or wrong, $\overline{G}_p$ would also rise, although usually remaining below G_p. As $\overline{G}_p$ rose, the indexation adjustment would come into play. But what would be indexed under policy Beta is only the monetary and fiscal accommodation to inflationary shocks, not the shocks themselves, which the domestic authorities might have been able to forecast but could not have prevented or warded off.

In terms of the so-called Scandinavian theory of inflation in small countries, as developed by Dr. Odd Aukrust in Norway:[9] Partial indexation is not proposed to compensate for inflation in "open" industries, whose prices and wages in the Aukrust schema merely reflect inflation of wages and prices in supplier or customer countries, but only for the further inflation of wages and prices in "sheltered" industries validated by measures like our policy Beta, which Aukrust supports or condones for reasons of equity between industrial sub-classes within the labor force.

Ad (2): I can devise no completely satisfactory or completely general ethical rationale for denying full indexation to sufferers from inflation. Most countries which have attempted indexation have, I believe, attempted an initial full-indexation basis on the principle of fiat iustitia ruat caelum. In some specific cases, however, including those already mentioned (p. 000), full indexation is itself objectionable on normative grounds after inflation-tax decisions have been openly or tacitly made. Another applicable analogy, permitting only partial indexation, may be wrung from the Anglo-American law of torts, in which a plaintiff must formally prove not only damages to himself but negligence by the tortfeasor, and where "Acts of God or the King's Enemies" constitute a sufficient defense.[1o]

---

9) Aukrust, "Prim I: A Model of the Price and Income Distribution Mechanism of an Open Economy", Artikler frå Statistisk Sentralbyrå (No. 35, 197o). See also Helmut Frisch, "Introduction - Inflation in Small Countries", in M.Beckmann and H.P. Künzi (eds.). Lecture Notes in Economics and Mathematical Systems (No. 119, 1974).

1o) This is not the case, however, under a "strict liability"rule, which applies in most American jurisdictions for claims arising from defects in manufacturing processes. Here the plaintiff must only prove damages - an analogy to full indexation in our own problem.

Most important than normative considerations is the danger of accelerating inflation in consequence of the indexing operations themselves. This danger always exists, but has often seemed minimal. The danger is greatest in small countries with high trade dependence in an environment of world-wide or nearly world-wide inflation. It is significantly less in larger countries more nearly self-sufficient. We do not and cannot prove that partial indexation by this scheme (or by most others[11)]) will always prevent acceleration of domestic inflation, or even hold such acceleration within pre-assigned bounds. The likelihood and the severity of such acceleration are however reduced quantitatively by our "minimum adjustment" rule as between G_p and $\overline{G}_p$.

Ad (3): Flexible exchange rate regimes tend to insulate a country's inflation rate from foreign shocks, while fixed rate regimes tend to strengthen international buffers against domestic shocks. Let me illustrate by hypothetical examples from the agricultural sector.

Bad crops overseas will raise prices less in an agricultural exporting country when they simultaneously raise export demand and up-value the country's exchange (flexible-rate regime) then when they simply raise export demand (fixed-rate regime). Bad domestic crops in an agricultural importing country, however, are less inflationary when fixed exchange rates permit imports at world prices than when they also raise the price of foreign exchange.

All such shocks, of course, whether temporary or long-range,

---

11) One exception to this generalization would be a partial-indexation scheme with a fixed maximum or "cap" (adjustments limited to inflation rates of, say, 5 % and below). Another exception would give some governmental authority discretion to disallow indexation adjustments which (in the authority's best judgement) would require financing by methods which would accelerate the inflation rate significantly. The first of these devices prevails, to some extent, in Brazil. (Compare Kleiman, op.cit., pp.153-168.)

affect primarily G_p rather than $\overline{G}_p$. If they eventually affect $\overline{G}_p$ as well, this will usually mean that fiscal and-or monetary policy has been affected by considerations of financing purchases or sales of foreign exchange, either to hold rates stable or to move them in one direction or the other. Many complexities are introduced by these and other exchange-market considerations, which earlier drafts of this paper had ignored entirely.[12)] I have considered several of these, "but evermore" as the Rubaiyat has it "came out by the same door wherein I went". Which is to say, I continue to recommend partial indexation by Min $(G_p, \overline{G}_p)$ regardless of the country's exchange regime, and regardless of the reactions of exchange rate considerations upon either estimated $\overline{G}_p$ or observed G_p.

ALTERNATIVES TO INDEXATION

Victims of inflation have not had to wait for, or rely on, indexations or escalations to defend themselves in some degree. The most popular defenses for the wealthy (or for those with access to substantial credit) have been the accumulation of inventories - land, precious metals, art objects, foreign exchange, equity securities - called "inflation hedges", which, the buyers anticipate, will be especially price-sensitive to inflation. In elasticity terms, if p is a general price level and p' the (anticipated) price of a potential inflation-hedge commodity:

$$E_{p'p} = \frac{d \log p'}{d \log p} = \frac{dp'}{dp} \frac{p}{p'} > 1$$

The practicability of inflation hedging (seldom high for the average citizen) is unaffected by indexation either partial or complete. But since the two devices are to some extent competitive

---

12) And which Professor Helmut Frisch then repeatedly urged me, in correspondence and conversation, to elaborate more explicitly.

in demand, the availability of indexation may be expected to lower somewhat both the anticipated inflation-hedge prices p' and the elasticity coefficients $E_{p'p}$ of the last equation. Indexation might conceivably displace certain marginal commodities from inflation-hedge status ($E_{p'p}$ significantly greater than unity) to normal commodity status ($E_{p'p} \leq 1$). Indexation would therefore arouse rational suspicion and opposition in the several inflation-hedge producing (and speculating) industries.

A second alternative to indexation for protection against inflation has been competition between currencies and precious metals, and likewise competition between currencies themselves. A historical example from the U.S. has been the "gold clause" popular in the early 2oth century but subsequently declared illegal in a famous (but probably erroneous) Supreme Court decision of 1935.[13] A gold cause in a 6 % bond issued in 192o and due in 198o entitled the holder in 198o to the number of ounces of gold represented by $ 1ooo in 192o, or alternatively, to the 198o dollar price of that weight of gold. Some but not all gold clauses also applied to the interest payments due over the 6o-year life of the bond.

The Nobel laureate Friedrich von Hayek has more recently suggested as an anti-inflationary device the reciprocal extension by the leading industrial countries of the legal-tender privilege to each others' currencies. This system would permit American

---

13) Baltimore and Ohio R.R. v Francis. My belief is that had the railroad bond owned by Mr. Francis fallen due only after the post-194o inflation developed substantially, the Supreme Court might well have decided "the other way". In 1935, unfortunately, Francis (the original plaintiff) appeared to be an unconscionable profiteer seeing a 75 percent capital gain from a 75 % rise on the price of gold, unaccompanied as yet by significant rises in living costs.

creditors today to stipulate future payment in whatever currency (U.S. dollars, British sterling, Swiss francs, German marks, Japanese yen, etc.) might seem most desirable today as a store of value or means of payment - or alternatively, in the dollar value of such currency when the debt fell due. This would not, of course, protect completely against truly world-wide inflation - nor did the gold clause protect against the "gold inflation" of 1896-1914 - but its degree of protection, assuming sufficiently anti-inflationary policy to be correctly anticipated for at least one country, might seem at least comparable to partial-indexation schemes like our own.

My worries about Professor Hayek's currency-competition proposal can be illustrated by supposing, first of all, some temporary reversal in the contemporary inflationary surge. Such a reversal occurred, to many people's surprise, in the United States in the two years prior to the Korean War, beginning in mid-1948. In such a deflationary episode, equity would seem to require that debtors have parallel rights to specify under the Hayek proposal the currency in which payment is to be made. And if inflation were subsequently to resume (as it did in the U.S. in mid-195o), there would seem no ethical reason to leave the rules of competition between paper and metals, or among rival currencies, to be determined unilaterally by creditor interests. But if the rules were not so determined, net deflation (disguised perhaps as "disinflation") would immediately involve Gresham's (or Bodin's) Law - bad money drives out good. In which case the Hayek proposal would have made matters worse rather than better in all countries but the one with the weakest (most inflationary) currency in the group of countries Hayek has in mind.[14)]

14) I accept Professor Émile Claasen's defense (on the Conference floor) of the Hayek proposal as even-handed between debtors and creditors, since "currency choice" is a matter jointly determined. This joint-determination feature, however, increases creditor's risk in inflationary times, and makes the plan less effective as a rival to indexation. For a restatement of the Hayek argument, see his Denationalisation of Money (London: Institute of Economic Affairs, 1978).

Illustrations of currency-competition and broadened legal-tender privileges gone bad are frequent in American history - first in the colonial period and repeatedly in the "wildcat banking", "greenback", and "free silver" controversies of the 19th century. Proposals to "monetize the land" were endemic at least until the closing of the frontier in the 189o's. The great revolutionary democratic and populist orator Patrick Henry first rose to prominence by supporting a Virginia ordinance requiring clergymen of the Established (Anglican) Church to accept their stipends in tobacco rather than specie when the price of tobacco was falling. The Constitution of 1789 contains a prohibition on the States (although not on the new Federal Government, despite the "Continental Currency" inflation of the Revolutionary War period shortly preceding) not only from issuing competitive currencies but from making anything but specie legal tender for debt payments. Such history as this, and its equivalents in other countries at many stages of development, suggests to me real danger in the Hayek proposal.

DEFLATION AND QUASI-DEFLATION

Any such sustained deflation as marked the final third of the 19th century in most Western countries may seem too fantastic for serious consideration. Indeed, I should not be interpreted as either desiring or forecasting any such development. But should some such deflation (or a smaller and shorter one) in fact occur, it may be worth considering whether and how our proposed partial-indexation rule might fit such radically-changed circumstances.

Our formula is, to repeat, deflation by the smaller of the observed inflation rate G_p and the "normal" (unshocked) rate $\bar{G}_p$, ascribable to monetary and fiscal policies and defined as:

$$G_o + h(G_m + G_v - G_y) + kG_a - jG_r$$

But this rule assumed both G_p and $\bar{G}_p$ to be positive, as per the standard definition of inflation. If our problem is instead deflation with G_p and $\bar{G}_p$ both negative, I propose instead "reflation" by the larger of the two, i.e., by Max (G_p, $\bar{G}_p$); the value closest to zero in absolute terms.

A positive rationale for such a choice is, as in the inflation case, to reduce the danger of acceleration - in this case, of accelerated deflation. A normative rationale, occasionally discussed by apostles of slow "neutral money" deflation in the 192o's and 193o's, is to permit fixed income receivers to share in the higher living standards brought on by technical progess (which the "neutral money" writers, at least, presumed to be the dominant cause of negative G_p in the absence of monetary growth).

One last case to be considered is the uncertain one which I propose as call quasi-deflation. Here the couplet (G_p, $\bar{G}_p$) is of opposite sign. In this case, which may have prevailed in the United States during some part of the 1946-48 period, I propose indexation by whichever of the couplet is closest to zero in absolute value. This is consistent with both our inflation and deflation proposals, although in such circumstances significant acceleration of either inflation or deflation can hardly be a serious problem.

COMMENT ON M. BRONFENBRENNER, "A PARTIAL INDEXATION SCHEME"

Emil-Maria Claassen

The two arguments given in favour of partial indexation and against full indexation are not very convincing.

The first concerns the well-known inflation acceleration hypothesis. The financing of indexational adjustments would "normally involve currency and credit expansion". This is a possible but not a necessary outcome. In this context it is important to know what are the motivations for which the government proposes the introduction of indexation. If the main reason is the neutralization of the real effects of inflation (employment, allocation and distribution effects) without any precise inflation target, the acceleration hypothesis is a possible case. However, if indexation is introduced as one instrument of an anti-inflationary policy where indexation should mainly correct wrong inflationary expectations, and if the other instrument is a monetary policy in terms of a monetary growth target, the possibility of inflation acceleration would be excluded. But still if monetary policy was conducted very badly, the acceleration of inflation could also happen with partial indexation even though to a lesser extent.

The second argument against full indexation is that of the fiscal implications it would have. But this is an argument - and an important one - against any anti-inflationary policy. We know that the State is the biggest winner of inflation. Consequently, any anti-inflationary measure and any indexation imply a fiscal reform or a reduction in the growth rate of public expenditures.

Generally, the notion of "partial" remains ambiguous for the reader. It could be partial in the sense that only a part of all contracts in the economy are indexed. This holds in Martin Bronfenbrenner's paper because only government expenditures and government receipts are indexed. The question remains open because one does not know that is happening in the private sector; probably individuals have the freedom to index their contracts. "Partial" can also mean to choose the lowest inflation indicator if there are several ones which differ from each other. The main bulk of the paper is devoted to this latter question.

There are two annual inflation rates (in the paper), the acutal one and the "normal" or "pure" one. The "normal" inflation rate represents the "pure" inflation phenomenon generated in Martin Bronfenbrenner's model by monetary and/or fiscal impulses. The formula for the "normal" inflation rate is so general that nearly each inflation theory could interprete it in its favour. My critical comment is not on that formula, but on the need to have a such formula.

The other inflation rate which is the observed one is sensible to changes in relative prices (due to external shocks like the increase in the oil price or in agricultural product prices as a consequence of a crop failure). This sensibility is either temporary or permanent.

In the first case where monetary policy is not changed there is a time lag in price flexibility. Some relative prices have increased and only after a certain time other relative prices will decline so that the actual inflation rate will decline as well. If this time lag in price flexibility covers normally a period longer than a year, the need for Bronfenbrenner's formula is justified. However, if this time lag is by far shorter, there is no urgent need for it because his indexation scheme refers to an annual indexation.

In the second case there is an increase in relative prices with an accommodation of monetary policy which allows that other relative prices do not need to fall. This monetary accommodation will affect all prices included those goods the relative price of which has increased.

In such a situation where the initial change in relative prices will be maintained, Bronfenbrenner's "normal" inflation rate will attain the actual inflation rate even though with a certain time lag depending on the time dimension between the monetary accommodation and its effect on the general price level. The case can even be made that the choice of the actual inflation rate as the basis of indexation is a better one than that of the "normal" inflation rate because it would imply a smooth and steady adjustment instead of an abrupt one in the case of the "normal" inflation rate as the indicator for indexation.

I do not see why the problems of indexation may be different in a system of fixed exchange rates versus a system of flexible exchange rates. What is different is the determination of the inflation rate: in the first case and depending on the size of the country it is determined mainly in the international economy and in the second case it is determined mainly in the national economy. If an indexation scheme is utilized as an anti-inflationary measure (together with a restrictive monetary policy), it is certain that its efficiency is limited in a regime of fixed rates because any anti-inflationary policy has to be conducted on a world-wide basis.

At the end of the paper the reader begins to recognize that the motivation of Bronfenbrenner's scheme is the protection against inflation because he discusses in length other alternatives to indexation as an "inflation hedge" like, for instance, the acquisition of certain physical assets or of certain less inflationary currencies.

Our comment should be read and understood in the sense that indexation is utilized as one instrument within the bundle of anti-inflationary measures in order to neutralize the inflationary expectations which can represent one cause of the acceleration of inflation or a cause of the unemployment effects when anti-inflationary measures are undertaken. Indexation as an anti-inflationary weapon does certainly not exclude that it constitutes simultaneously a protection against inflation.

When Bronfenbrenner discusses currency competition as a possible "inflation hedge", there is no need to go until the Hayek proposal. It would be already sufficient to eliminate the interdiction of interest payments on sight deposits and to assure that the banks are sufficiently competitive among each other.

That a deceleration of inflation or a deflation disfavours the debtors is a matter of course such that the debtors have the main interest to commit indexed credit contracts. Because Bronfenbrenner's scheme concerns only the indexation of transactions by the public sector, his scheme would be adopted even more easily by the government when it pursues simultaneously an anti-inflationary policy. So his discussion of indexation in the context of "disinflation" seems to me to constitute a "no problem".

INFLATION, THE TERMS OF TRADE AND FLEXIBLE EXCHANGE RATES*

Staffan Viotti

I. INTRODUCTION

The asset approach to exchange rate dynamics has brought a minor revolution to the theory of flexible exchange rates. As is amply demonstrated by for instance the contributions of the 1975 conference in Saltsjöbaden (see especially the papers by Dornbusch (1976) and Kouri (1976)), this approach explains in a very simple way the high volatility of the exchange rate in the short run. It also shows that the well-known propositions about the relation between inflation rates and the development of the exchange rate are propositions about the long run with little relevance for the explanation of short-run behavior.

The models used in the asset approach to exchange rate dynamics have been either explicitly partial or with the general equilibrium structure only vaguely sketched.[1)] The focus is on the monetary side of the economy, and the real side is neglected. This makes a comparison with the general equilibrium treatments of the fixed exchange rate case difficult. It also makes it difficult to study how traditional demand management policy influences the development of prices and exchange rates.

---

* This paper draws on earlier work done in collaboration with Lars Nyberg, who has also contributed to this paper with several helpful comments and suggestions. I am also indebted to Assar Lindbeck, Horst Herberg, Benjamin Cohen, Uwe Westphal and to the participants of the seminar at the Institute for International Economic Studies for comments on earlier drafts.

1) Two notable exceptions are Aoki (1978) and Henderson (1978)

The purpose of this paper is to integrate in the simplest possible way the monetary and real sectors in the analysis of flexible exchange rate dynamics. We focus explicitly on the interplay over time between the terms of trade, the exchange rate and the foreign and domestic rates of inflation and study how these time paths are influenced by international disturbances and domestic policy actions.

It is generally argued that under a regime of flexible rates the small country has the option to choose its own long-run rate of inflation independent of the rest of the world. In the paper we analyze what this freedom of choice implies for the formulation of long-run monetary policy.

The paper is organized in the following way. In section II the basic model is presented and in section III some important long-run properties of this model are analyzed. Section IV contains a discussion of the adjustment process in the case with static expectations, and in section V the effects of international disturbances and economic policy are investigated.

II. THE MODEL

The model consists of an asset sector and a real sector. The symbols used are summarized below.

y	real national income
r_d	domestic interest rate
r_f	foreign interest rate
ε^e	expected change of the exchange rate
M, m	money supply
B, b	domestic bonds
F, f	foreign securities
e	exchange rate (domestic currency/foreign currency)
A, a	total private wealth
D, d	public debt
δ	composition of public debt
i	imports (quantity)

x exports (quantity)

p_d price of domestic goods (in domestic currency)

p_f price of foreign goods (in domestic currency)

y_f world activity level

c private expenditure (real)

g government expenditure (real)

t taxes (real)

p domestic price level ($p = p(p_d, p_f)$)

π^e expected inflation

π_d inflation on domestic goods

π_f inflation on foreign goods

ν the terms of trade

z excess demand (for the domestic good)

A dot over a variable denotes its time derivate. All variables are functions of time, but this is suppressed in the notation. A bar over a variable denotes its steady state value. An asterisk indicates that the variable is expressed in foreign currency. Partial derivatives are denoted by numerical subscripts. Capital letters denote nominal values, while small letters stand for real values.

The asset sector

The asset sector is similar to those used by Branson (1976), Flood (1976) and Kouri (1976), which may all be considered simplified versions of the model formulated by Black (1973) in his pioneering analysis of the asset market determination of exchange rates. We distinguish between three assets, domestic money M, domestic bonds B and foreign securities F. Foreign money is not held in the portfolios of the private sector. Domestic bonds are issued by the government and are not held in portfolios outside the country. The sum of money and bonds constitutes total government debt D ($D = M + B$). The fraction made up of bonds is δ, a policy parameter ($B = \delta D$ and $M = (1 - \delta)D$).

Foreign securities are issued abroad and denominated in foreign currency. The domestic demand for these securities is such a small fraction of total demand that the (nominal) interest rate r_f can be regarded as given. For simplicity both domestic bonds and foreign securities are treated as fixed-price variable-yield assets, which means that we abstract from capital gains and losses caused by variations in interest rates.

The asset demand functions are specified in the following way.

$$(1)\quad M^d = L(y, r_d, r_f + \varepsilon^e)A \qquad L_1 > 0,\ L_2 < 0,\ L_3 < 0$$

$$(2)\quad B^d = H(y, r_d, r_f + \varepsilon^e)A \qquad H_1 < 0,\ H_2 > 0,\ H_3 < 0$$

$$(3)\quad eF^d = G(y, r_d, r_f + \varepsilon^e)A \qquad G_1 < 0,\ G_2 < 0,\ G_3 > 0$$

The arguments in the demand functions and the signs of the derivatives are standard.[2] From the definition of private wealth

$$(4)\quad A = eF + D$$

it follows that only two of the market equilibrium conditions (1), (2) and (3) are independent. At any given point of time, asset market equilibrium determines the domestic interest rate r_d and the exchange rate e (measured as domestic currency per unit of foreign exchange), given the inherited asset stocks, real income and exchange rate expectations. In this way r_d and e are continuously adjusted to make people willingly hold the given stocks in their portfolios.

The real sector

The model contains two composite goods, one foreign good and one home good. The home country is assumed to be small enough

---

2) Since all assets are nominal assets we need not distinguish between nominal and real asset yield in the demand functions.

to regard the supply of the foreign good as perfectly elastic. The demand for imports is a function of real private expenditure and the terms of trade.

$$(5) \qquad i = i\left(c, \frac{p_d}{p_f}\right) . \qquad i_1 > 0, \quad i_2 > 0$$

The home good is the only good produced in the domestic economy. With the assumption that all factors of production are always fully utilized, domestic output could be regarded as fixed.

The demand for exports varies with the activity level abroad and the terms of trade.

$$(6) \qquad x = x\left(y_f, \frac{p_d}{p_f}\right) \qquad x_1 > 0, \quad x_2 < 0$$

Total domestic expenditure is a function of real disposable income, real wealth and the real rate of interest.

$$(7) \quad c = C\left(\frac{p_d}{p}(y-t), \frac{A}{p}, r_d - \pi^e\right) \quad c_1 > 0, \quad c_2 > 0, \quad c_3 < 0$$

Equilibrium on the market for home goods can be written as

$$(8) \quad c + g + x - y - \frac{p_f}{p_d} . i = 0$$

where g is government expenditure.[3)]

At any given point of time the equilibrium condition determines the price of the domestic good (p_d). We assume that domestic and foreign price notations are always perfectly linked through arbitrage by the current exchange rate, i.e. $p_i = ep_i^*$ (i=d,f)

---

3) (8) looks like an ordinary Keynesian open economy equilibrium but is in fact quite different. National income y is not demand-determined and prices are not given.

where p_i are prices expressed in foreign currency. The price of the foreign good in terms of the foreign currency is given exogenously.

Dynamic relations

Changes in the stocks of foreign and domestic assets (F and D) move the system over time. The stock of foreign assets grows (diminishes) with a surplus (deficit) in the current account

$$(9) \quad \dot{F} = (p_d x - p_f i) \frac{1}{e} + r_f F$$

where $r_f F$ is interest payments on foreign assets. The government budget policy determines the development of the public debt

$$(1o) \quad \dot{D} = p_d (g - t)$$

Besides changes in the stocks of assets, expectations variables play an important role for the development of the system over time. Throughout this paper we assume extremely simple price expectations mechanisms for both prices and the exchange rate. The expected rate of inflation is taken to be equal to the long-run rate of inflation, i.e.

$$(11) \quad \pi^e = \bar{\pi}$$

Exchange rate expectations are assumed to be static, but correct in the steady state,[4)] i.e.

$$(12) \quad \varepsilon^e = \frac{\bar{e}}{e}$$

4) In an extended version of this paper available as Seminar Paper no 94, Institute for International Economic Studies, University of Stockholm,some other specifications of the exchange rate expectations mechanism are analyzed.

III. SOME LONG-RUN PROPERTIES

We shall now discuss some important steady state properties of the model presented in the preceding section. We assume that world inflation is given by π_f^*,[5] which means that the price of important goods grows at a steady rate in terms of foreign currency. In the steady state the price of import goods in terms of the domestic currency must grow at the same rate as the price of domestic goods, i.e.

$$(13) \quad \bar{\pi}_d = \pi_f^* + \frac{\dot{e}}{e} = \bar{\pi}_f$$

Unless (13) is satisfied, the terms of trade and the current account will change over time and the economy cannot be in a position of long-run equilibrium.

It is generally agreed that under a flexible exchange rate regime a country can choose its own rate of inflation independent of the rest of the world, even in the long run. It is not always recognized, however, that in a general equilibrium framework the rate of domestic inflation cannot be determined without an accommodating debt policy. In the simple case when real income is fixed, nominal debt must expand at the same rate as the target inflation rate

$$(14) \quad \frac{\dot{D}}{D} = \pi.$$

---

5) Not that world inflation is in principle equal to $\pi_w^* = \beta\pi_f^* + (1 - \beta)\,\pi_d^*$, where π_w^* is a weighted average of the inflation on foreign goods (the import good of the home currency) and domestic goods (the export good of the home country). In the steady state π_f^* must be equal to π_d^* so that $\pi_w^* = \pi_f^*$. Even outside the steady state π_f can be taken to represent world inflation, if the home country's exports are a very small fraction of total world trade and consumtion. In that case $\beta \to 1$ and $\pi_w^* = \pi_f^*$.

To see this consider first the case where the country accepts the world rate of inflation over time, i.e. $\pi = \pi_f^*$ implying $\frac{\dot{e}}{e} = 0$ in the steady state. To keep the exchange rate constant the stocks of all the three assets must grow at the same rate. Otherwise there will be attempts to redistribute portfolios in the private sector leading to changes in the exchange rate. Furthermore, the rate at which the stocks must grow in nominal terms must equal the target long-run inflation rate π_f^*. If they grow faster, real wealth will increase. With higher real wealth domestic absorption rises and the terms of trade change, which is again inconsistent with long-run equilibrium. To make nominal government debt grow at the same rate as long-run inflation, the authorities have to run a budget deficit such that the total debt always grows at the observed (and fixed) foreign rate of inflation π_f^*, i.e.

$$\frac{\dot{D}}{D} = \pi_f^* \qquad (14a)$$

This policy can be pursued also outside the steady state. It then serves as a signal to the public that the authorities intend to accept the foreign inflation on the average over time.

If the country chooses to have an inflation rate different from the rest of the world, it could announce that immediately by letting the public debt grow at the same rate as the desired long-run inflation, as shown in (14). It follows from (13) that if the chosen target rate is below (above) the world rate the exchange rate will steadily appreciate (depreciate).

What target rate of inflation is chosen by the government has important consequences for the formation of expectations. It should be clear from the previous discussion that there exists a long-run equilibrium level of the exchange rate only in the special case when foreign inflation is fully accepted. In all other cases the exchange rate moves indefinitely, although at a steady rate, and no equilibrium rate exists. If it is made clear to the public that the target rate for domestic inflation deviates from the world rate, people obviously cannot rationally base their decisions on any notion of an equilibrium level of the exchange rate.

IV. THE ADJUSTMENT PROCESS

We are now in a position to study the adjustment process implied by the model presented in section II. Without loss of generality we can assume that the policy-makers accept world inflation in the long run and hence let nominal debt expand at that rate. By assumption (12) people then have static, but asymptotically correct expectations about the exchange rate by always believing it to stay unchanged, i.e. $\varepsilon^e = 0$.

The short-run asset market equilibrium is illustrated in Fig. 1.[6] The MM, BB and FF lines show combinations of the domestic interest rate and the exchange rate consistent with equilibrium in the markets for money, domestic bonds and foreign securities, respectively (equations (1), (2) and (3)). The relative slopes of the curves follow unambiguously from the assumption of gross substitutability. If e rises the value of wealth in domestic currency increases, thus increasing the demand for all assets. To maintain equilibrium in the money market, r_d must rise to force money demand down and keep it equal to the fixed supply. Thus the slope of the MM-curve has to be positive. In a similar way the negative slopes of the FF and BB-curves are derived. It is also simple to demonstrate that the assumption of gross substitutability implies that the BB-curve has a steeper slope than the FF-curve.

If two of the markets clear the third will also be in equilibrium, which is to say that the three curves intersect at a single point. In this way the market clearing exchange rate and interest rate are determined.

---

6) For mathematical derivations see the mathematical appendix

FIGURE 1: Asset market equilibrium

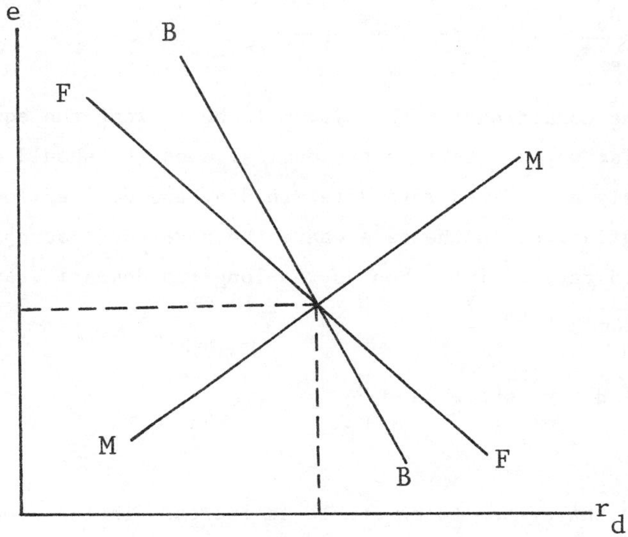

Given the values of r_d and e determined by portfolio equilibrium, the price (p_d) which clears the domestic market can be found from (8). Since the foreign price p_f^* is given, the terms of trade ($p_d/e\ p_f^*$) are also determined by the short-run equilibrium of the system.

The terms of trade in turn determine the position of the current account and thereby, via (9), the net accumulation of foreign securities ($\dot{F}$). Thus, in the following period a new value of F is fed into the system, generating a new short-run solution for the exchange rate, the terms of trade and the current balance. This story repeats itself (if stable) until a steady state is reached. But as we saw in the preceding section the steady state is not characterized by a fixed level of nominal holdings of foreign assets, i.e. by $\dot{F} = 0$. Instead we should expect nominal holdings (in terms of the home currency) to grow at the rate determined by long-run inflation. The true state variable of the system is therefore the real stock of foreign assets (in terms of foreign goods), i.e. $\frac{F}{p_f^*} = f$.

$$(15) \quad \dot{f} = \frac{p_d}{ep_f^*} x - i + (r_f - \pi_f^*) f = 0$$

is then the condition for the system to be in long-run equilibrium. In a similar way we realize that nominal debt (D) should expand continuously at a fixed rate determined by the desired long-run rate of inflation. In the case where the government accepts the given world rate of inflation as the long-run domestic target rate, if follows that[7)]

$$\dot{d} \quad 0 \quad \text{where} \quad d = \frac{D}{p_f^*} .$$

Stability

For the system to be stable an increase in the stock of foreign securities must lead to a deterioration of the current account.[8)] If the stock of foreign securities increases, the terms of trade will unambiguously improve. This is so partly because the exchange rate will have to appreciate to make people hold the increased amount of foreign assets in their portfolios and partly because the increase in real wealth will put an upward pressure on the price of home goods. If then the Marshall-Lerner condition

---

7) The assumption that $\dot{d} = 0$ identically is not essential to the argument, although it somewhat facilitates the analysis. If the target rate of inflation is different from the world rate, real debt will be constant in the steady state only. This will not, however, add any new element to the dynamic structure of the model. See e.g. Kouri (1976) and Nyberg-Viotti (1978).

8) The condition for stability requires that

$$\frac{d\nu}{df} (x_2 + x - i_2) + r_f - \pi_f^* < 0$$

As argued in the text the derivating appearing to the left is unambiguously positive. The factor $x_2 + x - i_2$ is the Marshall-Lerner condition.

is fulfilled the trade balance will deteriorate. Unless the real value of the increase in interest payments from abroad outweighs the negative trade account, the stock of foreign securities (in terms of foreign goods) will have fallen in the next period and the system is stable. Otherwise, i.e. if the Marshall-Lerner condition is not fulfilled or the interest payments on foreign assets increase more than enough to offset the negative effect on the trade account, the stock of foreign assets will go on accumulating indefinitely and the system is unstable. The second cause of instability could be analyzed in terms of a transfer problem. Take an initial fall in the stock of foreign assets for a change. The terms of trade must now deteriorate to create a surplus big enough in the trade balance to pay for the loss of interest payments from abroad. Otherwise the economy will never be able to compensate for this loss and the stock of foreign securities will fall indefinitely.

The adjustment process of the system is illustrated in Fig. 2. The flatter of the curves in the diagram shows combinations of the terms of trade and the stock of foreign securities consistent with long-run equilibrium ($\dot{f} = 0$). If the Marshall-Lerner condition is fulfilled but the real yield on foreign securities is positive ($r_f - \pi_f^* > 0$) the slope of the curve is positive.[9)] The system may then be either stable or unstable.[1o)] At points below the curve

---

9) The exact expression for the slope of the $\dot{f} = 0$ curve is

$$\frac{d\nu}{df}\Big|_{\dot{f}=0} = - \frac{r_f - \pi_f^*}{x_2 + x - i_2}$$, where the denominator is negative if the Marshall-Lerner condition is fulfilled.

1o) If the Marshall-Lerner condition holds and there is a real loss on the stock of securities the $\dot{f} = 0$ curve has a negative slope and the system is necessarily stable. This simple case is not further examined.

FIGURE 2: The adjustment process - a stable case

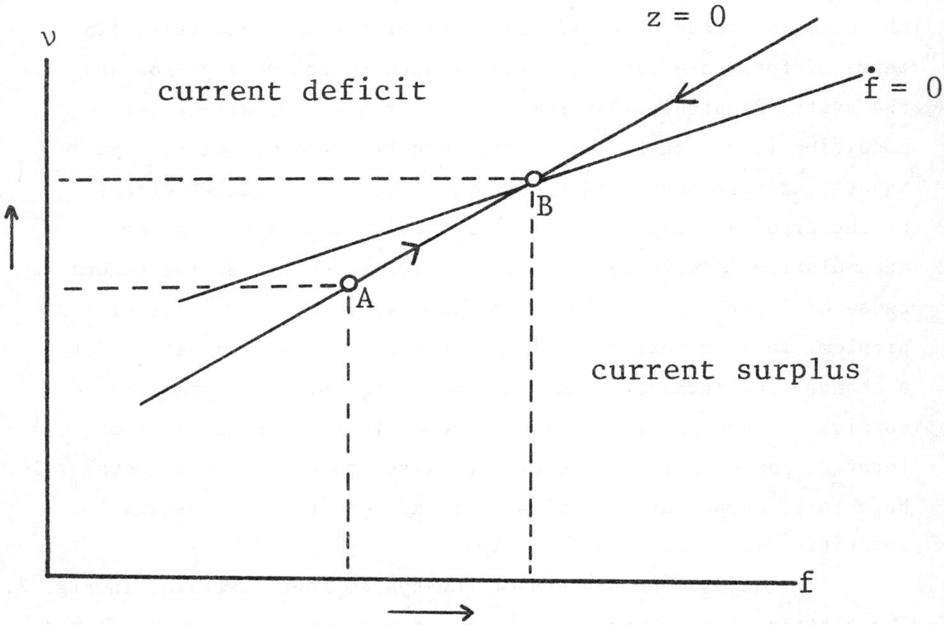

the terms of trade are lower than what is consistent with long-run equilibrium. In this region a deficit in the trade balance cannot be big enough to offset the real inflow of interest payments from abroad. Hence the stock of foreign securities must be increasing below the $\dot{f} = 0$ curve. From a similar reasoning it follows that the stock must decrease at points above the curve.

However, the economy is constrained by the short-run system to be at the steeper of the curves in the diagram. This curve shows combinations of the terms of trade and the stock of foreign securities consistent with equilibrium in the real sector. From the discussion in the previous paragraph we know that this curve ($z = 0$) has a positive slope.

With the help of these two curves the stability properties of the model can be illustrated. It is simple to show that stability is assumed if the $z = 0$ curve cuts the $\dot{f} = 0$ curve from below.[11] Assume that the economy is initially at point A in Fig. 2. Since A is below the $\dot{f} = 0$ curve, there is a current account surplus. The economy will thus be moving along the $z = 0$ curve towards the right until it reaches the steady-state point B, i.e. the system is stable.

Adjustment of the exchange rate and domestic inflation

Knowing the adjustment paths of the terms of trade and the stock of foreign securities, we can derive the paths of the exchange rate and the domestic rate of inflation. From the assumption of portfolio balance it follows that the elasticity of e with respect to f is equal to minus one ($\dot{e}/e = - \dot{f}/f$). If the stock of foreign securities increases monotonically towards the steady, as in Fig. 2, the exchange rate will appreciate all the way towards its equilibrium level. To make people willingly hold the increasing stock of foreign security in their portfolios, the exchange rate must continuously appreciate.

What can be said about the development of domestic inflation? Will domestic inflation be above or below world inflation during the adjustment process illustrated above? From the definition of the terms of trade we see that $\pi_d - \pi_f^* = \frac{\dot{\nu}}{\nu} + \frac{\dot{e}}{e}$, i.e. the difference between domestic and foreign rates of inflation is equal to the sum of the rates of change in the terms of trade and the exchange rate. If the terms of trade improve faster than the exchange rate appreciates, domestic inflation will be above foreign

11) The condition for (local) stability was derived in note 2 on the previous page.

$$\frac{d\nu}{df}\Big|_{z=0} > \frac{d\nu}{df}\Big|_{\dot{f}=0} = - \frac{r_f - \pi_f^*}{x_2 + x - i_2} \quad \text{implies that}$$

$$\frac{d\nu}{df} \cdot (x_2 + x - i_2) + r_f - \pi_f^* < 0.$$ This stability is assumed if the $\dot{f} = 0$ curve is steeper than the $z = 0$ curve.

inflation during the whole adjustment process, in the opposite case it will always be below. In Fig. 3 the former case is illustrated.

FIGURE 3: The adjustment of domestic inflation

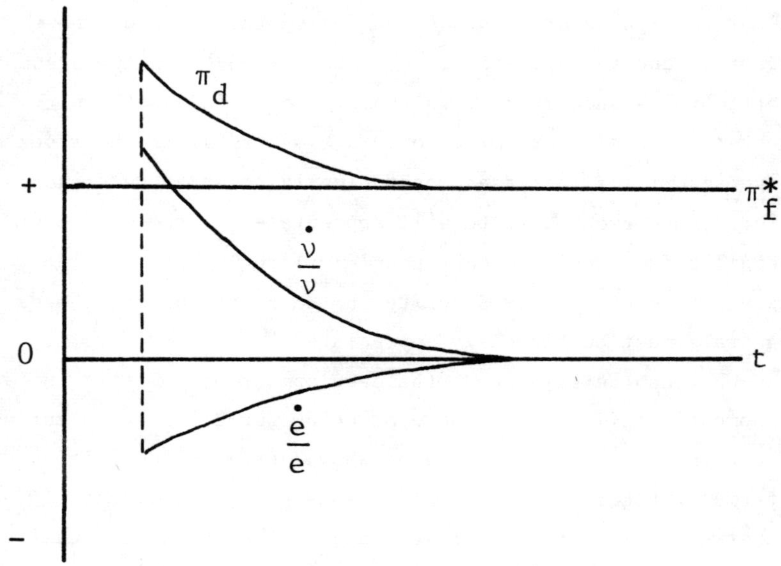

V. EFFECTS OF FOREIGN DISTURBANCES AND ECONOMIC POLICY

We are now in a position to analyze how the system reacts over time to various changes in exogenous variables. We first consider changes in international conditions such as the foreign interest rate (r_f), world inflation (π_f^*) and the world activity level, (y_f).

An increase in the interest rate on foreign securities

A rise in the interest rate on foreign securities has a direct impact effect on the exchange rate and the domestic interest rate through the asset market. As seen from Fig. 4 both the BB-curve and the FF-curve will shift outwards in response to a rise in r_f - for a given exchange rate, a higher domestic interest rate is now required to make people hold the existing stocks of both bonds and foreign securities. The impact effect on the exchange rate is unambiguously positive because of the gross substitutability assumption, but the effect on the domestic interest rate could be either positive or negative depending on whether bonds are a better or worse substitute for foreign assets than money.

FIGURE 4: Impact effect on e and r_d of a rise in the foreign interest rate

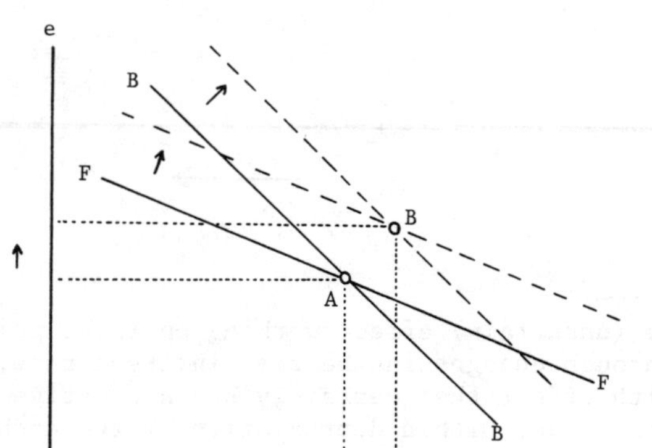

In Fig. 5 the dynamic response to a change in r_f is illustrated. If the impact effect on the domestic interest rate is positive as in Fig. 4 the terms of trade must certainly deteriorate[12] to maintain equilibrium in the real sector. In Fig. 6 this shows up as a downward shift of the z = 0 curve.

FIGURE 5: Dynamic response to a rise in r_f

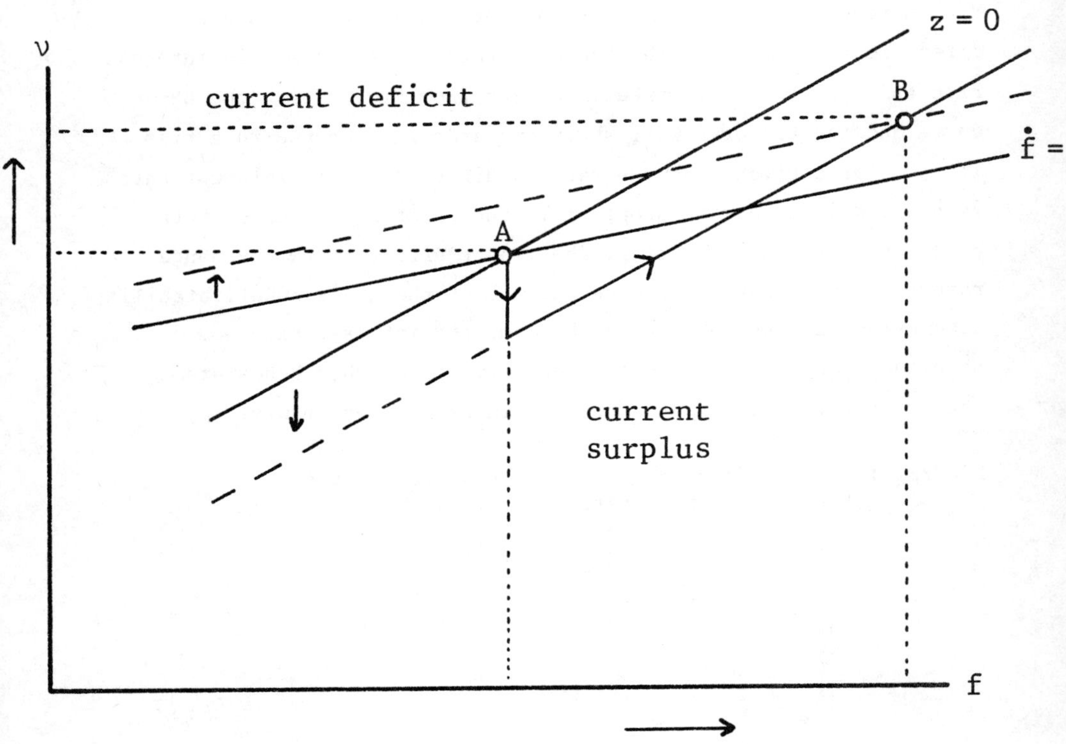

12) Apart from the (uncertain) effect working on total private expenditure through changes in the real interest rate, there is also a wealth effect that certainly has a negative influence on the terms of trade. With a depreciation of the exchange rate the price level rises and real wealth falls (at least the part that is denominated in the home currency).

FIGURE 6: Dynamic response to an increase in world inflation

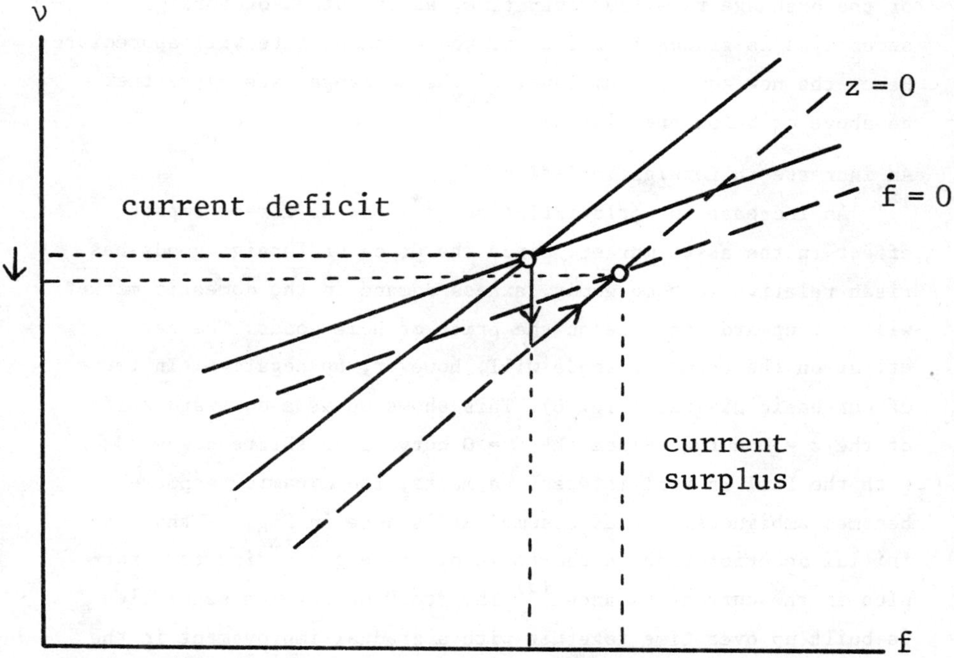

The $\dot{f} = 0$ curve will shift upwards because for a given real stock of foreign securities interest payments from abroad will rise. This allows for a bigger deficit in the trade balance and hence for a higher level of the terms of trade. The adjustment process is now easily read off from the diagram. The initial deterioration in the terms of trade is followed by an accumulation of foreign assets and a gradual improvement of the terms of trade. In the new steady state they will even be above the initial level. The negative impact effect is consequently more than offset in the long run.

The effect on the long-run equilibrium level of the exchange rate (if it exists) is not clear, however. As shown in Fig. 4 the immediate response to the rise in r_f is a depreciation of the exchange rate. But over time, as the stock of foreign securities is gradually built up, the exchange rate will appreciate. Hence the new equilibrium level of the exchange rate may either be above or below the old one.

An increase in foreign inflation

An increase in world inflation (π_f^*) has no direct impact effect in the asset market. Since the price of foreign goods has risen relative to home goods, excess demand in the domestic market will put upward pressure on the price of home goods. The net effect on the terms of trade will, however, be negative. In terms of our basic diagram (Fig. 6). This shows up as a downward shift of the z = 0 curve. Since the $\dot{f} = 0$ curve also shifts downwards with the fall in real interest payments, the dynamic response becomes ambiguous. Let us assume (as is done in Fig. 6) that the initial deterioration in the terms of trade gives rise to a surplus in the current balance.[13] The stock of foreign securities is built up over time together with a gradual improvement in the terms of trade and appreciation of the exchange rate. The long-run effect on the terms of trade is not clear, although in the "normal" case we may expect the terms of trade to have deteriorated over in the steady state (as depicted in Fig. 6). Since there was no impact effect on the exchange rate, it will appreciate continuously until the new higher equilibrium level is reached.

13) The positive effect on the trade account caused by the fall in the terms of trade may be counteracted by the fall in the real interest payments, in which case the current account will show a deficit.

An increase in world activity

An increase in world activity, finally, has also no impact effect on the asset market. The increased demand for domestic products from abroad will lead to an improvement of the terms of trade. The effect on the trade balance is uncertain, however, because the negative effect through increased imports may counteract the increase in the value of exports. If the latter dominates, which seems to be the reasonable case, the adjustment process is the one pictured in Fig. 7. With no impact effect on the exchange rate, its development is straight forward: a steady appreciation until the steady-state level is reaches.

FIGURE 7: Dynamic response to an increase in the world activity level

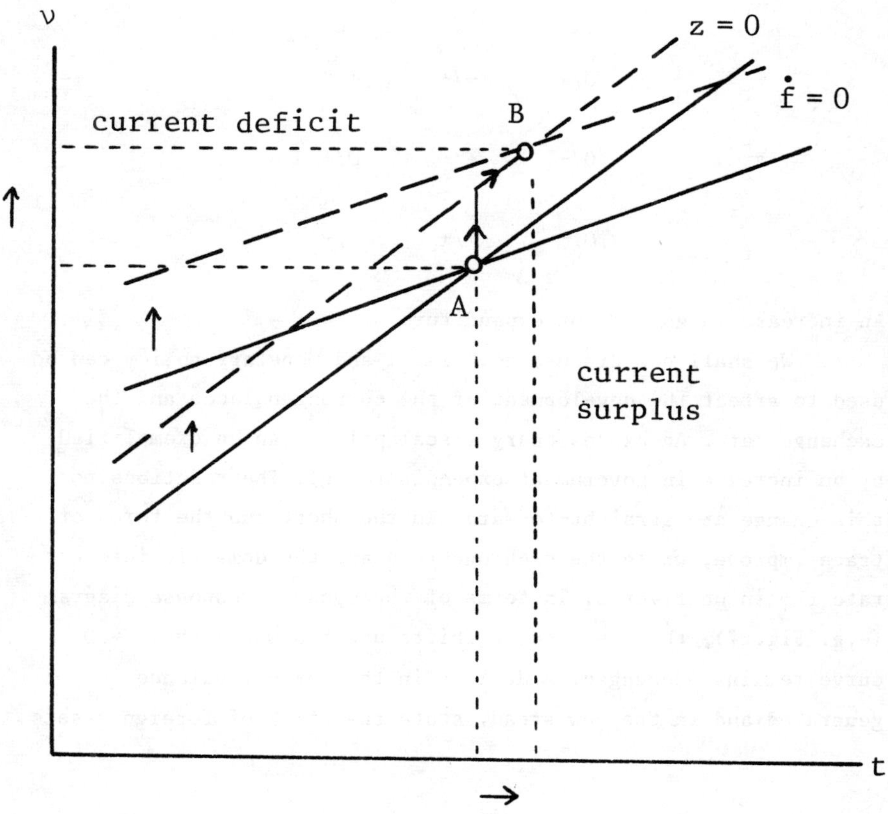

Table 1 summarizes the discussion about the effects of foreign impulses. In each entry of the table the short-run (impact) effect is shown to the left and above while the long-run effect is found to the right and below.

It is worth noting that these foreign impulses or disturbances usually appear in combination. For instance the case of inflation being imported into the small flexible exchange rate economy would probably be best characterized by increased inflation for foreign goods (π_f^*) and increased capacity utilization in the world y_f. The combined effect on the terms of trade is obviously uncertain, while the exchange rate effect is unambiguous - a steady appreciation.

TABLE 1: Impact and steady effects of foreign impulses

	f	ν	e
r_f	0/+	-/+	+/?
π_f^*	0/-	+/-	0/+
y_f	0/-	+/+	0/-

An increase in government expenditure

We shall now discuss how fiscal and monetary policy can be used to affect the development of the current balance and the exchange rate. An expansionary fiscal policy can be exemplified by an increase in government expenditure (g). The reactions to this change are straight-forward. In the short run the terms of trade improve, while the exchange rate and the domestic interest rate remain unaffected. In terms of the dynamic response diagram (e.g. Fig. 7), the $z = 0$ curve shifts upwards while the $\dot{f} = 0$ curve remains unchanged. A deficit in the current balance is generated and in the new steady state the stock of foreign assets has fallen, the exchange rate has depreciated and the terms of trade have deteriorated (below its original level).

An open market operation

The two instruments for monetary policy in the system are the rate of expansion of (nominal) debt and its composition. An increase in δ, i.e. an open market operation with the central bank selling bonds to the private sector, will have a direct impact effect on the asset markets, causing an appreciation of the exchange rate and a rise in the domestic interest rate.
The impact effect on the terms of trade is unclear, however. It depends on whether the positive real balance effect caused by the appreciation of the exchange rate dominates the negative effect of the higher interest rate. In Figure 8 the former effect is assumed to dominate. In this case the effect on the long-run equilibrium level of the exchange rate is ambiguous, because the immediate appreciation is offset over time by a gradual depreciation.

FIGURE 8: Dynamic response to open market operation

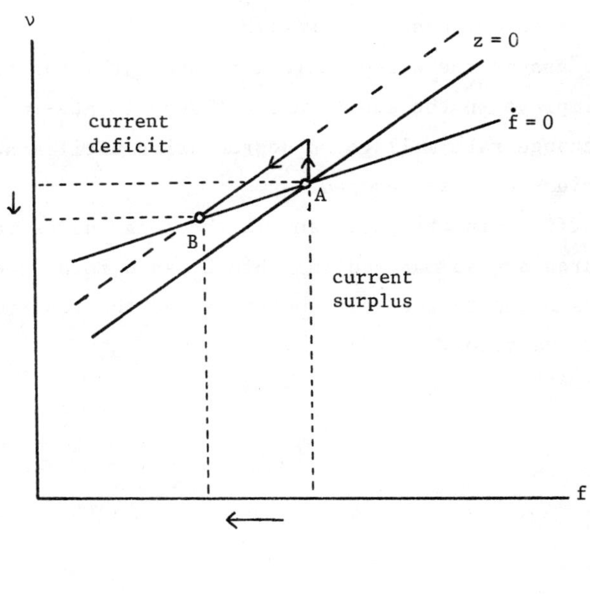

An expansionary debt policy

As argued in section III, the rate of expansion of the public debt must be pegged to world inflation if an equilibrium long-run level of the exchange rate is to exist. Apparently the average rate of expansion of the public debt is determined by long-run considerations and should therefore not be regarded as an instrument for short-run policy. However, the rate of expansion of the public debt can be increased (decreased) temporarily without changing the average long-run rate. In the model such a policy measure corresponds to a once and for all change in public debt, d. An increase in d at a given point in time can be interpreted as a temporary one-period increase in the rate of growth of nominal debt above the rate determined by average world inflation. The ensuing increase in private wealth will depreciate the exchange rate. Since the composition of debt remains the same the domestic interest rate is not influenced. The effect on the terms of trade will normally be positive due to the increase in private wealth following the issue of new debt. However, the direct positive effect on real wealth is counteracted by the fact that the depreciation of the exchange rate will move the price level up and hence work to decrease real wealth.

If we assume the direct effect to dominate, the terms of trade will improve in the short run, but deteriorate in the long run. The exchange rate will go on depreciating until a new long-run equilibrium level is reached.

The effects in the short and in the long run of various policy measures are summarized in table 2. As before, the short-run effect is shown to the left and above and the long-run effect to the right and below.

TABLE 2: Impact and steady state effects of economic policy

	f	ν	e
g	0/-	+/-	0/+
δ	0/?	?/?	-/?
d	0/+	+/-	+/+
	(-)	(-)(+)	(-)

VI. CONCLUSIONS

In this paper we have developed a simple general equilibrium model for the study of a small open economy under flexible exchange rates. Within this framework we have been able to analyze the effects of international disturbances and economic policy on the development of the exchange rate, the terms of trade, the current balance and domestic inflation. We have explored the connection between the target rate of inflation and the development of the exchange rate and discussed the specific long-run monetary policy implied by the choice of a target long-run inflation. It is pointed out that anything like an equilibrium rate exists only in the case when the country fully accepts average world inflation over time. The notion about a "normal" price of a currency often hinted at in the public debate thus has no real meaning except for this special case.

MATHEMATICAL APPENDIX

A. The short run

(1) e and r_d are derived from the conditions of equilibrium in the markets for bonds and foreign securities

$$\delta D = H(y, r_d, r_f)A$$

$$eF = G(y, r_d, r_f)A$$

After differentiation the following solution for e and r_d is obtained.

$$\begin{bmatrix} dr_d \\ de \end{bmatrix} = \frac{1}{\Delta} \begin{bmatrix} F(G-1) & -HF \\ -G_2 A & H_2 A \end{bmatrix} \begin{bmatrix} -He & -H_3 A & -H_1 A & D & \delta - H \\ -(G-1)e & -G_3 A & -G_1 A & 0 & -G \end{bmatrix} \begin{bmatrix} dF \\ dr_f \\ dy \\ d\delta \\ dD \end{bmatrix}$$

where $\Delta = AF\,[H_2(G-1) - G_2 H] < 0$ since ($H_2 > -G_2$ and $1 - G > H$).

Thus the relations between e and r_d and the (short-run) exogenous variables are

$$e = E(\overset{-}{F}, \overset{+}{r_f}, \overset{-}{y}, \overset{-}{\delta}, \overset{+}{D})$$

$$r_d = R(\overset{0}{F}, \overset{(\pm)}{r_f}, \overset{+}{y}, \overset{+}{\delta}, \overset{0}{D})$$

(2) Define $p_r = \frac{p_d}{p_f^*}$, $f = \frac{F}{p_f^*}$, $d = \frac{D}{p_f^*}$ and $a = \frac{A}{p_f^*}$.

Then $\frac{A}{p} = (ef+d) \cdot \frac{1}{\alpha p_r + (1-\alpha)e}$ (if $p = \alpha p_d + (1-\alpha)\, p_f$) and

$$y^{di} = \frac{p_d}{p}(y-t) = (y-t) \cdot \frac{p_r}{\alpha p_r + (1-\alpha)e}$$

If real taxes are taken to be the dependent policy instrument $\dot{d} = (g-t)\, p_r - \pi_f^* d = 0$ implies that $t = g - \pi_f^* d p_r^{-1}$.

Equilibrium in the goods market $z = c + g + x - y - e p_r^{-1}\, i = 0$ solves for p_r. Without loss of generality we assume that we differentiate around the stationary equilibrium point where $p_r = e = 1$. Differentiation of z gives

$$
\begin{aligned}
dz = & & + \mu\, dp_r\, + \\
& + (-E_1\mu - c_1 E_1 \pi_f^* d + c_2(1-E_1 d)) & df\, + \\
& + (-E_2\mu - c_1 E_2 \pi_f^* d + c_2 E_2 d + c_3 R_2) & dr_f\, + \\
& + \quad (c_1 d - c_3) & d\pi_f^*\, + \\
& + (-E_4\mu - c_1 E_4 \pi_f^* d + c_2 E_4 d + c_3 R_4 + c_1 - i_1 - 1) & dy\, + \\
& + \quad x_1 & dy_f\, + \\
& + \quad (1-c_1) & dg\, + \\
& + (-E_7\mu - c_1 E_7 \pi_f^* d + c_2 E_7 d + c_3 R_7) & d\delta\, + \\
& + (-E_8\mu - c_1 E_8 \pi_f^* d + c_2(1-E_8 d)) & dd
\end{aligned}
$$

where

$$\mu = c_1((y-g)(1-\alpha) - \alpha\pi_f^* d) - c_2\, a\alpha + x_2 + i - i_2 < 0 \text{ (by assumption).}$$

Thus the solution for p_r can be written

$$p_r = P(\overset{(\pm)}{f}, \overset{-?}{r_f}, \overset{+}{\pi_f^*}, \overset{-}{y}, \overset{+}{y_f}, \overset{+}{g}, \overset{?}{\delta}, \overset{(\pm)}{d})$$

Since the terms of trade ν are defined as $\dfrac{p_d}{ep_f^*}$

$$\nu_1 = \frac{dp_{r/e}}{df} = P_1 - e_1 = \frac{E_1\ \pi_f^* d - c_2(1-E_1 d)}{\mu} > 0$$

Then the function

$$\frac{p_d}{ep_f^*} = \nu(\overset{+}{f}, \overset{-?}{r_f}, \overset{+}{\pi_f^*}, \overset{+?}{y}, \overset{+}{y_f}, \overset{+}{g}, \overset{?}{\delta}, \overset{(\pm)}{d})$$

is derived, showing short-run effects on the terms of trade.

B. Stability

The condition for (local) stability is that

$$\frac{d\dot{f}}{df} = \nu_1\eta + r_f - \pi_f^* < 0$$

where $\eta = x_2 + x - i_2 < 0$ if the Marshall-Lerner condition is fulfilled. Since ν_1 is certainly positive the necessary condition for stability can be written

$$|\nu_1\eta| > (r_f - \pi_f^*)$$

C. The steady state

By implicit differentiation of $\dot{f} = 0$ we can solve for the long-run level of the real stock of foreign securities $\bar{f}$ as a function of the (long-run) exogenous variables

$$\bar{f} = K(\overset{+}{r_f}, \overset{-}{\pi^*_f}, \overset{-?}{y}, \overset{+?}{y_f}, \overset{-}{g}, \overset{?}{\delta}, \overset{(\pm)}{d})$$

where for instance

$$K_1 = - \frac{\nu_2 \eta + f}{\nu_1 \eta \, (r_f - \pi^*_f)}$$

From the knowledge of $\bar{f}$ the long-run equilibrium values of the exchange rate and the terms of trade can be derived as functions of the exogenous variables

$$\bar{e} = \bar{E}(\overset{?}{r_f}, \overset{+}{\pi^*_f}, \overset{-?}{y}, \overset{-?}{y_f}, \overset{+}{g}, \overset{?}{\delta}, \overset{(\pm)}{d})$$

where for instance

$$\bar{E}_1 = E_2 + E_1 K_1$$

for which the sign is uncertain, since the direct impact effect E_2 is positive, while the effect working via f over time is negative.

$$\bar{Tot} = \bar{\nu}(\overset{+}{r_f}, \overset{-}{\pi^*_f}, \overset{-}{y}, \overset{+}{y_f}, \overset{-}{g}, \overset{?}{\delta}, \overset{(\mp)}{d})$$

where

$$\bar{\nu}_1 = \nu_2 - \nu_1 \cdot \frac{\nu_2 \eta + f}{\nu_1 \eta + r_f - \pi^*_f} = (\nu_2 - \frac{\nu_2}{1 + \frac{r_f - \pi^*_f}{\nu_1 \eta}}) - \frac{\nu_1 f}{\nu_1 \eta + r_f - \pi^*_f}$$

which is certainly positive if $(r_f - \pi^*_f) > 0$ although the direct impact effect ν_2 is negative.

REFERENCES

Aoki, M. "Short-Run Asset and the Real Sector Dynamics of a Small Open Economy Under Flexible Exchange Rates", Kredit und Kapital 1978 (this issue)

Black, S. "International Money Markets and Flexible Exchange Rates", Priceton Studies in International Finance No. 32, Princeton, New Jersey, 1973.

Branson, W. "Asset Markets and Relative Prices in Exchange Rate Determination", Seminar Paper No. 66, Institute for International Economic Studies, University of Stockholm, 1976.

Dornbusch, R. "The Theory of Flexible Exchange Rate Regimes and Macroeconomic Policy", Scandinavian Journal of Economics, 1976, pp.255-275.

Flood, R. "Asset Trading, Exchange Rate Determination and Exchange Rate Dynamics", Paper presented at SSRC-Ford Foundation, Ware, England, 1976.

Henderson, D.W. "The Dynamic Effects of Exchange Market Intervention Policy: Two Extreme Views and a Synthesis", Kredit und Kapital, 1978 (this issue)

Kouri, P. "The Exchange Rate and the Balance of Payments in the Short Run and in the Long Run: A Monetary Approach", Scandinavian Journal of Economics, 1976, pp.28o-3o4.

Nyberg, L. and S. Viotti, "Unemployment, Inflation and the Balance of Payments: A Dynamic Analysis", in Stabilization Policy in Open Economies, edited by A. Lindbeck (forthcoming at North Holland).

COMMENT ON S. VIOTTI, "INFLATION, THE TERMS OF TRADE AND FLEXIBLE EXCHANGE RATES"

Benjamin J. Cohen

Staffan Viotti's paper represents a useful addition to the growing literature on exchange-rate dynamics. As the author himself points out, most recent contributions have tended to focus mainly on the monetary side of the economy, the real side being more or less neglected. His model, by contrast, explicitly integrates the monetary and real sectors. The result is a considerable new insight into the properties of a floating exchange-rate regime for a small open economy.

In this comment, I wish to focus not on the mechanics of Viotti's model - about which I have little quarrel - but rather on its implications for policy. Viotti refers to the "generally agreed" proposition that "under a flexible exchange rate regime a country can choose its own rate of inflation independent of the rest of the world, even in the long run". His own model, however, seems to cast doubt on that proposition. Indeed, I submit that if we are to take his analysis really seriously, we must arrive at precisely the opposite conclusion - that in reality a small country probably cannot choose its own inflation rate. For such a country, the presumed extra degree of freedom is likely to prove illusory. Domestic policy is still seriously constrained by external developments.

Consider Viotti's discussion of the formation of expectations. He correctly notes that if a country chooses to have an inflation rate different from the rest of the world, its exchange rate must steadily change, even in the long term (the domestic currency appreciating if the target rate is below the world rate, depreciating if it is above). But this then means that there can be no such thing as a long-run equilibrium level of the exchange rate except in the special case where foreign inflation is fully accepted. In all other cases, people cannot rationally base their exchange-rate expectations on any notion of an equilibrium level of the exchange rate. If they do, they will constantly and eternally prove to be incorrect. Since, however, this creates prospects of unrealized profits, the conclusion suggests itself that as the public's understanding of floating rates accumulates, speculators should rationally shift their expectations from the notion of a long-run equilibrium rate to one of a long-run equilibrium rate of change. This would seem likely to become the most typical basis for the formation of expectations.

But it max be easily demonstrated that an expectations mechanism such as this is quite likely to render an otherwise stable system unstable. This proposition in no way depends on the assumption that expectations are rational. Instability can ensue even if speculators lack perfect foresight. The outcome depends solely on two factors - (a) the speed with which expected changes of the exchange rate adjust to actual changes ; and (b) the elasticity of the exchange rate with respect to exchange-rate expectations. Once again, a conclusion suggests itself: in view of the prospects of unrealized profits, at least the first of these two factors is apt to increase as the public's understanding of floating rates accumulates. Consequently, the probability of an unstable adjustment process would in fact appear to be quite high.

What, then, may we conclude? We may conclude that a small country that tries to choose its own independent inflation rate faces the prospect of increased instability. And how can this instability be avoided? It can be avoided by moving the target rate of inflation toward the world rate of inflation - and, ultimately, by equating the two (in which case speculation becomes stabilizing rather than destabilizing). Stability can be preserved - but only at the loss of the country's presumed extra degree of freedom. In practice, the country does not appear able to choose its own rate of inflation.

There is a general point here. It is that in analyzing the dynamics of floating exchange rates, especially for a small open economy, it is essential to take account of the feedback effects of exchange-rate movements on domestic economic policy. Models like Viotti's treat policy as exogenous and the exchange rate as endogenous. But in reality the two are mutually interactive. Not only can a country's policy drive its exchange rate; its exchange rate can drive its policy too. To consider just one possibility: in Viotti's model, the impacts of certain types of exogenous policy changes (specifically, a change of the foreign interest rate or a domestic open market operation) on the equilibrium level of the exchange rate (if it exists) are ambiguous. Consequently, it is not impossible to imagine situations in which speculators, no matter how well informed, tend to overshoot the equilibrium rate by a very sizable margin. It is also not impossible to imagine these movements in turn generating considerable pressures on the authorities to modify their existing economic policies - for example, pressures on the monetary authorities to expand money supply to accommodate wage and price increases provoked by a sizable depreciation. This is the grain of truth in the so-called vicious-circle hypothesis linking domestic price inflation to exchange-rate depreciation. And it is a truth that must not be ignored in studying the economics of flexible exchange rates.

SHORT-RUN ASSET AND THE REAL SECTOR DYNAMICS OF A SMALL OPEN ECONOMY UNDER FLEXIBLE EXCHANGE RATES*

Masanao Aoki

1. INTRODUCTION

Recently, the exchange rate dynamics has been examined by a number of writers using asset (portfolio balance) models of international financial markets. These writers focus their attention primarily on the financial sector.[1)]

In addition to feedback between the financial variables such as the exchange rate and "interest" rates and stocks of various financial assets, there also exists feedback between financial variables and the real sector variables such as price and output levels. This additional source of dynamics in studying open economies has not been fully treated by these writers in order to gain a partial but clear view of one important channel of adjustment by a simplified analysis (Branson, 1976), or if treated, it is done so in the context of longer-run growth models or stationary models (Dornbusch (1974) and Genberg-Kierzkowski (1975) for example).

It is necessary to examine the interaction between the asset sector and the real sector in the context of a much shorter run than steady or stationary state and on equal footing, i.e., in the

---

* The author would like to acknowledge comments made by Peter B. Clark, W. Branson, R. Findley and S. Viotti on the earlier version of the paper.

1) See for example papers in Volumne 28, No. 2 of the Scandinavian Journal of Economics (1976), Henderson (1976) or Branson (1972, 1976).

context of a general equilibrium model.[2] Thus we detect at least two gaps in the literature; lack of examination of dynamic behavior in finite time, and use of only partial equilibrium models of open economy.

The aim of this paper is to attempt to partially fill these gaps for a small open economy. In the process, we also generate several implications on macroeconomic policies in a small open economy under flexible exchange rates, some of which seem new.

The model is described in Section 2. We assume that domestic financial assets and foreign financial assets are imperfect substitutes. As for the real sector, we abstract from the distinction between traded and non-traded goods, (this simplification is made to facilitate our exposition), and assume that the domestic economy produces a composite output which is also an imperfect substitute for foreign goods. Flow equilibrium between demand and supply is assumed to be (re-)established in short run following a disturbance.

---

2) It is important to examine the effects of the real sector explicitly since without the real sector it is difficult to study how traditional demand management policy affects the price and output levels and the exchange rate, and since we are never sure how good and how partial are the results of the financial sector dynamic analysis without explicit examination of the effects of linkage between the financial and the real sector. The only exception would be the study of the impact effect of open-market operations which exchange two or more stocks of financial assets. Since no time elapses in such impact analysis, real variables do not adjust. As the time span of analysis lengthens, effects of the government budget deficit (or surplus), and of the current account surplus (or deficit) on the real variables are expected to increase, and so do the effects of the real sector on the asset sector.

We thus examine flow equilibrium dynamics.[3)] Our real sector is therefore more aggregated than that of Dornbusch (1974), for example, but our examination of interactions between the asset and the real sectors and their dynamic behavior is more explicit and detailed.

Dynamic behavior and macroeconomic policy implications of this small open economy under flexible exchange rates are studied by systematic examination of deviations of endogenous variables from a set of mutually consistently chosen reference time paths. (These time paths may represent trends of the endogenous variables due to long-run policy decision.)

There are two sets of variational relations we need: One is obtained from the asset sector and the other from the real sector. The former expresses the variations of the domestic interest rate and the exchange rate in terms of variations in the policy instruments and real sector variables. The other represents the variational relations of the aggregate demand schedule and aggregate supply schedule, and expresses variations of the domestic price level and real output in terms of the variations of the domestic interest rate and the exchange rate among others.[4)] These derivations

---

3) Following a disturbance, the real and/or financial sector variables deviate from their reference or trend time paths. Deviations in the domestic interest rate and the exchange rate from their reference or trend time paths, for example, cause the real sector variables to change further to achieve flow equilibrium in the face of the given deviations of the domestic interest rate and the exchange rate, completing a feedback path between the two sectors. A period (discrete time) model description of the above process is conceptually straightforward but mathematically somewhat cumbersome. We therefore use the continuous time description in this paper.

4) Alternate specifications of the aggregate supply relation, for example, give rise to slightly different variational expressions. To fix ideas, our discussions are carried out with a specific choice of the aggregate supply schedule. Consequences of alternate specifications can easily be examined following the procedure of this paper.

are carried out in Sections 3.1 and 3.2.

These two sets of the variational equations, when solved together for the endogenous variables of the real and the asset sector, yield a kind of reduced form relations for the variations of the domestic interest rate, the exchange rate, the domestic price, the domestic real output and the current account expression. This is carried out in Section 3.3.

The variations of the two flow constraint equations, i.e., the domestic government budget constraint and the current account equation, yield dynamic equations for the variational variables.[5)] Section 4 describes this short-run dynamic equation. We show, for a specific policy reaction function and for two alternate adaptive expectations mechanisms of the exchange rate changes, how the endogenous variables behave dynamically and we derive finite-time policy multipliers and show how they depend on the sizes of the government budget deficit and the current account. We derive conditions (which involve both the current account and the government budget deficit (or surplus)) for the variational variables to exhibit stable damped oscillation, or for them to become unstable. This seems new. Explicit examination of interactions between the policy makers' long-run and short-run choices in dynamic models which we carry out seems also to be new.

Recently Viotti also provided general equilibrium analysis of a small open economy (1977). His analysis shares our concern stated above that the models commonly used in the asset approach are either partial, or have only a vague general equilibrium structure and are not very well suited to derive comparison with the general equilibrium treatments of the fixed exchange rate case nor suited to study

---

5) Variation of the domestic capital stock accumulation equation should also be included in a longer-run analysis. We ignore the effects of the variation of the domestic capital stock in this paper.

the effects of traditional demand management policy. Our analysis, however, differs from his in some important technical detail. In particular, the short-run dynamics for the economy is explicitly derived using the perturbation analysis and macroeconomic policy implications are explored in more detail.

2. MODEL

The economy produces a single (composite) domestic good (flow variable) which may be consumed, traded or used as capital. Its domestic currency price is P. There are three financial assets (stock variables); domestic money, domestic government bonds and domestic equities which are assumed to be perfect substitutes, and foreign bonds, as we explain next.

We assume that firms own all of the capital stock. Private equities reflect ownership of the firms; thus the value of private equities is the value of the existing capital stock, K, which can deviate from its replacement cost P since there is assumed to be no direct market for capital in place. The market value of the domestic private equities is then $B/(i-\pi)$ where $B = (F_K-\sigma)KP$ where i is the domestic interest rate, π is the expected value of the domestic inflation rate. F_K is the marginal product of capital, σ is capital depreciation rate per unit capital stocks.[6] Variation of B due to changes in output, domestic price and i forms an important linkage between the asset and the real sectors.

The government issues bonds, which are perfect substitutes for private equities. The government bonds are treated also as consols.

---

6) Two alternate specifications on bonds are commonly adopted in the literature; one is to treat them as fixed-price variable return bonds, the other as consols. One may say that the former is more suitable for a short-run study. As far as impact analysis of open market and foreign exchange operations are concerned, however, the alternate specifications give rise to equite analogous results. Flood (1976) makes similar comments. Analysis in this paper is carried out using the consol specification. Analysis using the alternate specification has also been partially carried out. See Aoki (1977).

There are B_g of them each of unit domestic currency interest payment per period. The market value (in domestic currency) of the total domestic bonds and equities held by the domestic private sector is therefore $V/(i-\pi)$ where $V = B+B_g$. International bonds are also treated as consols. The value of domestic private holdings of international bonds in domestic currency are denoted by $EB_p^*/(i^*-\pi^*)$ where E is the exchange rate (domestic money price of the unit of foreign currency). The foreign variables are indicated by *. The home government holds the foreign bonds as international reserves, the number of which is denoted by B_g^*. Domestic and foreign financial assets are assumed to be imperfect substitutes.

The demands for these assets depend on expected interest rate differentials and a scale variable.

Following the asset-market view, we assume that there is portfolio equilibrium with respect to the composition of assets at each point in time (see Dornbusch (1975)).

We assume that non-human capital wealth is held in the form of three financial assets according to (in domestic currency)

$$M = \alpha(i, PY/W, i^* + \varepsilon)W \tag{1.A}$$

$$V/(i-\pi) = \beta(i, PY/W, i^* + \varepsilon)W \tag{1.B}$$

and

$$EB_p^*/(i^*-\pi^*) = \gamma(i, PY/W, i^* + \varepsilon)W \tag{1.C}$$

where W is the non-human nominal wealth of the domestic private sector, M is the stock of domestic money, V is the number of the domestic bond-equities treated as consols and B_p^* is the number of international bond-equities held by the domestic residents. Y is the domestic real output. ε is the expected rate of change of E, i.e., of $\dot{E}/E$. This specification is similar to the one used by Clark and Kwack (1976). When α, β, and γ do not depend on Y, (1) is the same as that used by Girton and Henderson (1977). We assume that foreigners do not hold domestic bonds.[7]

---

7) The other case, where the domestic bonds are internationally traded, can be treated similarly with suitable changes in asset equations (1). We do not do this here to develop our method for a simple case.

From the wealth constraint on the asset demand functions we have

$$\alpha + \beta + \gamma = 1, \ \gamma > 0$$

$$\alpha_i + \beta_i + \gamma_i = 0, \ i = 1{\sim}3 \ . \qquad (1.D)$$

We assume that $\alpha_2 > 0$, $\beta_1 > 0$, $\gamma_3 > 0$, and that the signs of all other partial derivatives are non-positive.[8)] These signs follow from the assumption of wealth normality and gross substitutability of the financial assets. When the wealth elasticity is assumed to be one as in (1), the domestic price level P_I (defined for example by $P_I = p^a(EP^*)^{1-a}$, $0 < a < 1$ where a is the weight assigned to the domestic price level) disappears from the asset equation and the direct effect of the change in the exchange rate is felt in the asset sector only if $\gamma > 0$. We assume $\gamma > 0$ from now on.[9)10)] The change

---

8) According to Dornbusch (p. 261 in Scan.J. Econ., 78, (1976)), $\alpha_1 \simeq -0.05\alpha/i$. We then write $\gamma_1 = -(0.05\nu/i)\nu$ where ν is some positive scalar number to indicate the relative degree by which wealth holders move out of the foreign securities as compared with that of domestic money. For example, $\nu = 1$ means that an increase in the domestic interest rate causes wealth holders to move out of domestic money and foreign securities by equal percentage. From (1.D), $\beta_1 = (0.05\alpha/i)(1+\nu)$.

9) The set of asset composition equations as given in (1) is a simplification of a more complex set of portfolio balance equation such as

$$M/P_I = L(i,Y,W/P_I)$$

$$V/(i-\pi)P_I = H(i,Y,W/P_I)$$

$$EB_p^*/(i^* - \pi^*)P_I = J(i,Y,W/P_I)$$

where

$$W = M + V/(i-\pi) + EB_p^*/(i^*-\pi^*),$$

where P_I is a domestic price level.

With the above, the instantaneous change in E, which we denote by ΔE causes the real non-human wealth to change discontinuously, since $\Delta P_I/P_I$ is a nonzero when $\Delta E \neq 0$. Hence, the changes in i and E in response to open-market operations include effects due to the instantaneous change in P_I. This effect is absent in the model of (1). See Aoki (1977) for the analysis of open market operations.

10) If $\gamma = 0$, then the matrix Φ in (4) is singular. This is because the composition of the wealth and the portfolio is independent of E when $\gamma = 0$. Thus we assume $\gamma > 0$. If the wealth and portfolio compositions are specified as in footnote 9, then even if $\gamma = 0$, we can show that the matrix corresponding to (4) is nonsingular, since E affects W/P_I because $\Delta P_I \neq 0$ when $\Delta E \neq 0$.

in P_I due to change E is captured in the real sector. See (12) below. In order to facilitate our presentation, we derive all the formulas assuming that $i*$ and $\pi*$ are constants.

3. SHORT-RUN ANALYSIS

We now present a systematic procedure to discuss interactions between the asset sector variables and the real sector variables in the short run, taking into account cumulative effects of past open market and/or foreign exchange operations on the real variables as well as effects of changes (over time) of other instruments.[11] We use the notation δ to indicate variation of variables in short run. For example $\delta i(t)$ is defined by

$$i^{\mu}(t) = i^{o}(t) + \mu\delta i(t) + o(t,\mu) , \quad t \geq t_o$$

where μ is the perturbation or variational parameters, i^{μ} and i^{o} are perturbed and reference time paths of the interest rate, i.e., $\mu\delta i(t)$ is the difference between the perturbed and a reference time path of i. If an open-market operation is conducted at time t_o, then $\delta i(t_o) = \Delta i(t_o) \neq 0$ where $\Delta i(t_o)$ is the discontinuous (instantaneous) change in i at the time of the open-market operation conducted at t_o, but $\delta i(t_o+\delta t) \neq \Delta i(t_o)$ generally. Here $\delta t > 0$ denotes a small time interval. Expressions such as δP and δY are defined analogously.

Changes in the stock variables are also expressed using δ notation, for example, as $M^{\mu}(t) = M^{o}(t)(i+\mu\delta m(t)) + o(t\ ,\mu)$ where we shall denote proportional changes by lower case letters except for i. The exact magnitudes of δm, δb_g, ... are constrained by the government budget equation and the current account equation, as we discuss them later. From now on, we drop the supercript μ for simpler notation.

---

11) Our procedure is similar in spirit to the one described by Branson (1976). Ours is better, since in addition to the government budget constraint, we use a more detailed specification of the real sector as well.

3.1 ASSET SECTOR

We obtain short-run variational expressions for i and E from the portfolio balance equations in the asset sector. Since one of the three equations (1.A) ~ (1.C) is redundant, we drop (1.C). To convey the main idea simply, we neglect δk. (In a longer-run analysis, δk has non-negligible effects on the dynamic multipliers we derive later.)

Following our notational convention, we write

$$\delta b_p^* = \delta B_p^*/B_p^* .$$

The variational expressions obtained from (1.A) and (1.B) can be arranged as

$$\Phi \begin{bmatrix} \delta i \\ \delta e \end{bmatrix} = \begin{bmatrix} 1-\alpha \\ -\alpha \end{bmatrix} \delta m + \begin{bmatrix} -\beta \\ 1-\beta \end{bmatrix} (\delta v + \frac{\beta_p}{\beta} \frac{\delta\pi}{r}) - \gamma \begin{bmatrix} 1 \\ 1 \end{bmatrix} \delta b_p^* - \begin{bmatrix} \alpha_3/\alpha \\ \beta_3/\beta \end{bmatrix} \delta\varepsilon + z \quad (2)$$

where $r = i-\pi$ is the domestic reat rate of interest, δv is defined by (5) below and where the term z, defined by

$$z = \frac{PY}{W} \begin{bmatrix} \alpha_2/\alpha \\ \beta_2/\beta \end{bmatrix} \{(\alpha\delta m + \beta\delta v + \gamma\delta b_p^*) - (\beta/r)\delta\pi - (\delta p + \delta y)\}, \quad (3)$$

collects all the terms expressing the effect of the transaction demands for the domestic money and the domestic securities, and where

$$\Phi = \begin{bmatrix} \Phi_1 & \Phi_2 \\ \Phi_3 & \Phi_4 \end{bmatrix} \quad \text{with} \quad (4)$$

$\Phi_1 = \alpha_1/\alpha - \beta/r' + (\beta/r)(\alpha_2/\alpha)PY/W, \quad \Phi_2 = \gamma - \gamma(\alpha_2/\alpha)PY/W,$

$r' = r/(1 - \frac{\beta_p}{\beta} \frac{\pi}{i})$

$\Phi_3 = \beta_1/\beta + (1-\beta)/r' + (\beta/r)(\beta_2/\beta)PY/W - \gamma(\beta_2/\beta)PY/W,$

$\Phi_4 = \gamma - \gamma(\beta_2/\beta)PY/W.$

Since the determinant of Φ, $|\Phi|$ is proportional to γ, the matrix Φ is nonsingular provided $\gamma > 0$. Its determinant is approximately given by

$$\gamma(\alpha_1/\alpha - \beta_1/\beta - 1/r')$$

when we ignore terms proportional to $\gamma PY/W$ as being small.

In the above, δv is expressible from its definition as

$$\delta v = (\beta_p/\beta)\delta b + (\beta_g/\beta)\delta b_g \qquad (5)$$

where $\beta_p = \beta - \beta_g$, where δb is expressible as $\delta b = h\delta y + \delta p$ and where $h = F_k/(F_k - \sigma) > 1$ is a parameter (this follows from $B = (F_k - \sigma)KP$ where we assume the Cobb-Douglas production function with the parameter $\bar{\alpha}$ hence $F_k = \bar{\alpha}Y/K$).

After replacing δv by (5), we solve (2) to obtain the first set of the variational equations:

$$\begin{bmatrix} \delta i \\ \delta e \end{bmatrix} = \begin{bmatrix} -\sigma_1 \\ \theta_1 \end{bmatrix} \delta m + \begin{bmatrix} \sigma_2 \\ \theta_2 \end{bmatrix} \delta bg - \begin{bmatrix} \sigma_3 \\ \theta_3 \end{bmatrix} \delta b_p^* + \begin{bmatrix} \sigma_4 \\ \theta_4 \end{bmatrix} \delta \varepsilon \qquad (6)$$

$$+ \begin{bmatrix} \sigma_5 \\ \theta_5 \end{bmatrix} \delta \pi + \begin{bmatrix} \sigma_6 \\ \theta_6 \end{bmatrix} \delta p + \begin{bmatrix} \sigma_7 \\ \theta_7 \end{bmatrix} \delta y \quad .$$

See Appendix 1 for the exact expressions for σ's and θ's in (6). (6) describes how short-run behavior of the financial variables i and E depends on specific assumptions we make about the asset composition and their interest and income elasticities.

3.2 REAL SECTOR

We derive next deviations of the real variables by variations of the aggregate demand and supply schedules. This analysis takes the place of more traditional IS-LM analysis.

Putting these two sets of variational equations together, we later deduce the effects of feedback between the two sectors. In this way, we can also distinguish primary effects that some policy instruments, such as the government expenditures, have on the endogenous variables and their secondary (or feedback) effects. First, we write the GNP identity by purchasers as $Y^D = \dot{K}+\sigma K+C+X+G$, where C is the real demand for the domestic output by the domestic residents. X is the real exports. The real rate of investment is assumed to be given by (we assume that only domestic goods are used for investment) $\dot{K}=I=I(F_K-\sigma-i+\pi)$, $I' > 0$. We assume that[12)]

$$C = C(Y',\nu,\varepsilon),\ C_1 > 0,\ C_2 < 0,\ C_3\ ?\ , \tag{7}$$

$$X = X(\nu,\varepsilon),\ X_1 < 0,\ X_2\ ?\ , \tag{8}$$

where $\nu = P/EP*$, (this is the terms of trade) and where Y' is the disposable income. Consequences of including W and C are discussed in Footnote 12.

The variational expression for Y^D is (dropping superscript D)

$$\delta y = d_o\delta g + d_1\delta y' - d_2\delta r - d_3(\delta p-\delta e) + d_4\delta\varepsilon \tag{9}$$

where

$$d = Y - I'F_K$$
$$d_o = G/d$$
$$d_1 = C_1Y'/d$$
$$d_2 = I'/d$$
$$d_3 = -(X_1+C_2)\nu/d$$
$$d_4 = (X_2+C_3)/d$$

These coefficients are assumed to be positive except for d_4 which is ambiguous. We take Y' to be approximately given by (see Wallace (1972))

$$P_IY' = P(Y-\sigma K-T) + B_g + EB_p^* \tag{1o}$$

---

12) If we include W as an argument of C, Eq. (13) in the text will additionally contain δC terms due to the change in wealth;

$$\delta W/W = \alpha\delta m + \beta_p\ \delta b + \beta_g\delta b_g + \gamma(\delta e + \delta b_p^*) - \beta\delta r/r\ .$$

Referring to (11) and (13), we see that two new terms due to δm and δb_g are introduced by this modification. If these terms are ignored, then (13) is formally the same regardless of the dependence of C on W, except for the facts that coefficients in (13) are somewhat modified. With δm and δbg terms in (16), (17.A) contains these two terms. Consequently in (17.A) and (17.B), δm and δb_p^* terms in addition to δg and δT/T terms have direct as well as secondary feedback effects which tends to reduce the direct effects δm has on δi and δe.

where T is the real tax receipt, σ is the depreciation rate of capital stock per unit stock, and P_I is the price index which is the weighted geometric average of home and foreign prices. We treat the weight a as fixed. The foreign price is also assumed to be held fixed.

Then taking the variation of (1o), and collecting like terms together, we relate the variation in Y' to those of P, Y, K, i, E, B_g, etc. as approximately

$$\delta y' \approx \bar{\ell}_1(\delta p - \delta e) + \bar{\ell}_2 \delta y - (\bar{\ell}_2 - 1)\delta T/T \tag{11}$$

where $\bar{\ell}$'s are the elasticities of the real disposable income with respect to the domestic price, real GNP and so on. The expressions for $\bar{\ell}$'s simplify when we ignore the interest receipts, B_g and EB_p^*, as being small compared with $P_I Y'$. Furthermore, $\bar{\ell}_1$ then becomes approximately equal to $\bar{\ell}_1 \approx (1-a)$, and $\bar{\ell}_2 \approx 1+\bar{\ell}_8$, if we ignore σK term in (1o). Here, $\bar{\ell}_1$ represents approximately the direct effect of the exchange rate change on the domestic price level since

$$\delta P_I / P_I = (1-a)\ \delta e + a\delta p\ . \tag{12}$$

See Appendix 1 for the exact expressions of the coefficients.

Eliminate $\delta y'$ from (9) and (11). The result is the expression for δy^D, δp in terms of $\delta T/T, \delta i, \delta e$ and the instruments

$$\mu_1 \delta y^D + \mu_2 \delta p = -\mu_4 \delta r + \mu_2 \delta e + \mu_o \delta g - \mu_8 \delta T/T + \mu_3 \delta \varepsilon \tag{13}$$

where the expressions for μ's are found in the Appendix 1.

This is the variational expression for the aggregate demand schedule in the short run, valid when the interest receipts and capital stock depreciation are negligible compared with $P_I Y'$. The slope of (13) is given by $\delta p/\delta y^D = -\mu_2/\mu_1$. The aggregate demand is downward sloping, therefore, if $d_3 - d_1 \bar{\ell}_1 > 0$ or if

$$-\ (X_1 + C_2)\nu / Y' > (1-a)\ C_1\ . \tag{14}$$

Roughly speaking, if the total demand of the domestic output is more responsive to direct price effect than to change in the disposable income due to the exchange rate change, then the aggregate demand is downward sloping.

Eq. (13) shows that an expansionary fiscal policy $\delta g > 0$ shifts the variational curve out directly. An expansionary monetary policy $\delta m > 0$ does not have a direct effect but has an expansionary effect which works through δi and δe. (See footnote 12.) This can be seen from (6) and (13).

To separate δy from δp in (13) we need another relation. We could postulate δp by a mark-up relation or we would specify an aggregate supply schedule. We adopt the latter approach and assume that flow equilibrium is (re-)established in short run between variations of the aggregate supply and demand to determine δy and δp. We take as the variational espression for our aggregate supply curve[13)]

$$\delta y^s = s_1 \delta k + s_2 \delta p - s_3 \delta e \simeq s_2 \delta p - s_3 \delta e \ . \qquad (15)$$

---

13) We used a production function $Y^s = F(K,L)$, together with the equation for demand for labor, in which the real wage is equated to the marginal product of labor, taking the money wage as fixed in the short-run, to produce (15). There are alternatives to the price equation (16) which was derived using the aggregate supply curve of the open economy (15) together with the aggregate demand equation (13).
One alternative is to modify the expression for the marginal product of labor according to some measure of demand pressure. Shafter (1976) adopts this tack. Another possibility that is suggested in the literature is to relate the price to marginal cost with variable mark-up in which the mark-up is made to depend on some measure of market demand, typically capacity utilization. In models of closed economy, Nordhaus, (1972), de Menil and Gordon (1975) have discussed such schemes. In models of open economy, Howard Howe (1976) proposed to use this scheme of price determination with suitable modification to account for the effects of price of imports. This approach seems appropriate in open economies since the production sector may have some monopolistic power. We do not examine implications of this alternative in this paper, since the procedure of analysis is identical to the one given in the paper, although the coefficients in (16) will be altered.

See for example Salop (1974) for derivation. Her procedure can be extended to include the effect on the aggregate supply of the exchange rate change. Fixed money wage as well as some change in the money wage can be accommodated by (15). If we assume that the labor market clears, then $s_2 = s_3 > 0$. If the labor market does not necessarily clear, then $s_2 > s_3$.

From the assumed flow equilibrium, we set $\delta y^S = \delta y^D = \delta y$. Then (13) and (15) are used to solve for δp and δy. We can express δp as

$$\delta p \simeq \pi_o \delta g - \pi_1 \delta r + \pi_2 \delta e - \pi_3 \delta \varepsilon + \pi_6 \delta T/T \qquad (16)$$

where the coefficients are given in Appendix 1. Only when I' is zero, $\pi_1 = 0$ and δi has no effect on δp and δy. On the other hand, if $s_2 = s_3 = 0$, then $\delta y = 0$, i.e., δi and δe affect only δp.[14)] Eq. (15) and (16) summarize how the real sector variables respond to deviations in the financial variables and the fiscal instruments G and T. We have $\pi_1 \geq \pi_2$ or $\pi_1 \leq \pi_2$, depending on whether the relative sensitivity of the demand for investment with respect to the interest change is greater or less than the demand of domestic goods for domestic consumption and exports due to the change in the terms of trade.

If $\mu_2 > 0$ (for example by satisfying (14)) then π's are all positive except for π_3 which is ambiguous. The elasticities of the exports with respect to the real disposable income all affect π_1, and π_2 in (16). With $s_2 = s_3$, π_2 becomes one indicating that δe is fully reflected in δp in (16) and $\delta y = 0$. We would expect that $s_2 > s_3$. This implies that $\pi_2 < 1$ so that δe is not fully reflected in δp in (16) with nonzero δy.

---

14) We thus see the very special nature of the assumptions such as $\delta y = 0$ and/or $\delta p = 0$.

3.3 FEEDBACK PATHS

We solve (6), (15) and (16) to obtain the reduced form expression for δi, δe, δp and δy:

$$\begin{matrix}\delta i \\ \delta e\end{matrix} = \begin{bmatrix}\rho_1 \\ \rho_2\end{bmatrix} \delta b_p^* + \begin{bmatrix}f_1 \\ f_2\end{bmatrix} \delta g + \begin{bmatrix}\varepsilon_1 \\ \varepsilon_2\end{bmatrix} \delta m + \begin{bmatrix}\delta_1 \\ \delta_2\end{bmatrix} \delta b_g + \begin{bmatrix}\zeta_1 \\ \zeta_2\end{bmatrix} \delta \varepsilon + \begin{bmatrix}\eta_1 \\ \eta_2\end{bmatrix} \delta \pi \quad (17.A)$$

and

$$\begin{matrix}\delta p \\ \delta y\end{matrix} = \begin{bmatrix}\rho_3 \\ \rho_4\end{bmatrix} \delta b_p^* + \begin{bmatrix}f_3 \\ f_4\end{bmatrix} \pi_0 \delta g + \begin{bmatrix}\varepsilon_3 \\ \varepsilon_4\end{bmatrix} \delta m + \begin{bmatrix}\delta_3 \\ \delta_4\end{bmatrix} \delta b_g + \begin{bmatrix}\zeta_3 \\ \zeta_4\end{bmatrix} \delta \varepsilon + \begin{bmatrix}\eta_3 \\ \eta_4\end{bmatrix} \delta \pi \quad (17.B)$$

where

$$\Sigma = \begin{bmatrix}\overset{+}{\sigma_6} & \overset{+}{\sigma_7} \\ \overset{-}{\theta_6} & \overset{?}{\theta_7}\end{bmatrix}, \qquad \Pi = \begin{bmatrix}-\overset{-}{\pi_1} & \overset{+}{\pi_2} \\ -s_2\pi_1 & \overset{?}{s_2\pi_2 - s_3}\end{bmatrix},$$

$$\begin{bmatrix}\rho_1 \\ \rho_2\end{bmatrix} = -(I - \Sigma\Pi)^{-1} \begin{bmatrix}\sigma_3 \\ \theta_3\end{bmatrix}, \quad \begin{bmatrix}\rho_3 \\ \rho_4\end{bmatrix} = \Pi \begin{bmatrix}\rho_1 \\ \rho_2\end{bmatrix}, \quad (18)$$

$$\begin{bmatrix}f_1 \\ f_2\end{bmatrix} = (I - \Sigma\Pi)^{-1}\Sigma \begin{bmatrix}1 \\ s_2\end{bmatrix} \pi_0, \quad \begin{bmatrix}f_3 \\ f_4\end{bmatrix} = \begin{bmatrix}1 \\ s_2\end{bmatrix} \pi_0 + \Pi \begin{bmatrix}f_1 \\ f_2\end{bmatrix} \pi_0,$$

$$\begin{bmatrix}\varepsilon_1 \\ \varepsilon_2\end{bmatrix} = (I - \Sigma\Pi)^{-1} \begin{bmatrix}-\sigma_1 \\ \theta_1\end{bmatrix}, \quad \begin{bmatrix}\varepsilon_3 \\ \varepsilon_4\end{bmatrix} = \Pi \begin{bmatrix}\varepsilon_1 \\ \varepsilon_2\end{bmatrix}, \quad \begin{bmatrix}\zeta_1 \\ \zeta_2\end{bmatrix} = (I - \Sigma\Pi)^{-1} \begin{bmatrix}\sigma_4 \\ \theta_4\end{bmatrix},$$

$$\begin{bmatrix}\delta_1 \\ \delta_2\end{bmatrix} = (I - \Sigma\Pi)^{-1} \begin{bmatrix}\sigma_1 \\ \theta_2\end{bmatrix}, \quad \begin{bmatrix}\delta_3 \\ \delta_4\end{bmatrix} = \Pi \begin{bmatrix}\delta_1 \\ \delta_2\end{bmatrix} \begin{bmatrix}\zeta_3 \\ \zeta_4\end{bmatrix} = \Pi \begin{bmatrix}\zeta_1 \\ \zeta_2\end{bmatrix} + \pi_3 \begin{bmatrix}1 \\ s_2\end{bmatrix},$$

$$\begin{bmatrix}\eta_1 \\ \eta_2\end{bmatrix} = (I - \Sigma\Pi)^{-1} \begin{bmatrix}\sigma_5 \\ \theta_5\end{bmatrix}, \quad \begin{bmatrix}\eta_3 \\ \eta_4\end{bmatrix} = \Pi \begin{bmatrix}\eta_1 \\ \eta_2\end{bmatrix} + \pi_1 \begin{bmatrix}1 \\ s_2\end{bmatrix}.$$

We can treat variation in the real tax receipt as exogenous or endogenize $\delta T/T$ by $\delta T/T = \kappa \delta y$ where $\kappa = T'(Y)Y/T$ is the real income elasticity of the real tax receipt, and treat κ as one of the instruments. The former is simpler. Read $\pi_o \delta g$ to stand for $\pi_o \delta g - \pi_o \delta T/T$ for this case and set $\kappa = 0$. The expressions for f_3 and f_4 show that δg has the direct effect on the real variables given by the first term as well as the secondary effect from the financial sector. As discussed in footnote 12, inclusion of the wealth effect in the consumption function specification would introduce direct effects due to δm and δb_g into the above as well.

3.4 THE CURRENT ACCOUNT

Although (17) is useful in assessing short-run effects of fiscal and monetary policies, they do not tell the whole story since δm, δb_g, δb_p^* and δg are interconnected through the government budget constraint and the current account. We next derive the variational expression for the current account, U, since it changes with time as the real and financial variables such as i, e, p and y' change with time. The current account is defined to be

$$U = E(B_g^* + B_p^*) + F \tag{19}$$

where

$$F = PX - EP^*IM$$

where the second term represents the trade balance in domestic currency, where IM is the real import assumed to be specified by $IM(Y', \nu, \varepsilon)$, $IM_1 > 0$, $IM_2 > 0$, $IM_3 ?$.

Variation in U, caused by variations in the financial and real sector variables, is expressible as

$$\delta U = \{\frac{\partial U}{\partial i}\,\delta i + \frac{\partial U}{\partial e}\,\delta e + \frac{\partial U}{\partial p}\,\delta p + \frac{\partial U}{\partial y} \cdot \delta y'\} \tag{2o}$$
$$+ \text{(terms due to instrument variations).}$$

We can calculate the partial derivatives as follows:

$$\partial U/\partial i = E\, B_p^*(1 + B_g^*/B_p^*)(\gamma_1/\gamma - \beta/(i-\pi))$$

since $\partial F/\partial i \approx 0$.

Differentiation of (19) with respect to e, p and y' yield respectively

$$\partial U/\partial e = \partial F/\partial e + E\,(B_p^* + B_g^*)$$

where

$$\partial F/\partial e = (PX'-EP^{*}IM_2)\tau - EP^{*}IM\text{, and}$$

$$\partial U/\partial p = \partial F/\partial p = pX + (PX' - EP^{*}IM_2)(-\tau),$$

and finally $\partial U/\partial y' = \partial F/\partial y' = - EP^{*}IM_1 < 0.$

The term $\partial F/\partial p$ is the one associated with the Marshall-Lerner condition. From (19) and (2o), we can write δU as

$$\delta U = \lambda_1 \delta b_p^* + f_5 \delta g + \varepsilon_5 \delta m + \delta_5 \delta b_g + \zeta_5 \delta\varepsilon + \eta_5 \delta\pi \qquad (21)$$

The expression for λ_1 is given in Appendix 2. It is likely to be negative. In Section 4, we need signs of δ's of (18) and (21). It is likely that $\delta_1 > 0$, $\delta_2 < 0$, $\delta_3 < 0$, $\delta_5 < 0$. The sign of δ_4 is somewhat ambiguous but is likely to be negative if $s_3 < s_2$.

4. SHORT-RUN DYNAMIC EQUATION

We are now ready to derive the differential equations for the perturbed time paths of the stocks of B_p^*, B_g^*, M and B_g. Coupled with (17) and (21), the differential equations also describe the time paths for δi, δe, δy, δp and δU.

Short-run decisions by the policy makers can, of course, deviate from their long-run decision. In the short run, the proportion of the government deficit to be financed by money and the degrees of intervention in the foreign exchange market, for example, can differ from their long-run or steady-state rates. We later show how policy makers' choice of the long-run (trend or growth) rates of the stocks of money, the government bonds, and of the international bonds affect stability of short-run dynamics of the perturbed variables.

The long-run policies determine the rates of growth of what we call the reference time paths. We assume that the reference growth rates are given by

$$\dot{B}_g^{*o}/B_g^{*o} = \ell_1, \quad \dot{B}_p^{*o}/B_p^{*o} = \ell_2, \quad \dot{M}_d^o/M_d^o = \ell_3, \quad \dot{B}_g^o/B_g^o = \ell_4$$

(they could be time-varying) where M_d is the domestic component of the money base. (The superscript ^{o} refers to the reference time paths.

We drop it in the following.) The rates of growth $\ell_1 \sim \ell_4$ are not independent but are subject to the constraints on long-run policy choices. We do not discuss the long-run policy choices here but assume that $\ell_1 \sim \ell_4$ are consistently chosen.

The short-run dynamic analysis is subject to two constraints on the flow variables. One is the government budget constraint $\dot{M}_d + \dot{B}_g/(i-\pi) = D$ where $D = P(G-T) + B_g - EB_g^*$ is the budget deficit when $D > 0$. It states that the government deficit (in the domestic currency) must be financed either by (the domestic component of) money or issuing the government bonds. Because of the assumption that the bonds are perpetuities, B_g and EB_g^* are the interest on the government bonds and on the international reserves. The other constraint is expressed in terms of the current account, which describes the rate at which the small economy is accumulating the international bonds $\dot{B}_p^* + \dot{B}_g^* = (U/E)(i*-\pi*)$, where U is defined by (19). The variation of the budget constraint yields

$$\delta\dot{m}_d + \ell_3\delta m + \phi(\delta\dot{b}_g + \ell_4\delta b_g) - \ell_4\phi(\delta r/r) = \delta D/M_d \qquad (22)$$

where

$$\phi = B_g/(r\ M_d),$$

$$\delta\dot{M}_d/M_d = \delta\dot{m}_d + \ell_3\delta m_d,$$

and

$$\delta\dot{B}_g/B_g = \dot{b}_g + \ell_4\delta b_g\ . \qquad (23)$$

and where, taking the variation of the government budget deficit, we have

$$\delta D/M_d = m_o\delta g + m_1\delta p - m_2\delta y + m_3\delta b_g - m_4(\delta e + \delta b_g^*). \qquad (24)$$

Here we define

$$m_o = PG/M_d,\ m_1 = P(G-T)/M_d$$

$$m_2 = PT(Y)\kappa/M \text{ where } \kappa = T'(Y)Y/T(Y),$$

$$m_3 = B_g/M_d,\ m_4 = EB_g^*/M_d\ .$$

We assume for simplicity that m_3 and m_4 are small and neglect them in what follows. Note that $m_1 \lesseqgtr 0$ depending on the status of the budget. The sign of m_1 will be important in the stability conditions we derive below. The variational expression of the current account equation is

$$\delta\dot{b}_p^* + \ell_2\delta b_p^* + (B_g^*/B_p^*)(\delta\dot{b}_g^* + \ell_1\delta b_g^*) = (r^*/EB_p^*)(\delta U - U\delta e). \quad (25)$$

This equation states how the total accumulation of the international bonds by the small economy deviates from the reference (or planned) time path. The manner by which the total deviation is divided into the private and the government holding is determined in part by a short-run policy of the government foreign exchange market intervention.

Eq. (22) and (25) can be solved for two of the variational expressions of the instrumente, or we can examine various alternate policy (reaction) functions (behavioral rules) in which the variation of the instruments are made to depend on current (and past) values of δi, δe, δp, etc., subject to these two constraints.

We illustrate our procedure for analyzing dynamic implication of policy functions with a behavioral rule $\delta\dot{M}_d = \bar{\theta}(\delta y, \delta\pi)$ and $\delta\dot{B}_g^* = \bar{s}(\delta e)$; the domestic component of the money stock is varied as a function of deviations of the real output and the inflation rate, and the stock of international reserve is varied as the exchange rate deviates from its reference value.

In terms of the proportional (lower case) variables they are expressible as

$$\delta\dot{m}_d = \theta_1\delta y + \theta_2\delta\pi - \ell_3\delta m_d \quad (26)$$

and

$$\delta\dot{b}_g^* = s\delta e - \ell_1\delta b_g^* \quad (27)$$

where

$$\theta_1 = \bar{\theta}_1/(\bar{\theta}\ M_d), \quad \theta_2 = \bar{\theta}_2/(\bar{\theta}\ M_d)$$

$$s = \bar{s}'/(\bar{s}\ B_g^*)\ .$$

To conserve space, we assume $\delta\pi = 0$ from now on, even though $\delta\pi \neq 0$ can be incorporated with no difficulty. Eq. (26), (22), (27) and (25) jointly determine the set of differential equations for δm_d, δb_g, δb_g^* and δb_p^* that is implied by the two flow constraint equations. They are

$$dz/dt = L_1 z + L_2 \begin{bmatrix} \delta p \\ \delta y \end{bmatrix} + L_3 \begin{bmatrix} \delta e \\ \delta U/R^* \end{bmatrix} + L_4 \delta i + L_5 \delta g, \quad (28)$$

where

$$z = (\delta b_g^*, \delta b_p^*, \delta m_d, \delta b_g)', \quad L_1 = \text{diag}\,(-\ell_1, -\ell_2, -\ell_3, -\ell_4)$$

$$L_2 = \begin{bmatrix} 0 & 0 \\ 0 & 0 \\ 0 & \theta_1 \\ m_1/\phi & -(m_2+\theta_1)/\phi \end{bmatrix}, \quad L_3 = \begin{bmatrix} s & 0 \\ -\mu s - U & 1 \\ 0 & 0 \\ 0 & 0 \end{bmatrix}, \quad L_4 = \begin{bmatrix} 0 \\ 0 \\ 0 \\ 1 \end{bmatrix} (\ell_4/r)$$

$$L_5 = \begin{bmatrix} 0 \\ 0 \\ 0 \\ 1 \end{bmatrix} \frac{m_2}{\phi} \qquad \phi = B_g/rM_d, \quad \mu = B_g^*/B_p^*, \quad R^* = EB_p^*/r^*.$$

When δi, δe, δp and δe given by (17) are substituted into the above, (28) is converted into

$$dz/dt = Z_1 \delta z + \zeta_1 \delta\varepsilon + \zeta_2 \delta g \quad (29)$$

The exact expression of Z_1, ζ_1 and ζ_2 are given in Appendix 2.

To incorporate dynamics of $\delta\varepsilon$, we examine two alternate adaptive expectation mechanisms: One is adaptation to the level of e

$$\varepsilon = -a(e-\bar{e}), \quad a > 0 \quad (3o)$$

where $\bar{e}$ is the (logarithm of the) equilibrium exchange rate which is assumed to exist. In equilibrium

$$e = \bar{e} \text{ and } \varepsilon = 0.$$

The other is the mechanism for adaptation to the rate

$$d\varepsilon/dt = -b(\varepsilon-\dot{e}) \ , \quad b > 0 \ . \tag{31}$$

Here $\varepsilon = \dot{e}$ = constant holds in the steady state.
With (3o), $\delta\varepsilon = -a\delta e$, when δe is substituted out using (17). (29) becomes

$$dz/dt = Z_1{}' \ \delta z + \zeta_2{}'\delta g \tag{32}$$

where Z_1' and $\zeta_2{}'$ are Z_1 and ζ_2 modified respectively by a matrix of rank one. The eigenvalues of Z_1' are shown to be the roots (for the case $\theta = 0$ and $s = 0$.)

$$0 = |\lambda I - Z_1'| = (\lambda+\ell_1)(\lambda+\ell_3)\ [(\lambda+\ell_4-\psi_\delta')(\lambda+\ell_2-\lambda_2') - \nu_\delta\psi_\delta']$$

where[15]

$\psi_\delta' = \psi_\delta - a' \ \psi_\zeta\delta_2$, $a' = a/(1+a\zeta_2)$

$\lambda_2' = \lambda_2 - a'\nu_\zeta\delta_2$ and where ψ_δ and ν_ζ are defined in Appendix 2. Since $\ell_1 > 0$ and $\ell_3 > 0$, (32) is stable if and only if the roots of the quadratic polynominal in the square bracket is stable. We can assume that $\ell_4 - \psi_\delta' > 0$ and $\ell_2 - \lambda_2' > 0$ for positive ℓ_2 and ℓ_4 (i.e., unless ℓ_2 and ℓ_4 are both zero). Assuming that ℓ_2 and $\ell_4 > 0$, Z_1' is stable if $\nu_\delta\psi_\delta' < 0$. If $\nu_\delta\psi_\delta' > 0$ and smaller, there can be one unstable root. When we write out the expression for $\nu_\delta\psi_\delta'$, the sign condition can be expressed equivalently as follows:
Theorem. The variational dynamics with an adaptive expectations mechanism (32) ist stable for $\theta_1 = 0$ and $s = 0$ if

(i) $\ell_1 > 0$, $\ell_3 > 0$, $\ell_2-\lambda_2' > 0$ and $\ell_4-\psi_\delta' > 0$, and

(ii) $U \geq \underline{U}$ and $m_1 \geq \underline{m}_1$ or $U \leq \underline{U}$ and $m_1 \leq \underline{m}_1$

where $\underline{U} = (\delta_5 - a'\delta_2\zeta_5)(1+a'\zeta_2)/\delta_2 > 0$

---

15) ζ_2 is likely to be positive so that $a' > 0$. If $\zeta_2 < 0$, choose a small enough so that $a' > 0$.

and $\underline{m}_1 = [(\ell_4\phi/r)(\delta_1-a'\zeta_1)-m_2(\delta_4-a'\zeta_4)]/(\delta_3-a'\zeta_3)$. In both cases damped oscillations are possible for small $|\nu_\delta\psi_\delta'|$[16]. Condition (ii) states that for the time path with m_1 larger than its critical value $\underline{m}_1$, the current account must be sufficiently positive for (32) to be stable. The possibility of damped oscillation for $|\nu_\delta\psi_\delta'|$ small seems to be new.

When (32) is unstable, there is no oscillations. The variables diverge exponentially. With the other expectations mechanism (31), its variation equals

$$\delta\dot{\varepsilon} = -b(\delta\varepsilon - \delta\dot{e}), \quad b > 0. \tag{33}$$

Differentiating δe of (17) with respect to time and substituting it in (33), we can solve the result as

$$\delta\dot{\varepsilon} = -b'\delta\varepsilon + b'(b_2\delta\dot{g} + \varepsilon_2\delta\dot{m})$$

where

$$b' = b/(1-b\zeta_2).$$

To avoid a possibility of b' becoming negative if $\zeta_2 > 0$ and b is sufficiently large, we consider only those b with $b\zeta_2 < 1$. Combined with (29), it produces now a differential equation of dimension five: However, with $\theta_1 = 0$ and $s = 0$, the new eigenvalue introduced by this expectations mechanisms is just $-b'$. Thus, the dynamics is essentially the same as that of (32), except for one additional stable eigenvalue $-b'$.

5. DISCUSSIONS AND CONCLUSIONS

Eigenvalues of (32) are functions of $\ell_1 \sim \ell_4$, i.e., long-run rates of growth of the stock variables. Given these long-run rates, the solution of (32) is the finite-time dynamic policy multiplier since

---

16) We assume that $\delta_2/(1+a'\zeta_2) > 0$ and $(\delta_3-a'\zeta_3) < 0$. Both signs are likely to hold.

$$z(t) = \phi(t,t_o)\, z(t_o) + \int_{t_o}^{t} \phi\, (t,\tau)\zeta_2'\delta g(\tau)d\tau \qquad (34)$$

where $\phi(t,\tau)$ is the fundamental matrix of solution of (32). For specific form of $\delta g(\cdot)$, (34) can be evaluted to give the finite-time fiscal multiplier. For example, if $\delta g(\tau) = 0$ outside of a small neighborhood of $\tau = s$, i.e., if

$$\delta g(\tau) = \begin{cases} \delta g_o & u \leq \tau \leq u + \delta u \\ 0 & \text{otherwise} \end{cases},$$

then assuming $z(t_o) = 0$, $z(t) = \phi(t,u)\zeta_2'\delta g_o \delta u$, i.e., $\phi(t,u)\zeta_2'\delta u$ is the policy multiplier. Other types of variations in δg can be equally accommodated in this framework. See Aoki (1978) and Aoki-Canzoneri (1976) for additional detail.

Although we have examined a single policy function, other policy functions can similarly be examined and the resultant time paths of the endogenous variables can be compared. For example, consequences of 1oo % monetization of the budget deficit or various degrees of intervention in the foreign exchange markets can be analyzed, and the time paths compared.

In this paper we have given a systematic procedure for evaluating the variational dynamics and for deriving dynamic policy multipliers. We have given conditions for stability of the variational dynamics for a particular policy reaction function which requires certain inequalities be satisfied for the budget deficit and the current account. We have also shown that a damped oscillatory time behavior is possible for the small open economy under the flexible exchange rates.

In our analysis of the dynamics, which encompass both the financial and the real sector of a small open economy, we can exhibit a set of elasticities which determine the "strength" of dynamic interactions between the two sectors, and obtain relation or restrictions that must exist between various counteracting influences in order for the economy to behave "normally" (although we have not elaborated on it due to space limitation). We show that both current account and the public debt are important linkages. They jointly, together with various combinations of instruments, affect the dynamic of the interest rate, real output rate, the price level, and the exchange rate. By this analysis, we are able to exhibit explicitly the nature of the approximation of dynamic analysis which ignores the real sector.

APPENDIX 1

Define the parameters σ_1 and θ_1 by

$$\begin{bmatrix} -\sigma_1 \\ \theta_1 \end{bmatrix} = \Phi^{-1} \begin{bmatrix} 1-\alpha \\ -\alpha \end{bmatrix} + \alpha \frac{PY}{W} \begin{bmatrix} \alpha_2/\alpha \\ \beta_2/\beta \end{bmatrix}$$

$$\approx \begin{bmatrix} -a_1 \\ b_1 \end{bmatrix} + \alpha \frac{PY}{W} \begin{bmatrix} \omega_1 \\ \omega_2 \end{bmatrix} - \frac{PY}{W} \frac{\omega}{|\Phi|} \begin{bmatrix} \alpha \\ \beta/r \end{bmatrix}$$

where $a_1 = -\gamma/|\Phi| > 0$,

$$b_1 = -[(1-\alpha)(\beta_1/\beta) + \alpha(\alpha_1/\alpha) + \gamma/r]/|\Phi| > 0$$

$$\omega = (1-\alpha)\beta_2/\beta + \alpha(\alpha_2/\alpha),$$

$$\begin{matrix} \omega_1 \\ \omega_2 \end{matrix} = \Phi^{-1} \begin{bmatrix} \alpha_2/\alpha \\ \beta_2/\beta \end{bmatrix},$$

where

$$\omega_1 = (\gamma/|\Phi|)(-\beta_2/\beta + \alpha_2/\alpha) = -\alpha(-\beta_2/\beta + \alpha_2/\alpha)/(\beta_1/\beta - \alpha_1/\alpha + 1/r)$$

$$\omega_2 = (\alpha_1/\alpha)(\beta_2/\beta) - (\alpha_2/\alpha)(\beta_1/\beta) - \omega_3,$$

where

$$\omega_3 = -[\beta(\beta_2/\beta) + (1-\beta)\alpha_2/\alpha]/\gamma(\beta_1/\beta - \alpha_1/\alpha + 1/r)$$

a_1 is of the order r and b_1 is of the order 1.
By calculation we see that

$$\Phi^{-1} \begin{bmatrix} -\beta \\ 1-\beta \end{bmatrix} = \begin{bmatrix} a_1 \\ 1-b_1 \end{bmatrix} - \begin{bmatrix} 1 \\ \beta/r \end{bmatrix} \omega_3 \, (PY/W)$$

$$\Phi^{-1} \begin{bmatrix} 1 \\ 1 \end{bmatrix} = \begin{bmatrix} 0 \\ 1 \end{bmatrix} + \begin{bmatrix} 0 \\ \omega_1 \end{bmatrix} (\beta/r)(PY/W)$$

$$\begin{bmatrix}\sigma_2\\ \theta_2\end{bmatrix} = (\beta_g/\beta)\ \Phi^{-1} \begin{bmatrix}-\beta\\ 1-\beta\end{bmatrix} + \beta_g (PY/W \begin{bmatrix}\omega_1\\ \omega_2\end{bmatrix} ,$$

$$\begin{bmatrix}\sigma_3\\ \theta_3\end{bmatrix} \approx \gamma\ \Phi^{-1} \begin{bmatrix}1\\ 1\end{bmatrix} + \frac{PY}{W}\gamma \begin{bmatrix}\omega_1\\ \omega_2\end{bmatrix}$$

$$= \gamma \begin{bmatrix}0\\ 1\end{bmatrix} + \gamma(PY/W) \begin{bmatrix}\omega_1\\ \omega_2\end{bmatrix} + (\beta/r)\ (PY/W) \begin{bmatrix}0\\ \omega_1\end{bmatrix} ,$$

$$\begin{bmatrix}\sigma_4\\ \theta_4\end{bmatrix} = \Phi^{-1} \begin{bmatrix}\alpha_3/\alpha\\ \beta_3/\beta\end{bmatrix} ,$$

$$\begin{bmatrix}\sigma_5\\ \theta_5\end{bmatrix} = (1/r)\ \Phi^{-1} \begin{bmatrix}-\beta\\ 1-\beta\end{bmatrix} -(\beta/r)(PY/W) \begin{bmatrix}\omega_1\\ \omega_2\end{bmatrix} ,$$

$$= (1/r) \begin{bmatrix}a_1\\ 1-b_1\end{bmatrix} - (\omega_3/r)(PY/W) \begin{bmatrix}1\\ \beta/r\end{bmatrix} -(\beta/r)(PY/W) \begin{bmatrix}\omega_1\\ \omega_2\end{bmatrix} ,$$

$$\begin{bmatrix}\sigma_6\\ \theta_6\end{bmatrix} = (\beta_p/\beta_g) \begin{bmatrix}\sigma_2\\ \theta_2\end{bmatrix} - \frac{PY}{W} \begin{bmatrix}\omega_1\\ \omega_2\end{bmatrix} ,$$

$$\begin{bmatrix}\sigma_7\\ \theta_7\end{bmatrix} = (\beta_p/\beta_g)\ h \begin{bmatrix}\sigma_2\\ \theta_2\end{bmatrix} - \frac{PY}{W} \begin{bmatrix}\omega_1\\ \omega_2\end{bmatrix} .$$

The coefficients in (11) are given as follows: These are approximate values valid near $\nu \approx 1$ and $(F_k-\sigma) \approx (i-\pi)$:

$$\delta y' = \bar{\ell}_1 \delta p + \bar{\ell}_2 \delta y - \bar{\ell}_5 \delta e + \bar{\ell}_6 \delta b_g + \bar{\ell}_7\ \delta b_p^* - \bar{\ell}_8 \delta T/T$$

where

$$\bar{\ell}_1 = -a + P(Y-\sigma K-T)/P_I Y'$$

$$\bar{\ell}_2 = PY/P_I Y' > 1$$

$\bar{\ell}_5 = (1-a) + EB_p^*/P_I Y' > 0$

$\bar{\ell}_6 = B_g/P_I Y' > 0$

$\bar{\ell}_7 = EB_p^*/P_I Y' > 0$

$\bar{\ell}_8 = PT/P_I Y' > 0$. (Note that $\ell_8 = \ell_2 T/Y$).

$\mu_o = d_o$

$\mu_1 = 1-d_1\bar{\ell}_2$

$\mu_2 = d_3 - d_1\bar{\ell}_1 = d_3 - (1-a)d_1$

$\mu_3 = d_4$, $\mu_4 = d_2$, $\mu_8 = d_1(\bar{\ell}_2-1)$.

$\pi_o = \mu_o/(\mu_2+\mu_1 s_2) = d_o/d_5$, $\pi_1 = \mu_4/(\mu_2 + \mu_1 s_2) = d_2/d_5$

$\pi_2 = (\mu_1 s_3 + \mu_2)/(\mu_2 + \mu_1 s_2) = [d_3 + s_3 - d_1(\bar{\ell}_1 + s_3\bar{\ell}_2)] / d_5$

$\pi_3 = \mu_3/d_5 = d_4/d_5$

$\pi_6 = \mu_8/(\mu_2 + \mu_1 s_2) = d_1(\bar{\ell}_2-1)/d_5$

where

$d_5 = d_3 + s_2 - d_1(\bar{\ell}_1+s_2\bar{\ell}_2)$.

APPENDIX 2

Calculation of λ_1 (the case where $\omega_i = 0$, $i = 1,2$).

$$\lambda_1 = (\partial U/\partial i)\rho_1 + (\partial U/\partial e)\rho_2 + (\partial U/\partial p)\rho_3 + (\partial U/\partial y')\rho_4'$$

$$= \rho_2 \; [E(B_p^*+B_g^*) \; \{1+(\gamma_1/\gamma-\beta/(i-\pi) \; (\rho_1/\rho_2)\}$$

$$- (PX - (PX' - EP^* IM_2)\tau)(1-\pi_2) + F$$

$$- EP^* IM_1 \rho_4'/\rho_2 \qquad (*)$$

where $\pi_1\rho_1/\rho_2 \approx 0$ and $\rho_3/\rho_2 = \pi_2$, and $\rho_4'/\rho_2 = (\bar{\ell}_1+s_2\bar{\ell}_2)\pi_2 - (\bar{\ell}_1+s_3\bar{\ell}_2)$.

If $s_2 = s_3$, then $\pi_2 \gtrsim 1$ and (*) simplifies to

$$\lambda_1 \approx \rho_2 \{E(B_p^* + B_g^*) [1+ (\gamma_1/\gamma - \beta/(i-\pi))](\rho_1/\rho_2) + F\}.$$

Under $s_2 = s_3$ we have $\pi_2 \approx 1$ and $\tau_2 = 1$, hence

$$\rho_1/\rho_2 = (\beta_p/\beta)\sigma_1.$$

$$< \sigma_1 \leq i-\pi \quad ,$$

Thus, $[\gamma_1/\gamma - \beta/(i-\pi)]$ $(i-\pi)$is $-$ $(o.oo5\alpha\nu/\gamma + \beta)$ (see footnote 8 for the definition of ν), the magnitude $(o,o5\alpha\nu/\gamma + \beta)$ is expected to be less than one. Thus normally $1 + (\gamma_1/\gamma - \beta/(i-\pi))$ (ρ_1/ρ_2) is positive, and less than $(1-\beta)$, hence

$$\lambda_1 \simeq \{-[1-(\beta_p/\beta)(\sigma_1\tau_1)] + E(B_p^* + B_g^*)(1-\beta) + F\}/[1 + (\beta_p/\beta)\xi] .$$

Signs of f_5, ε_5 and δ_5

The combination of the instruments affecting U is seen to be given by

$$x_u = (\partial U/\partial i)x_i + (\partial U/\partial e)x_e + (\partial U/\partial p)x_p + (\partial U/\partial y')x_y .$$

where

$$x_y' = \ell_1(x_p - x_e) + \ell_2 x_y.$$

The way in which ∂g, ∂bg, ∂m appear in x_u can be found by writing out x_u. The signs of the coefficients are generally ambiguous. At F = 0 and if $s_2 = s_3$, then $\partial U/\partial e + \partial U/\partial p =$
$= E(B_p^* + B_g^*)$.

We can write x_u as

$$x_u = E(B_p^* + B_g^*)[(\gamma_1/\gamma - \beta/(i-\pi))(f_1\delta g + \varepsilon_1 \delta m + \delta_1 \delta b_g) + f_2\delta g + \varepsilon_2\delta m + \delta_2\delta b_g]$$

$$+ (\partial U/\partial p + \ell_1 \partial U/\partial y') [(f_2 - f_3\delta g + (\varepsilon_2 - \varepsilon_3) \delta m]$$

$$+ \ell_2 (\partial U/\partial y') (f_4\delta g + \varepsilon_4\delta m).$$

$$Z = \begin{bmatrix} -\ell_1 & s\rho_2 & s\varepsilon_2 & s\delta_2 \\ 0 & -\ell_2+\lambda_2 & \nu_\varepsilon & \nu_\delta \\ 0 & \theta_1\rho_4 & -\ell_3+\theta_1\varepsilon_4 & \theta_1\delta_4 \\ 0 & \psi_\rho & \psi_\varepsilon & -\ell_4+\psi_\delta \end{bmatrix}, \quad \zeta_1 = \begin{bmatrix} s\zeta_2 \\ \nu_\zeta \\ \theta_1\zeta_4 \\ \psi_\zeta \end{bmatrix},$$

$$\zeta_2 = \begin{bmatrix} sf_2 \\ \nu_f \\ \theta_1 f_4 \\ \psi_f \end{bmatrix},$$

where

$$\psi_\delta = \ell_4\delta_1/r + (m_1\delta_3-(m_2+\theta_1)\delta_4)/\phi$$

$$\nu_\delta = (\delta_5- (\mu s+U)\delta_2)/R^*$$

$$\lambda_2 = \{\lambda_1 + (s(1-\mu)-U)\rho_2\}/R^*$$

ψ_ρ, ν_ρ, etc., are analogously defined.

REFERENCES

Aoki, M., Optimal Control and System Theory in Dynamic Economic Analysis, North Holland, Amsterdam, 1976.

Aoki, M., "How Robust are Impact Money Multipliers of a Small Open Economy with a Regime of Flexible Exchange Rate", working paper May 1977.

Aoki, M., "Perturbation and Robustness Analysis of a Macroeconomic Model", Econometric Soc. Meeting, Chicago, August 1978.

Aoki, M., and M. Canzoneri, "Macroeconomic Policy in a Dynymic Two Country Model", Annals of Economic and Social Measurements 6/5, 631-650, 1978.

Branson, W.H., "Macroeconomic Equilibrium with Portfolio Balance in Open Economies," Institute of International Economic Studies, Univ. of Stockholm, Paper No. 22, November 1972.

Branson, W.H., "Asset Markets and Relative Prices in Exchange Rate Determination", Institute for International Economic Studies, Univ. of Stockholm, September 1976.

Clark, P., and S.Kwack, "Asset Markets and Interest Rate Determination in the Multi-Country Model", International Finance Discussion Papers, No. 94, Board of Governors,Federal Reserve System, December 1976.

Dornbusch, R., "Real and Monetary Aspects of the Effects of Exchange Rate Changes", in R.Z. Aliber (ed.), National Monetary Policies and the International Financial System, Univ. of Chicago Press, 1974.

Dornbusch, R., "A Portfolio Balance Model of the Open Economy," Journal of Monetary Economics, 1, 3-2o, 1975.

Dornbusch, R., "Expectations and Exchange Rate Dynamics," Journal of Political Economy, 84, 1161-1176, December 1976.

Flood, R., "Asset Trading, Exchange Rate Determination and Exchange Rate Dynamics," presented at SSRC-Ford Foundation Conference on Macroeconomic Policy and Adjustment in Open Economies, Ware, England, 1976.

Genberg, H. and H.Kierzkowski, "Short-Run, Long-Run, and Dynamics of Adjustment under Flexible Exchange Rate," Graduate Institute of International Studies, June 1975.

Girton, C. and D. Henderson, "Central Bank Operations in Foreign and Domestic Assets under Fixed and Flexible Exchange Rates," in Peter B. Clark, Dennis E. Logue, Richard James Sweeney (eds.), The Effects of Exchange Rate Adjustments, U.S. Government Printing Press, 1977.

Gordon, R.J., "The Impact of Aggregate Demand on Prices", Brooking Paper on Economic Activities, 3, 613-655, 1975.

Henderson, D.W., "Macroeconomic Theory: Modelling the Interdependence of National Money and Capital Markets", presented at ASSA Meeting, Atlantic City, September 1976.

Henderson, D.W., "Monetary, Fiscal, and Exchange Rate Policy in a Two Country, Short-Run, Macroeconomic Model," Working Paper, December 1974.

Howe, Howard, "Price Determination in the Multi-Country Model", International Finance Discussion Paper No. 98, December 1976.

Nordhaus, W.D., "Recent Developments in Price Dynamics" in The Econometrics of Price Determination, Otto Eckstein, Ed., Board of Governors of the Federal Reserve System, Washington, D.C., 1972.

Salop, J., "Devaluation and the Balance of Trade under Flexible Wages," in G.Horwich and P.A. Samuelson (eds.), Trade, Stability and Macroeconomics, Academic Press, New York, 1974.

Sargent, T. and N. Wallace, "Market Transaction Costs, Asset Demand Functions and the Relative Potency of Monetary and Fiscal Policy", J. Money, Credit and Banking, 1, 15-29, February 1969.

Shafer, J.R., "The Macroeconomic Behavior of a Large Open Economy with a Floating Exchange Rate", Ph.D. Dissertation, Yale Univ. May 1976.

Tobin, J., "A General Equilibrium Approach to Monetary Theory", J. Money, Credit and Banking, 1, 15-29, February 1969.

Viott, S., "General Equilibrium Analysis of the Small Open Economy Under Flexible Exchange Rates,"Institute for International Economic Studies, April 1977.

Wallace, N., "The Role of Stock Portfolio Shifts under Alternative Exchange Rate Regimes", Staff Report WP-18, Fed.Res. Bank, Minneapolis, 1972.

COMMENT ON M. AOKI, "SHORT-RUN ASSET AND THE REAL SECTOR DYNAMICS OF A SMALL OPEN ECONOMY UNDER FLEXIBLE EXCHANGE RATES"

Dieter Bender

The asset market approach of exchange rate analysis which constitutes an innovating application of Tobin's general equilibrium analysis to open economies, is the analytical framework used and extended by Aoki. Like in Viotti's contribution (1978) his starting point is the asset sector presented in the pioneering analysis of Branson (1976). Because the line of thought and the conclusions of the Aoki-model are somewhat hidden behind a very intricate structure of dynamic relations it might be useful to interpret this model as a marriage of Branson's asset market equilibrium approach with the "Marshallian cross" developed from conventional Hicks-IS-LM-analysis. This interpretation of the model as a combination of neo-keynesian assumption schemes with asset market approaches does allow me to offer some comments on such a model's capacity to explain fluctuations of exchange rates under conditions of variable output and prices by considering all underlying determinants of major importance.

While there exists a relative abundance of open economy portfolio models with comparative static properties little has been done to construct short run dynamic models of the general equilibrium type by integrating the monetary and the real sector. Trying to answer the question how monetary or fiscal disturbances affect the interdependent time paths of interest rate, exchange rate, output and prices, the Aoki-model offers a very interesting method by which this deficit could be closed. Assuming that domestic and foreign assets are regarded as imperfect substitutes no interest parity theorem holds in the short run which would force the domestic interest rate in every moment to deviate from the exogenously given world interest rate exactly by the expected depreciation or appreciation of the exchange rate. Neither strong purchasing power parity assumptions are introduced, because - with all goods internationally traded - domestic and foreign outputs are considered as imperfect substitutes making the price of domestic output dependent upon aggregate demand instead of being determined directly by world market prices. I want to stress and so far agree with this presentation that the implications of these assumptions are very well suited with the short run dynamics of a small country whose policy activities induce no foreign repercussions but have command over domestic interest rates, exchange rates and prices in the short run (the often assumed "law of one price" reduces this influence on price level of domestic output or exchange rate).

First, let me clarify the structure of this model by a rather simplified geometrical (comparative static) presentation of the causal relations subjected to Aoki's dynamic analysis. This is done in Fig. 1 which explains the overshooting of exchange rates after a monetary shock by the interaction of instantaneous asset market adjustment and lagged real market reactions.

Fig. 1 see last page

Such geometrical treatment now enables me to suggest two extensions whose recognition will lead to some major modifications of those exchange rate adjustment paths analyzed by Aoki.

Will real exports X (and real imports) in fact respond to every short run exchange rate change according to a behavioural function $X(P/EP^*, \varepsilon)$ with $X_1 < 0$ if this short run exchange rate variability is recognized as an overshooting effect and therefore as a temporary change? What are the consequences of introducing more refined behavioural assumptions linking real trade flows to the expected change of the equilibrium exchange rate? In a world of flexible exchange rates it is not unrealistic to assume that prices of exported goods are contracted in the currency of the exporting country. If there are substantial time lags between contracting (fixing export volume and export price by contract), delivery and payment, the real demand for a country's exports will depend on the future exchange rate expected in the period of contracting.[1)] Therefore we have

$X = X\,(P/\overline{E}P^*)$	X - home country's real exports
$X^* = X^*\,(P/\overline{E}P^*,\ A)$	X^* - foreign country's real exports
	$\overline{E}$ - expected (trend) value of the price of foreign currency
	A - real absorption of home country

With real absorption A depending on real disposable income Y' and the real rate of interest it can be shown that demand for domestic production

$$Y^d = A\,(Y',\, i - \pi) + X\,(P/\overline{E}P^*) - \frac{P^* E}{P}\, X^*\,(P/\overline{E}P^*,\ A)$$

might possibly decline in the short run if the (overshooting) movement of E is still regarded as temporary (and $\overline{E}$ does not change yet) and if investment demand remains relatively interest-inelastic. This primary reaction of real markets after asset market adjustment (A → B)[2)] will especially become effective where long run exchange rate expectations are reacting slower to falling interest rates and rising exchange rates than real demand for domestic goods does react (negatively) on the actual appreciation of E. In such a case of short run real sector dynamics we would observe a primary shift of the aggregate demand curve to the left creating a temporary

---

1) Forward covering of liabilities by importing units does not change this conclusion if expected exchange rates and forward exchange rates are closely tied together.

2) This possibility of real trade flows not fulfilling the Marshall-Lerner condition in the short run of a flexible exchange rate regime was regarded first by Niehans (1975) and analyzed further by Dornbusch (1976).

decline of Y and P which, by inducing a falling demand for money leads to a new asset market equilibrium with E higher and i lower than in point B. Only after $\overline{E}$ slowly starts to adjust to the exogenous forces which drove up E those "normal" reactions of real trade flows become effective and - accompanied by interest rate effects on real investment - shift Y^d to the right creating the real market process G → F analyzed already by Aoki. Introducing such short run demand effects of exchange rate changes into the asset market approach will magnify the overshooting of E and will generate adjustment processes in the real sector with a more complex and a more realistic lag structure. By this consideration I tried to show that complete analysis of short run exchange rate dynamics must build upon the interaction of short run exchange rate expectations and an endogenous explanation of expectations about the long run exchange rate or the trend growth of the exchange rate. Since these expectational effects have significant influence on instantaneous and short run exchange rate and interest rate changes, especially the magnitude of overshooting and the speed of adjustment to long run equilibrium values, they should not be disregarded in an analysis of feedback mechanismus operating through these channels on the time paths of real sector variables.

The model's lag structure (lags due to different adjustment speeds of asset and goods markets) will become even more difficult as well as more developed if the hypothesis of a stable Phillips-curve is substituted by a shifting aggregate supply curve the shiftability of which is generated by lagged reactions of nominal wage demands to inflationary expectations forming themselves in a process of lagged adjustment to price effects induced by those demand changes and exchange rate dynamics shown to us by Aoki's model. A major progress in macroeconomic model building of open economies would be to introduce such a dynamic model of an expectations-augmented Phillips-relation with endogenous inflationary expectations.

Because the formation of expectations about changes in the consumer price level in small open economies partly depends on exchange rate expectations, this task requires a more complex lag structure than the same type of macro-model in a closed economy.

Admittedly, I am well aware that these extensions could complicate a dynamic general equilibirium model like the one presented by Aoki in a way that makes economic meaningful results totally disappear behind the elegance of mathematical systems. After confronting Aoki's contribution with some - in my opinion - necessary extensions of open economy macro-models I must still agree with Henderson (1977) who points to the difficulty of working with dynamic models that contain more than a few endogenous variables and expects that "dynamic problems will be addressed using a number of special purpose models rather than a single model". These difficulties show that - as a starting point of such necessary extensions - the (less ambitious) comparative-static methods still remain useful as tools to analyze refined macro-models of the Tobin-type which by displaying the interaction of short run (temporary) equilibrium states should be able to generate a picture of exchange rate variability in a world of "floating".

REFERENCES

Branson, W.H., Asset Markets and Relative Prices in Exchange Rate Determination, Institute for International Economic Studies, University of Stockholm 1976.

Dornbusch, R., Exchange Rate Expectations and Monetary Policy, Journal of International Economics 6 (1976).

Henderson, D.W., Modelling the Interdependence of National Money and Capital Markets, American Economic Review 67 (1977).

Niehans, J., Some Doubts about the Efficacy of Monetary Policy under Flexible Exchange Rates, Journal of International Economics 6 (1975).

Viotti, S., Inflation, the Terms of Trade and Flexible Exchange Rates, presented at the conference on "The Economics of Flexible Exchange Rates", Vienna, March 29 - 31, 1978.

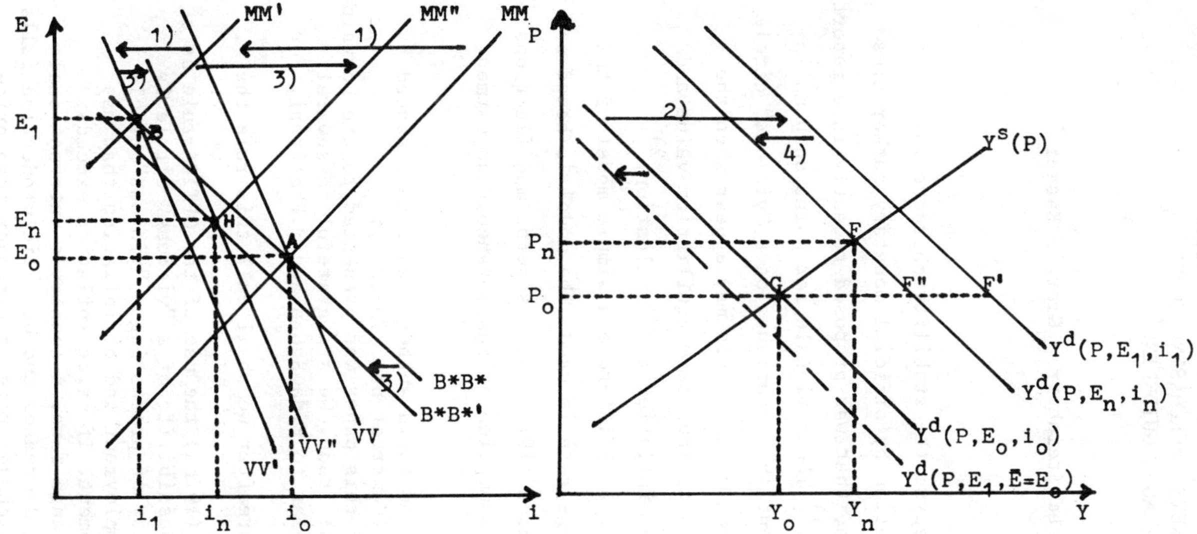

ASSET MARKETS

Fig. 1

REAL MARKET

MM: $M = \alpha(i, PY/W, i^* + \varepsilon)W$

VV: $V'/i - \pi = \beta(i, PY/W, i^* + \varepsilon)W$

B*B*: $EB^*/i^* - \pi^* = \gamma(i, PY/W, i^* + \varepsilon)W$

1)
A→B : Instantaneous effect of expansive open market policy (before lagged reaction of goods markets)

3)
B→H : Instantaneous asset market adjustment to rising Y and P (after real market reaction)

$Y^s(P) = Y^d(P, E, i)$

2) G→F' : Lagged demand effect of overshooting E_o-E_1-change and i_o-i_1-movement

4)
F→F" : Lagged demand effect after process 3 starts correcting the overshooting effects on E and i

G→F : Y-and P-movements generated by the demand effects

THE DYNAMICS OF INTERVENTION IN FOREIGN EXCHANGE MARKETS: PURCHASING POWER PARITY AS A GUIDELINE*

Paul De Grauwe - Alfred Steinherr - Giorgio Basevi

1. INTRODUCTION

In this paper we analyze the stability characteristics of a rule for guiding intervention by official monetary authorities in foreign exchange markets, that was proposed recently in a report to the European Commission.[1)] The rationale for using such an intervention rule is to prevent the occurrence of a "vicious" circle of inflation and depreciation. This circle may appear when the exchange rate deviates from its long-term equilibrium value and engenders a spiral of higher inflation and devaluation.[2)]

For the analysis of the OPTICA-rule a simple model of the determination of the exchange rate is used. The model is based on Dornbusch (1976) and Mathieson (1977), with several modifications added. In particular, the assumption of instantaneous adjustment

---

*) Research by the second and third authors has been financed by a Ford Foundation Grant (Contract no. 775-oo43).
A preliminary version of this paper was presented to the Louvain Workshop in International Trade. We are grateful to several participants, in particular to E.de Souza and M.Fratianni, for comments.

1) Optica Report (1976). Hereafter we shall call this rule the OPTICA-rule.

2) In Basevi and De Grauwe (1978a) the use of the OPTICA-rule as a means to eliminate the possibility of a "vicious" circle is analyzed. The desirability of preventing a "vicious" circle is based on the costs of employment and of inflation that may accompany such a development. If price inflation exceeds depreciation of the exchange rate, a country's international competitiveness is being decreased and domestic production falls. If depreciation of the exchange rate is stronger than price inflation, the competitiveness of foreign producers and therefore employment abroad will be damaged.

in the financial markets is dropped. This model is then used to derive the dynamic properties of the OPTICA-rule. Our aim is to determine whether intervention in the foreign exchange market according to the OPTICA-rule tends to stabilize the system, eliminates cycles, and increases the speed of adjustment to long-run equilibrium.

2. THE BASIC MODEL

We shall use capital letters to denote variables in natural units, smaller case letters for logarithms, and greek letters for coefficients, which are all defined positively. The model pertains to a small country, with its financial and goods markets.

2.1 Financial markets

The specification of financial markets in based on the explicit treatment of money and foreign exchange markets, while bond markets are left implicit. The demand for money is specified in loglinear form, so that we have:

$$m - p = \phi\bar{y} - \lambda R \qquad (1)$$

where: m = the log of the money supply

p = the log of the price level

$\bar{y}$ = the log of the full-employment level of income[3)]

R = the nominal rate of interest

and ϕ and λR are elasticities.

The domestic price level is defined as a geometric average of home and imported goods prices, so that, in logarithms, one obtains:

---

3) Full-employment income is used here as a proxy for permanent income. Alternatively, with the corresponding interpretation in the goods market, production could be considered as being fixed at full employment. For more detailed discussion see Dornbusch (1976). Later we shall allow for current income to determine the demand for money.

$$p = \alpha p_H + (1 - \alpha)\ p_T \tag{2}$$

where: α = the weight of the home good in the price index

p_H = the log of the price of home goods

p_T = the log of the price of imported goods

and

$$p_T = p_W + e \tag{3}$$

where: p_W = the log of the world price level (assumed constant)

e = the log of the spot exchange rate.

The domestic interest rate is tied to the foreign interest rate by the interest parity relationship, i.e.:

$$R = R^f + \frac{F - E}{E} \tag{4}$$

where: R^f = the foreign interest rate

F = the forward exchange rate

E = the spot exchange rate.

With an infinitely elastic speculative schedule the forward rate is always equal to the expected future spot rate.[4)] We then have:

$$F = E^* \tag{5}$$

where E^* is the expected future spot rate. We shall later introduce two alternative assumptions about the formation of expectations.

---

4) If the speculative schedule is less than infinitely elastic the forward rate will also be influenced by the interest rate differential and the level of the spot rate. Even in the case of a perfectly elastic speculative schedule our assumptions do not imply the absence of net capital flow, and hence allows for the possibility of a trade surplus or deficit, because commercial hedgers can find in speculators or arbitrageurs the counterpart of their net forward cover.

2.2 The goods market

The demand for home goods is related to real income, the price of home goods relative to foreign goods and the difference between the real interest rate and the marginal productivity of capital.[5)] In the short run, demand is assumed to determine production. The deviation of short-run output from potential output can then be written in loglinear form as:

$$y - \bar{y} = \mu \, [\delta(p_T - p_H) - \sigma(R - \dot{p}^* - R_K)] \tag{6}$$

where: μ = the Keynesian multiplier

$\dot{p}^*$ = the expected rate of inflation[6)]

R_K = the marginal productivity of capital

Note that, while δ is an elasticity, σ is a semi-elasticity. It is assumed that foreign and home goods are imperfect substitutes; hence their relative price $(p_T - p_H)$ influences demand for home goods in domestic and foreign markets.

The term $R - \dot{p}^*$ is the real rate of interest. If this exceeds the marginal productivity of capital a decline in purchases of investment goods will be induced. In general R_K is not constant but depends on the level of economic activity. We therefore postulate:

$$R_K = R_K^f + \kappa(y - \bar{y}) \tag{7}$$

where R_K^f is the foreign marginal productivity of capital, and $\kappa < 0$.

---

5) While in the long run real rates of interest and marginal productivities of capital are equal, their short-run divergence affects investment and hence aggregate demand. See, for example, Tobin (1969).

6) A dot over a variable denotes its time derivative. Thus, a dotted smaller case letter indicates the rate of change of the variable with respect to time. A star transforms a variable into its expected value.

In steady state equilibrium, demand is equal to full-employment supply ($y = \bar{y}$), and capital flows equalize the marginal productivities of capital throughout the world.

2.3 The conditions of equilibrium

The model consisting of equations (1) - (7) can be simplified so as to obtain three equations describing the equilibrium conditions of the system:

$$m - \alpha p_H - (1 - \alpha)p_W - (1 - \alpha)e = - \lambda R + \phi \bar{y} \tag{8}$$

$$R = R^f + \dot{e}^* \tag{9}$$

$$[\delta(e + p_W - p_H) - \sigma(R - \alpha \dot{p}_H^* - (1 - \alpha)\dot{e}^* - R_K)] = 0 . \tag{1o}$$

Note that for equation (1o) to be satisfied in long run equilibrium, both purchasing power parity and interest parities must be satisfied: for investment to level off to zero one must have $R = R_K$; since the same equilibrium condition should hold for the rest of the world, steady state requires also absence of capital flows, i.e., $R = R_K = R^f = R_K^f$.

3. EXPECTATIONS

In the previous section the process whereby expectations are formed was left unspecified. We now introduce two alternative assumptions about this process.

3.1 Rational expectations

In a deterministic model rational expectations are equivalent to perfect foresight.[7] In other words, the expected values of the

---

7) Since we disregard information costs, rational expectations are also efficient. Taking these costs into account gives rise to semi-rational expectations; they are incorporated into the analysis of Mathieson (1977). In a stochastic model rational expectations imply knowledge of the long run equilibrium solution but not necessarily of the entire adjustment path.

price level and the exchange rate are always equal to their realized values. Thus, equation (9) becomes

$$R = R^f + \dot{e}. \tag{11}$$

Similarly in equation (10) we substitute the expected rates of change of home goods prices and of the exchange rate by their actual values.

3.2 Adaptive expectations

In log-linear form we now have:

$$\dot{e}^* = \beta(e - e^*) \tag{12}$$

and

$$\dot{p}_H^* = \zeta(p_H - p_H^*) \tag{13}$$

where, as before, starred variables refer to expected values.

4. THE OPTICA-RULE

The OPTICA-rule requires a country's monetary authorities to buy foreign exchange whenever domestic inflation exceeds foreign inflation, in order to prevent the domestic currency from depreciating more than the difference in inflation rates, but does not require them to prevent the currency from appreciating if this results from market pressures. The converse is true for a country whose rate of inflation is below the foreign one.

In this paper a stronger intervention rule is considered. Authorities should intervene whenever the level of the exchange rate is below or above the one consistent with purchasing power parity. This is stronger than the rule proposed in the OPTICA report, since authorities have to intervene even if the rate of domestic inflation is matched by the rate of depreciation of the exchange rate, as long as absolute purchasing power parity is not obtained. With this stronger rule asymmetrical intervention is not required anymore to cope with monetary disturbances: however, it is still required as a means to adjust after real shocks.[8] Obviously, the final result is independent of the choice between the relative and absolute versions of purchasing power parity.

The rule can then be written as $\dot{z} = \omega(p - e - p_W)$, which, using (2) and (3), becomes:[9]

$$\dot{z} = \omega\alpha(p_H - e - p_W) \tag{14}$$

where: ω = the speed of adjustment (with $\omega = \infty$ the exchange rate will always be maintained at par with its purchasing power value)

$\dot{z}$ = the rate of change in the stock of international reserves.

5. STABILITY ANALYSIS WITH RATIONAL EXPECTATIONS

We shall assume, in what follows, that at least one solution for our economic system exists, and we shall limit the analysis to exploring the conditions for stability of that solution.[10]

In this section we analyze the stability characteristics of the model assuming that economic agents behave according to

---

8) The OPTICA report recommends asymmetrical intervention. This means that reference rates are defended in one direction only, i.e., against excessive depreciation for relatively inflationary countries, and against excessive appreciation for relatively deflationary countries. As shown in Basevi and De Grauwe (1978b), this technical feature allows for necessary changes in the real exchange rate.

9) Intervention based on lagged deviations from PPP is neglected here but analyzed in a separate paper.

1o) An explicit treatment of the problem of existence is provided in a separate paper, already referred to.

rational expectations.[11)]

The equilibrium conditions of the model consist of equations (8), (1o) and (11), where the expected values of the exchange rate and of the price level have been replaced by their actual values. However, equilibrium is not attained instantaneously, and the following dynamic adjustment is postulated. In the home goods market the rate of price change is assumed to depend upon the deviation between the actual and full employment level of income. Similarly, in the money market the rate of change of the exchange rate is made dependent upon the deviation between supply and demand for money. The following dynamic equations are then obtained:

$$\dot{p}_H = \pi(y - \bar{y})$$

$$= \frac{\pi\ \mu}{1 - \mu\sigma\kappa}\left[\delta(e + p_W - p_H) - \sigma(R - \alpha\dot{p}_H - (1-\alpha)\ \dot{e}) + \sigma R_K^f\right] \quad (15)$$

$$\dot{e} = \eta[z - \alpha p_H - (1-\alpha)p_W - (1-\alpha)\ e - \phi\bar{y} + \lambda R] \quad (16)$$

where π and η are the speeds of adjustment in the goods market and in the money market respectively.[12)]

11) This hypothesis is of particular interest for our analysis, because the introduction of an intervention rule will affect expectations. Since rational expectations imply that agents take all available information into account, they also reckon with the intervention rule. With our specification of adaptive expectations this is not the case, so that our analysis will suffer, at that point, from this limitation.

12) With instantaneous adjustment in the money market, $\eta = \infty$. A finite speed of adjustment may seem to be in contradiction with interest rate parity maintained at any instant. However, actual banking practice is to compute forward exchange rates from the interest parity formula.

After substitution of R from (11), equation (16) becomes

$$\dot{e} = T\,[z - \alpha p_H - (1-\alpha)e] \; - T\,[(1-\alpha)p_W + \phi\bar{y} - \lambda R^f] \tag{17}$$

where $T = \frac{\eta}{1 - \eta\lambda}$.

Similarly from (11) and (17), we transform (15) into:

$$\dot{p}_H = B\,[(\delta + (1-\alpha)\alpha\sigma\, T)e - (\delta - \alpha^2\sigma\, T)p_H - \alpha\sigma T z] \; +$$

$$+ B\,[(\delta + (1-\alpha)\alpha\sigma\, T)p_W - \sigma(1-\alpha T\lambda)R^f + \sigma R^f_K + \sigma\alpha\, T\phi\,\bar{y}] \tag{18}$$

where $B = \frac{\pi\,\mu}{1 - \sigma\mu(\kappa+\pi\alpha)}$.

Setting $\dot{p}_H = \dot{e} = 0$ yields the equilibrium relations between p_H and e. These are represented in figure 1. The $\dot{e} = 0$ line always has a negative slope equal to $-\frac{1-\alpha}{\alpha}$. The $\dot{p}_H = 0$ line has a slope equal to

$$\frac{\delta + (1-\alpha)\,\alpha\sigma\, T}{\delta - \alpha^2\,\sigma\, T}$$

which can be positive or negative. As will be shown, sufficient conditions for stability yield a positive slope. Moreover, if any one of the three parameters α, σ or T approaches zero, the slope of the $\dot{p}_H = 0$ line tends to unity.

Equation (14), (17) and (18) constitute a dynamic system, determining the adjustment path of e, p, and z. In matrix notation, this can be written as:

$$\dot{v} = \Omega v + \Lambda x \tag{19}$$

where $\dot{v}$ is the column vector $(\dot{z}\ \dot{e}\ \dot{p}_H)'$

$v = (z\ e\ p_H)'$

$x = (p_W\ \bar{y}\ R^f\ R^f_K)'$

and Ω and Λ are coefficient matrices for the endogenous and exogenous variables respectively. In particular, the first matrix is:

$$\Omega = \begin{bmatrix} 0 & -\omega\alpha & \omega\alpha \\ T & -T(1-\alpha) & -T\alpha \\ -\alpha\sigma TB & B\,[\delta+(1-\alpha)\alpha\sigma T] & -B(\delta - \alpha^2\,\sigma T) \end{bmatrix}$$

5.1 Free floating

This case implies that $\omega = 0$, so that $\dot{z} = 0$ and the dynamic system is reduced to two equations only. Correspondingly we should consider the matrix $\hat{\Omega}$, obtained from Ω by deleting its first row and column.

The necessary and sufficient conditions for stability are, in this case, that the determinant of $\hat{\Omega}$ be positive and its trace be negative.

$$\det \hat{\Omega} = TB\delta > 0 \qquad (2o)$$

$$\text{trace } \hat{\Omega} = -T(1-\alpha) - B(\delta - \alpha^2\sigma\, T) < 0. \qquad (21)$$

From (2o) we notice that T and B must have the same sign, while from (21) we infer that this sign must be positive. Thus, necessary conditions for stability are:

$$T = \frac{\eta}{1 - \eta\lambda} > 0 \quad \text{and} \quad B = \frac{\pi\mu}{1 - \mu\sigma(\kappa \;\; + \pi\alpha)} > 0. \qquad (22)$$

These conditions also become sufficient if α, σ or T are small, or δ is large enough.[13)] From (22) we obtain the conditions to be imposed on the speeds of adjustment:

---

13) As already posited out, these are the sufficient conditions that make the $\dot{p}_H = 0$ line slope positively in figure 1.

$$\eta < \frac{1}{\lambda} \qquad \text{and} \qquad \pi < \frac{1 - \sigma\kappa\mu}{\alpha\sigma\mu} \tag{23}$$

thus, with σ tending to zero, π can take any positive value less than infinite. Moreover, with a low interest elasticity of the demand for money stability is more likely than with a high interest elasticity. Note also that if the adjustment in the money market were instantaneous ($\eta = \infty$), the system would become necessarily unstable, as the first inequality in (23) could not be satisfied even with $\lambda = 0$.[14)]

Assuming stability, it is worth exploring whether the adjustment path is cyclical or not. This question is interesting, as it can shed some light on the overshooting problem.[15)] In order to answer it we must consider the discriminant of the characteristic equation:

$$\Delta \;=\; [B(\delta - \alpha^2 \sigma T) + T(1 - \alpha)]^2 - 4\,TB\delta. \tag{24}$$

There are no a priori reasons to decide whether this expression is positive or negative. If negative, the adjustment path will be cyclical and overshooting occurs; if positive, there is no overshooting. We therefore conclude that, under pure floating and rational expectations, overshooting is not a necessary outcome of the adjustment process.[16)]

---

14) This result is obtained also by Mathieson (1977). However, contrary to him, we do not necessarily obtain a saddle point solution: a saddle point occurs only if (2o) and (21) are negative.

15) In the analysis by Dornbusch (1976) overshooting is purely due to differential speeds of adjustment in the money and goods markets. In our case, cyclical adjustment, and hence overshooting, is possible even without making specific assumptions as to the relative speeds of adjustment.

16) This is at variance with the results obtained by Dornbusch and by Mathieson, because they assume a higher speed of adjustment in the money market than in the goods market. Mathieson, who also holds income constant in the demand for money, obtains

In figure 2 a phase diagram is represented, assuming stability. The initial equilibrium point is A. After a monetary shock, such as an increase in the foreign interest rate, equilibrium will be displaced to point B. Purchasing power parity will be realized at both points of equilibrium, so that they are located along a 45°-line. Two alternative paths from A to B are shown in figure 2, with and without cyclical behaviour.[17)]

The possibility of a cyclical movement of prices and exchange rates is particularly linked with the values of the speeds of adjustment π and η.

The smaller is the speed of adjustment in the goods market (π) and the larger is the speed of adjustment in the money market (η), the more a monetary expansion will depreciate the exchange rate compared to the movement in prices. Conversely, the larger is the elasticity of demand to relative prices (δ) and the lower is its sensitivity to the interest rate (as expressed by σ), the stronger is the tendency to move directly to PPP, without overshooting.

5.2 OPTICA-intervention

The stability conditions of the system are less stringent when the OPTICA-rule is used than when floating is free. In fact, as shown in Appendix 1.1, while T must still be positive for stability, B can be negative in the OPTICA-rule case, provided T is sufficiently large (i.e., η is sufficiently small) and α, σ or δ are sufficiently small.

---

16) (continued)
in fact an unstable solution. It can also be shown that the equilibrium condition $T > 0$ only results from holding income fixed in the demand for money; relaxation of this assumption allows T to become negative. This is the reason why Dornbusch can assume η large and still has a stable model.

17) In Appendix 1.5 it is shown that the adjustment path necessarily starts off below the PPP line.

Also, assuming that the respective stability conditions are met, the two systems - free floating and OPTICA intervention - are different with respect to the adjustment mechanism. In particular, as shown in Appendix 1.2, with the OPTICA-rule a cyclical behaviour of the exchange rate and the price level during the adjustment period is more likely.

From these results one can infer that in the presence of rational expectations an OPTICA intervention rule may stabilize the system when the latter is unstable under free floating. However, if the system is stable, the OPTICA-rule increases the likelihood of a cyclical behaviour of the exchange rate and the price level. On the other hand, it can also be shown, as done in Appendix 1.3, that if the system is stable and non-cyclical, then the OPTICA-rule increases the speed of adjustment of the system from one equilibrium point to the other. Moreover, although the adjustment path necessarily becomes oscillatory when the speed of OPTICA intervention tends to infinity ($\omega \rightarrow \infty$), the system in this case is stabilized at its initial equilibrium point (as shown in Appendix 1.4).

Thus, at least with perfect foresight of economic agents, intervention according to the OPTICA-rule exhibits attractive but also unattractive features.

6. STABILITY ANALYSIS WITH ADAPTIVE EXPECTATIONS

The stability analysis under adaptive expectations is considerably more complicated than under rational expectations. To simplify the case it will be assumed that adjustment in the money market is instantaneous, which is also the assumption underlying the Dornbusch and Mathieson models.

We assume that the demand for money, in nominal terms, is a function of expected prices and expected real income:

$$m - p^{*} = \phi y^{*} - \lambda R \qquad (25)$$

where expected real income is a weighted geometric average of current and full employment real income:

$$y^* = \theta y + (1 - \theta) \bar{y}. \tag{26}$$

In addition, we assume adaptive expectations on prices and the exchange rate, as described by (12) and (13), here reproduced:

$$\dot{e}^* = \beta(e - e^*)$$

$$\dot{p}_H^* = (p_H - p_H^*).$$

The remaining equations of the system are the same as equations (2) - (7), plus the OPTICA-rule equation (14).

Assuming stable foreign prices ($\dot{p}_W = 0$) for simplicity, and considering as before only the homogeneous part of the dynamic system, we can write the system as:

$$\dot{v} = H\ v \tag{27}$$

where $\dot{v} = (\dot{z}\ \dot{p}_H^*\ \dot{e}^*\ \dot{p}_H)'$

$v = (z\ p_H^*\ e^*\ p_H)'$

and H is a 4x4 matrix whose elements are listed in Appendix 2.1.

6.1 Free floating

In this case, with $\omega = 0$, the matrix of the system is reduced to a 3 x 3 matrix $\hat{H}$, derived from the matrix H by deleting the first row and the first column.

Necessary conditions for stability are

trace $\hat{H} < 0$, and det $\hat{H} < 0$.

As for the first condition, it is more likely to be verified (as shown in Appendix 2.2) when either the elasticity of the demand for money with respect to real income (ϕ) is high or the weight of current relative to full employment income in determining expected income (θ) is large, provided expectations about the exchange rate are adapted more rapidly than about the price level ($\zeta < \beta$).

The determinant of $\hat{H}$ is too cumbersome to be derived and given economic interpretation. We are therefore compelled to leave open to further analysis the full treatment of necessary and sufficient stability conditions, and of the monotone or cyclical nature of the adjustment path, in this adaptive expectations model. In the following we shall compare the free floating with the OPTICA-intervention case only with regard to the necessary condition on the trace of the system matrix.

6.2 OPTICA-intervention

In this case the conditions for stability must be referred to the full 4 x 4 matrix H. Again, necessary but not sufficient conditions are

$$\text{trace } H < 0 \quad , \qquad \text{and} \quad \det \; H > 0.$$

Limiting our analysis to the first inequality, we show in Appendix 2.3 that the same conditions that tend to verify it in the free-floating case apply also in the OPTICA-intervention case.

In addition, and similarly to what was found in the rational expectations model, a system which is unstable without the OPTICA-intervention, may become stable when the OPTICA-rule is applied to it.

Secondly, if the system is stable the OPTICA-rule will increase the speed of adjustment between two equilibria. As shown in Appendix 2.3 the use of the OPTICA-rule has the effect of increasing the sum of the absolute values of the characteristic roots of the system. Provided this sum is negative, OPTICA-intervention will therefore speed up the movement of the variables of the system.

One can conclude that an OPTICA-intervention rule makes sense also when expectations are adaptive. However, these results are less general and complete than those obtained with rational expectations;in particular, in specifying adaptive expectations we neglected the fact that agents are likely to modify their behaviour when an intervention rule is introduced.

7. CONCLUSIONS

In this paper we have analyzed the stability characteristics of an intervention rule in the foreign exchange market based on purchasing power parity. This rule, which was initially proposed by the OPTICA 1976 report to the E C Commission, has been discussed here in the framework of a simple theoretical model derived from Dornbusch's recent contributions.

The main results are the following. When expectations are rational an OPTICA-intervention rule may stabilize a system which is unstable under free floating. However, if the system is stable, the OPTICA-rule increases the likelihood of a cyclical behaviour of the exchange rate and the price level. On the other hand, the OPTICA-rule increases the speed of adjustment of the system from one equilibrium point to the other.

Similar conclusions are obtained when expectations are assumed to be formed on the basis of an adaptive process. In this case, however, the analysis has not been fully developed, due to the cumbersome nature of the system matrix, while allowance has not been made for the effect of the authorities behaviour on the adaptive expectation process.

Thus, further research is needed in order to give a more complete evaluation of the OPTICA proposal for the management of exchange rates.

APPENDIX

1. Rational expectations

1.1 When the OPTICA-rule is adopted, the characteristic equation of the dynamic system becomes

$$\rho^3 + b\,\rho^2 + c\rho + d = 0$$

or

$$\rho^3 + [B(\delta - \alpha^2\,\sigma T) + (1 - \alpha)T]\,\rho^2 + T\,[B\delta + \omega(1 + \sigma\alpha B)]\rho = 0. \quad \text{(A1)}$$

Since $d = 0$, one characteristic root is equal to zero and (A1) can be rewritten as $\rho^2 + b\rho + c = 0$. To obtain stability it is necessary that the coefficients of ρ^2 and ρ in (A1) be positive:

$$B(\delta - \alpha^2\sigma\,T) + (1 - \alpha)T > 0. \quad \text{(A2)}$$

and

$$T\,[B\delta + \omega(1 + \alpha\sigma B)] > 0. \quad \text{(A3)}$$

In order for both (A2) and (A3) to hold, it is necessary that

$$T > 0$$

as in the case of free floating. As for B, it can either be positive or negative, but in the latter case T must be sufficiently large (i.e. η is sufficiently small) to make (A2) positive, while δ, α, σ or B (in absolute value) must be sufficiently small to make (A3) positive.

1.2 In order to analyze the possibility of a cyclical behaviour of the adjustment path it is necessary to analyze the discriminant of the characteristic equation. Under free floating this is represented by the expression (24) in the text, where it is also discussed. With the operation of the OPTICA-rule the discriminant becomes

$$\Delta = [B(\delta - \alpha^2\sigma T) + (1 - \alpha)T]^2 - 4T[B\delta + \omega(1 + \alpha\sigma B)]. \quad (A4)$$

If both B and T are positive, this expression is more likely to be negative the larger is ω. This is also the case when, with $T > 0$, B is negative but the system is stable (i.e. the expression within the second square bracket in (A4) is positive).

1.3 What happens to the speed of adjustment of the system, when ω is increased? Since with cyclical adjustment the system speed of adjustment is independent of ω, let us assume that there is an ω below which adjustment is non-cyclical. From (A1) it can be seen that an increase of ω increases c but does not affect b in the quadratic equation $\rho_1, \rho_2 = 1/2 [-b \pm (b^2 - 4c)^{1/2}]$.
For monotonic adjustment $b^2 - 4c > 0$; hence $b^2 - 4c$ decreases when ω increases. For stability both roots must be negative; thus, a lower value of $(b^2 - 4c)^{1/2}$ implies that, in absolute value, the lower root is increased by the same amount that the higher root is decreased. Since the speed of adjustment depends on the smallest root, it follows that stronger intervention brings about faster adjustment.

1.4 The dynamic system can be solved explicity to yield:

$$z(t) = C_1 - \omega T(B\sigma\alpha + 1)(C_2 \exp(\rho_2 t) + C_3 \exp(\rho_3 t)) \quad (A5)$$

$$e(t) = C_1 + T(B\delta + \rho_2) C_2 \exp(\rho_2 t) + T(B\delta + \rho_3) C_3 \exp(\rho_3 t) \quad (A6)$$

$$p(t) = C_1 + T(B\delta - \sigma\alpha\rho_2) C_2 \exp(\rho_2 t) + TB(\delta - \sigma\alpha\rho_3) C_3 \exp(\rho_3 t) \quad (A7)$$

where

$$C_1 = \frac{TB\delta}{\rho_2\rho_3} z(0) + \frac{B\sigma\alpha\omega T}{\rho_2\rho_3} e(0) + \frac{T\omega}{\rho_2\rho_3} p(0) \quad (A8)$$

$$C_2 = \frac{z(0)}{(\rho_2-\rho_3)\rho_2} + \frac{\rho_2-B\sigma\alpha T}{(\rho_2-\rho_3)\rho_2(1+B\sigma\alpha)T} e(0) - \frac{(\rho_2+T)}{\rho_2(\rho_2-\rho_3)(1+B\sigma\alpha)T} p(0) \quad (A9)$$

$$C_3 = \frac{z(0)}{(\rho_2-\rho_3)\rho_3} - \frac{(\rho_2-B\sigma\alpha T)}{\rho_3(\rho_2-\rho_3)(1+B\sigma\alpha)T} e(0) + \frac{(T+\rho_3)}{\rho_3(\rho_2-\rho_3)(1+B\sigma\alpha)T} p(0) \quad (A1o)$$

and the constants x_i are normalized to zero. This implies that an initial equilibrium is characterized by $z(0) = p(0) = e(0)$.

(i) In the case of pure floating $\omega = 0$. Then one has

$$\rho_2\rho_3 = T\ (B\delta + \omega) + \omega B\sigma\alpha = TB\delta$$

Hence $C_1 = z(0)$ and when $t \to \infty$ one has

$$z(t) \to z(0),\ e(t) \to z(0),\ p(t) \to z(0)$$

(ii) With $\omega \to \infty$ one has $\rho_2\rho_3 \to \infty$ and

$$C_1 \to \frac{Tp(0) + TB\sigma\alpha e(0)}{T(1 + B\sigma\alpha)} \to p(0) = e(0).$$

Hence, when $t \to \infty$

$$z(t) \to p(0),\ e(t) \to p(0),\ p(t) \to p(0).$$

1.5 We now wish to show that following, say, a positive disturbance of z, the initial adjustment path lies necessarily below the PPP line. Using the fact that $z(0) = p(0) = e(0)$ the expressions for C_2 and C_3 simplify to

$$C_2 = \frac{z(0) - p(0)}{(\rho_2 - \rho_3)\rho_2}\ ; \qquad C_3 = \frac{-z(0) + p(0)}{(\rho_2 - \rho_3)\rho_3}.$$

Then one obtains

$$e(t) - p(t) = T(1+\sigma\beta\alpha)\ [\frac{z(0) - p(0)}{\rho_2 - \rho_3} \exp\ (\rho_2 t) - \frac{z(0) - p(0)}{\rho_2 - \rho_3} \exp\ (\rho_3 t)].$$

If the roots are real and if $\rho_2 < 0$, $\rho_3 < 0$ then a monetary expansion with $z = z(0) + \Delta z$ implies $e(t) - p(t) \geq 0$ for any t.

2. Adaptive expectations

2.1 The matrix of the homogeneous part of the system is composed, in this case, of the following elements:

$$H_{11} = \omega\alpha\frac{A}{D} ;$$

$$H_{12} = -\omega\alpha^2 \frac{A - \sigma\zeta\phi\theta\mu}{D} ;$$

$$H_{13} = -\omega\alpha \frac{A(1 - \alpha + \lambda\beta) + \alpha\beta\sigma\phi\theta\mu}{D} ;$$

$$H_{14} = \omega\alpha\frac{D - \phi\theta\mu\ (\alpha\sigma\zeta - \delta)}{D} ;$$

$$H_{21} = 0; \quad H_{22} = -\zeta ; \quad H_{23} = 0; \quad H_{24} = \zeta$$

$$H_{31} = -\frac{\beta A}{D} ; \quad H_{32} = \frac{\alpha\beta(A - \sigma\zeta\phi\theta\mu)}{D} ;$$

$$H_{33} = \frac{\beta[(1 - \alpha)\ A + \phi\theta\mu\delta]}{D} ; \quad H_{34} = \frac{\beta\phi\theta\mu\ (\alpha\sigma\zeta - \delta)}{D}$$

$$H_{41} = \frac{\pi B\ (\alpha\beta\sigma - \delta)}{C} ; \quad H_{42} = \frac{\alpha\pi B\ [\delta - \beta\sigma(\alpha + \zeta\lambda)]}{C}$$

$$H_{43} = \frac{\pi B\ [\beta\delta\lambda - (1 - \alpha)(\alpha\beta\sigma - \delta)]}{C} ; \quad H_{44} = \frac{\beta\pi\lambda B\ (\alpha\sigma\zeta - \delta)}{C}$$

where $A = 1 - \mu\sigma\kappa$

$B = \pi\mu/A$

$C = \pi\lambda\beta + \phi\theta B(\alpha\beta\sigma - \delta)$

$D = \lambda\beta + \phi\theta\mu(\alpha\beta\sigma - \delta)$

2.2 With free floating, we have:

$$\text{trace}\ \hat{H} = -\zeta + \frac{\beta}{C} \{\pi(1-\alpha) + B\ [\phi\theta\delta + \pi\lambda\ (\alpha\sigma\zeta - \delta)]\}.$$

Notice that B contains neither of β, ζ or θ, while C does not contain ζ. If, as already done in the rational expectations model of section 5, we take as part of the necessary conditions for stability that B > 0, we have:

$$\lim_{\beta \to 0^+} C = -\phi\theta\delta\, B < 0.$$

If either ϕ or θ are sufficiently large, we also have:

$$\lim_{\beta \to 0^+} \beta\{\pi(1-\alpha) + B\,[\phi\theta\delta + \pi\lambda(\alpha\sigma\zeta - \delta)]\} = 0^+.$$

Thus:

$$\lim_{\beta \to 0^+} \text{trace}\ \hat{H} = -\zeta + \frac{0^+}{-\phi\theta\delta B} < 0.$$

Moreover

$$\lim_{\zeta \to 0^+} \beta\{\pi(1-\alpha) + B\,[\phi\theta\delta + \pi\lambda(\alpha\sigma\tau - \delta)]\} = \beta[\pi(1-\alpha) + B\delta(\phi\theta - \pi\lambda)]$$

which is positive for ϕ or θ sufficiently large. Then:

$$\lim_{\zeta \to 0^+} \text{trace}\ \hat{H} = \frac{\beta[\pi(1-\alpha) + B\delta\,(\phi\theta - \pi\lambda)]}{\pi\lambda\beta + B\phi\theta\,(\alpha\sigma\beta - \delta)} = E$$

which is negative for ϕ or θ sufficiently large.

Thus, if both $\beta \to 0^+$ and $\zeta \to 0^+$, always with $\zeta < \beta$, we have

$$\lim_{\substack{\beta \to 0^+ \\ \zeta \to 0^+}} E = \frac{0^+}{-\phi\theta\delta B} = 0^- \quad \text{for } \theta \text{ and/or } \phi \text{ sufficiently large.}$$

2.3 With OPTICA-intervention, we have:

$$\begin{aligned} \text{trace}\ H &= H_{11} + \text{trace}\ \hat{H} \\ &= \omega\alpha\frac{A}{D} + \text{trace}\ \hat{H} \\ &= \omega\alpha\frac{AB}{\mu C} + \text{trace}\ \hat{H}. \end{aligned}$$

With $B > 0$ (and hence $A > 0$), we see that H_{11} is negative when $C < 0$. Since C tends to be negative for large values of θ and ϕ, and for small values of β, we can see that the same conditions that tend to make the trace of $\hat{H}$ negative in the free-floating case, make also the trace of H negative in the OPTICA-intervention case.

In addition, if in the free floating case instability were due to the non-fulfillment of the condition on the trace of $\hat{H}$, then the OPTICA-rule with a sufficiently high ω may stabilize the system by making trace H negative.

Moreover, the larger the size of ω, i.e. the faster the OPTICA-intervention speed, the faster will be the speed of convergence of the system toward equilibrium, if this is stable.

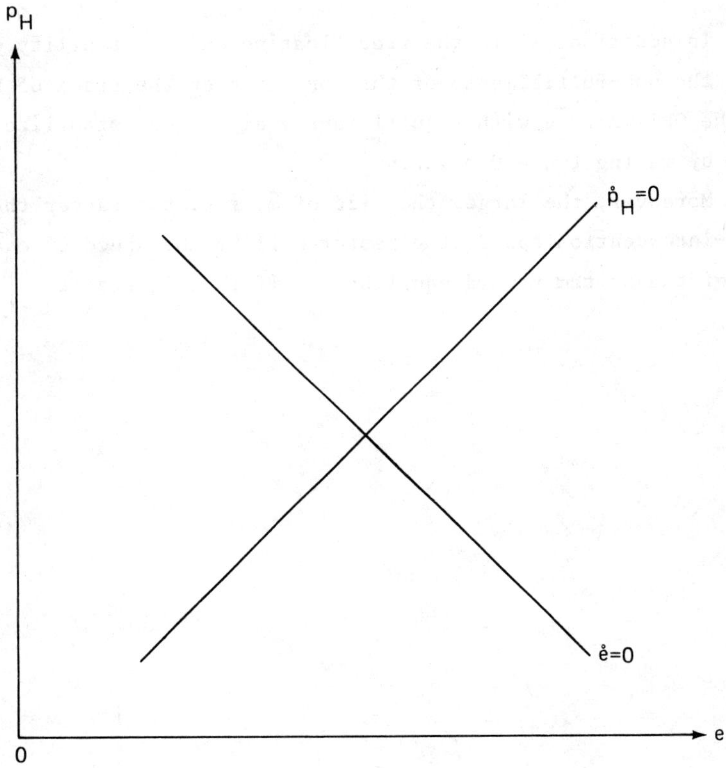

FIGURE 1

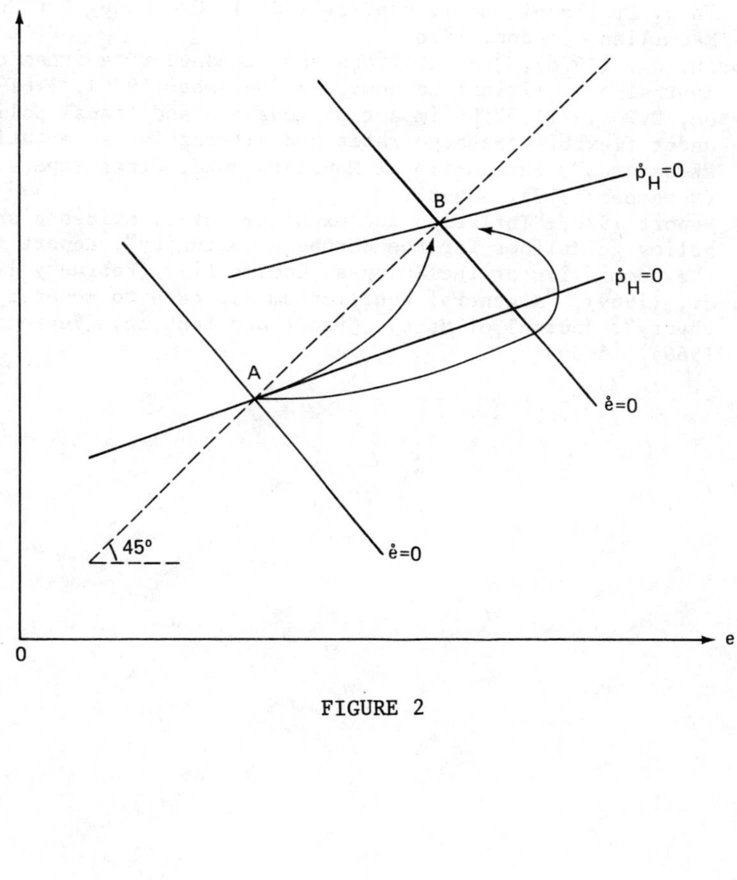

FIGURE 2

REFERENCES

Basevi, G. and De Grauwe, P., (1978a), "Vicious and virtuous circles. A theoretical analysis and a policy proposal for managing exchange rates", European Economic Review, 1978, no. 3.

Basevi, G. and De Grauwe, P., (1978b), "Vicious and virtuous circles and the OPTICA proposal: a two countries analysis", in M. Fratianni and T. Peeters (eds.), One Money for Europe, Macmillan, London, 1978.

Dornbusch, R., (1976), "Expectations and exchange rate dynamics", Journal of Political Economy, 84 (December 1976), 1161-76.

Mathieson, D., (1977), "The impact of monetary and fiscal policy under flexible exchange rates and alternative expectations structures", International Monetary Fund, Staff Papers, 24 (November 1977), 535-68.

OPTICA Report 1976, "Inflation and exchange rates: evidence and policy guidelines for the European Community", Report to the Commission of the European Communities (February 1977).

Tobin, J., (1969), "A general equilibrium approach to monetary theory", Journal of Money, Credit and Banking, (February 1969), 15-3o.

COMMENT ON P.DE GRAUWE, A.STEINHERR AND G.BASEVI, "THE DYNAMICS OF INTERVENTION RULES IN FOREIGN EXCHANGE MARKETS"

Emil-Maria Claassen

The conclusion of the paper is that the Optica-intervention rule works normally well if expectations are of the adaptive type. This information is already implicitly contained in the Dornbusch-type model (which the authors use) because, on a ceteris paribus basis, adaptive expectations give generally rise to a higher degree of variability than rational expectations.

It should be credited to Giorghiu Basevi, the chairman of the Optica-group, to have initiated such a study because it was him who proposed principally the Optica-rule. I was member of the Optica-group only during the first year of its existence when it proposed a European Parallel Currency. In the second year the Optica-rule was conceived so that I can comment on it rather freely.

However, my comment concerns the need of the Optica-rule within the Dornbusch-type model. If the shocks giving rise to the variability of the exchange rate are mainly monetary, the policy to reduce the variability is equally monetary by avoiding the monetary shocks at the very beginning. If, for instance, the change in the rate of interest leading to the variability of the exchange rate is the main result of monetary policy (in the domestic country or abroad), monetary policy should remain stable such that it avoids such a change in the interest rate.

In the framework of the analysis by de Grauwe - Steinherr - Basevi, it would be useless and even costly to intervene directly on the market for foreign exchange (according to the Optica-rule or not) in order to reduce the variability in the exchange rate.

If the latter had been caused by monetary policy, it is true that an intervention on the market for foreign exchange would nullify the expansionary or restrictive effect of the former monetary policy because of the changes in international reserves which constitute one of the components of the monetary base. But why should there be first (for example) an expansionary monetary policy and afterwards a reduction of the quantity of money via the sale of foreign exchange? It would be better not to pursue an expansionary monetary policy in the very beginning. However, if the monetary authorities follow a neutralization policy by maintaining the expansionary policy, they succeed in reducing the variability (with or without the Optica-rule) only by influencing the expectations with respect to the future exchange rate (in our example of an expansionary monetary policy the individuals should expect an appreciation - an attempt the success of which is difficult to imagine.

Consequently, our proposition to reduce the variability of the exchange rate - within the framework of the Dornbusch model - concerns a stable monetary policy which may be in terms of a constant rate of interest or in terms of a constant monetary growth rate. Such a rule, however, would be confronted with two difficulties. On the one hand, the variability of the exchange rate is a phenomenon of the very short run, while from a technical point of view the growth rate of the quantity of money cannot be regulated very strictly in the very short run. However, it would be better to fix it in this way than not at all. Furthermore, such a monetary policy would help to know better the long-run level of the exchange-rate; (it would also imply that expectations would become more of the rational type; consequently, an Optica-intervention rule which involves a non-stable monetary policy, would destabilize the system under rational expectations as the authors have detected). On the other hand, the variability of the exchange rate is influenced by the monetary policy of two countries because the exchange rate is the relative price of two currencies; consequently, the stable monetary policy should be realized in the two countries concerned. If all exchange rates should have a lower degree of variability (a similar concern of the Optica-rule), all countries should realize a stable monetary policy.

THE DEMAND FOR INTERNATIONAL RESERVES UNDER PEGGED AND FLEXIBLE EXCHANGE RATE REGIMES AND ASPECTS OF THE ECONOMICS OF MANAGED FLOAT*

Jacob A. Frenkel

I. INTRODUCTION

One of the striking features characterizing the international monetary system since the early 1970's has been the continued use of international reserves even though, legally, the system has been characterized as a flexible exchange rate regime.

In this paper I analyze the interrelationship between the determinants and patterns of reserve holdings and the international monetary system. Section II contains an empirical analysis of the demand for international reserves. In this context I analyze the differences in behavioral patterns of developed and less-developed countries. Section III deals with the empirical question of the timing at which the system moved from pegged to floating rates. The interest in this question stems from the belief that timing of changes in economic behavior need not correspond to, or be

---

* Previous drafts of this paper were presented at the conference on "The Economics of Flexible Exchange Rates", Institute for Advanced Studies, Vienna, Austria, March 29-31, 1978 and the Carnegie-Rochester Conference held at Carnegie-Mellon University, November 18-19, 1977. I am indebted to Craig Hakkio for helpful comments, suggestions and efficient research assistance. In revising the paper I have benefited from useful comments by Russell Boyer, Kenneth Clements, Robert Hodrick, Edi Karni and David Laidler. The present version draws on Frenkel (1978); it extends the discussion by including a framework for the analysis of managed float and by modifying the definitions of the measures of variability and scale that are used in the empirical work, which is extended to cover the period up to 1977. This version corrects some errors in the data for LDC's and incorporates more recent revisions of the IMF data base.

associated with, the timing of changes in legal commitments. One of the conclusions emerging from the analysis is that the extent of the change in economic behavior (as far as the holdings of international reserves are concerned) has not been as large as one might have predicted. Countries have preferred to move to a system of managed floating that is intermediate between the extremes of fixed rates and of clean float. Section IV provides a sketch of an analytical framework for the analysis of a managed float regime. Some concluding remarks and suggested extensions are contained in Section V.

II.1 THE DETERMINANTS OF THE DEMAND FOR INTERNATIONAL RESERVES

Earlier studies of the demand for reserves considered the variability of international receipts and payments as an important argument in the demand function (e.g., Kenen and Yudin, 1965; Clower and Lipsey, 1968; Archibald and Richmond, 1971). In addition, it has been suggested that the demand function also depends on the propensity to import (e.g., Heller, 1966; Kelly, 1970; Clark, 1970a; Flanders, 1971; Frenkel, 1974a, 1974b, 1978; Hipple, 1974; Iyoha, 1976). These and other studies have recently been surveyed by Grubel (1971), Williamson (1973), Claassen (1974) and Cohen (1975).

The choice of a variability measure as an argument in the demand function stems directly from the role of international reserves in serving as a buffer stock accommodating fluctuations in external transactions. Consequently, it has generally been expected that the demand for reserves is positively associated with the extent of these fluctuations.

The rationale for the use of the propensity to import as an argument is more involved. It stems from an application of the Keynesian priceless model of the foreign trade multiplier. According to that model, an external disequilibrium that is induced by a decline in export earnings, could be corrected by a decline in output proportional to the multiplier. The cost of output adjustment could be saved if the monetary authorities are able to run down their stock of international reserves thereby enabling them to finance the external deficit. Since the foreign trade multiplier (and thus the required output dampening due to the fall in exports) is inversely related to the marginal propensity to import, the popular approach argues that the cost of not having reserves, and hence the demand for reserves, is inversely related to the marginal propensity to import (see references op.cit.). In the absence of data on the marginal propensity to import, earlier empirical studies have replaced it by the ratio of imports to income, i.e., by the average propensity (typically referred to as the degree of "openness" of the economy). The coefficient of the average propensity to import frequently appeared with the "wrong" (positive) sign when used to estimate the demand for reserves.

Using an adjustment mechanism which emphasizes the role of relative prices, price level and demand for money, it was previously shown (Frenkel, 1974a) that under certain assumptions, the demand for reserves was expected to be associated positively with the average propensity to import. This association was shown to be consistent with data for the period 1963 - 1967 for both Developed and Less-Developed Countries (Frenkel, 1974b). A simplified derivation of the association between reserve holdings and the propensity to import is presented in Appendix A. It is shown that the relationship between these two variables is, in general, not clear cut, although, under some assumptions this relationship is expected to be positive.

In what follows I present cross-sectional estimates of the demand for international reserves where, in addition to the above mentioned variables, I have also included a scaling variable as one of the determinants of the demand.[1)]

II.2 CROSS-SECTIONAL ESTIMATES OF THE DEMAND FOR INTERNATIONAL RESERVES

The empirical analysis includes data from 22 Developed Countries and 32 Less-Developed Countries (LDC's) and covers the period 1963 - 77. Appendix B contains the list of countries and definitions of variables used in the analysis. The classification of countries as Developed and Less-Developed is based on that of the IMF. The choice of countries and the period of analysis was determined by the availability of continuous series of data.[2)]

---

1) An additional variable which in principle should have been included in the list of the determinants of reserve holdings is the opportunity cost of holding reserves. In practice, a large fraction of international reserves is held in the form of short term interest-bearing assets and thus, the opportunity cost is the difference between the alternative yield and the rate of return on reserves. Previous studies faced serious difficulties in estimating this cost. Clark (1970a) decided to exclude this variable from his estimation. Heller (1966) assumed that the cost was the same for all countries (5 percent). Kenen and Yudin (1965) used income per capita as a proxy, and found that it had the "wrong" sign and was not significant. Kelly (1970) used in addition to per capita income, the value of foreign assets and liabilities as proxies, but found that in all cases the latter appeared with the "wrong" sign while in some cases the former had the "wrong" sign. Courchene and Youssef (1967) used the long-term interest rate as a proxy, and found that in five out of nine cases its coefficient was not significantly negative. All these attempts taken together, provided the rationale for not including this variable in the estimating equations. For an incorporation of the rate of interest into a stochastic framework see Frenkel and Jovanovic (1979).
2) From the list of countries for which data were available, two countries - Canada and the United States - were excluded from the analysis. Canada was excluded since it had a flexible exchange rate system during most of the period for which the variability measure was calculated. Since the discussion focuses on the behavior of countries as demanders of reserves, the exclusion of the United States as the main supplier seems justified. This relates to one of the limitations of the present approach of estimating the demand for reserves by means of a single regression equation. To the best of my knowledge, the potential difficulty of an identification problem is shared by all previous empirical studies of the demand for reserves.

TABLE 1: Estimated equation:

$$\ell n\ R = \alpha_0 + \alpha_1\ \ell n\ \sigma + \alpha_2\ \ell n\ Y + \alpha_3\ \ell n\ m + \mu$$

Developed Countries, N = 22
(standard errors in parentheses)

Year	Constant	$\ell n\ \sigma$	$\ell n\ Y$	$\ell n\ m$	R^2	s.e.
1963	4.141	.618	.441	.781	.90	.436
	(.701)	(.211)	(.214)	(.271)		
1964	4.243	.608	.399	.738	.88	.480
	(.809)	(.255)	(.259)	(.276)		
1965	4.464	.507	.546	.867	.85	.538
	(.916)	(.294)	(.292)	(.314)		
1966	4.448	.596	.506	1.042	.86	.540
	(.914)	(.288)	(.286)	(.329)		
1967	4.291	.650	.495	1.096	.86	.556
	(.899)	(.280)	(.270)	(.316)		
1968	4.254	.570	.582	1.019	.85	.587
	(1.114)	(.324)	(.280)	(.341)		
1969	4.282	.510	.483	.735	.84	.551
	(.940)	(.269)	(.239)	(.298)		
1970	4.006	.569	.446	.627	.85	.534
	(.817)	(.249)	(.225)	(.292)		
1971	4.378	.352	.661	.405	.86	.539
	(.771)	(.242)	(.230)	(.303)		
1972	3.568	.733	.209	.265	.90	.425
	(.620)	(.219)	(.212)	(.237)		
1973	3.915	.675	.291	.533	.88	.475
	(.667)	(.272)	(.248)	(.283)		
1974	3.171	.803	.257	.676	.87	.533
	(.796)	(.325)	(.319)	(.334)		
1975	3.366	.668	.510	1.012	.85	.606
	(.944)	(.348)	(.298)	(.414)		
1976	3.226	.809	.330	1.088	.84	.588
	(.946)	(.352)	(.301)	(.374)		
1977	3.126	.851	.435	1.422	.93	.410
	(.616)	(.219)	(.195)	(.236)		

TABLE 2: Estimated equation:

$$\ell n\ R = \alpha_0 + \alpha_1\ \ell n\ \sigma + \alpha_2\ \ell n\ Y + \alpha_3\ \ell n\ m + \mu$$

Less-Developed Countries, N = 32
(standard errors in parentheses)

Year	Constant	$\ell n\ \sigma$	$\ell n\ Y$	$\ell n\ m$	R^2	s.e.
1963	5.864	.297	.946	1.598	.84	.523
	(.684)	(.174)	(.204)	(.280)		
1964	5.751	.241	.955	1.491	.80	.553
	(.723)	(.190)	(.219)	(.287)		
1965	5.596	.188	.937	1.223	.79	.539
	(.647)	(.179)	(.197)	(.263)		
1966	4.924	.380	.734	1.129	.73	.627
	(.724)	(.201)	(.220)	(.321)		
1967	4.228	.586	.666	1.110	.70	.753
	(.851)	(.223)	(.254)	(.399)		
1968	4.611	.425	.791	1.101	.74	.684
	(.749)	(.193)	(.219)	(.334)		
1969	4.610	.297	.909	.947	.77	.655
	(.754)	(.204)	(.224)	(.305)		
1970	4.281	.293	.913	.784	.76	.719
	(.801)	(.222)	(.248)	(.321)		
1971	4.877	.240	.997	1.071	.77	.684
	(.829)	(.235)	(.256)	(.312)		
1972	5.036	.269	.964	1.062	.83	.592
	(.713)	(.203)	(.213)	(.248)		
1973	3.782	.549	.641	.599	.86	.537
	(.612)	(.187)	(.193)	(.204)		
1974	2.882	.703	.400	.292	.78	.700
	(.772)	(.257)	(.263)	(.264)		
1975	3.328	.603	.467	.538	.75	.737
	(.665)	(.205)	(.236)	(.276)		
1976	3.615	.462	.696	.545	.74	.807
	(.754)	(.224)	(.249)	(.288)		
1977	3.368	.569	.572	.503	.76	.759
	(.802)	(.255)	(.301)	(.298)		

As indicated above,the demand function was assumed to depend on three variables: (i) a measure of variability of international receipts and payments denoted by σ; the value of σ for each year was estimated by computing the standard deviation over the previous 15 years of the trend-adjusted annual changes of the level of reserves;[3)] (ii) a scaling variable measuring the size of international transactions represented by the level of GNP, Y; in the few cases where this was not available, it was replaced by Gross Domestic Products, GDP, and (iii) the average propensity to import, $m = IM/Y$, where IM denotes imports.

The functional form of the demand function was assumed to be:

$$(1) \quad \ln R = \alpha_0 + \alpha_1 \ln\sigma + \alpha_2 \ln Y + \alpha_3 \ln m + \mu$$

where u denotes an error term.

Tables 1 and 2 present for each year the cross-sectional ordinary-least-squares estimates of the demand for reserves by Developed and Less-Developed Countries. In all case the coefficients have the expected positive sign and in most cases these coefficients are statistically significant at the 95 percent confidence level.

In summary it should be noted that the overall fit of the regressions reported in Tables 1 and 2 (as measured by the coefficients of determination R^2) is very satisfactory.[4)] This point

---

3) A limitation of this measure is that actual changes in reserves need not provide an exact measure of the disturbance, since countries may use other policies. Kenen and Yudin (1965) and Heller (1966) who have used similar measures, have assumed that its estimates are not materially affected by national policies.

4) The estimates for LDC's in this paper differ from those in Frenkel (1978) due to revisions and some errors in the data used in the previous paper. The errors however affected mainly the values of the constant terms without altering any of the basic qualitative results.

is noteworthy since these results pertain to cross-sectional estimates. Of special interest is the good fit of the cross-sectional regressions for the last few years reported in Tables 1 and 2. During the latter years of the sample period, the international monetary system moved towards a greater flexibility of exchange rates. This move was expected to result in different as well as in less stable estimates of the parameters of the demand for reserves. Since, as will be shown below, the cross-sectional estimates seem to have remained stable (at least during the periods 1963 - 72 and 1973 - 77), more efficient estimates may be obtained by pooling the time-series with cross-sections.

II.3 POOLED TIME-SERIES AND CROSS-SECTIONS: PEGGED VERSUS FLOATING EXCHANGE RATES

In order to examine the effect of the move to a regime of flexible exchange rates, I have divided the sample into two periods: the pegged exchange rate period (1963 - 72) and the flexible exchange rate period (1973 - 77). In Section III I provide a formal justification for this division.

TABLE 3: Estimated equation:

$$\ell n\ R = \alpha_0 + \alpha_1\ \ell n\ \sigma + \alpha_2\ \ell n\ Y + \alpha_3\ \ell n\ m + \mu$$

Pooled time series-cross section
(standard errors in parentheses)

Year	Group	Constant	$\ell n\ \sigma$	$\ell n\ Y$	$\ell n\ m$	R^2	s.e.
1963-72	DC's	4.129	.593	.467	.760	.86	.504
	NOB = 220	(.247)	(.076)	(.072)	(.089)		
1963-72	LDC's	4.907	.323	.865	1.103	.76	.623
	NOB = 320	(.226)	(.062)	(.067)	(.092)		
1973-77	DC's	3.469	.708	.379	.826	.84	.549
	NOB = 110	(.366)	(.139)	(.125)	(.147)		
1973-77	LDC's	3.356	.572	.532	.434	.77	.696
	NOB = 160	(.310)	(.097)	(.106)	(.113)		

TABLE 4: Tests for difference between Developed and Less-Developed Countries (standard errors in parentheses)

Year	Estimated Dummies for Developed Countries				F-statistic
	Constant	$\ell n\ \sigma$	$\ell n\ Y$	$\ell n\ m$	for Chow-Test
1963-72	-.778	.270	-.398	-.343	5.069
	(.353)	(.104)	(.104)	(.133)	
1973-77	.113	.136	-.153	.392	2.564
	(.514)	(.185)	(.176)	(.20)	

Note: The estimated dummies measure the differential values of the constant and the slope coefficients for Developed Countries from the corresponding estimates for LDC's. The F-statistics for the Chow-test correspond to the null hypothesis that the regression coefficients are the same for Developed and Less-Developed Countries. The relevant degrees of freedom for the two periods are F(4, 532) and F(4, 262), respectively. The null hypothesis is rejected since the values of the F-statistics exceed the critical values at the 95-percent confidence levels.

To the extent that the coefficients of the cross-sectional equations remained stable within each of the periods 1963 - 72 and 1973 - 77, one may obtain more efficient estimates by pooling the time-series with the cross-sections. Table 3 contains the ordinary-least-squares estimates of the pooled regression for both periods. In all cases the coefficients are positive and significant at the 95 percent confidence level.

I turn now to a comparison of the regression coefficients between Developed and Less-Developed Countries during the two periods. The first method used for this comparison was the dummy variables method as outlined by Gujarti (1970). According to this method, each and every coefficient was allowed to differ between Developed and Less-Developed Countries by including dummy variables pertaining to data for Developed Countries. The estimated coefficients of the dummy variables are reported in Table 4 where it is seen that for the first period the coefficients of the constant term, of income and of the average propensity to imports are significantly lower for Developed Countries while the coefficient of the variability measure is higher. For the latter period, however, the behavior of the two groups with respect to international reserves is much more similar. These estimates reveal a larger degree of economies of scale in the demand for reserves (as measured by the income elasticity) in Developed Countries than in LDC's. It is also apparent that the demand for reserves by LDC's is less sensitive to the variability measure than the demand by Developed Countries. The differencesin the income elasticities may reflect differences in the character of the financial systems. The financial system in Developed Countries is more sophisticated than its counterpart in LDC's, thus entailing larger possibilities for economies of scale in reserve management. In addition, Developed Countries have a larger access to world capital markets and greater facilities for swap agreements.[5)] The higher sensitivity of Developed Countries to the variability measure may reflect larger reluctance to cope with unexpected shocks by imposing trade controls and

---

footnote 5) see page 127

restrictions.[6] These differences have diminished significantly with the move towards greater flexibility of exchange rates.

The dummy variables method focuses on comparisons between individual coefficients. The second method that was employed in the comparison between Developed and Less-Developed Countries was that of the Chow-test following the procedure described by Fisher (1970). The results of this test are also reported in Table 4 where the F-statistics correspond to the null-hypothesis that the OLS regressions in Table 4 do not differ from each other. The null hypothesis is rejected since the values of the F-statistics exceed the critical values at the 95 percent confidence level. Thus, also the Chow-test leads to the conclusion that Developed and Less-Developed Countries reveal different behavior concerning the holdings of international reserves. It should be noted however that for the second period the statistical significance of the difference between the groups is marginal. It is of interest to explore in greater detail the patterns of the move to the floating rates regime, as are implied by the characteristics of reserve holdings.

III. WHEN DID THE SYSTEM MOVE FROM PEGGED TO FLOATING RATES?

The analysis in the previous sections made a distinction between the periods 1963-72 und 1973-77. The presumption was that the evolution of the international monetary system from pegged exchange rates to floating exchange rates might have resulted in a structural change in the demand for international reserves. In the present section I examine formally the timing and extent of the structural change following the method proposed by Quandt (1958, 1960).[7]

---

5) The interpretation of the estimates of the income elasticities as measuring economies of scale should be taken only as suggestive since the variability measure is not free of units and might therefore pick up some of the effect of size.

6) For further elaboration of these and other interpretations see Frenkel (1974b).

7) For this and other methods of analyzing switching regressions see Goldfeld and Quandt (1976, Chs. 1, 4).

Consider a situation in which a structural change occurred at year t* within the period 1,...,T and assume that the demand for reserves corresponding to the two regimes (before and after t*) can be characterized by two distinct regression equations like (2) - (3)

$$(2) \qquad y_{nt} = x'_{nt}\beta_1 + u_{1nt}, \qquad t \leq t^*$$

$$(3) \qquad y_{nt} = x'_{nt}\beta_2 + u_{2nt}, \qquad t > t^*$$

where u_{1nt} and u_{2nt} are the error terms that are assumed to be distributed as $N(0, \sigma_1^2)$ and $N(0, \sigma_2^2)$, β_1 and β_2 are the vectors of the regression coefficients corresponding to the two regimes, and where n = 1,...,N denote the countries (for the Developed countries N = 22 and for the LDC's N = 32). The analysis of the timing of the structural change amounts to searching for the value of t*. Quandt's method of estimating t* involves the following: first, a maximization of the likelihood function (4) conditional on t*:

$$(4) \qquad L(y|t^*) = \left(\frac{1}{2\pi}\right)^{NT/2} \sigma_1^{-Nt^*} \sigma_2^{-N(T-t^*)} \exp$$

$$\left\{-\frac{1}{2\sigma_1^2} \sum_{t=1}^{t^*} \sum_{n=1}^{N} (y_{nt} - x'_{nt}\beta_1)^2 - \frac{1}{2\sigma_2^2} \sum_{t=t^*+1}^{T} \sum_{n=1}^{N} (y_{nt} - x'_{nt}\beta_2)^2\right\}$$

(where N denotes the number of countries and T denotes the number of years), and second, determination of the breakpoint t* as the value which yields the highest maximum likelihood L(y|t*). The application of this procedure to determining the breakpoint in the demand for reserves, yields 1973 and 1972 as the estimates for t* for Developed and Less-Developed Countries, respectively.

Based on these results, 1972 is used as the estimate of the break point for both the Developed and the Less Developed Countries, implying that the two subperiods are 1963-72 and 1973-77.

This choice is based on the fact that while for LDC's 1972 seems to be an unambiguous estimate for the data of the structural change, the case for Developed Countries is less clear cut; it is therefore assumed that, by analogy with the LDC's, the break point for Developed Countries also occurred in 1972 (even though it should be noted that the choice between 1972 and 1973 is somewhat arbitrary). The validity of this assumption can be tested by applying the likelihood-ratio test to the null hypothesis that no switch took place between 1972 and 1973. The likelihood ratio statistic is

$$\phi = \hat{\sigma}_1^{N\hat{t}*} \hat{\sigma}_2^{N(T-\hat{t}*)} / \hat{\sigma}^{NT}$$

where $\hat{\sigma}^{NT}$ is the estimated standard deviation of the residuals from the single regression estimated over the entire period 1963-77.

According to the null hypothesis, $-2 \ln \phi$ is distributed $\chi^2(5)$. The null hypothesis is rejected for both groups of countries. For the LDC's the value of $-2 \ln \phi$ is 26.6 while the corresponding value of Developed Countries is 37.8, both exceeding 15.1 - the critical value at the 99 percent confidence level.[8)] The practical implication is that for the purpose of estimation, data from the period 1963-72 should not be pooled with those from the period 1973-77 and that the structural change occurred by the end of 1972.

---

8) It should be noted that the application of this method to the problem at hand is not without conceptual difficulties since it requires differentiating the likelihood function with respect to t*.
It should also be noted that the analysis assumes that the structural change has taken place at a given point in time. An alternative approach would allow for a gradual evolution, and would estimate regression equations with variable coefficients. For references and discussion of the properties of the distribution of $-2 \ln \phi$ see Goldfeld and Quandt (1976, Ch. 1).

In addition to the above tests one may also use a Chow-test to test for the equality of the regression coefficients between the two periods.[9] The resulting values of the F-statistics relevant for testing the null hypothesis are 9.45 for Developed Countries and 6.12 for LDC's - well above the critical values at the 99 percent confidence level. Thus, the Chow-test as well leads to the rejection of the null hypothesis. The overall inference is that the system has changed by the end of 1972. It is this conclusion which provides the rationale for the pattern of the intertemporal pooling that is employed in Tables 3 - 4.[10] It should be noted that even though, as a statistical matter, the system underwent a structural change, the extent of the change has not been large enough to make obsolete parameter estimates that are based on the period 1963-72. In fact, forecasting reserve holdings during the period 1973-77 based on parameter estimates from 1963-72, yield extremely good predictions (for details see Frenkel, 1978).

The interpretation of the relative stability of the patterns of reserve holdings is quite obvious: during the pegged rate regime the rate was adjustable rather than fixed and during the so-called floating rate regime the rate has been managed rather than free. Economic behavior seems to be more stable than legal arrangements. Central banks have revealed that their choice is for neither of the extreme exchange rate systems, but have rather preferred to have the intermediate system of managed floating. Since managing the float requires international reserves, it seems relevent to

9) In implementing the Chow-test one pretends that t* was known a priori. Goldfeld and Quandt (1976, Ch. 1) provide reference to evidence that the Chow-test yields satisfactory results.

10) The above discussion associated the structural change with the change in the exchange rate regime; it could of course reflect other (not necessarily unrelated) phenomena which occurred in the early 1970's like the oil crisis and the commodity price boom.

analyze the determinants of the degree to which countries will attempt to manage the float. In the following section I deal with some analytical aspects of managed floating.

IV. A SKETCH OF A FRAMEWORK FOR THE ANALYSIS OF MANAGED FLOAT[11)]

In this section I provide a sketch of an analytical framework for the analysis of the economics of managed floating. The analysis will highlight some variables which should be included as determinants of the demand for reserves under a regime of managed float.

Earlier discussions of the optimal exchange rate regime centered around comparisons between fixed and flexible exchange rate systems. More recent explorations - originating with Mundell's contributions in the early 1960's - have shifted to the determination of optimal currency areas within which exchange rates are fixed and between which exchange rates are flexible. The following analysis of the optimal managed float recognizes that the spectrum of possibilities is broader and that the rate of exchange between any pair of currencies need not be entirely fixed or flexible but rather it might be some optimal mix of the two extremes. In what follows I will sketch a simple analytical framework that highlights some of the determinants of the optimal degree of exchange rate flexibility. The analysis will emphasize the role of the stochastic structure of the various shocks which affect the economy, and its purpose is to suggest an additional set of variables which might be incorporated into the specification of the demand for international reserves under a regime of managed float.

Consider a small economy that is subject to two types of repetitive and serially uncorrelated shocks. These shocks, which

---

11) I am indebted to Michael Bazdarich for research assistance and suggestions concerning the material in this section. The material in this section draws on Frenkel (1976b).

are specified below in a manner similar to that of Fischer (1977), are referred to as real and monetary shocks.

Denote the supply of output by Y_t and let

$$(5)\qquad Y_t = ye^{\mu} \quad ; \qquad \mu \sim N(-\sigma_{\mu}^2/2,\ \sigma_{\mu}^2)$$

where μ is a stochastic shock (the "real" shock) with a constant variance σ_{μ}^2. The mean of the distribution of the real shock is chosen to be $-\sigma_{\mu}^2/2$ so as to assure that the expected value of output equals y (permanent income).

The second shock arises from the monetary sector. Let the demand for nominal cash balances L_t be

$$(6)\qquad L_t = kP_tY_te^{\varepsilon} \quad ; \qquad \varepsilon \sim N(-\sigma_{\varepsilon}^2/2,\ \sigma_{\varepsilon}^2)$$

where k denotes the desired money-income ratio, P denotes the domestic price level and ε denotes the stochastic shock to the demand for money (the "monetary" shock).

The domestic price level is linked to the foreign price level through the purchasing power parity relationship. Thus

$$(7)\qquad P_t = S_tP_t^*$$

where P_t^* denotes the foreign price level and S_t denotes the exchange rate (the price of foreign currency in terms of domestic currency). To simplify the analysis it is assumed that foreign prices are fixed, (and thus it will be denoted henceforth as P*), that purchasing power parity holds deterministically and that μ and ε are independent.[12)]

12) A more elaborate analysis would allow for disturbances which originate from the foreign sector and which are allowed to be correlated with domestic shocks. Another extension would allow for possible short run deviations from purchasing power parity in which case, in the short-run changes in the exchange rate induce changes in relative prices. For a rationale for managed

Assume that the flow demand for money ΔM^d corresponds to a stock adjustment process such that

$$(8) \qquad \Delta M^d = \alpha(L_t - \overline{M}_t)$$

where $\overline{M}_t$ denotes the money stock at the beginning of the period.

Using equations (5) and (7) we may express the demand for money (6) as

$$(9) \qquad L_t = kS_t P^* y e^{\mu+\varepsilon}.$$

When the exchange rate is flexible, it will adjust so as to eliminate any stock disequilibrium in the money market, and thus ensuring that $L_t - \overline{M}_t = 0$. Using (9) it follows that when the exchange rate is flexible

$$(10) \qquad kS_t P^* y e^{\mu+\varepsilon} - \overline{M}_t = 0.$$

The equilibrium exchange rate can be written as

$$(11) \qquad S_t = (\overline{M}_t / kP^* y) e^{-(\mu+\varepsilon)}$$

and the percentage change thereof is

$$(12) \qquad \ln S_t - \ln S_{t-1} = \ln (\overline{M}_t / kS_{t-1} P^* y) - (\mu + \varepsilon).$$

The other extreme system is the fixed exchange rate system for which

---

12) (continued)
float that is based on this phenomenon see Mussa (1976); for recent empirical evidence on the short-run relationship between exchange rates and relative prices see Dornbusch and Krugman (1977). In a recent analysis of the optimal foreign exchange intervention Boyer (1976) extends and applies Poole's framework (1970) to the problem at hand. Boyer assumes that real income is fixed and that the objective function is to minimize variability of prices.

(13) $\ln S_t - \ln S_{t-1} = 0.$

Using (12) and (13) we may define an index γ such that $0 \leq \gamma \leq 1$:

(14) $\gamma = (\ln S_t - \ln S_{t-1})/[\ln(\overline{M}_t/kS_{t-1}P^*y) - (\mu + \varepsilon)].$

The coefficient γ characterizes the whole spectrum of exchange rate regimes. When $\gamma = 0$, the system is that of a fixed exchange rate, and when $\gamma = 1$ the system is that of a freely flexible exchange rate. An intermediate value of γ indicates an intermediate degree of exchange rate flexibility. We will refer to the coefficient γ as the coefficient of managed float, or the intervention index. From the policy perspective, the basic question is to determine the optimal value of γ, and thus to determine the optimal degree of exchange rate flexibility.

In principle, if shocks were identifiable, the optimal policy would be to allow the exchange rate to correct monetary disturbances but not real disturbances.[13)] We will assume, however, that information is incomplete and that during a given period only the joint outcome of the shocks $\mu + \varepsilon$ is known but not the separate values of μ and ε. It is this lack of complete information which necessitates a second-best policy of managed float.[14)]

Assume that the objective is to minimize the losses due to imperfect information and that the policymaker wishes to minimize the quadratic loss function H:

(15) Minimize $H = E[c_t - E(Y_t)]^2$

where c_t denotes the rate of consumption which, from the budget

---

13) For an analysis of the proposition see Fischer (1977).
14) The assumption of the lack of complete information has been used by Gray (1976) to analyze partial wage indexation.

constraint, equals the rate of income minus the real value of additions to real cash balances

$$(16) \qquad c_t = Y_t - \frac{\Delta M}{P_t} .$$

The previous relationships imply that

$$(17) \quad [c_t - E(Y_t)] = y(e^{\mu} - 1) - \alpha ky[e^{\mu+\varepsilon} - (\overline{M}_t / kS_{t-1} P^* y)^{1-\gamma} e^{\gamma(\mu+\varepsilon)}],$$

and using (17) in (15) yields the loss function which is to be minimized with respect to the intervention index γ.

The above analysis has not specified the value of the money stock $\overline{M}_t$ at the beginning of the period. It is assumed, following Fischer (1977), that at the beginning of each period the monetary authority changes the money supply so as to compensate for past disturbances according to

$$(18) \qquad \overline{M}_t = kS_{t-1} P^* y.$$

Substituting (18) and (17) and minimizing the loss function with respect to γ yield the following implications concerning the choice of the optimal degree of exchange rate flexibility:

(i) In general, the optimal value of γ will be within the range (0, 1), so that the optimal exchange rate regime will correspond to neither of the extremes of a completely fixed or of a completely flexible rate regime.

(ii) The intermediate solution is more likely the higher is αk - the propensity to save out of transitory income.

(iii) When the only shocks to the system are real ($\sigma_{\varepsilon} = 0$), the optimal solution is that of fixed rates ($\gamma = 0$); and conversely, when the only source of shocks is monetary ($\sigma_{\mu} = 0$), the optimal solution is that of freely floating rates ($\gamma = 1$).

(iv) The higher the variance of the monetary shock, the larger will be the optimal value of γ while the higher is the variance of the real shock the lower will be the optimal value of γ. That is, high variance of real shocks, ceteris paribus, tends to raise the desirability of greater fixity of exchange rates and conversely for high variance of monetary shocks.

Table 5 contains the results of illustrative computations of the optimal degree of the intervention index γ for alternative values of αk - the propensity to save out of transistory income - and for alternative assumptions concerning the magnitudes of the various shocks. These results illustrate the above propositions.

The analysis in this section provides a simple framework for determining the optimal degree of exchange rate flexibility. It highlights the unique role of the stochastic structure of the economy and suggests, therefore, that the magnitude of and the relationship between these variables are among the determinants of the demand for reserves and should be incorporated into the analysis of the demand for international reserves under a regime of managed float.

TABLE 5: Optimal managed float for alternative values of real and monetary disturbances and saving propensities

σ_μ \ σ_ε	$\alpha k = .5$					$\alpha k = 1$				
	.01	.03	.05	.07	.09	.01	.03	.05	.07	.09
.01	.0	.80	.92	.96	.98	.50	.90	.96	.98	.99
.03	.0	.47	.69	.80	.87	.10	.50	.74	.85	.90
.05	.0	.0	.0	.33	.53	.04	.27	.50	.67	.77
.07	.0	.0	.0	.0	.25	.02	.16	.34	.50	.63
.09	.0	.0	.0	.0	.0	.01	.10	.24	.38	.51

As a general comment on the analysis in this section it should be noted that monetary policy and foreign exchange intervention are treated as close substitutes. In fact, as a first approximation, these two policies are indistinguishable. It is believed that this feature of the model is much closer to reality than would be the other extreme in which monetary policy and foreign exchange policies are viewed as two independent policy instruments.

The special role of the exchange rate should also be noted. In the above framework the exchange rate (and thereby the price level) is determined by considerations of asset market equilibrium. This characteristic is in accord with the recent developments of the asset market approach to the analysis of exchange rates.[15] An important limitation of the model is the absence of an explicit incorporation of an integrated world capital market which would reflect itself in the capital account of the balance of payments.

Finally, it should be noted that the present specification of the nature of the shocks is somewhat biased in favor of government intervention since the shocks have been presumed to originate from the instability of the private sector rather than from the actions of government policies. Furthermore, the concept of the optimal managed float and thereby the derived demand for international reserves were developed as a policy prescription for the monetary authorities. This was motivated by realism and could be rationalized in terms of the assumption that the monetary authorities possess superior information concerning its own actions as well as concerning the official holdings of international reserves. In principle, however, much of the optimal mix could also be performed by the private sector.

V. CONCLUDING REMARKS

This paper contained an analysis of the role of international reserves under a regime of pegged exchange rates and under a regime of managed float. It presented evidence on the stability of the demand for reserves during the periods 1963-72 and 1973-77. It was

15) See for example Dornbusch (1976), Frenkel (1976a), Kouri (1976), Mussa (1976), Bilson (1978) and Frenkel and Johnson (1978).

shown that the demand for reserves by Developed countries differs from that of Less-Developed countries and that the system underwent a structural change by the end of 1972. In view of the drastic changes in the international monetary system, the extent of the structural change (in particular with reference to the behavior of Developed countries) has not been as large as one might have expected.[16] This finding led to the observation that economic behavior seems to be more stable than legal arrangements. The evidence suggests that countries have continued to hold and use international reserves. Likewise, countries have chosen to manage their exchange rates rather than let it float freely. From the policy perspective, it follows that the problems concerning the provision of international reserves and the discussions concerning the role of the IMF in this context are as relevant at the present as they were in the past.[17] The paper concluded with a sketch of a stochastic framework for the analysis of the optimal degree of managed floating.

The analysis in this paper would benefit from several extensions. First, it was assumed that, during the sample period, countries were "on" their long-run demand functions. An extension would allow for a distinction between short-run and long-run demand functions and would examine the determinants of the speed of adjustment along the lines of Clark (1970b). Second, an examination of the residuals from the estimated equations reveals the existence of persistent negative residuals for some countries (e.g., U.K. and New Zealand) and positive residuals for other (e.g., Switzerland). An extension would refine the grouping of countries by allowing for country-specific factors. In this connection it would be of

---

16) For analyses of the effects of the move to floating exchange rates on the demand for and the optimal provision of international reserves see Grubel (1976), Makin (1974) and Williamson (1976). For evidence on reserve use during the two regimes see Suss (1976) and for a comparison on the estimated coefficients in the Canadian case see Saidi and Barro (1977) and for further evidence on structural change see Heller and Kahn (1978).

17) On this issue see, however, Haberler (1976).

interest to test the hypothesis that countries behave so as to trade off large stocks of reserves for high speeds of adjustment; some preliminary results in Bilson and Frenkel (1979) are consistent with this hypothesis.

Third, the specification of the demand for reserves was assumed to remain unchanged as between the two exchange rate regimes. In principle, however, the specification of the demand for reserves during a regime of managed float should be derived from the analysis of the determinants of countries' decisions concerning the degree of optimal foreign exchange intervention (i.e., the optimal managed float). In Section IV it was shown that the optimal degree of managed float depends on the details of the stochastic structure of the various shocks which affect the economy. It suggests, therefore, that these stochastic characteristics should be incorporated into the specification of the demand for reserves under a regime of managed float.[18)]

Finally, the analytical framework underlying the literature on the demand for international reserves needs to be tied up with the framework underlying the literature on the monetary approach to the balance of payments. The monetary approach to the balance of payments emphasizes the considerations of monetary equilibrium and highlights the fact that when the monetary authorities peg the rate of exchange, they lose control over the nominal monetary stock. In many of the simplified versions of the monetary approach to the balance of payments, credit policies are viewed as the exogenous variable which, along with the path of the demand for money, determine (as a residual) the path of international reserves.[19)] In this framework little attention has been paid to

---

18) On the relationship between the stochastic structure of the economy and the estimated coefficients see Lucas (1976).

19) See for example the various studies in Frenkel and Johnson (1976).

incorporating into the analysis the possibility that the monetary authorities may have preferences concerning the composition of their assets.[20] These preferences are emphasized in the analytical framework underlying the demand for international reserves. In that literature, however, little attention has been paid to the conditions of monetary equilibrium. A useful extension would combine these two strands of analysis. In such an extension, credit policies would not be viewed as exogenous but rather, international reserves and domestic credit would be determined jointly so as to satisfy simultaneously equilibrium in the money market as well as equilibrium in the composition of central banks' assets.

20) For an exception which incorporates the monetary authorities' reaction function into the analytical framework of the monetary approach to the balance of payments see Ujiie (1978).

APPENDIX A

Reserve Holdings and the Average Propensity to Import

In this appendix I derive the relationship between long-run holdings of international reserves and the average propensity to import. It is shown that in contrast with the implications of the simple foreign trade multiplier, the relationship is not a clear cut one. Furthermore, it is shown that, according to a specific interpretation of the "small country assumption", there exists a positive long-run relationship between openness (the average propensity to import) and reserve holdings.

Consider the following simple two-goods model of a fully employed economy. The economy produces and consumes the quantities $[X_1, X_2]$ and $[x_1, x_2]$ respectively, and exports the first commodity. Nominal income (Y) is:

$$(A.1) \qquad Y = P_1X_1 + P_2X_2$$

where P_1 and P_2 are the money prices of the two goods. Denoting a percentage change in a variable by a circumflex (e.g., $\hat{X} = dX/X$), and using the fact that for small changes $P_1dX_1 + P_2dX_2 = 0$ (the envelope theorem), one may write the percentage change in nominal income as:

$$(A.2) \qquad \hat{Y} = \theta_1\hat{P}_1 + \theta_2\hat{P}_2$$

where

$$\theta_1 = \frac{P_1X_1}{Y} \; ; \qquad \theta_2 = \frac{P_2X_2}{Y}$$

and

$$\theta_1 + \theta_2 = 1.$$

In equation (A.2), θ_i denotes the relative share in production of good i (i = 1, 2). Let consumer price level (P) be a linear homogenous function of the money prices of goods with constant elasticities that are equal to the relative shares of expenditures on these goods in total expenditures. Thus:

$$(A.3) \qquad \hat{P} = \beta_1\hat{P}_1 + \beta_2\hat{P}_2$$

where

$$\beta_1 = \frac{P_1x_1}{Y} \quad ; \qquad \beta_2 = \frac{P_2x_2}{Y}$$

and

$$\beta_1 + \beta_2 = 1.$$

In equation (A.3), β_i denotes the average propensity to consume good i (i = 1, 2). The following analysis is confined to the long run when expenditures are equal to income.

The real value of income in terms of the consumer basket is y = Y/P:

$$(A.4) \qquad y = \frac{P_1X_1 + P_2X_2}{P}.$$

Using (A.2) - (A.3) in (A.4), the percentage change in real income is

$$(A.5) \qquad \hat{y} = (\beta_2 - \theta_2)(\hat{P}_1 - \hat{P}_2).$$

Equation (A.5) emphasizes the fact that a change in the terms of trade (P_1/P_2) raises real income if the relative share in production of the good whose relative price has risen exceeds its relative share in consumption. In particular, since the second commodity is the imported good, $\beta_2 > \theta_2$ and thus when $\hat{P}_1 - \hat{P}_2 > 0$ real income rises. Using the above notations, the average propensity to import is $(\beta_2 - \theta_2)$.

The stock demand for nominal cash balances (M^d) is assumed to depend on the price level and on real income. This demand function is homogenous of degree one in all prices:

$$\text{(A.6)} \qquad M^d = PL(y).$$

The long-run holdings of international reserves by the monetary authorities is assumed to be an increasing function of the central bank's assets. For simplicity, it is assumed that in the long run the money supply is proportional to the stock of reserves as it is when the money multiplier is fixed and when the operations of the monetary authorities are confined to pegging the exchange rate. By an appropriate choice of units, the proportionality factor is set to equal unity. Is should be noted, however, that the following qualitative results do not depend on this simplification.

At equilibrium the existing stock of cash balances (reserves) equals the desired stock:

$$\text{(A.7)} \qquad R = PL(y)$$

where R denotes the stock of reserves.

The percentage change of (A.7) is

$$\text{(A.8)} \qquad \hat{R} = \hat{P} + \eta\hat{y}; \qquad \eta = (\partial L/\partial y)y/L$$

where η denotes the income elasticity of the demand for real cash balances. Using (A.3) and (A.5) in (A.8) yields

$$\text{(A.9)} \qquad \hat{R} = \beta_1\hat{P}_1 + \beta_2\hat{P}_2 + \eta(\beta_2 - \theta_2)(\hat{P}_1 - \hat{P}_2).$$

Equation (A.9) expresses the proportional change in reserves as a function of the proportional change in prices. The first two terms describe the effects of the change in the price level due to changes in its components, and the third term describes the effects of the change in real income due to a change in relative prices.

As can be seen from (A.9), for any given price level (so that the sum of the first two terms in (A.9) vanishes), the effect of a given change in the terms of trade on reserve holdings increases with $(\beta_2 - \theta_2)$. On these grounds alone one may expect to find a positive relationship between reserves and the average propensity to import. In general, however, the price level will also change and therefore, in addition to the value of the parameters, the relationship depends on whether the changes are due to variations in the price of exportables or in the price of importables. It is in this sense that the effect of openness on reserve holdings is not a clear cut one. However, if we adopt some variant of the "small country assumption" and assume that the price of importables (P_2) is given by the rest of the world, then equation (A.9) can be written as:

$$\text{(A.1o)} \qquad \hat{R}/\hat{P}_1 = 1 - \beta_2 + \eta(\beta_2 - \theta_2)$$

which describes the effects of a given change in price on the holdings of international reserves.[21)]

The effects of the magnitude of the average propensity to import on reserve holdings can be ascertained by differentiating (A.1o) with respect to $(\beta_2 - \theta_2)$. An increase in the average propensity to import could result from either a decline in the production of importables and/or from an increase in the consumption of importables. Thus, from (A.1o):

---

21) Clearly, this variant of the "small country assumption" does not imply that the terms of trade are fixed since the price of exportables is determined endogenously.

$$\text{(A.11)} \qquad \left.\frac{\partial(\widehat{R/P_1})}{\partial(\beta_2 - \theta_2)}\right|_{\beta_2 = \text{constant}} = \eta$$

$$\text{(A.12)} \qquad \left.\frac{\partial(\widehat{R/P_1})}{\partial(\beta_2 - \theta_2)}\right|_{\theta_2 = \text{constant}} = \eta - 1$$

Equation (A.11) states that for given consumption conditions the induced changes in international reserves (due to a given change in export price) are positively related to the average propensity to import. The smaller the production of importables, the larger will be the resulting change and thus the holdings of reserves. Equation (A.12) states that for given production conditions, the induced changes in international reserves are also positively related to the average propensity to import if the income elasticity of the demand for money does not fall short of unity.[22)] Cross-sectional differences in the average propensity of import reflect differences in both production and consumption shares. Since empirical studies on the demand for money suggest that, in general, η does not fall short of unity, one can expect reserve holdings to depend positively on the average propensity to import.

---

22) It was previously shown (Frenkel, 1974a) that in this case the positive association between reserve holdings and the average propensity to import will be maintained as long as η exceeds some critical number which is smaller than unity. The difference arises from the simplification adopted in the present analysis: the present analysis takes the change in export prices as being the exogenous disturbance while the previous analysis allowed export prices to be endogenously determined while taking changes in foreign demand as the exogenous factor. In the latter case, the average propensity to import will also determine (via the Marshall-Lerner condition) the effect of a given change in foreign demand on the price of exportables.

Further, if the main differences among countries are in production patterns rather than in consumption patterns (as in the Heckscher-Ohlin model of international trade), equation (A.11) implies that the positive association between reserves and the average propensity to import will be maintained as long as the income elasticity of the demand for money is positive. It should, however, be emphasized that the above conclusions have been derived for a specific interpretation of the "small country assumption" and for a specific assumption concerning the nature and origin of disturbances. In general the relationship between reserve holdings and the average propensity to import depends on the nature and origin of disturbances and is not clear cut. Furthermore, the formulation in this appendix assumes that under a pegged exchange rate system, the operation of the monetary authorities are confined to pegging the rate and thus yielding a "passive" path of reserves along the lines described by the monetary approach to the balance of payments. Consequently, the terms used were "reserve holdings" rather than the "demand for reserves". An extension would modify the assumption concerning the operations of the monetary authorities and would allow for credit policies that are aimed at achieving the desired stock of international reserves.

APPENDIX B

List of Countries and Definitions of Variables

1. List of Countries[a)]

Developed Countries	Less-Developed Countries	
United Kingdom	Argentina	Jamaica
Austria	Brazil	Israel
Belgium	Chile	Jordan
Denmark	Columbia	Egypt
France	Costa Rica	Burma
Germany	Dom.Republic	Sri Lanka
Italy	Ecuador	China
Netherlands	El Salvador	India
Norway	Guatemala	Korea
Sweden	Honduras	Malaysia
Switzerland	Mexico	Pakistan
Japan	Nicaragua	Philippines
Finland	Panama	Thailand
Greece	Paraguay	Ghana
Iceland	Peru	Sudan
Ireland	Venezuela	Tunesia
Portugal		
Spain		
Turkey		
Australia		
New Zealand		
South Africa		

a) Classification based on the International Monetary Fund.

2. Definitions of Variables

All data sources are from the IFS tape obtained from the International Monetary Fund.

R - International reserves are measured in end-of-period 10^6 U.S. dollars. Reserves are defined as the sum of gold, SDR's, foreign exchange and reserve position at the Fund. When reserves are reported in local currency, they were converted to U.S. dollars using the end-of-period exchange rate.

IM - Imports are reported as cif in local currency units. These figures were then converted to U.S. dollars using the period average exchange rate. The figures used are measured in 10^9 U.S. dollars.

GNP - GNP and GDP are reported in local currency units. These figures were converted to U.S. dollars using the period average exchange rate. The figures are measured in 10^9 U.S. dollars.

m - The average propensity to import was defined as the ratio of imports to GNP. When the latter was unavailable, GDP was used instead.

σ - The variability measure. To calculate the value of σ_T^2 for year T for a given country, the following regression was first run:

$R_t = \alpha + \beta_T t + u$ over $t = T - 15, \ldots, T-1$, and then using the estimated trend $\hat{\beta}_T$, σ_T^2 was defined

$$\sigma_T^2 = \sum_{t=T-15}^{T-1} (R_t - R_{t-1} - \hat{\beta}_T)^2/14$$

(except for 1963 for which, due to lack of data, σ_T^2 is based on the previous 14 observations). Thus, σ^2 is defined as the variance of the trend-adjusted changes in the stock of international reserves. A plot of the time-series of reserves revealed that the assumption of a linear trend seems more appropriate than that of an exponential trend.

REFERENCES

Archibald, G.C., and Richmond, J. "On the Theory of Foreign Exchange Reserve Requirements." The Review of Economic Studies XXXVIII (April 1971): 245-263.

Bilson, John F.O. "Rational Expectations and the Exchange Rate." In Frenkel, J.A. and H.G. Johnson (eds.) The Economics of Exchange Rates: Selected Studies. Reading, Mass.: Addison-Wesley Publishing Co., 1978.

Bilson, John, F.O. and Frenkel, Jacob A. "International Reserves and the Dynamics of Adjustment." Unpublished manuscript, University of Chicago, 1979.

Boyer, Russell S. "Optimal Foreign Exchange Market Intervention." Journal of Political Economy 86, No.6 (December, 1978): 1045-1055.

Claassen, Emil M. "The Optimizing Approach to the Demand for International Reserves." Weltwirtschaftliches Archiv 3, (1974): 353-398.

Clark, Peter B. "Demand for International Reserves: A Cross-Country Analysis." Canadian Journal of Economics III (November 197o): 577-594.

Clower, Robert and Lipsey, Richard. "The Present State of International Liquidity Theory." American Economic Review LVII (May 1968): 586-594.

Cohen, Benjamin J. "International Reserves and Liquidity: A Survey." In Peter B. Kenen (ed.) International Trade and Finance. Cambridge: Cambridge University Press, 1975. Pp. 411-451.

Courchene, Thomas J. and Youseff, G.M. "The Demand for International Reserves." Journal of Political Economy 75, No. 4, Part I (August 1967): 4o4-13.

Dornbusch, Rüdiger. "The Theory of Flexible Exchange Rate Regimes and Macroeconomic Policy." Scandinavian Journal of Economics, 78, No. 2 (May 1976): 255-75.

Dornbusch, Rüdiger and Krugman, Paul. "Flexible Exchange Rates in the Short Run." Brookings Papers on Economic Activity, No. 3 (1976): 537-75.

Fischer, Stanley. "Stability and Exchange Rate Systems in a Monetarist Model of the Balance of Payments." In R.Z. Aliber (ed.) The Political Economy of Monetary Reform. Cambridge: Cambridge University Press, 1977. Pp. 59-73.

Fisher, Franklin M. "Tests of Equality between Sets of Coefficients in Two Linear Regressions: An Expository Note". Econometrica XXXVIII (197o): 361-366.

Flanders, M. June. "The Demand for International Reserves." Princeton Studies in International Finance 27 (1971): 1-5o.

Frenkel, Jacob A. "Openness and the Demand for International Reserves." In R.Z. Aliber (ed.) National Monetary Policies and the International Financial System. Chicago, III.: University of Chicago Press, 1974a, Pp.289-298.

Frenkel, Jacob A. "The Demand for International Reserves by Developed and Less-Developed Countries". Economica 41, No. 161 (February 1974b): 14-24.

______. "A Monetary Approach to the Exchange Rate: Doctrinal Aspects and Emiprical Evidence". Scandinavian Journal of Economics 78, No. 2 (May 1976a): 200-24.

______. "Comments on Exchange Rate Flexibility and Currency Areas". Presented at a conference on Money and International Monetary Problems, Martinique, 1976b. Forthcoming in E. Claassen and P. Salin (eds.) Exchange Rate Regimes and Currency Areas, Zeitschrift der Wirtschaftswissenschaften, 1918-9.

______. "International Reserves: Pegged Exchange Rates and Managed Float". In Brunner, K. and Meltzer, A.H. (eds.) Economic Policies in Open Economies Vol. 9 of the Carnegie-Rochester Conference Series on Public Policy, a Supplementary Series of the Journal of Monetary Economics, July 1978.

Frenkel, Jacob A. and Harry G. Johnson (eds.) The Monetary Approach to the Balance of Payments. London: Allen and Unwin and Toronto: University of Toronto Press, 1976.

______. The Economics of Exchange Rates: Selected Studies. Reading, Mass.: Addison-Wesely, 1978.

Frenkel, Jacob A. and Jovanovic, Boyan. "Optimal International Reserves: A Stochastic Framework," Unpublished manuscript, University of Chicago, 1979.

Goldfeld, Stephen M. and Quandt, Richard E. (eds.) Studies in Nonlinear Estimation. Cambridge: Ballinger, 1976.

Gray, JoAnna. "Wage Indexation: A Macroeconomic Approach". Journal of Monetary Economics 2, No. 2 (April 1976): 231-46.

Grubel, Herbert G. "The Demand for International Reserves: A Critical Review of the Literature". Journal of Economic Literature 9 (December 1971): 1148-1166.

______. "The Optimum Supply of International Reserves in a World of Managed Floating." Presented at the Marcus Fleming Memorial Conference on The New International Monetary System, Washington, D.C., November, 1976.

Gujarti, Damodar. "Use of Dummy Variables in Testing for Equality between Sets of Coefficients in Linear Regressions: A Generalization." The American Statistician (December 1970): 18-22.

Haberler, Gottfried. "How Important is Control over International Reserves?" Presented at the Marcus Fleming Memorial Conference on The New International Monetary System, Washington, D.C., November, 1976.

Heller, Robert H. "Optimal International Reserves". Economic Journal LXXVI (June 1966): 296-311.

Heller, Robert H. and Kahn, Mohsin S. "The Demand for International Reserves Under Fixed and Floating Exchange Rates", International Monetary Fund, Staff Papers 25, 4 (December, 1978): 623-49.

Hipple, F. Steb. "The Disturbances Approach to the Demand for International Reserves." Princeton Studies in International Finance, No. 35 (May 1974).

Iyoha, Milton A. "Demand for International Reserves in Less Developed Countries: A Distributed Lag Specification." The Review of Economics and Statistics 58, No. 3 (August 1976): 351-55.

Kelly, Michael G. "The Demand for International Reserves." American Economic Review 60 (September 1970): 655-667.

Kenen, Peter B. and Yudin, Elinor B. "The Demand for International Reserves." Review of Economics and Statistics 47 (August 1965): 242-250.

Kouri, Pentti J.K. "The Exchange Rate and the Balance of Payments in the Short Run and in the Long Run: A Monetary Approach." Scandinavian Journal of Economics 78, No. 2 (May 1976): 280-304.

Makin, John H. "Exchange Rate Flexibility and the Demand for International Reserves." Weltwirtschaftliches Archiv 110, No. 2 (1974): 229-43.

Mundell, Robert A. International Economics. Macmillan: New York, 1968.

Mussa, Michael: "The Exchange Rate, the Balance of Payments, and Monetary and Fiscal Policy under a Regime of Controlled Floating". Scandinavian Journal of Economics 78, No. 2 (May 1976): 229-49.

Poole, William. "Optimal Choice of Monetary Policy Instruments in a Simple Stochastic Macro-Model." Quarterly Journal of Economics 84 (May 1970): 197-216.

Quandt, Richard E. "The Estimation of the Parameters of a Linear Regression System Obeying Two Separate Regimes". Journal of the American Statistical Association 53 (Sept., 1958): 873-80.

______. "Tests of the Hypothesis that a Linear Regression System Obeys Two Separate Regimes." Journal of the American Statistical Association 55 (June, 1960): 324-30.

Saidi, Nasser and Robert J. Barro. "Unanticipated Money Growth and Unemployment in Canada." Unpublished manuscript, University of Rochester, 1977.

Suss, Esther C. "A Note on Reserve Use under Alternative Exchange Rate Regimes". IMF Staff Papers 23, no. 2 (July 1976): 387-94.

Ujiie, Junichi. "A Stock Adjustment Approach to Monetary Policy and the Balance of Payments." In Frenkel, J.A. and H.G. Johnson (eds.) The Economics of Exchange Rates: Selected Studies. Reading, Mass.: Addison-Wesley, 1978.

Williamson, John. "International Liquidity: A Survey". Economic Journal 83 (September 1973): 685-746.

______. "Generalized Floating and the Reserve Needs of Developing Countries." In D.M. Leipziger (ed.) The International Monetary System and Developing Nations. Washington, D.C.: Agency for International Development, 1976. Pp. 75-86.

COMMENT ON J.A. FRENKEL, "INTERNATIONAL RESERVES: PEGGED EXCHANGE RATES AND MANAGED FLOAT"

Heidi Schelbert

In the main part of this paper, Frenkel analyzes the demand for international reserves. Among others, he poses the following specific questions:

1. Do Developed and Less-Developed Countries differ significantly in their demand for international reserves?
2. Did the drastic change in the monetary system from pegged to floating exchange rates cause a structural change in the demand for international reserves?

This questions are of great interest. Frenkel combines economic theory and empirical research (cross sectional and pooled time-series/cross-section data) to find the answers and this seems to me the preferable if not the only practicable way.

Nevertheless, I have doubts about the specifications of the demand for international reserves. This demand function is assumed to depend on three variables: 1. a measure of the variability of international receipts and payments, 2. a scaling variable, measuring the size of international transactions (imports only) and 3. the average propensity to import.

This specification is similar to long-known formulations of money demand functions. All three variables account for the transaction demand, but the second and third do not allow for capital movements. So the specification is incomplete, at least for quite a few European countries, such as Switzerland, where imports and exports of capital can dominate the stock and the growth rate of international reserves. The next point is of greater importance. Mechanical theories of transaction demand were replaced some time ago by models of optimizing behavior. The variables, Frenkel included, can serve as proxis for the benefits of international reserves, but a variable picking up the cost of the stock of reserves is missing. The author writes in footnote 3, that previous studies faced serious difficulties in estimating this cost. I suppose this is so because the analogy between money demand and the demand for international reserves does not work. Under a regime of pegged exchange rates, the monetary authorities can not optimize the stock of international reserves according to cost-benefit calculations. Instead, they have to purchase (sell) reserves, when the market rate of their currency rises (falls).

Obviously, no target is completely fixed. The central bank must stop selling before it runs out of reserves, and buying can get rather expensiv in the long run, as we have learned in Switzerland. Fixed exchange rates can be changed and have been changed, when other policy targets predominated, e.g. the control of inflation.

I therefore propose to formulate the demand for international reserves as a policy reaction function as it is done in other papers at this conference.[1)] Arguments in this function are the exchange rate, the rate of monetary expansion and other policy targets. Frenkel writes on the first page, that "a flexible exchange rate regime enables savings on resources that under a fixed exchange rate system would have been allocated to reserve holdings". This statement is obviously correct, but it is beside the main point, at least for the small open economies dominating his cross-section sample of the Developed Countries. For these countries not the savings on resources but the possible benefits of a more independent monetary policy was the motive for switching over to flexible rates.

In spite of these doubts about the specification of the demand function, the overall fit of the regressions is impressive, at least

---

1) e.g. the papers of P. De Grauwe, D.W. Henderson, M.M.G. Fase/ A.P. Huijser.

when the coefficient of determination is considered. The differences in the demand for international reserves between the Developed and the Less-Developed Countries are amazingly small, and we can see no drastic structural change when the monetary system changed from pegged to floating exchange rates. Empirical research is a hard, sometimes even nasty, job. There are no controlled experiments, so it is easy to criticize empirical work and it is difficult to do any better. Nevertheless, I venture some suggestions:

1. OLS is surely not the best method, and the evidence of the estimated parameters and the test statistics is questionable. Of course, Frenkel is aware of this point and as I understand, he plans to reestimate the demand function with other methods. It will be instructive to compare the results.

2. The model explains the stock of international reserves. This quantity is rather sluggish compared with the volatile flow of reserves. With regard to this fact, the high coefficients of determination are less impressive. A stronger test for the hypothesis would be to estimate the model with the change of international reserves as the dependent variable.
The measure of variability of international receipts and payments was proxied by computing the variance of the trend-adjusted annual changes of the level of reserves over the previous 15 years. By summing up the annual changes, the stock of reserves is obtained. So, I cannot completely dismiss the idea that Frenkel has explained, at least partly, reserves with reserves.

3. The central banks entered the period of flexible exchange rates with a stock of reserves that was piled up during the period of fixed rates. It is likely that "hard currency" countries like Switzerland or Germany had too much reserves considering cost-benefit calculations for the stock. In order to attain the optimal stock, flows have to be changed. A sudden stock adjustment requires large changes in the flows and might be very expensive when considering other policy goals. Therefore I am not at all amazed by the estimated stock equations showing no drastical structural change when the

monetary system changed from pegged to floating exchange rates. The hypothesis "structural change" can only be tested correctly with a stock adjustment model.

4. In the concluding remarks on page 24 we read: "an examination of the residuals from the estimated equations reveals the existence of persistent negative residuals for some countries (e.g. U.K. and New Zealand) and positive residuals for other (e.g. Switzerland)". I bet that the residuals for Germany are mostly positive too. The regressions have been estimated assuming that during the sample period countries were "on" their long-run demand function as specified by the model. I presume that during the period of fixed exchange rates the "demand" for reserves was determined by the compulsion to peg this rates. As a consequence,"hard currency" countries show positive,"soft currency" countries negative residuals.

In the concluding remarks,Frenkel writes that the analysis in his paper would benefit from several extensions. The central point seems to me to tie up the analytical framework underlying the literature on the demand for international reserves with the framework underlying the literature on the monetary approach to the balance of payments. I wait for this results with close attention. In appendix C,there is a very promising sketch of a framework for the analysis of the managed float. The idea of the optimal intervention index being suggestiv, this model should be analyzed further.

THE DYNAMIC EFFECTS OF EXCHANGE MARKET INTERVENTION POLICY: TWO EXTREME VIEWS AND A SYNTHESIS

Dale W. Henderson*

I. INTRODUCTION

Under a regime of managed floating, one policy instrument available to the authorities is exchange market intervention policy, purchases or sales of assets denominated in foreign currency in exchange for assets denominated in home currency. Since, in general, an economy does not reach its new long-run equilibrium immediately following an exchange market intervention, a complete analysis of the effects of this policy must include a description of the path followed by the economy as it adjusts to its new long-run equlibrium. This paper is a study of the dynamic effects of a particular type of intervention policy, a purchase of foreign money with home money.[1)]

---

* Economist, International Finance Division, Board of Governors of the Federal Reserve System. Discussions with Ralph Bryant, Rudiger Dornbusch, Lance Girton, Gene Grossman, and Bennett McCallum have resulted in improvements in the paper. Betty Daniel, Barry Eichengreen, Peter Isard, Richard Meese, Walter Salant, Michael Schmid, Jürgen Siebke, Carl Van Duyne, and Janet Yellen made helpful comments on earlier drafts. No one but the author is responsible for the remaining shortcomings of the paper. This paper represents the views of the author and should not be interpreted as reflecting the views of the Federal Reserve System or other members of its staff.

1) Girton and Henderson (1977) offer some alternative specifications of intervention policy and analyze the short-run effects of these alternative specifications. Kouri (1976) studies the short-run, medium-run, and long-run effects of the type of intervention policy investigated in this paper.
Most of the analysis of this paper would also apply to the case in which the exchange market intervention consists of a sale of home securities and a purchase of foreign securities by the home authorities so long as it is assumed that the authorities in both countries are pegging nominal interest rates. However, when

Recent studies of exchange rate dynamics contain two extreme views about why an economy does not reach its new long-run equilibrium immediately following a shock. One extreme view is based on the assumption that changes in real wealth affect spending decisions and asset demands.[2] Under this assumption the intervention policy considered here gives rise to an incentive for residents of the home country to accumulate assets and for foreigners to decumulate assets. This incentive leads to an asset transfer which occurs slowly over time at a rate which is equal in magnitude to the home trade account surplus. During the slow buildup of assets by home residents through the trade account surplus, the short-run equilibrium position of the economy continues to change because of wealth effects on spending decisions and asset demands. The economy cannot come to rest at its new long-run equilibrium until there is no longer an incentive for asset transfers to take place so that the trade account is once again in balance.

The other extreme view is based on the assumption that prices adjust slowly when output exceeds "normal" supply.[3] Under this assumption the intervention policy considered here gives rise to an excess of output of the home good over "normal" supply. This excess must ultimately be removed by a rise in the price of the home good which occurs slowly over time. While the price of the home good is rising, the short-run equilibrium position of the economy continues to change since increases in the

---

1) (continued) securities are included in the model, exchange market intervention has service account effects, which, while they may be important, complicate the analysis and obscure other, more important effects.

2) Kouri's (1976) fundamental contribution to the analysis of exchange rate dynamics puts forward this view. Branson (1976) has also participated in the development of this view.

3) Dornbusch's (1976a) path-breaking work on exchange rate dynamics is the source of this view.

price of the home good affect spending decisions and asset demands. The economy cannot come to rest at its new long-run equilibrium until the adjustment of the price of the home good is complete.

The effects of intervention policy are explored using three specialized versions of the model of a single open economy which is now in general use.[4)] Each of the first two versions embodies one of the extreme views about why the economy adjusts slowly to its new long-run equilibrium. In the first version, changes in wealth affect the spending decisions and asset demands of home residents, but the home wage rate and the price of the home good are perfectly flexible so that output is always at its full employment level. In the second version, the wage rate and the price of the home good adjust slowly when output exceeds normal supply, but there are no wealth effects. The third version is a synthesis of the first two which incorporates both wealth effects and slow wage and price adjustment.

Since attention is to be focused on the adjustment path of the economy after an exchange market intervention under alternative assumptions about what affects this path, the three versions of the model have been constructed so that the long-run effects of exchange market intervention are particularly simple. In the long run the exchange market intervention causes all nominal variables to increase by the same proportion as the supply of home money increases and leaves all real variables unchanged.

The effects of intervention policy are investigated under the assumption that in forming their exchange rate expectations

---

4) A description of a general version of this model, a discussion of some of its properties, and references to other applications of the model are provided in Henderson (1977).

consumers have long-run perfect foresight.[5)] Under this regime the stationary equilibrium value of the exchange rate is known to consumers, and they expect that the exchange rate will move from its current value toward that stationary equilibrium rate. Expectations are correct in the long run, but they may be incorrect while the system is adjusting toward its stationary equilibrium.

The analysis begins with a description of the building blocks for the three versions of the model in Section II. A consideration of the effects of exchange market intervention when only asset transfers accomplished through a trade surplus affect the adjustment path of the economy is contained in Section III. Then, in Section IV, the case in which only slow adjustment of the price of the home good influences the path of the economy is discussed. Both the trade surplus and slow price adjustment affect the path of the economy in the version of the model explored in Section V. Section VI contains some concluding remarks.

II. THE BUILDING BLOCKS FOR THE THREE VERSIONS OF THE MODEL

Home Consumers

Consumers in the home economy make four basic decisions: a saving decision, an expenditure-allocation decision, a wealth-allocation decision, and a labor market decision. In the description of how consumers make these decisions it is assumed that all real variables are obtained by deflating nominal variables by a

---

5) Dornbusch (1976b) uses this assumption about expectations formation. He (1976a) also shows that assuming long-run perfect foresight is equivalent to assuming complete perfect foresight under some conditions. Under complete perfect foresight the stationary equilibrium value of the exchange rate is known to consumers, and their expectations are correct both in stationary equilibrium and while the system is adjusting to the stationary equlibirium. Kouri (1976) considers three possible assumptions about how exchange rate expectations are formed: static expectations, adaptive expectations, and complete perfect foresight.

price index (P_I):

$$P_I = k_1 P + k_2 E, \qquad k_1, k_2 > 0, \; k_1 + k_2 = 1, \qquad (1)$$

where P is the home currency price of the single home good, and E is the home currency price of foreign currency. The foreign authorities keep the foreign currency price of the single foreign good, which is different from the home good, constant at one unit of foreign currency.[6)]

Consumers' real saving ($\frac{S}{P_I}$) rises with increases in real income ($\frac{Py}{P_I}$) and falls with increases in real wealth ($\frac{A}{P_I}$):

$$\frac{S}{P_I} = s_1 \frac{Py}{P_I} - s_2 \frac{A}{P_I} + s_6, \qquad 0 < s_1 < 1, \; s_2, s_6 > 0, \qquad (2)$$

where S is nominal saving, y is output of the home good measured in physical units, and A is nominal wealth.

Consumers allocate part of their real expenditure to the home good and the rest to the foreign good. Real imports ($\frac{M}{P_I}$) depend positively on real spending ($\frac{Py}{P_I} - \frac{S}{P_I}$), negatively on the ratio of the exchange rate to the price index ($\frac{E}{P_I}$), and positively on the ratio of the price of the home good to the price index ($\frac{P}{P_I}$):[7)]

$$\frac{M}{P_I} = m_1 \left(\frac{Py}{P_I} - \frac{S}{P_I}\right) - m_3 \frac{E}{P_I} + m_4 \frac{P}{P_I}, \qquad 0 < m_1 < 1, \; m_3, m_4 > 0, \qquad (3)$$

where M is nominal imports.

---

6) The foreign authorities could use balanced budget variations in government spending to accomplish this objective.

7) By implication consumers' demand for the home good is given by

$$\frac{J}{P_I} = j_1 \left(\frac{Py}{P_I} - \frac{S}{P_I}\right) + j_3 \frac{E}{P_I} - j_4 \frac{P}{P_I}, \qquad 0 < j_1 < 1, \; j_3, j_4 > 0,$$

where J is nominal spending on the home good, and

$m_1 + j_1 = 1$, $m_3 - j_3 = 0$, $m_4 - j_4 = 0$.

They allocate their real wealth between home money and foreign money. Their demand for real holdings of home money ($\frac{Q^d}{P_I}$) depends positively on real income and real wealth and negatively on the expected rate of depreciation of the home currency (e):[8)]

$$\frac{Q^d}{P_I} = q_1 \frac{Py}{P_I} + q_2 \frac{A}{P_I} - q_5 e + q_6, \quad q_1, q_2, q_5, q_6 > 0, \qquad (4)$$

where Q^d is consumers' demand for nominal holdings of home money. It is assumed that foreign consumers do not hold domestic money. Therefore, home consumers' nominal wealth in terms of home currency is equal to the total supply of domestic money (Q) plus the product of the exchange rate and home consumers' holdings of foreign money measured in foreign currency (F):

$$A = Q + EF. \qquad (5)$$

Consumers also make a labor market decision. Two alternative forms of labor market behavior by consumers are considered. In the first version of the model explored below it is assumed that consumers supply a fixed amount of labor services ($\tilde{N}$) no matter what the real wage.[9)] In this version the nominal wage (W) is determined in a competitive labor market. In the other two versions explored below it is assumed that at a point in time consumers supply whatever amount of labor firms want at the prevailing nominal wage. In these versions consumers set the percentage rate of change

---

8) By implication consumers' demand for foreign money is given by

$$\frac{(EF)^d}{P_I} = -f_1 \frac{Py}{P_I} + f_2 \frac{A}{P_I} + f_5 e - f_6, \quad f_1, f_2, f_5, f_6 > 0,$$

and

$$q_1 - f_1 = 0,\ q_2 + f_2 = 1,\ q_5 - f_5 = 0,\ q_6 - f_6 = 0.$$

9) Alternatively it could be assumed that labor supply depends positively on the real wage defined as the ratio of the nominal wage to the price index ($\frac{W}{P_I}$). Salop (1974) analyzes the momentary equilibrium effects of a devaluation under this assumption.

of the nominal wage. They attempt to raise (lower) the real wage by increasing (decreasing) the nominal wage when labor demand (N^d) exceeds (falls short of) a fixed "normal" supply ($\tilde{N}$):[10)]

$$\frac{\dot{W}}{W} = u(N^d - \tilde{N}), \qquad u > 0. \tag{6}$$

Home Firms

Firms in the home economy produce output using only labor and a production function with a fixed labor-output ratio (n). In the version in which the supply of labor is inelastic, the supply of output is inelastic at the full employment level:

$$y = \bar{y} = \frac{1}{n}\tilde{N}. \tag{7}$$

Firms take the price of output as given and bid the nominal wage up or down to the point at which profits are zero:

$$W = \frac{1}{n}P. \tag{8}$$

In the versions in which labor is supplied perfectly elastically at a point in time, firms produce enough output to satisfy aggregate demand, and labor demand is given by

$$N^d = ny. \tag{9}$$

---

10) Alternatively it could be assumed that "normal" labor supply depends on the real wage ($\frac{W}{P_I}$) and that consumers attempt to raise the anticipated real wage ($\frac{\dot{W}}{W} - k_1 p - k_2 e > 0$) by raising the nominal wage when labor demand exceeds "normal" supply:
$\frac{\dot{W}}{W} = u[N^d - \tilde{N}(\frac{W}{P_I})] + k_1 p + k_2 e,$
where p is the anticipated rate of change in the price of the home good. This wage adjustment equation is one type of expectations augmented Phillips curve. Daniel (1977) analyzes the relationship between inflation and unemployment in a small open economy using a similar expectations augmented Phillips curve.

Competition among firms assures that the price of the domestic good is set so that it just covers costs at the prevailing nominal wage:

$$P = Wn, \tag{10}$$

so the percentage rate of change in the price of the domestic good is equal to the percentage rate of change in nominal wages:

$$\frac{\dot{P}}{P} = \frac{\dot{W}}{W}. \tag{11}$$

Home Authorities

The home authorities determine the nominal supply of home money. They undertake exchange market intervention by purchasing foreign money from home residents with home money subject to

$$dQ + EdF = 0, \tag{12}$$

or in percentage terms

$$q\hat{Q} + f\hat{F} = 0, \tag{13}$$

where a hat over a variable indicates a percentage change in the variable and where q is the fraction of wealth held in domestic money and f is the fraction of wealth held in foreign money.

Foreigners

Consumers in the foreign country have a real demand for the home good ($\frac{X}{P_I}$) which depends positively on the ratio of the exchange rate to the price index and negatively on the ratio of the price of the home good to the price index:

$$\frac{X}{P_I} = x_3 \frac{E}{P_I} - x_4 \frac{P}{P_I}, \qquad x_3, x_4 > 0, \tag{14}$$

where X is foreign consumers' nominal demand for the home good measured in home currency. As stated above, foreign consumers do not hold home money, and the foreign authorities keep the foreign currency price of the foreign good constant at one unit of foreign currency. It is important to observe that the assumptions that foreign demand for the home good is independent of foreign wealth and that foreigners do not hold home money insure that transfers of wealth from foreigners to home residents lead to increases in demand for home goods and home money.

Expectations Formation

Home consumers are assumed to possess long-run perfect foresight. Under this assumption, consumers correctly calculate the stationary state value of E, denoted by $\bar{E}$, and expect that E will adjust toward this stationary state value at a rate which is proportional to the ratio of the gap between its stationary state value and its current value to its stationary state value:[11)]

$$e = \varepsilon(1 - \frac{E}{\bar{E}}), \qquad \varepsilon > 0. \tag{15}$$

---

11) The technique employed by Dornbusch (1976a) can be used to show that in the first two versions of the model assuming that expectations are formed according to (15) is equivalent to assuming that consumers have complete perfect foresight when ε is chosen properly.
If expectations regarding the rate of change of the price of the home good were assumed to affect the rate of change of wages in the manner suggested in footnote 10, it would be natural to assume that consumers correctly calculate the stationary value of P, denoted by $\bar{P}$, and expect that P will adjust toward this stationary state value at a rate which is proportional to the ratio of the gap between its stationary state value and its current value to its stationary state value:

$$p = \pi(1 - \frac{P}{\bar{P}}), \qquad \pi > 0.$$

In the limiting case in which $\varepsilon = 0$, consumers have static expectations.

III. THE EFFECTS OF INTERVENTION POLICY WHEN ONLY THE TRADE SURPLUS AFFECTS THE ADJUSTMENT PATH OF THE ECONOMY

The Conditions for Momentary Equilibrium

In order to focus attention on the effects of the trade surplus on the path of the economy following exchange market intervention it is assumed in the version of the model of this Section that prices and wages are perfectly flexible so that output is always at its full employment level ($\bar{y}$).[12] The position of the economy at a point in time is referred to as momentary equilibrium.

In order to lay a foundation for the discussion of the conditions for momentary equilibrium it is useful to derive an expression for the real trade balance ($\frac{T}{P_I}$) from equations (3) and (14):

---

12) The version of the model discussed in Section III is similar to the model of Kouri (1976) who analyzes the effects of the type of intervention policy investigated in this paper. The only important difference is that the version of Section III allows for changes in the terms of trade which are ruled out in Kouri's model by his assumption that the home good is a perfect substitute for the foreign good. Flood (1978) analyzes the effects of an increase in the rate of expansion of the home money supply under the assumption that the home good and the foreign good are perfect substitutes. The version of Section III is also similar to the model of Calvo and Rodriguez (1977). Both models allow for changes in a relative price. In this model the variable relative price is the price of the foreign good in terms of the home good; in the Calvo and Rodriguez model the variable relative price is the price of a traded good in terms of a non-traded good. Calvo and Rodriguez analyze the effects of an increase in the rate of expansion of home money rather than those of a one time increase in the home money supply through a purchase of foreign money by the home authorities.

$$\frac{T}{P_I} = \frac{X}{P_I} - \frac{M}{P_I} = -t_1 \frac{Py}{P_I} - t_2 \frac{A}{P_I} + t_3 \frac{E}{P_I} - t_4 \frac{P}{P_I} + t_6, \tag{16}$$

$$t_1 = m_1(1 - s_1),\ t_2 = m_1 s_2,$$

$$t_3 = x_3 + m_3,\ t_4 = x_4 + m_4,\ t_6 = m_1 s_6,$$

where T is the nominal trade surplus measured in terms of home currency.

Three conditions determine the momentary equilibrium values of the exchange rate, the price level, and the change in home consumers' holdings of foreign money ($\dot{F}$). The first condition is that the domestic goods market must clear. For the excess demand for domestic goods to equal zero, the real trade surplus must equal real saving:

$$\frac{T}{P_I} - \frac{S}{P_I} = 0. \tag{17}$$

When equations (2), (5), and (16) are substituted into equation (17) the condition for goods market equilibrium becomes

$$-g_1 \frac{P\bar{y}}{P_I} + g_2 \frac{Q + EF}{P_I} + g_3 \frac{E}{P_I} - g_4 \frac{P}{P_I} - g_6 = 0, \tag{18a}$$

$$g_1 = s_1 + m_1(1 - s_1),\ g_2 = s_2(1 - m_1),$$

$$g_3 = x_3 + m_3,\ g_4 = x_4 + m_4,\ g_6 = (1 - m_1)s_6.$$

A second condition for momentary equilibrium is that the excess demand by consumers for home money must equal zero. When equations (5) and (15) are substituted into equation (4), this condition can be written as

$$q_1 \frac{P\bar{y}}{P_I} + q_2 \frac{Q + EF}{P_I} - q_5 \varepsilon(1 - \frac{E}{\bar{E}}) + q_6 - \frac{Q}{P_I} = 0. \tag{18b}$$

The third and final condition states that the change in real domestic holdings of foreign money ($\frac{E}{P_I}\dot{F}$) must equal the trade surplus:

$$-t_1 \frac{P\bar{y}}{P_I} - t_2 \frac{Q + EF}{P_I} + t_3 \frac{E}{P_I} - t_4 \frac{P}{P_I} + t_6 - \frac{E}{P_I}\dot{F} = 0. \qquad (18c)$$

The Stationary State Effects

Since knowledge of the stationary state effects of intervention policy is necessary for determining the impact effects and the paths of the variables under long run perfect foresight, it is useful to begin by describing these stationary state effects. In a stationary state foreign money accumulation by domestic residents is zero, and the exchange rate is expected to remain unchanged:

$$\dot{F} = e = 0. \qquad (19)$$

Imposing these restrictions on the three equations (18) after eliminating P_I using equation (1) yields three equations which are sufficient to determine the stationary state values of the price level ($\bar{P}$), the exchange rate ($\bar{E}$), and home consumers' holdings of foreign money ($\bar{F}$) given full employment output ($\bar{y}$) and the stationary state stock of domestic money ($\bar{Q}$). The stationary state effects of a purchase of foreign money by the authorities on $\bar{P}$, $\bar{E}$, and $\bar{F}$ can be determined by inspection. The system of equations obtained by imposing the stationary state restrictions (19) on equations (18) is homogenous of degree zero in the three nominal variables $\bar{P}$, $\bar{E}$, and $\bar{Q}$, and $\bar{Q}$ is the only exogenous nominal variable.[13] So, if $\bar{Q}$ increases, $\bar{P}$ and $\bar{E}$ must

13) That is, the model exhibits neutrality with respect to a change in the home money supply. An economic model may be said to exhibit neutrality with respect to changes in a particular nominal variable if (1) the model is homogenous of degree zero in all nominal variables and (2) the nominal variable being changed is the only exogenous nominal variable. This way of describing sufficient conditions for neutrality is due to Don Roper (1975).

increase by the same proportion, and $\bar{F}$ must remain unchanged:

$$\hat{\bar{P}} = \hat{\bar{E}} = \hat{\bar{Q}}, \tag{20a}$$

$$\hat{\bar{F}} = 0. \tag{20b}$$

The Impact Effects

The impact effects of a purchase of foreign money by the authorities on the exchange rate and the price of the domestic good are shown in Figure 1 which is constructed using equations (18a) and (18b) with P_I eliminated through equation (1). The G_0G_0 schedule shows the pairs of (the natural logarithms of) E and P which are compatible with equilibrium in the market for the home good. The Q_0Q_0 schedule shows the pairs of E and P which are compatible with equilibrium in the home money market.

The GG schedule has a slope which is greater than positive one as shown in Figure 1 under plausible assumptions. First, consider the effects of an increase in the price of the home good on excess demand for the home good. This price increase reduces the excess demand for the home good for three reasons: (1) the price increase raises real income thereby reducing the trade surplus and increasing saving; (2) it lowers real wealth, and this decline in real wealth raises saving by more than it improves the trade account; and (3) it lowers the ratio of the exchange rate to the price index and raises the ratio of the price of the home good to the price index, and both of these changes cause home and foreign residents to shift spending from the home good to the foreign good thereby reducing the trade surplus.

Next, consider the effects of a depreciation of the home currency (a rise in E) on the excess demand for the home good. This depreciation tends to raise excess demand for two reasons: (1) it lowers real income, and (2) it raises the ratio of the exchange rate to the price index and lowers the ratio of the price of the home good to the price index. However, the depreciation may

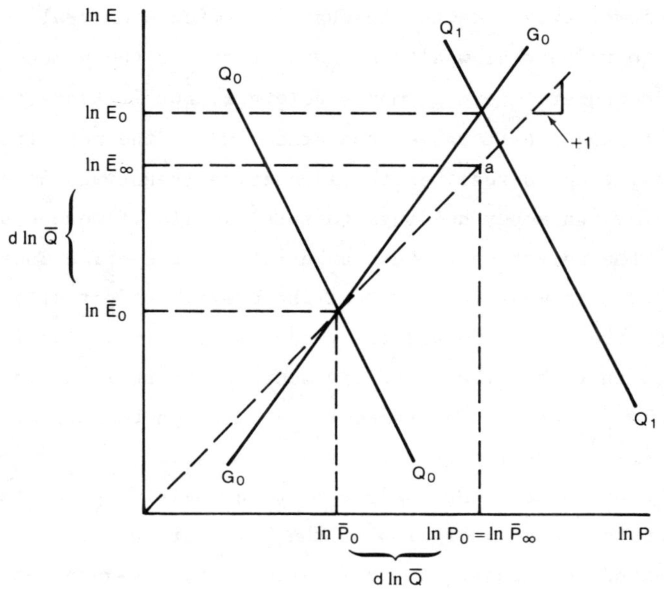

FIGURE 1

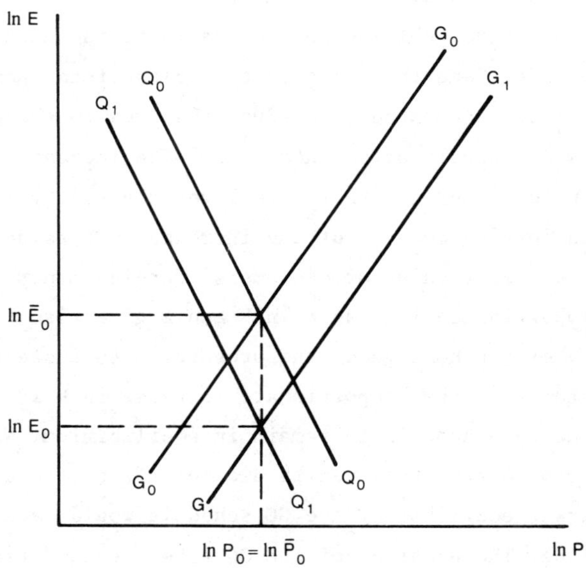

FIGURE 2

raise or lower excess demand through its effects on real wealth. It tends to raise real wealth because it raises the home currency value of consumers' foreign money holdings, but it tends to lower real wealth because it raises the price index. The net effect of the depreciation on real wealth is positive (negative) if the ratio of foreign money holdings to total wealth (f) exceeds (falls short of) the weight on the exchange rate in the price index (k_2). It is assumed in what follows that the overall effect of a depreciation on the excess demand for goods is positive; that is, it is assumed that the effects of the decrease in real income, the increase in $\frac{E}{P_I}$, and the decrease in $\frac{P}{P_I}$ outweigh the effect of the decrease in real wealth if f is less than k_2.

The slope of the GG schedule must be positive given the assumption that a depreciation of the home currency raises the excess demand for goods. An increase in P creates an excess supply of goods, so the domestic currency must depreciate if the goods market is to remain in equilibrium. The slope of the GG schedule must exceed positive one. Increases in P and E by the same proportion leave real income, the ratio of the exchange rate to the price index, and the ratio of the price of the home good to the price index unchanged but reduce real wealth thereby giving rise to an excess supply of the home good. The increases in P and E raise the price index and therefore lower the real value of both home and foreign money, but the increase in E raises only the domestic currency value of consumers' foreign money holdings. Since equiproportionate increases in P and E give rise to an excess supply of the home good, the proportionate increase in E must be greater than the proportionate increase in P if the market for the home good is to remain in equilibirium. Note that if g_2 were zero so that real wealth did not affect the condition for goods market equilibrium, the GG schedule would have a slope of positive one. The equation of the GG schedule is derived by differentiating equation (18a) in the neighborhood of stationary equilibrium to obtain

$$-(g + g_2\bar{A}k_1)\hat{P} + [g + g_2\bar{A}(\bar{f} - k_2)]\,\hat{E} + g_2\bar{A}\,\bar{q}\hat{Q} + g_2\bar{A}\,\bar{f}\hat{F} = 0, \quad (21)$$

$$g = g_1\bar{y}k_2 + g_3k_1 + g_4k_2 > 0,$$

where units are chosen such that P = E = 1 in stationary equilibrium.

The QQ schedule has a negative slope as shown in Figure 1 under plausible assumptions. First, consider the effect of an increase in the price of the home good on the excess demand for home money. This price increase raises the excess demand for home money because it raises nominal income. However, the increase in the price of the home good may raise or lower excess demand because it raises the price index. The increase in the price index reduces the supply of real balances; however, it also reduces the demand for real balances because it reduces real income and real wealth. The net effect of an increase in the price index is to raise the excess demand for home money if the sum of the real income and real wealth elasticities of demand for real balances is less than one ($q_1\bar{y} + q_2\bar{A} < \bar{Q}$). It is assumed in what follows that this condition is met so that an increase in the price index raises the excess demand for money. Under this assumption the overall effect of an increase in the price of the home good is definitely to raise the excess demand for money.

Next, consider the effect of a depreciation of the home currency on the excess demand for home money. This depreciation raises the excess demand for money for three reasons: (1) it increases nominal wealth; (2) it increases the price index; and (3) it induces money holders to expect an appreciation of the home currency.

The slope of the QQ schedule must be negative given the assumption that the sum of the real income and real wealth elasticities of demand for real balances is less than one. An increase in P creates an excess demand for money, so the domestic currency must appreciate if the money market is to remain in equilibrium. The equation of the QQ schedule is derived by differentiating (18b) in the neighborhood of stationary equilibrium and recognizing the fact that $\hat{\bar{E}} = \hat{\bar{Q}}$ to obtain

$$[(\bar{Q} - q_1\bar{y} - q_2\bar{A})k_1 + q_1\bar{y}]\,\hat{P} + [(\bar{Q} - q_1\bar{y} - q_2\bar{A})k_2$$

$$+ q_2\bar{A}\,\bar{f} + q_5\varepsilon]\,\hat{E} + (q_2\bar{A}\,\bar{q} - \bar{Q} - q_5\varepsilon)\hat{\bar{Q}} + q_2\bar{A}\,\bar{f}\hat{F} = 0. \qquad (22)$$

A purchase of foreign money by the home authorities $(\bar{q}\,\hat{\bar{Q}} + \bar{f}\hat{F} = 0)$ shifts the QQ schedule up to Q_1Q_1. The QQ schedule must shift farther than point a along the dashed line which has a slope of positive one in Figure 1. Point a is the point which corresponds to increases in both E and P by the same proportion as the increase in $\bar{Q}$ $(\hat{E} = \hat{P} = \hat{\bar{Q}})$. Equiproportionate increases in E, P, and $\bar{Q}$ leave real balances, real income, and the expected rate of depreciation unchanged but reduce real wealth thereby giving rise to an excess supply of money. Thus, if equilibrium in the home money market were to be reestablished with equal percentage changes in E and P following an exchange market intervention which increases $\bar{Q}$, the percentage changes in E and P would have to exceed the percentage change in $\bar{Q}$. Note that if q_2 were equal to zero so that real wealth did not influence the demand for real balances, Q_1Q_1 would pass through point a.

The impact effects of an exchange market intervention are shown by the intersection of Q_1Q_1 and G_0G_0. The home currency depreciates, and the price of the home good rises. The exchange rate overshoots its stationary equilibrium level; that is, E rises initially to a value that is higher than the one associated with the new stationary equilibrium, $\bar{E}_\infty$, where the subscript ∞ indicates the value of a variable in the new stationary equilibrium.[14] This result arises because changes in real wealth affect the markets for the home good and home money. If changes in wealth affect either market (g_2 or $q_2 > 0$), the exchange rate overshoots.[15] The price of the home good may overshoot or undershoot its new stationary

---

14) Solving equations (21) and (22) for $\hat{E}$ subject to $\bar{q}\,\hat{\bar{Q}} + \bar{f}\hat{F} = 0$ yields

$$\hat{E} = -\frac{1}{\Delta_1}\,[(\bar{Q} + q_5\varepsilon)(g + g_2\bar{A}k_1)]\,\hat{\bar{Q}} > 0,$$

$$\hat{E} = [1 - \frac{1}{\Delta_1}\,(gq_2 + q_1\bar{y}k_2g_2)\bar{A}\,\bar{q}\,]\hat{\bar{Q}} > \hat{\bar{E}} = \hat{\bar{Q}},$$

$$\Delta_1 = -(g + g_2\bar{A}k_1)\,[(\bar{Q} - q_1\bar{y} - q_2\bar{A})k_2 + q_2\bar{A}\,\bar{f} + q_5\varepsilon]$$

$$- [g + g_2\bar{A}(\bar{f} - k_2)][(\bar{Q} - q_1\bar{y} - q_2\bar{A})k_1 + q_1\bar{y}] < 0.$$

Δ_1 is negative because it has been assumed that the sum of the real income and real wealth elasticities of the demand for real balances is less than one ($q_1\bar{y} + q_2\bar{A} < \bar{Q}$) and that a depreciation of the home currency raises excess demand for the home good $[g + g_2\bar{A}(\bar{f} - k_2) > 0]$.

15) That is, if $q_2 = 0$ and g_2 is positive or if $g_2 = 0$ and q_2 is positive, E overshoots. A general analysis of the effects of increases in g_2 and q_2 on the changes in E and P resulting from a given percentage change in $\bar{Q}$ is somewhat more complicated. It can be shown that raising g_2 makes the GG schedule steeper thereby raising $\hat{E}$ and reducing $\hat{P}$. Raising q_2 reduces the responsiveness of the excess demand for money to changes in the price of the home good, so the QQ schedule shifts out farther for a given value of E. Raising q_2 raises (lowers) the responsiveness of the excess demand for money to changes in the exchange rate if $\bar{f} - k_2$ is greater than (less than) zero. Thus, if $\bar{f} - k_2$ is positive so that the QQ schedule shifts up less far for a given value of P, an increase in q_2 raises (lowers) $\hat{E}$ and $\hat{P}$ for slopes of the GG schedule less than (greater than) a critical value which is smaller the larger is $\bar{f} - k_2$. If $\bar{f} - k_2$ is negative so that the QQ schedule shifts up farther for a given value of P, an increase in q_2 raises $\hat{E}$ and $\hat{P}$ for all possible slopes of the GG schedule.

equilibrium level.[16] A borderline case in which the price of the home good rises only as much as is necessary to reach its new stationary equilibrium level is shown in Figure 1. The proportionate rise in E is greater than the proportionate rise in P, so the relative price of the foreign good ("the real exchange rate") definitely rises. This result is quite important: a policy change which leaves the real exchange rate unchanged in the long run causes it to rise in the short run even though wages and prices are completely flexible. It follows from the fact that changes in real wealth affect the market for the home good. If there were no wealth effect in either market ($g_2 = q_2 = 0$), both E and P would rise by the same proportion as $\bar{Q}$ rises; the new momentary and stationary state equilibria would be at point a.

The Adjustment Process

In order to lay a foundation for the discussion of the adjustment process it is useful to derive two additional relationships. The changes in the exchange rate and the price of the home good which are required to clear the markets for the home good and home money when home consumers' holdings of foreign money increase are shown in Figure 2. An increase in F shifts the GG schedule down to G_1G_1. A rise in F raises the demand for the home good, so for a given value of P, E must fall if the market for the home good is to remain in equilibrium. An increase in F also shifts the QQ schedule down to Q_1Q_1. A rise in F raises the demand for home money, so for a given value of P, E must fall if the home money market is to remain in equilibrium. The new equilibrium values of E and P are

16) Solving equations (21) and (22) for $\hat{P}$ subject to $\bar{q}\,\hat{\bar{Q}} + \bar{f}\hat{F} = 0$ yields

$$\hat{P} = -\frac{1}{\Delta_1}\{(\bar{Q} + q_5\varepsilon)\,[g + g_2\bar{A}(\bar{f} - k_2)]\}\hat{\bar{Q}} > 0,$$

$$\hat{P} = \left\{1 - \frac{1}{\Delta_1}\{gq_2 - g_2\,[(\bar{Q} - q_1\bar{y})k_2 + q_5\varepsilon]\}A\bar{q}\right\}\hat{\bar{Q}} \gtrless \hat{\bar{Q}}.$$

given by the intersection of Q_1Q_1 and G_1G_1. The home currency definitely appreciates.[17)] The price of the home good may rise or fall; a borderline case in which P remains unchanged is shown in Figure 2.[18)]

The adjustment process for the system following the exchange market intervention is shown in Figure 3. The downward-sloping GQ_0GQ_0 schedule shows the pairs of the exchange rate and home consumers' holdings of foreign money which are compatible with equilibrium in both the market for the home good and the market for home money before the exchange market intervention. It has just been established that increases in F cause E to fall.

The $\dot{F}_0\dot{F}_0$ schedule shows the pairs of the exchange rate and home consumers' holdings of foreign money which are compatible both with equilibrium in the market for the home good and with zero foreign money accumulation before the exchange market intervention. It can be shown that (1) the $\dot{F}\dot{F}$ schedule is upward-sloping, and (2) the left of (the right of) the $\dot{F}\dot{F}$

---

17) Solving equations (21) and (22) for $\hat{E}$ subject to $\hat{\bar{Q}} = 0$ yields

$$\hat{E} = \frac{1}{\Delta_1}\,[q_2 g + g_2(\bar{Q}k_1 + q_1\bar{y}k_2)]\bar{A}\bar{f}\hat{F} < 0.$$

18) Solving equations (21) and (22) for $\hat{P}$ subject to $\hat{\bar{Q}} = 0$ yields

$$\hat{P} = \frac{1}{\Delta_1}\,\{gq_2 - g_2\,[(\bar{Q} - q_1\bar{y})k_2 + q_5\varepsilon\,]\}\bar{A}\bar{f}\hat{F} \gtrless 0.$$

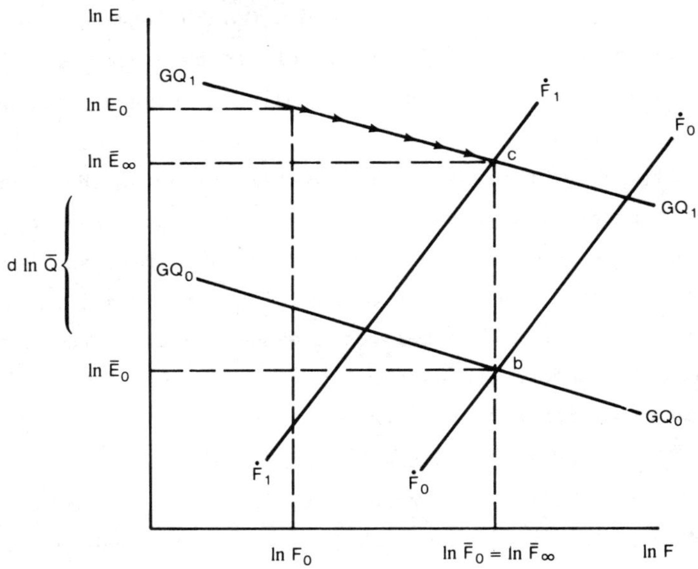

FIGURE 3

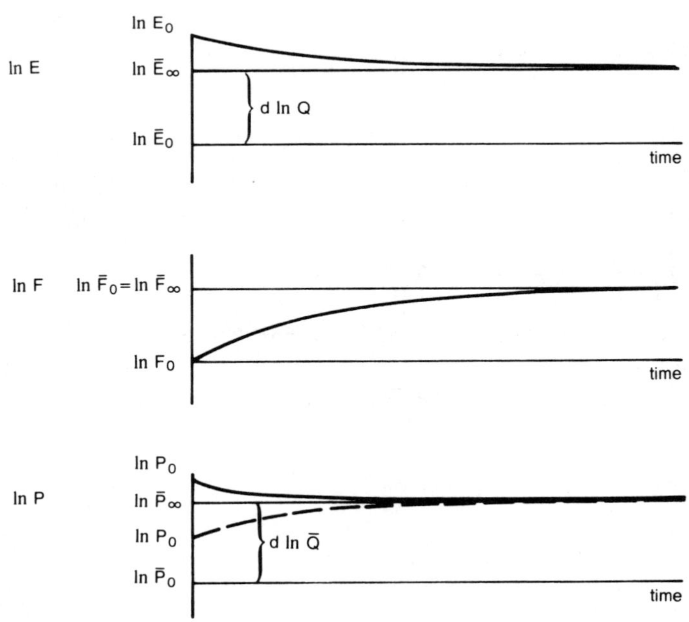

FIGURE 4

schedule, foreign money accumulation is positive (negative).[19)]

Just before the exchange market intervention the home economy is at point b in Figure 3 with foreign money holdings of $\bar{F}_0$ and with an exchange rate of $\bar{E}_0$. The stationary equilibrium which the economy approaches following the exchange market intervention is at point c. It has been shown that an exchange market intervention which increases $\bar{Q}$ raises the stationary state exchange rate by the same proportion $[(\bar{E}_\infty - \bar{E}_0)/\bar{E}_0 = \hat{\bar{E}} = \hat{\bar{Q}}]$ and leaves consumers' stationary state foreign money holdings unchanged $(\bar{F}_\infty = \bar{F}_0)$. Thus, the exchange market intervention must cause the GQGQ and $\ddot{F}\ddot{F}$ schedules to shift upward to GQ_1GQ_1 and $\dot{F}_1\dot{F}_1$.

The economy approaches the new stationary equilibrium over time. The exchange market intervention initially reduces home residents' holdings of foreign money from $\bar{F}_0$ to F_0. Given home residents' holdings of foreign money, the exchange rate must be the one which is compatible with equilibrium in the home good and home money markets. Thus, at the moment of the exchange market intervention, the exchange rate jumps up from $\bar{E}_0$ to E_0,

19) Linearizing equation (18c) in the neighborhood of stationary equilibrium yields

$$\dot{F} = -(t - t_2\bar{A}k_1)\hat{P} + [t - t_2\bar{A}(\bar{f} - k_2)]\hat{E} - t_2\bar{A}\,\bar{f}\hat{F} - t_2\bar{A}\,\bar{q}\hat{Q},$$

$$\iota = t_1\bar{y}k_2 + t_3k_1 + t_4k_2 > 0.$$

Solving vor $\hat{P}$ using equation (21), the total differential of the equilibrium condition for the market for the home good, and substituting the resulting expression into the equation for $\dot{F}$ yields the equation of the $\ddot{F}\ddot{F}$ schedule:

$$\dot{F} = \{[(tg_2 + gt_2)\bar{A}]/(g + g_2\bar{A}k_1)\}(\bar{q}\hat{E} - \bar{f}\hat{F} - \bar{q}\hat{Q}).$$

Strictly, the two propositions in the text are true if and only if it is assumed, as it has been implicitly throughout this Section, that home consumers' initial holdings of foreign money are positive $(\bar{E}_0\bar{F}_0 > 0)$.

the value of the exchange rate on the GQ_1GQ_1 schedule which corresponds to F_0. Since the pair (E_0, F_0) lies to the left of the $\dot{F}_1\dot{F}_1$ schedule, the trade surplus is positive, and home residents begin accumulating foreign money. The economy moves along GQ_1GQ_1 until the new stationary equilibrium pair $(\bar{E}_\infty, \bar{F}_\infty)$ is reached. After its initial depreciation the home currency appreciates steadily from E_0 to $\bar{E}_\infty$.

The time paths of E and F and two alternative time paths for P are shown in Figure 4. The time paths of E and F have already been discussed, but the two possible paths of P require a little further comment. It has been shown that P may initially overshoot or undershoot its stationary equilibrium value. It can be shown that if P initially overshoots (undershoots), increases in F cause decreases (increases) in P.[20)] Since F is always rising while the economy is adjusting, P steadily approaches its new stationary equilibrium value from either above or below.

IV. THE EFFECTS OF INTERVENTION POLICY WHEN ONLY SLOW PRICE ADJUSTMENT AFFECTS THE ADJUSTMENT PATH OF THE ECONOMY

The Conditions for Momentary Equilibrium

In order to focus attention on the effects of slow price adjustment on the path of the economy following exchange market intervention, it is assumed that the price level adjusts slowly and that output is variable.[21)] It is also assumed that neither

---

20) A comparison of the expressions in footnotes 16 and 18 reveals that if P initially overshoots (undershoots), increases in F cause decreases (increases) in P.

21) The version of the model discussed in Section IV is similar to the model presented in the Appendix to Dornbusch (1976a). There are three main differences between the assumptions made here and those made by Dornbusch: (1) here home wealth is allocated between home and foreign money, but in Dornbusch's model home wealth is allocated between home money and holdings of a single world security; (2) here there is no rate of return effect in the market for the home good, but in Dornbusch's model increases in the nominal rate of interest reduce demand

saving nor the demand for home money depend on real wealth so that $s_2 = q_2 = 0$. This assumption implies that changes in real wealth do not affect either the excess demand for goods ($g_2 = 0$) or the trade surplus ($t_2 = 0$). For convenience the position of the economy at a point in time is still referred to as momentary equilibrium even though the labor market is not in full equilibrium.

Under the assumptions stated above four conditions determine the momentary equilibrium values of the exchange rate, output, the rate of inflation, and the change in home consumers' holdings of foreign money:

$$-g_1 \frac{Py}{P_I} + g_3 \frac{E}{P_I} - g_4 \frac{P}{P_I} - g_6 = 0, \tag{23a}$$

$$q_1 \frac{Py}{P_I} - q_5 \varepsilon (1 - \frac{E}{\bar{E}}) + q_6 - \frac{Q}{P_I} = 0, \tag{23b}$$

$$u(ny - \tilde{N}) - \frac{\dot{P}}{P} = 0, \tag{23c}$$

$$-t_1 \frac{Py}{P_I} + t_3 \frac{E}{P_I} - t_4 \frac{P}{P_I} + t_6 - \frac{E}{P_I} \dot{F} = 0. \tag{23d}$$

Equation (23c) which determines the rate of inflation of the price of the home good is obtained by substituting equations (9) and (11) into equation (6).

---

21) (continued)
for the home good; and (3) here a price index is used to deflate nominal income and the money supply, but in Dornbusch's model the price of the home good is used to deflate these nominal magnitudes. One by-product of the first difference is that the method of increasing the home money supply is different in the two models. Here the home authorities purchase foreign money, but in Dornbusch's model they purchase the single world security. When the policy considered is an increase in the home money supply, the differences in assumptions lead to no important differences in results. For a demonstration that there is only a minor change in the condition for overshooting see footnote 22.

The Stationary State Effects

As before it is useful to begin the analysis of the effects of intervention policy by describing the stationary state effects. In a stationary state the rate of inflation is zero, and the exchange rate is expected to remain unchanged:

$$\frac{\dot{P}}{P} = e = 0. \tag{24}$$

Imposing these restrictions on the four equations (23) after eliminating P_I using equation (1) yields four equations which are sufficient to determine the stationary state equilibrium values $\bar{y}$, $\bar{P}$, $\bar{E}$, and $\bar{\dot{F}}$ given $\bar{Q}$. These four equations actually describe a pseudo stationary state equilibrium since wealth continues to change because $\bar{\dot{F}}$ is not equal to zero, but in what follows the equilibrium is referred to as a stationary state for convenience. The four equations which describe stationary state equilibrium are homogenous of degree zero in the three nominal variables $\bar{P}$, $\bar{E}$, and $\bar{Q}$, and $\bar{Q}$ is the only exogenous nominal variable. So, if $\bar{Q}$ increases, $\bar{P}$ and $\bar{E}$ must increase by the same proportion, and $\bar{y}$ and $\bar{\dot{F}}$ must remain unchanged:

$$\hat{\bar{P}} = \hat{\bar{E}} = \hat{\bar{Q}}, \tag{25a}$$

$$\hat{\bar{y}} = \hat{\bar{\dot{F}}} = 0. \tag{25b}$$

The Impact Effects

The impact effects of a purchase of foreign money by the authorities on the exchange rate and physical output are shown in Figure 5 which is constructed using equations (23a) and (23b) with P_I eliminated through equation (1). The G_0G_0 schedule shows the pairs of the exchange rate and output which are compatible with equilibrium in the market for the home good. The Q_0Q_0 schedule shows the pairs of the exchange rate and output which

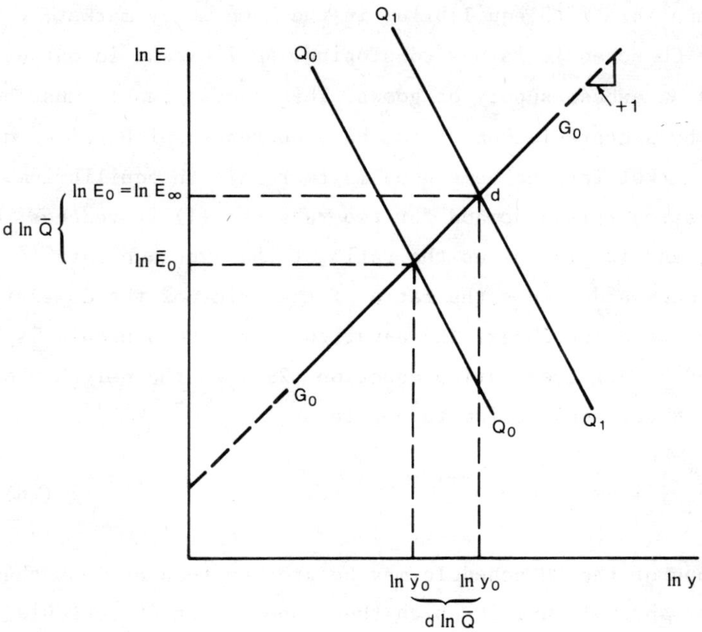

FIGURE 5

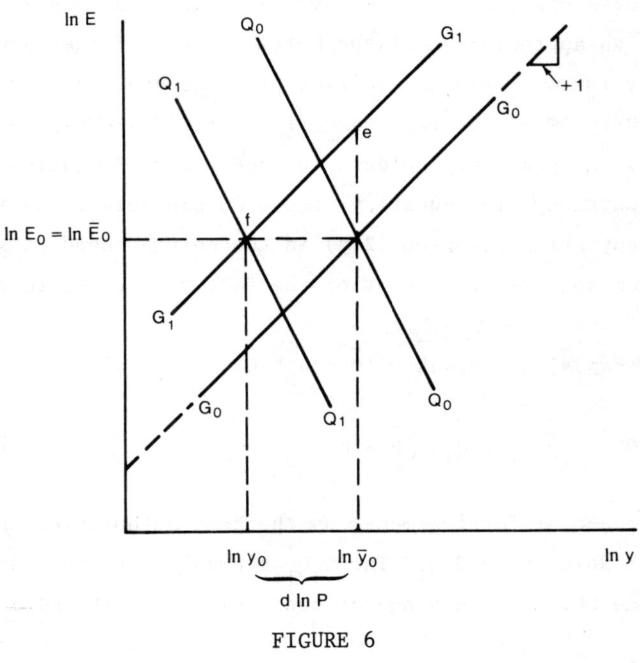

FIGURE 6

are compatible with equilibrium in the home money market.

The GG schedule is upward-sloping. An increase in output creates an excess supply of goods. This excess supply must be offset by a depreciation of the home currency which raises demand if the market for the home good is to remain in equilibrium. A depreciation raises demand for two reasons: (1) it reduces real income; and (2) it raises the ratio of the exchange rate to the price index and lowers the ratio of the price of the domestic good to the price index. The equation of the GG schedule is obtained by differentiating equation (23a) in the neighborhood of stationary equilibrium to obtain

$$- g_1 \bar{y}\hat{y} + g\hat{E} - g\hat{P} = 0. \tag{26}$$

The slope of the GG schedule may be greater than or less than one. The special case in which the slope of the GG schedule is exactly equal to one is shown in Figure 5.

The QQ schedule is downward-sloping. An increase in output creates an excess demand for money. This excess demand must be offset by an appreciation of the home currency if the market for home money is to remain in equilibrium. An appreciation reduces excess money demand for two reasons: (1) is lowers the price index, and (2) it induces money holders to expect a depreciation of the home currency. The equation of the QQ schedule is derived by differentiating equation (24a) in the neighborhood of stationary equilibrium and taking account of the fact that $\hat{\bar{E}} = \hat{\bar{Q}}$ to obtain

$$q_1 \bar{y}\hat{y} + [(\bar{Q} - q_1 \bar{y})k_2 + q_5 \varepsilon]\hat{E} - (\bar{Q} - q_5 \varepsilon)\hat{\bar{Q}}$$

$$+ [(Q - q_1 \bar{y})k_1 + q_1 \bar{y}]\,\hat{P} = 0. \tag{27}$$

A purchase of foreign money by the home authorities shifts the QQ schedule up to Q_1Q_1. The Q_1Q_1 schedule must intersect the dashed line which has a slope of positive one in Figure 5 at or above point d. Point d corresponds to proportionate increases in E and y equal to the proportionate increase in $\bar{Q}$ ($\hat{E} = \hat{y} = \hat{\bar{Q}}$). Equiproportionate changes in E, y, and $\bar{Q}$ leave the expected rate of depreciation unchanged and raise real balances and real income by the same percentage. If the real income elasticity of the demand for money is less than one, equal percentage increases in real balances and real income give rise to an excess supply of money. Thus, if equilibrium were to be established with equal percentage increases in E and y following an exchange market intervention which increases $\bar{Q}$, the percentage changes in E and y would have to exceed the percentage change in $\bar{Q}$. The special case in which the real income elasticity of demand for real balances is exactly equal to one so that Q_1Q_1 intersects the dashed line at point d is shown in Figure 5.

The impact effects on E and y are shown by the intersection of Q_1Q_1 and G_0G_0. The home currency depreciates, and the exchange rate may overshoot or undershoot its stationary equilibrium value.[22)]

---

22) Solving equations (26) and (27) for $\hat{E}$ subject to $\bar{q}\,\hat{\bar{Q}} + \bar{f}\hat{F} = 0$ yields

$$\hat{E} = -\frac{1}{\Delta_2}\left[g_1\bar{y}(\bar{Q} + q_5\varepsilon)\right]\hat{\bar{Q}} > 0,$$

$$\hat{E} = \{1 - \frac{1}{\Delta_2}\left[q_1\bar{y}(g_1\bar{y} - g) + g_1\bar{y}(\bar{Q} - q_1\bar{y})k_1\right]\}\hat{\bar{Q}} \gtrless \hat{\bar{E}} = \hat{\bar{Q}},$$

$$\Delta_2 = -g_1\bar{y}\left[(\bar{Q} - q_1\bar{y})k_2 + q_5\varepsilon\right] - gq_1\bar{y} < 0.$$

Δ_2 is negative because it has been assumed that the real income elasticity of demand for real balance is less than one ($q_1\bar{y} < \bar{Q}$).
The condition under which the exchange rate overshoots in this version of the model is quite similar to the condition under which the exchange rate overshoots in the model presented in the Appendix to Dornbusch (1976a). Here the exchange rate overshoots if

$$q_1\bar{y}(g_1\bar{y} - g) + g_1\bar{y}\left[(\bar{Q} - q_1\bar{y})k_1\right] > 0,$$

or equivalently if

$$k_1 + \frac{q_1\bar{y}}{\bar{Q}}k_2 - \frac{1}{g_1\bar{y}}\frac{q_1\bar{y}}{\bar{Q}}g > 0.$$

Physical output rises, and the proportionate increase in output may exceed or fall short of the proportionate increase in the home money supply.[23] The special case in which $\hat{E} = \hat{\hat{E}} = \hat{\hat{Q}}$ and $\hat{y} = \hat{\hat{Q}}$ is shown in Figure 5. If the GG schedule were steeper (flatter) than one, the exchange rate would overshoot (undershoot), and the proportionate increase output would fall short of (exceed) the proportionate increase in the home money supply. If the real income elasticity of the demand for real balances were less than one, the exchange rate would overshoot and $\hat{y}$ would exceed $\hat{\hat{Q}}$. In general, the steeper the GG schedule and the lower the real income elasticity of the demand for real balances, the more likely it is that the exchange rate will overshoot; the flatter the GG schedule and the lower the real income elasticity of the demand for real balances, the more likely it is that $\hat{y}$ will exceed $\hat{\hat{Q}}$.

---

22) (continued)
If $k_1 = 1$ (and $k_2 = 0$) this condition is identical to Dornbusch's since
$\frac{1}{g_1\bar{y}}$ is his μ, $\frac{q_1\bar{y}}{\bar{Q}}$ is his $\emptyset$, and g is his δ. The condition here is more stringent because when a price index is employed a depreciation of the home currency has a larger positive effect on the excess demand for money, so the home currency need not depreciate as much to offset a given increase in the home money supply.

23) Solving equations (26) and (27) for $\hat{y}$ subject to $\bar{q}\,\hat{\hat{Q}} + \bar{f}\hat{F} = 0$ yields

$$\hat{y} = -\frac{1}{\Delta_2}\,[(\bar{Q} + q_5\varepsilon)g]\hat{\hat{Q}} > 0,$$

$$\hat{y} = \{1 + \frac{1}{\Delta_2}\,[(g_1\bar{y}k_2 - g)\,(\bar{Q} - q_1\bar{y}) + (g_1\bar{y} - g)q_5\varepsilon]\}\,\hat{\hat{Q}} \gtrless \hat{\hat{Q}}.$$

The Adjustment Process

In order to lay a foundation for a discussion of the adjustment process it is useful to derive two additional relationships. The changes in the exchange rate and physical output which are required in order to clear the markets for the home good and home money when the price of the home good changes are shown in Figure 6. An increase in the price of the home good shifts the GG schedule up to G_1G_1. A rise in P creates an excess supply of the home good for two reasons: (1) it raises real income; and (2) it lowers the ratio of E to P_I and raises the ratio of P to P_I. In order to offset this excess supply so that the market for the home good remains in equilibrium, the home currency must depreciate for a given value of output. G_1G_1 must intersect the vertical dashed line at point e which corresponds to a proportionate increase in E equal to the proportionate increase in P since equiproportionate increases in P and E with y held constant leave the goods market in equilibrium. A rise in the price of the home good shifts the QQ schedule to the left to Q_1Q_1. An increase in P creates an excess demand for real balances because it lowers real balances and raises real income. In order to offset this excess demand for real balances so that the market for home money remains in equilibrium, physical output must fall for a given value of the exchange rate. Q_1Q_1 must intersect the horizontal dashed line at or to the left of point f which corresponds to a proportionate decrease in y equal to the proportionate increase in P. If y decreases by the same proportion as P increases, real balances and real income fall by the same proportion. If the real income elasticity of the demand for real balances is less than one, equal percentage decreases in real balances and real income give rise to an excess demand for money. Thus, when the real income elasticity of demand for real balances is less than one, the percentage decrease in y must exceed the percentage increase in P if the market for home money is to remain in equilibrium; that is, Q_1Q_1 must cut the horizontal dashed line to the left of f. The special case in which the real income elasticity is equal to one so that Q_1Q_1 passes through point f is shown in Figure 6.

The new equilibrium values of E and y are given by the intersection of G_1G_1 and Q_1Q_1. The home currency may depreciate or appreciate.[24)] Real output must fall, and the absolute value of the proportionate decrease in y may exceed or fall short of the proportionate increase in P.[25)] In the special case shown in Figure 6 the GG schedule has a slope of one and the real income elasticity of the demand for real balances is equal to one. In this case $\hat{E} = 0$ and $\hat{y} = -\hat{P}$. If the GG schedule were steeper (flatter) than one, the home currency would appreciate (depreciate), and the absolute value of the proportionate decrease in output would be less than (exceed) the proportionate rise in the price of the home good. If the real income elasticity of the demand for real balances were less than one, the exchange rate would appreciate and the absolute value of $\hat{y}$ would exceed $\hat{P}$. In general, the steeper the GG schedule and the lower the real income elasticity of demand for real balances, the more likely it is that $\hat{E}$ will be negative; the flatter the GG schedule and the lower the real income elasticity of the demand for real balances, the more likely it is that the absolute value of $\hat{y}$ will exceed $\hat{P}$. It is

---

24) Solving equations (26) and (27) for $\hat{E}$ subject to $\hat{\bar{Q}} = 0$ yields

$$\hat{E} = \frac{1}{\Delta_2} [q_1\bar{y}(g_1\bar{y} - g) + g_1\bar{y}(\bar{Q} - q_1\bar{y})k_1]\ \hat{P} \gtrless 0.$$

25) Solving equations (26) and (27) for $\hat{y}$ subject to $\hat{\bar{Q}} = 0$ yields

$$\hat{y} = \frac{1}{\Delta_2} [g(Q + q_5\varepsilon)]\ \hat{P} < 0.$$

important to observe that the conditions under which an increase in Q causes E to overshoot its stationary equilibrium value are exactly the same as the conditions under which an increase in P causes E to fall.[26)]

The adjustment process for the system following the exchange market intervention is shown in Figure 7. The downward-sloping GQ_0GQ_0 schedule shows the pairs of E and P which are compatible with equilibrium in both the market for the home good and the market for home money before the exchange market intervention. Although the GQGQ schedule has been drawn with a negative slope in Figure 7, it follows from the analysis above that the slope of this schedule may be positive. What happens when GQGQ has a positive slope is discussed at the end of this section.

The $\dot{P}\dot{P}$ schedule shows the pairs of E and P which are compatible both with equilibrium in the market for the home good and with zero inflation. It has a slope of positive one because equiproportionate changes in E and P leave the market for the home good in equilibrium at an unchanged value of physical output and, therefore, lead to no change in the rate of inflation. To the left of (the right of) the $\dot{P}\dot{P}$ schedule the rate of inflation is positive (negative). For any given value of the exchange rate a fall in the price of the home good raises the value of physical output which clears the goods market. This increase in output raises the rate of inflation because it increases the demand for labor.[27)]

---

26) A comparison of the expressions in footnotes 22 and 24 reveals that if E initially overshoots (undershoots), increases in P cause decreases (increases) in E.

27) Linearizing equation (23c) in the neighborhood of stationary equilibrium yields

$$\dot{P} = un\bar{y}\hat{y}.$$

Solving for $\hat{y}$ using equation (26), the total differential of the equilibrium condition for the market for the home good, and substituting the resulting expression into the equation for $\dot{P}$ yields the equation of the $\dot{P}\dot{P}$ schedule:

$$\dot{P} = [ung/g_1](\hat{E} - \hat{P}).$$

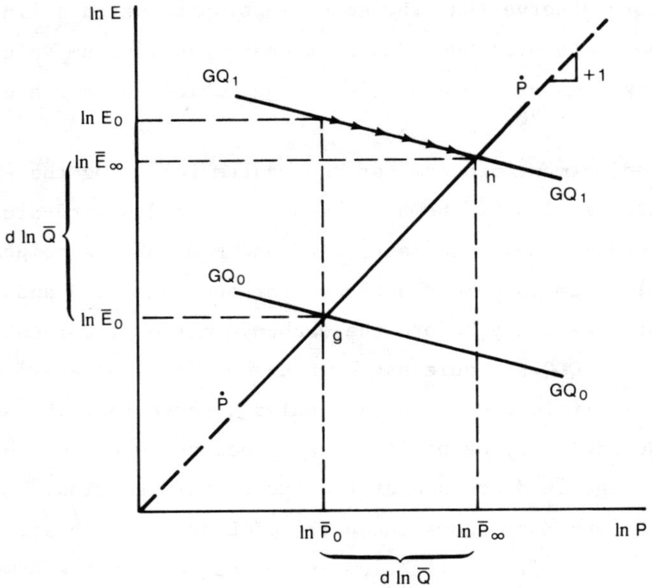

FIGURE 7

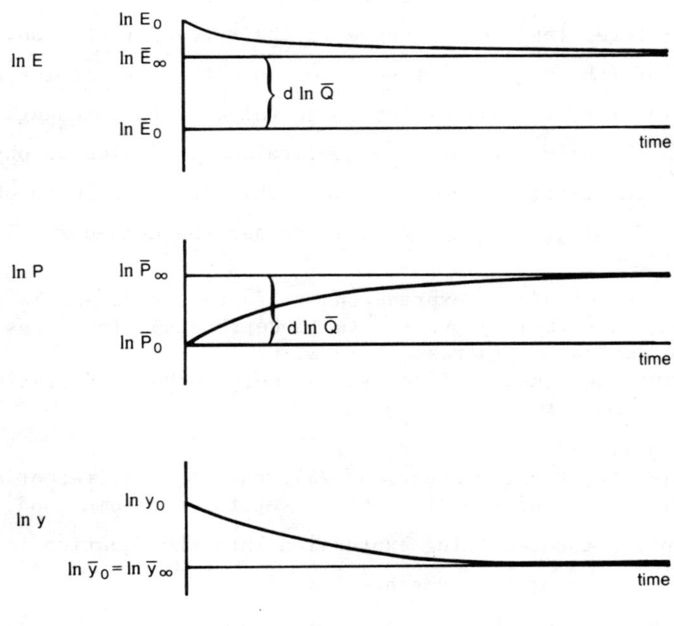

FIGURE 8

Just before the exchange market intervention the economy is at point g in Figure 7 with a price level of $\bar{P}_0$ and with the exchange rate at $\bar{E}_0$. The exchange market intervention shifts the GQGQ schedule up to GQ_1GQ_1. It has been established above that, given P, E must rise when $\bar{Q}$ rises if both the goods and money markets are to remain in equilibrium.

From the analysis of the stationary state effects of the intervention policy, it follows that the exchange market intervention must shift the GQGQ schedule in such a way that it intersects the $\dot{P}\dot{P}$ schedule, which is unaffected by the increase in $\bar{Q}$, at point h. This point represents proportionate increases in P and E equal to the proportionate increase in $\bar{Q}$. The new stationary values of P and E are represented by $\bar{P}_\infty$ and $\bar{E}_\infty$.

Given the price level, the exchange rate at any time must be that one which is compatible with equilibrium in the markets for the home good and home money. Thus, at the moment of the exchange market intervention the exchange rate jumps from $\bar{E}_0$ to E_0, the value of the exchange rate on the GQ_1GQ_1 schedule which corresponds to $\bar{P}_0$. As has been established above the exchange rate overshoots its stationary equilibrium value when the GQGQ schedule is downward sloping. Since the point corresponding to the pair $(E_0, \bar{P}_0)$ lies to the left of $\dot{P}\dot{P}$, the inflation rate is positive. The economy moves downward along GQ_1GQ_1 until the new stationary equilibrium pair $(\bar{E}_\infty, \bar{P}_\infty)$ is reached. After this initial jump up, the exchange rate declines steadily from E_0 to $\bar{E}_\infty$, and the price level rises steadily from $\bar{P}_0$ to $\bar{P}_\infty$.

The time paths of the three endogenous variables are shown in Figure 8. The time paths of E and P have already been discussed. It has been demonstrated above that y increases initially. Since increases in P cause decreases in y, physical output declines steadily back to its unchanged stationary value.

If the GQGQ schedule has a positive slope as in Figure 9, the exchange rate rises but undershoots its stationary equilibrium value as a result of an exchange market intervention. Since the slope of the GQGQ schedule must be less than one, the inflation rate becomes positive. The economy moves upward along its new GQGQ schedule until the new stationary equilibrium exchange rate and price level are reached. After its initial jump up, the exchange rate continues to rise as the price level rises. Output rises initially and then declines steadily back to its unchanged stationary value.

V. THE EFFECTS OF INTERVENTION POLICY WHEN BOTH THE TRADE SURPLUS AND SLOW PRICE ADJUSTMENT AFFECT THE ADJUSTMENT PATH OF THE ECONOMY

The Conditions for Momentary Equilibrium

When both the trade surplus and slow price adjustment affect the path of the economy, the conditions for momentary equilibrium are

$$-g_1 \frac{Py}{P_I} + g_2 \frac{Q + EF}{P_I} + g_3 \frac{E}{P_I} - g_4 \frac{P}{P_I} - g_6 = 0, \qquad (28a)$$

$$q_1 \frac{Py}{P_I} + q_2 \frac{Q + EF}{P_I} - q_5 \varepsilon(1 - \frac{E}{\bar{E}} + q_6 - \frac{Q}{P_I} = 0, \qquad (28b)$$

$$u(ny - \tilde{N}) - \frac{\dot{P}}{P} = 0, \qquad (28c)$$

$$-t_1 \frac{Py}{P_I} - t_2 \frac{Q + EF}{P_I} + t_3 \frac{E}{P_I} - t_4 \frac{P}{P_I} + t_6 - \frac{E}{P_I} \dot{F} = 0. \qquad (28d)$$

These conditions are identical to the conditions for momentary equilibrium in the version of Section IV except that the excess demand for the home good, the excess demand for home money, and the trade surplus all depend on real wealth.

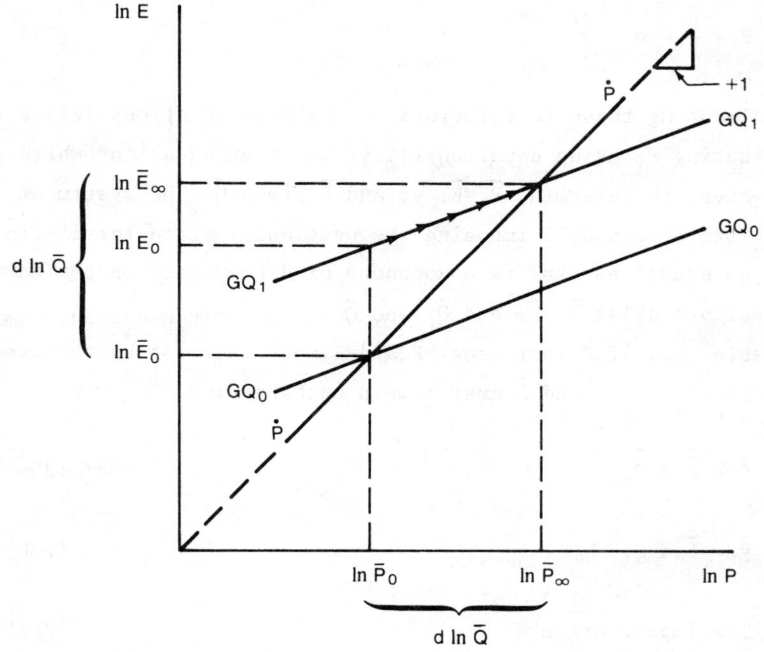

FIGURE 9

The Stationary State Effects

Once again it is useful to begin the analysis of the effects of intervention policy by describing the stationary state effects. In a stationary state no variable is changing and no variable is expected to change, so

$$\dot{F} = \frac{\dot{P}}{P} = e = 0. \tag{29}$$

Imposing these restrictions on the four equations (28) after eliminating P_I using equation (1) yields four equations which are sufficient to determine $\bar{P}$, $\bar{E}$, $\bar{y}$, and $\bar{F}$ given $\bar{Q}$. The system of equations obtained by imposing the stationary state restrictions (29) on equations (28) is homogenous of degree zero in the three nominal variables $\bar{P}$, $\bar{E}$, and $\bar{Q}$, and $\bar{Q}$ is the only exogenous nominal variable. So, if $\bar{Q}$ increases, $\bar{P}$ and $\bar{E}$ must increase by the same proportion, and $\bar{y}$ and $\bar{F}$ must remain unchanged:

$$\hat{\bar{P}} = \hat{\bar{E}} = \hat{\bar{Q}}, \tag{30a}$$

$$\hat{\bar{y}} = \hat{\bar{F}} = 0. \tag{30b}$$

The Impact Effects

The impact effects of a purchase of foreign money by the authorities on the exchange rate and output are shown in Figure 10 which is constructed using equations (28a) and (28b) with P_I eliminated through equation (1). The G_0G_0 schedule shows the pairs of the exchange rate and physical output which are compatible with equilibrium in the market for the home good. The Q_0Q_0 schedule shows the pairs of E and y which are compatible with equilibrium in the market for home money.

The GG schedule is upward-sloping given the assumption of Section III that a depreciation of the home currency raises demand for the home good. An increase in output creates an excess

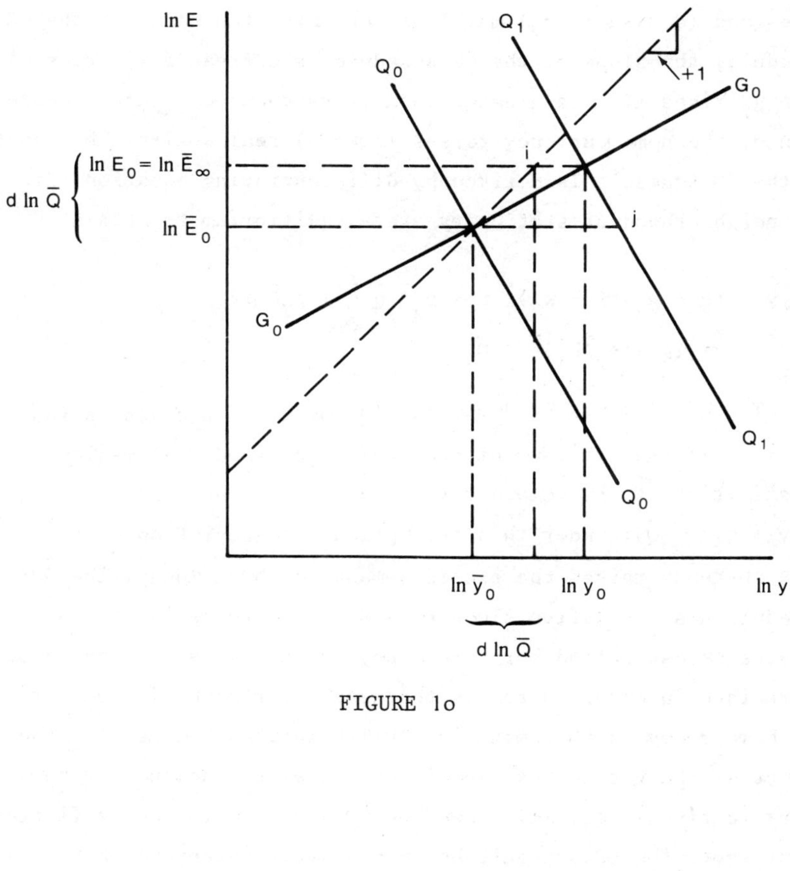

FIGURE 1o

supply of the home good, so the home currency must depreciate in order to increase demand if the market for the home good is to remain in equilibrium. The slope of the GG schedule may be less than one as it is in Figure 10 or greater than one. An increase in the effect of changes in real wealth on excess demand for the home good (a rise in g_2) may lower or raise the slope of the GG schedule; the slope of the GG schedule is decreased (increased) when g_2 rises if f is greater than (less than) k_2 since a depreciation of the home currency raises (lowers) real wealth. The equation of the GG schedule is derived by differentiating equation (28a) in the neighborhood of stationary state equilibrium to obtain

$$-g_1\bar{y}\hat{y} + [g + g_2\bar{A}(\bar{f} - k_2)]\,\hat{E} + g_2\bar{A}\,\bar{q}\,\hat{\bar{Q}} + g_2\bar{A}\,\bar{f}\hat{F} - (g + g_2\bar{A}k_1)\hat{P} = 0. \qquad (31)$$

The QQ schedule is downward-sloping given the assumption of Section III that the sum of the real income and real wealth elasticities of the demand for money is less than one ($q_1\bar{y} + q_2\bar{A} < \bar{Q}$). Under this assumption a depreciation of the home currency raises the excess demand for home money. The QQ schedule has a negative slope because an increase in real output creates excess demand for home money, so the home currency must appreciate in order to reduce the demand for money if the market for home money is to remain in equilibrium. An increase in the effect of changes in real wealth on the excess demand for home money (a rise in q_2) may cause the QQ schedule to become flatter or steeper; the QQ schedule becomes flatter (steeper) when f is greater than (less than) k_2 since a depreciation of the home currency raises (lowers) real wealth. The equation of the QQ schedule is derived by differentiating (28b) in the neighborhood of stationary equilibrium and recognizing the $\hat{\bar{E}} = \hat{\bar{Q}}$ to obtain

$$q_1\hat{\bar{y}}y + [(\bar{Q} - q_1\bar{y} - q_2\bar{A})k_2 + q_2\bar{A}\,\bar{f} + q_5\varepsilon]\hat{E} + (q_2\bar{A}\,\bar{q} - \bar{Q} - q_5\varepsilon)\hat{\bar{Q}}$$

$$+ q_2A\bar{f}\hat{F} + [(\bar{Q} - q_1\bar{y} - q_2\bar{A})k_1 + q_1\bar{y}]\,\hat{P} = 0. \qquad (32)$$

A purchase of foreign money by the home authorities ($\bar{q}\,\hat{\bar{Q}} + \bar{f}\hat{F} = 0$) shifts the QQ schedule up to Q_1Q_1. The QQ schedule must shift farther than point i along the dashed line which has a slope of positive one in Figure 10. Point i is the point which corresponds to increases in E and y by the same proportion as the increase in $\bar{Q}$ ($\hat{E} = \hat{y} = \hat{\bar{Q}}$). Equiproportionate increases in E, y, and $\bar{Q}$ raise real balances and real income by the same proportion. These changes raise (lower) real wealth if f is greater than (less than) k_2. However, even if these changes raise real wealth, they increase it by a smaller proportion than real balances and real income are increased since only the foreign money component of nominal wealth is increased by increases in E. Thus, equiproportionate changes in E, y, and $\bar{Q}$ give rise to an excess supply of real balances since it has been assumed that the sum of the real income and real wealth elasticities of demand for real balances is less than (or, in the extreme, equal to) one. If equilibrium in the market for home money were to be established with equal percentage changes in E and y following an exchange market intervention which raises $\bar{Q}$, the percentage increases in E and y would have to exceed the percentage change in $\bar{Q}$.

The impact effects on E and y are shown by the intersection of Q_1Q_1 and G_0G_0. Both E and y definitely increase.[28)29)] E may

---

28) Solving equations (31) and (32) for $\hat{E}$ subject to $\bar{q}\,\hat{\bar{Q}} + \bar{f}\hat{F} = 0$ yields

$$\hat{E} = -\frac{1}{\Delta_3}[g_1\bar{y}(\bar{Q} + q_5\varepsilon)]\hat{\bar{Q}} > 0,$$

$$\hat{E} = \Big\{1 - \frac{1}{\Delta_3}\{q_1\bar{y}[g_1\bar{y} - g - g_2\bar{A}(\bar{f} - k_2)]$$

$$+ g_1\bar{y}\,[(\bar{Q} - q_1\bar{y})k_1 - q_2\bar{A}(\bar{f} - k_2)]\}\Big\}\,\hat{\bar{Q}} \gtrless \hat{E} = \hat{\bar{Q}},$$

overshoot or undershoot its stationary equilibrium level; a borderline case in which E rises only as much as is necessary to reach its new stationary equilibrium level is shown in Figure 10. Note that since Q_1Q_1 must intersect the dashed line with a slope of positive one to the right of point i, the exchange rate may overshoot even if the slope of the GG schedule is less than one. The percentage increase in y may be greater than or less than the percentage change in $\bar{Q}$. If E undershoots $\hat{y}$ definitely exceeds $\hat{\bar{Q}}$; if E overshoots $\hat{y}$ may be greater than or less than $\hat{\bar{Q}}$.

Since the only difference between this version of the model and the one of Section IV is the presence of wealth effects in the market for the home good and the market for home money, it is important to investigate how changes in these wealth effects alter the impact effects of intervention policy. An increase in g_2 causes the GG schedule to become flatter (steeper) if f is greater than (less than) k_2 and therefore makes it more likely that the exchange rate will undershoot (overshoot) and that $\hat{y}$ will be

---

28) (continued)

$$\Delta_3 = - g_1\bar{y} [(\bar{Q} - q_1\bar{y} - q_2\bar{A})k_2 + q_2\bar{A}\,\bar{f} + q_5\varepsilon]$$
$$- q_1\bar{y} [g + g_2A(\bar{f} - k_2)] < 0.$$

Δ_3 is negative because it has been assumed that the sum of the real income and real wealth elasticities of demand for real balances is less than one $(q_1\bar{y} + q_2\bar{A} < \bar{Q})$ and that a depreciation of the home currency raises excess demand for the home good $[g + g_2\bar{A}(\bar{f} - k_2) > 0]$.

29) Solving equations (31) and (32) for $\hat{y}$ subject to $\bar{q}\,\hat{\bar{Q}} + \bar{f}\hat{F} = 0$ yields

$$\hat{y} = - \frac{1}{\Delta_3} \{[g + g_2\bar{A}(\bar{f} - k_2)]\ (\bar{Q} + q_5\varepsilon)\}\hat{\bar{Q}} > 0,$$

$$\hat{y} = \Big\{1 - \frac{1}{\Delta_3} \{(\bar{Q} - q_1\bar{y} + q_5\varepsilon)\ [g + g_2\bar{A}(\bar{f} - k_2)]$$
$$-g_1\bar{y}\ [(\bar{Q} - q_1\bar{y} - q_2\bar{A})k_2 + q_2\bar{A}\,\bar{f} + q_5\varepsilon]\}\Big\}\ \hat{\bar{Q}} \gtrless \hat{\bar{Q}}.$$

greater than (less than) $\hat{\bar{Q}}$. An increase in q_2 causes the Q_1Q_1 schedule to rotate around point j which corresponds to the old equilibrium exchange rate, $\bar{E}_0$, since the real income elasticity of the demand for real balances remains unchanged. An increase in q_2 causes the QQ schedule to become flatter (steeper) if f is greater than (less than) k_2 and therefore makes it more likely that the exchange rate will undershoot (overshoot) and that $\hat{y}$ will be less than (greater than) $\hat{\bar{Q}}$.[30)]

The Adjustment Process

In order to lay a foundation for a discussion of the adjustment process it is useful to derive four additional relationships. The changes in the exchange rate and physical output which are required in order to clear the market for the home good and home money when the price of the home good changes are shown in Figure 11. An increase in P shifts the GG schedule to the left to G_1G_1. A rise in P decreases excess demand for the home good, so, for a given value of E, y must fall if the goods market is to remain in equilibrium. A rise in P also shifts the QQ schedule to the left to Q_1Q_1. A rise in P creates an excess demand for home money, so, for a given value of E, y must fall if the money market is to remain in equilibrium. The new equilibrium values of E and y are given by the intersection of G_1G_1 and Q_1Q_1.[31)] E may

---

30) Note that increases in q_2 can never cause the Q_1Q_1 schedule to cut the dashed line with a slope of positive one to the left of point i under the assumption that the sum of the real income and real wealth elasticities of the demand for real balances is less than (or, in the extreme, equal to) one.

31) Solving equations (31) and (32) for $\hat{E}$ and $\hat{y}$ subject to $\hat{\bar{Q}} = \hat{F} = 0$ yields

$$\hat{E} = \frac{1}{\Delta_3} \{g_1\bar{y}\,[(\bar{Q} - q_1\bar{y} - q_2\bar{A})k_1 + q_1\bar{y}] - q_1\bar{y}(g + g_2\bar{A}k_1)\}\,\hat{P} \gtrless 0,$$

$$\hat{y} = \frac{1}{\Delta_3} \{(g + g_2\bar{A}k_1)\,[(\bar{Q} - q_1\bar{y} - q_2\bar{A})k_2 + q_2\bar{A}\,\bar{f} + q_5\varepsilon]$$

$$+ [(\bar{Q} - q_1\bar{y} - q_2\bar{A})k_1 + q_1\bar{y}][g + g_2\bar{A}(\bar{f} - k_2)]\}\,\hat{P} < 0.$$

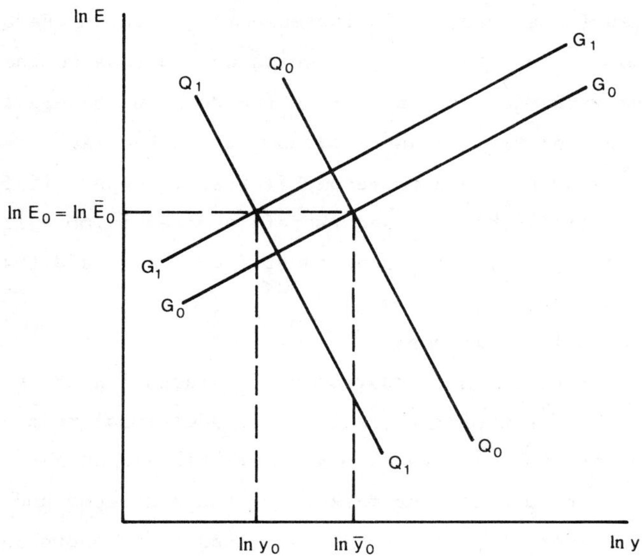

FIGURE 11

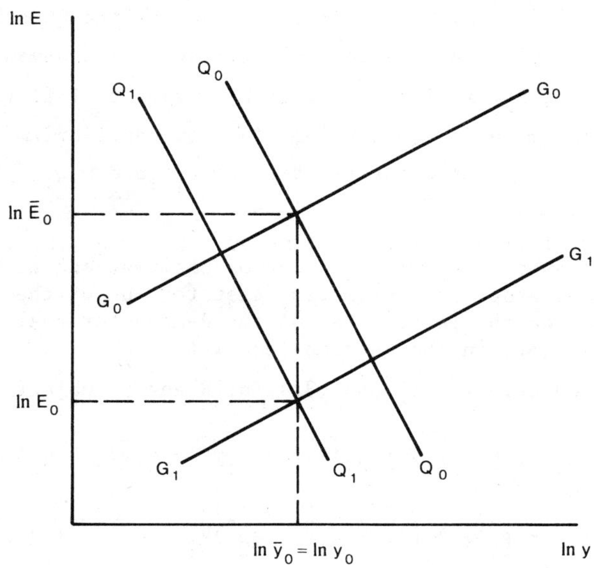

FIGURE 12

rise or fall; the borderline case in which E remains unchanged is shown in Figure 11. y definitely falls. The larger g_2, the more GG shifts to the left; the larger q_2, the less QQ shifts to the left. Therefore, the larger g_2 and q_2, the more likely it is that E will rise. E is more likely to rise when P rises in the version of this Section than in that of Section IV in which $g_2 = q_2 = 0$.

The changes in the exchange rate and output which are required to clear the markets for the home good and home money when home residents' holdings of foreign money change are shown in Figure 12. An increase in F shifts the GG schedule down to G_1G_1. A rise in F raises the demand for the home good, so, for a given value of y, E must fall if the market for the home good is to remain in equilibrium. An increase in F also shifts the QQ schedule down to Q_1Q_1. A rise in F creates an excess demand for home money, so, for a given value y, E must fall if the market for home money is to remain in equilibrium. The new equilibrium values of E and y are given by the intersection of G_1G_1 and Q_1Q_1.[32)] E definitely falls. y may rise or fall; a borderline case in which y remains unchanged is shown in Figure 12. The larger are g_2 and q_2, the larger the appreciation in the home currency since both the GG and QQ schedules shift down farther.

---

32) Solving equations (31) and (32) for $\hat{E}$ and $\hat{y}$ subject to $\hat{Q} = \hat{P} = 0$ yields

$$\hat{E} = \frac{1}{\Delta_3} (g_1 q_2 + q_1 g_2)\bar{A}\ \bar{f}\ \bar{y}\hat{F} < 0,$$

$$\hat{y} = \frac{1}{\Delta_3} \{-g_2\bar{A}\ \bar{f}\ [(\bar{Q} - q_1\bar{y} - q_2\bar{A})k_2 + q_2\bar{A}\ \bar{f} + q_5\varepsilon]$$

$$+ q_2\bar{A}\ \bar{f}\ [g + g_2\bar{A}(\bar{f} - k_2)]\}\ \hat{F} \gtrless 0.$$

The adjustment process for the system following the exchange market intervention is described by the two differential equations (28c) and (28d) which are reproduced here for convenience:

$$\frac{\dot{P}}{P} = u(ny - \tilde{N}), \tag{28c}$$

$$\frac{E}{P_I}\dot{F} = -t_1\frac{Py}{P_I} - t_2\frac{Q + EF}{P_I} + t_3\frac{E}{P_I} - t_4\frac{P}{P_I} + t_6. \tag{28d}$$

Linearizing these equations in the neighborhood of stationary equilibrium after eliminating P_I through (1) yields:

$$\dot{P} = un\bar{y}\hat{y}, \tag{33a}$$

$$\dot{F} = -t_1\bar{y}\hat{y} + [t - t_2\bar{A}(\bar{f} - k_2)]\hat{E} - [\bar{t} - t_2\bar{A}k_1]\hat{P}$$
$$- t_2\bar{A}\,\bar{f}\hat{F}. \tag{33b}$$

It has been shown above that $\hat{E}$ and $\hat{y}$ depend on $\hat{P}$ and $\hat{F}$.[33] Substituting for $\hat{E}$ and $\hat{y}$ using these relationships transforms equations (33) into

$$\dot{P} = B_{11}\hat{P} + B_{12}\hat{F}, \tag{34a}$$

$$\dot{F} = B_{21}\hat{P} + B_{22}\hat{F}, \tag{34b}$$

$$B_{11} = \frac{1}{\Delta_3}\, un\bar{y}[(g_1\bar{y}k_2 + C_1)C_2 - q_2\bar{A}\,\bar{q} + g_2\bar{A}k_1C_3 - \bar{A}\,\bar{q}\,\bar{y}k_2C_4] < 0,$$

$$B_{12} = \frac{1}{\Delta_3}\, un\bar{y}\,[-g_2C_5 + \bar{y}k_2C_4 + q_2C_1]\,\bar{A}\,\bar{f} \gtrless 0,$$

$$B_{21} = \frac{1}{\Delta_3}\,[s_1C_1C_2 - \bar{A}\bar{q}C_1C_6 - m_1s_2k_1\bar{A}C_3]\,\bar{y} \gtrless 0,$$

$$B_{22} = \frac{1}{\Delta_3}\,[C_1C_6 + m_1s_2C_5]\,\bar{A}\,\bar{f}\,\bar{y} < 0,$$

---

33) These relationships are contained in footnotes 31 and 32.

$$\Delta_3 = -g_1\bar{y}C_5 - \bar{A}\,\bar{y}(\bar{f} - k_2)C_4 - q_1\bar{y}C_1 < 0,$$

$$C_1 = g_3k_1 + g_4k_2 = t_3k_1 + t_4k_2,$$

$$C_2 = \bar{Q} + q_5\varepsilon,$$

$$C_3 = \bar{Q}\,\bar{f} + q_5\varepsilon,$$

$$C_4 = g_1q_2 + g_2q_1,$$

$$C_5 = \bar{Q}k_2 + q_5\varepsilon,$$

$$C_6 = s_1q_2 + s_2q_1.$$

The adjustment process is definitely stable since the trace of the matrix of coefficients of the pair of differential equations (34) is negative,[34)]

$$B_{11} + B_{22} < 0, \tag{35}$$

and the determinant is positive,[35)]

$$B_{11}B_{22} - B_{12}B_{21} = -\frac{1}{\Delta_3}\,un\bar{y}\,\bar{A}\,\bar{f}\,(s_2C_1 + m_1s_2\bar{y}k_2)(\bar{Q} + q_5\varepsilon) > 0. \tag{36}$$

---

34) It is not apparent from the expression for B_{11} that it must be negative. However, $B_{11} = un\bar{y}\,\frac{\hat{y}}{\hat{P}}$, and, as can be verified by referring to footnote 31, $\frac{\hat{y}}{\hat{P}}$ is negative under the assumptions of this paper that $q_1\bar{y} + q_2\bar{A} < \bar{Q}$ and that $g + g_2\bar{A}(\bar{f} - k_2) > 0$.

35) The derivation of (36), which is very tedious, is available from the author on request.

Given that two out of the four coefficients in the dynamic system have ambiguous signs, it is not surprising that it is not possible to make unambiguous statements about the path followed by the system to stationary equilibrium. The adjustment path may be non-cyclical or cyclical. Each of these possibilities can be illustrated with a special case of system (34).

First, a case in which the adjustment path is non-cyclical is considered. If s_1 is large enough, B_{12} and B_{21} are both negative. Under this assumption the adjustment paths for P and F can be analyzed using the phase diagram shown in Figure 13. The $\ddot{P}\ddot{P}$ schedule shows the pairs of P and F which are consistent with zero inflation. It must be downward-sloping since B_{11} and B_{12} are both negative:

$$\left.\frac{\hat{P}}{\hat{F}}\right|_{\ddot{P}\ddot{P}} = - \frac{B_{12}}{B_{11}} < 0. \tag{37}$$

The $\ddot{F}\ddot{F}$ schedule shows the pairs of P and F which are consistent with zero foreign money accumulation. This schedule must also be downward sloping since B_{21} and B_{22} are both negative:

$$\left.\frac{\hat{P}}{\hat{F}}\right|_{\ddot{F}\ddot{F}} = - \frac{B_{22}}{B_{21}} < 0. \tag{38}$$

The $\ddot{P}\ddot{P}$ schedule must be flatter than the $\ddot{F}\ddot{F}$ schedule as shown in Figure 13 since $B_{11}B_{22} - B_{12}B_{21}$ is positive:

$$\left.\frac{\hat{P}}{\hat{F}}\right|_{\ddot{P}\ddot{P}} - \left.\frac{\hat{P}}{\hat{F}}\right|_{\ddot{F}\ddot{F}} = \frac{1}{B_{11}B_{21}}(B_{11}B_{22} - B_{12}B_{21}) > 0. \tag{39}$$

Just before the exchange market intervention the economy is at point k. From the analysis of the stationary equilibrium effects it follows that in the new stationary state F is unchanged ($\bar{F}_0 = \bar{F}_\infty$), and P rises by the same proportion as the increase in $\bar{Q}$. Initially the exchange market intervention moves the economy to point m; F is reduced from $\bar{F}_0$ to F_0, and P remains unchanged at $\bar{P}_0$. Both P and F rise during the early phase of adjustment while the economy is in Region I. Eventually the economy moves into either Region II (solid path) or Region IV (dashed path) in which P and F move in opposite directions and proceeds directly to the new stationary equilibrium. The adjustment paths for P and F for the case in which the economy moves into Region II are shown in Figure 14.

The adjustment paths for E and y must possess two properities in the case in which s_1 is large. First, since in this case increases in P and F reduce both E and y during the adjustment process ($\frac{\hat{E}}{\hat{P}}, \frac{\hat{E}}{\hat{F}}, \frac{\hat{y}}{\hat{P}}, \frac{\hat{y}}{\hat{F}} < 0$), both E and y fall while the economy is in Region I. [36] Second, E and y continue to fall for a time after the economy enters Region II or Region IV. These properties are displayed by the adjustment paths for E and y shown in Figure 14 which is constructed on the assumption that the economy moves into Region II.

Some of the other properties of the paths for E and y in Figure 14 are possible but not necessary consequences of the assumption that the economy moves into Region II. In Figure 14, E overshoots, and both E and y first fall below their new stationary equilibrium values and then rise back up to these values. It is also possible when E overshoots that the adjustment of both E and y to their stationary equilibrium values is monotonic. Another possibility is that E may undershoot in which case the paths for E and y have the same general shapes as the paths in Figure 14. It is a necessary consequence of the assumption that the economy moves into Region II that if both E and y increase for a time at the end of the adjustment process, y must begin to increase before

---

36) This statement can be verified by letting s_1 become large in the expressions contained in footnotes 31 and 32.

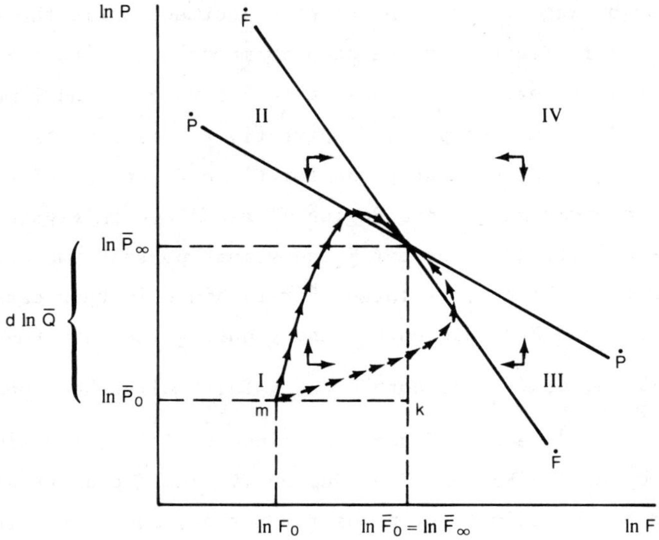

FIGURE 13

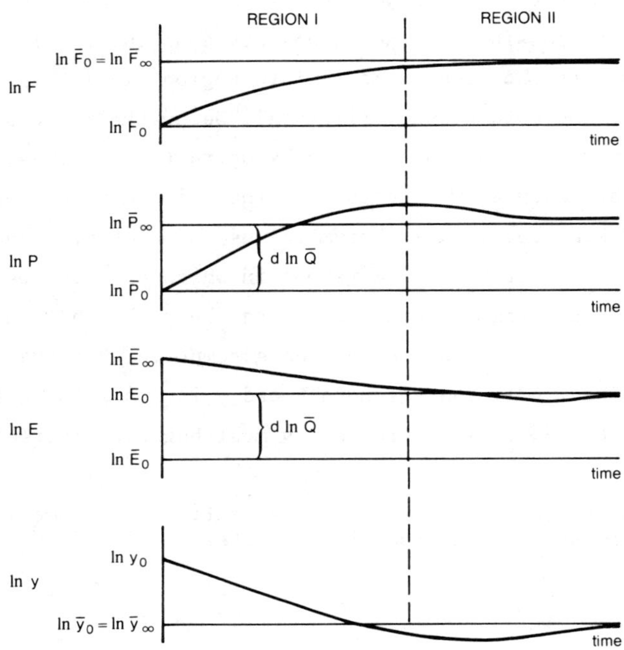

FIGURE 14

E begins to increase.[37)]

Now a case in which the adjustment process is cyclical is considered. If q_2 is large enough, B_{12} is negative, and B_{21} is positive. Under this assumption the adjustment paths for P and F can be analyzed using the phase diagram shown in Figure 15. The $\dot{F}\dot{F}$ schedule is downward-sloping, but the $\dot{P}\dot{P}$ schedule is upward-sloping in this case. When the two schedules have slopes of the opposite sign, the approaches of P and F to stationary equilibrium may be cyclical as in Figure 15. If the paths of P and F are cyclical, there must be cycles in the adjustment paths of both the exchange rate and output.

VI. CONCLUDING REMARKS

The analysis of the dynamic behavior of open economies under managed floating exchange rates is still in its early stages. This paper is an attempt to consolidate some of the gains that have been made and to build upon them by considering the dynamic effects of one type of intervention policy in three versions of a

---

37) The adjustment process is also non-cyclical if s_2 is large enough. In this case B_{12} and B_{21} are both positive. With B_{12} and B_{21} both positive $\frac{\hat{P}}{\hat{F}}\Big|_{\dot{P}\dot{P}}$ and $\frac{\hat{P}}{\hat{F}}\Big|_{\dot{F}\dot{F}}$ are both upward-sloping.

It follows from the argument in the text that $\frac{\hat{P}}{\hat{F}}\Big|_{\dot{P}\dot{P}}$ is flatter than $\frac{\hat{P}}{\hat{F}}\Big|_{\dot{F}\dot{F}}$. Given this relationship between the two schedules the economy must eventually enter a phase in which both P and F rise directly toward the new stationary equilibrium. A description of the adjustment paths for E and y for the case of large s_2 is not attempted here. In this case $\frac{\hat{E}}{\hat{F}}$ and $\frac{\hat{y}}{\hat{P}}$ are negative, as they are in all cases, but $\frac{\hat{E}}{\hat{P}}$ and $\frac{\hat{y}}{\hat{F}}$ are positive.

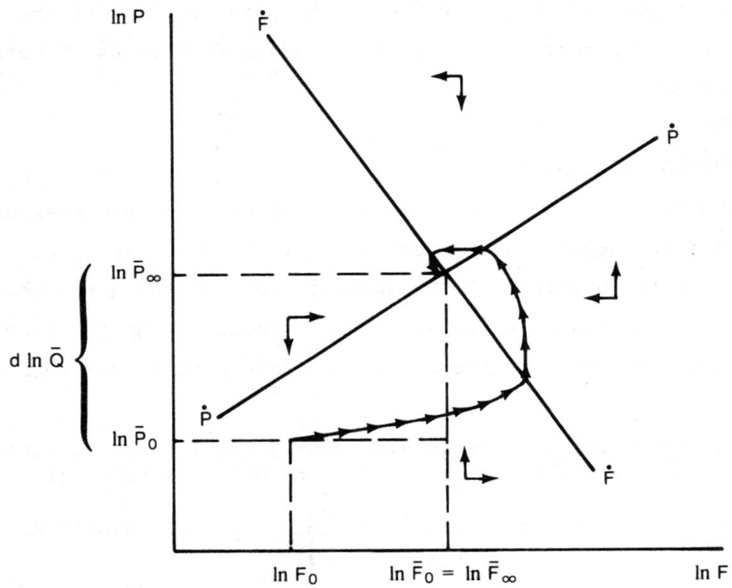

FIGURE 15

single model. The three versions of the model are designed to highlight two reasons why the exchange rate may not attain its new long-run equilibrium value immediately after a shock to the economy: wealth effects and slow price adjustment.

It has been shown that robust conclusions can be drawn regarding the impact effects of a purchase of foreign money with home money by the authorities. The home currency depreciates and home nominal income rises. The price of the home good rises if it is flexible and output is always at its full employment level; home output rises if the price of the home good adjusts slowly when output of the home good exceeds normal supply.

The exchange rate definitely overshoots its new long-run value in the first version of the model; it may overshoot or undershoot in the second and third versions. What is remarkable is not the ambiguity in the second and third versions but the result that the exchange rate must overshoot in the first version. In early studies of exchange rate dynamics in which overshooting is a necessary result, the exchange rate is the only variable which can move in the short run to remove excess supply in the home money market.[38)] During the adjustment to long-run equilibrium other variables, such as home holdings of foreign money or the home price level, change in a way that raises demand for home money, so the home currency must appreciate as the economy adjusts. Here, either the price of the home good or home output is free to increase in the short run. Increases in these variables raise the demand for home money, so the home currency need not depreciate as much as would be necessary if both of these variables were fixed. It remains to be determined whether or not exchange rate overshooting in the very short run in which both

38) The exchange rate must overshoot in the model of Kouri (1976) and the model in the text of Dornbusch (1976a).

prices and output are fixed is a general result which emerges in models which allow for a wider range of financial assets than those of this and earlier studies.

The adjustment process following an exchange market intervention is stable in all three versions of the model.[39)] In the first two versions all of the variables which are free to move in the short run jump initially and then adjust monotonically to their long-run equilibrium values. That the adjustment paths have this simple form is a direct consequence of stability and the fact that there is only one variable which must adjust slowly, home holdings of foreign money or the price of the home good, in each of the first two versions. It is somewhat disappointing, if not too surprising, that it is not possible to reach definite conclusions regarding the adjustment paths of the variables in version three, in which there are two variables which must adjust slowly, without making additional assumptions about the relative sizes of the parameters of the model.

It would be relatively easy to extend the model to allow for interest bearing assets so that the effects of exchange market intervention on the service account could be considered. To begin with it could be assumed that the authorities at home and abroad peg nominal interest rates; then this assumption could be relaxed. As it stands the model could be used to analyze the dynamic effects of other shocks to the economy such as shifts in preferences for home and foreign goods or for home and foreign money, policy actions aimed at the trade account, and conventional fiscal measures.

---

39) If the expectations augmented Phillips curve of footnote 10 rather than equation (6) described wage adjustment in versions two and three of the model additional assumptions would be required in order to guarantee stability.

REFERENCES

Branson, William H., "Asset Markets and Relative Prices in Exchange Rate Determination", Seminar Paper No. 66, Institute for International Economic Studies, University of Stockholm, Stockholm, Sweden, December 1976.

Daniel, Betty C., "Inflation and Unemployment in Open Economies", International Finance Discussion Papers No. 114, Board of Governors of the Federal Reserve System, Washington, D.C., December 1977.

Dornbusch, Rudiger, "Expectations and Exchange Rate Dynamics", Journal of Political Economy, Vol. 84, No. 2, December 1976a.

Dornbusch, Rudiger, "The Theory of Flexible Exchange Rate Regimes and Macroeconomic Policy" The Scandinavian Journal of Economics, Vol. 78, No. 2, 1976b.

Flood, Robert P., "An Example of Exchange Rate Overshooting", unpublished paper, University of Virginia, February 1978.

Girton, Lance and Dale W. Henderson, "Central Bank Operations in Foreign and Domestic Assets Under Fixed and Flexible Exchange Rates" in Peter B. Clark, Dennis E. Logue, and Richard James Sweeney, eds., The Effects of Exchange Rate Adjustments, U.S. Government Printing Office, Washington, D.C., 1977.

Henderson, Dale W., "Modeling the Interdependence of National Money and Capital Markets", American Economic Review, Vol. 67, No. 1, February 1977.

Kouri, Pentti J.K., "The Exchange Rate and the Balance of Payments in the Short Run and in the Long Run: A Monetary Approach", The Scandinavian Journal of Economics, Vol. 78, No. 2, 1976.

Calvo, Guillermo A., and Carlos Alfredo Rodriguez, "A Model of Exchange Rate Determination Under Currency Substitution and Rational Expectations", Journal of Political Economy, Vol. 85, No. 3, June 1977.

Roper, Don, "Two Ingredients of Monetarism in an International Setting", Intermountain Economic Review, Vol. 6, No. 1, 1975.

Salop, Joanne, "Devaluation and the Balance of Trade Under Flexible Wages" in George Horwich and Paul A. Samuelson, eds., Trade, Stability, and Macroeconomics, Academic Press, New York, 1974.

COMMENT ON D.HENDERSON, "THE DYNAMIC EFFECTS OF EXCHANGE MARKET INTERVENTION POLICY: TWO EXTREME VIEWS AND A SYNTHESIS"

Walter S. Salant

Dale Henderson's paper is extremely difficult to read - for me, at least. On the assumption that others may also find it difficult, I shall devote the first part of my comments to an effort to help others understand it, and then I shall raise some questions about wealth effects.

The purpose of the paper is to compare the paths that the exchange rate follows over time in three models when the monetary authority buys foreign money. Two of the models are similar to but not identical with those of Kouri in the Scandinavian Journal of Economics and of Dornbusch in the Journal of Political Economy and the third, created by Henderson in this paper, synthesizes the other two models. In the quasi-Kouri model, wealth affects the demand for goods and for domestic money. Also, prices and wages are perfectly flexible and the supply of labor is fixed, so that output is always at its full-employment level. In the quasi-Dornbusch model, in contrast, changes in real wealth do not affect the demand for output or for money and the price level adjusts only slowly, so that output is variable. In Henderson's synthesizing model, assets are transferable and changes in real wealth do affect the demands for output and money, as in the "Kouri" model, but the price level adjusts slowly and output is a variable, as in the "Dornbusch" model.

Naturally, such a synthesizing model gets complicated. It should be noted, however, that it abstracts from the real world in one respect that must be important for some purposes. Presumably in order to keep the complexity of the model to a minimum, it includes no securities and no explicit rate of interest.

I shall try now to interpret the paper not by considering what happens at all stages in the path of change for one model at a time but by considering what happens in all models for one stage at a time, so as to bring out the differences among the models. I think this may best be done by using a table that summarizes the results.

IMPACT EFFECTS

The "Kouri" model assumes that prices and wages are perfectly flexible, so that output is always at the full-employment level. It also assumes that changes in real wealth affect both the demand for domestic goods and the demand for domestic money. When the monetary authority buys foreign money, the quantity of domestic money rises and creates an excess supply of that money. Demand for domestic goods is not directly affected because wealth is unchanged, the increase in holdings of domestic money being offset by a decrease in domestic residents' holdings of foreign money. But the excess supply of domestic money arising from the public's desire to restore the original currency composition of their total money holdings raises the price of the foreign currency. This, in turn, increases the demand for domestic goods. It does so for two reasons. Insofar as domestic residents hold foreign money, the increase in the domestic price of foreign money increases their wealth and this is one influence that, in this model, increases the demand for domestic goods. Another influence increasing it is that domestic goods have become cheaper relative to foreign goods, causing both domestic and foreign demand to shift from foreign to domestic goods, an influence that operates also in the "Dornbusch" model. These two influences raise the domestic price level.

The proportionate rise in the price of the foreign currency exceeds the proportionate rises in both the domestic price level and the supply of domestic money. Why?

If a change in wealth did not affect the demand for home goods or home money, the price level and the exchange rate would immediately go to their new stationary-state levels. Because in this model a change in wealth does affect those demands, a rise in the foreign currency not only shifts domestic and foreign demand from foreign to domestic goods but increases domestic wealth, and that increases domestic demand for goods, including imports and exportables, thereby raising the price of the foreign currency by more than it would rise otherwise. As a result, the exchange rate must rise by more than the price level if the market for goods is to remain in equilibrium.

Furthermore, if the price of the foreign currency rose only in the same proportion as the supply of domestic money, the excess supply of domestic money, although lower than if the exchange rate had remained unchanged, would not have been eliminated. Demand for domestic money would have increased only by the increase in transactions demand, and that is less than the increase in supply. Since holders of domestic money want to restore the initial proportion of their assets held in foreign currency, they would still seek to convert some of the increment in their domestic money holdings into foreign money. Thus, influences in the money market require that the price of the foreign currency at first rise more than in proportion to the increase in domestic money.

If expectations as to the exchange rate are "static", i.e., no change is expected, the price level also initially rises above its new stationary-state level. But if the overshooting of the exchange rate creates expectations that the price of the foreign currency, having overshot its stationary-state value, will drop back, the domestic price level is less likely to overshoot. The more rapid the expected reversal of the exchange rate, the more likely it is that the price level will undershoot its stationary-state value. (The paper gives two reasons for this.)

Comparison of Effects of Official Purchase of Foreign Currency in Three Models

A. Impact Effects and Adjustments	"Kouri" Model	"Dornbusch" Model	Henderson Model
1. Domestic price of foreign currency (E)	Rises and overshoots stationary equilibrium level.	Rises. Overshoots if for equilibria in home goods and money markets, lower price level requires higher foreign currency price. Undershoots if it requires lower foreign currency price.	Rises and may overshoot or undershoot. Rises less than in "Dornbusch" model if fraction of wealth held in foreign money (f) exceeds weight of foreign goods (k_2) in price index because rise in wealth raises demand for both domestic goods and domestic money ($g_2>0<q_2$). Rises more than in "Dornbusch" model if $f<k_2$.
2. Price of home goods (P)	Rises but may overshoot or undershoot, depending on sensitivity of (a) expectations of change in exchange rate to gap between its current and stationary-state values, and (b) demand for goods to change in wealth. (Greater sensitivity raises probability of undershooting.)	Unchanged at impact; then rises steadily to stationary-state value.	Unchanged at impact. Then rises to stationary-state value. May or may not overshoot in duing so.
3. Domestic output (y)	No change (by assumption of perfect price-wage flexibility and	Rises, then falls back to initial level as price level rises.	Rises, either by more or less than money supply and than in "Dornbusch" model

Comparison of Effects ... (continued)

A. Impact Effects and Adjustments (cont'd)	"Kouri" Model	"Dornbusch" Model	Henderson Model
	perfectly inelastic labor supply)		If fraction of wealth held in foreign money (f) exceeds weight of foreign goods (k_2) in domestic price index, it rises more, the greater is marginal wealth demand for domestic goods and the smaller it is for domestic money, but reverse if $f<k_2$
4. Domestic holdings of foreign money (in foreign money) (F)	Falls immediately but then rises gradually back to initial (and stationary-state) level.	Falls immediately. Change is equal and opposite to change in domestic money but does not affect domestic economy.	Falls immediately. Then rises to stationary-state value. May or may not overshoot in doing so.
5. Domestic acquisition of foreign money ($\dot{F}$)	Becomes positive on impact, then falls steadily to zero.	(Not worked out.)	Predominantly positive, although not necessarily throughout adjustment period.
B. Stationary-State Effects			
1. Domestic price of foreign currency ($\bar{E}$)	Stable at level above initial level in proportion to rise in domestic money.	Same as in "Kouri" model.	Same as in "Kouri" and "Dornbusch" models.

Comparison of Effects ... (continued)

B. Stationary-State Effects (cont'd)	"Kouri" Model	"Dornbusch" Model	Henderson Model
2. Domestic price level ($\bar{P}$)	Stable at level above initial level in proportion to rise in domestic money.	Same as in "Kouri" model.	Same as in "Kouri" and "Dornbusch" models.
3. Domestic output ($\bar{y}$)	Unchanged by assumption.	Unchanged from pre-intervention level.	Unchanged from pre-intervention level.
4. Domestic holdings of foreign money (in foreign money) ($\bar{F}$)	Unchanged from pre-intervention level.	Indeterminate.	Unchanged from pre-intervention level.
5. Domestic acquisition of foreign money ($\bar{\dot{F}}$)	Zero (pre-intervention level).	Pre-intervention level (not necessarily zero).	Zero (pre-intervention level).

In the "Dornbusch" model the price level adjusts slowly and the short-run supply of labor is variable so that output is variable. Also, changes in wealth do not affect the demands for goods or for money. The results may be compared with those of the "Kouri" model by reference to the table.

Henderson's model synthesizes the other two models by assuming that changes in wealth affect the demands for domestic goods and domestic money, as in the "Kouri" model, that prices and wages adjust slowly, and that employment varies with aggregate demand, as in the "Dornbusch" model.

The effect of official purchases of foreign currency on both the "Dornbusch" and Henderson models is to increase domestic output in the short run. It may be worth noting that Dornbusch and Paul Krugman, in a later paper,[1)] pointed out that domestic monetary expansion may have the effect of reducing domestic output. This result occurs if the domestic demand for imports is sufficiently inelastic so that when depreciation of the domestic currency raises import prices, domestic spending on imports rises, the current account deteriorates, and domestic demand for domestic output falls. In the short run, owing to a lag in adjustment of trade flows, foreign demand for domestic output may not rise enough to offset this fall, so total domestic output may decline.[2)] Henderson does not get this result in his model, even as a possibility, because he assumes that the Marshall-Lerner condition is fulfilled. The inclusion of a wealth effect increases the stimulus that depreciation of the domestic currency gives to domestic output if the fraction

---

1) "Flexible Exchange Rates in the Short Run" in Brookings Papers on Economc Activity, 3:1976 (Washington: Brookings Institution, 1976), pp.537-75. The point mentioned is made on p.553.

2) Dornbusch and Krugman note that this possibility was suggested by Niehans in "Some Doubts about the Efficacy of Monetary Policy under Flexible Exchange Rates" in the Journal of International Economics, August 1975.

of wealth held in foreign money (f) exceeds the weight of foreign goods (k_2) in the price index, so a reduction of domestic output is less likely in his model than in the Dornbusch-Krugman model, which has no wealth effect. But a reduction of output is a possibility if the Marshall-Lerner condition is not fulfilled.

Let me end with one observation and one question about wealth effects on the exchange rate. As I understand the influence on exchange rates attributed to changes in wealth, that influence occurs because the aggregated portfolio preferences of asset holders in countries with current-account surpluses for assets denominated in different currencies differ from the aggregated portfolio preferences of asset holders in the countries with current-account deficits. My observation is that the fact of differences in national asset preferences implies something that is concealed in a model with only two "countries" or regions: viz, that, owing to differences in asset preferences among foreign countries, a country's average exchange rate may be affected as much by the distribution of a given current-account imbalance among its partner countries as it is by the size of its total current-account imbalance. In other words, the average exchange rate can be affected by the identity of the foreign countries to which or from which the imbalance shifts wealth. Although this point would emerge explicitly in a model with three or more regions, it is concealed in a two-country model and therefore may be overlooked.

The question that I would raise about the effects of shifts of wealth on the exchange rate concerns the relative quantitative importance of shifts in wealth caused by current-account imbalances and of shifts arising from other causes that are not mentioned in discussions of what determines exchange rates. Shifts arising from current-account imbalances transfer part of the total of wealth among countries. Let us assume that there are national differences in portfolio preferences but that within a country the relative preferences for assets of different currency denominations are unaffected by the absolute size of total national wealth, so that the distribution of world asset preferences (at given relative yields) is affected only by the relative shares of each country in world wealth. Then any given change in the relative national shares of world wealth would affect exchange rates equally, whatever the cause of that change. If that is correct, a shift in relative wealth caused by current-account imbalances would have no more effect on exchange rates than the same shift in relative wealth caused by national differences in the rate of domestic capital formation.

Casual observation, in fact, suggests that imbalances in current accounts are very small in relation to total wealth, so small as to raise a question how great, in general, is the effect on the foreign-exchange markets of the shifts that they cause in the distribution of aggregate wealth among countries compared to the effect of the much larger shifts caused by differences in national rates of domestic capital formation.

If current-account imbalances are less important than differences in national rates of domestic capital formation as an influence on the distribution of wealth among countries, this fact raises a question as to whether they do not have less effect on exchange rates. But it only raises the question; it does not, alone, imply the answer. I think one must compare the distribution within countries of the changes in asset-holding caused by current-account imbalances with the distribution of such changes caused by differences in domestic capital formation. Perhaps the difference among countries in asset preferences of those firms and households whose wealth is changed by current-account imbalances is greater than in the case of firms and households whose relative wealth is changed by differences in domestic capital formation.

In these last comments I am raising, not answering, questions. It appears that we need further analytical and empirical research about whose wealth is changed and about the relative asset preference of those economic entities before we can form some judgment about the relative influence on exchange rates of the wealth effect of current-account imbalances, which is now receiving much attention, and the wealth effect of differences in domestic capital formation, which appears to be totally ignored.

COMMENT ON D.HENDERSON, "THE DYNAMIC EFFECTS OF EXCHANGE MARKET INTERVENTION POLICY: TWO EXTREME VIEWS AND A SYNTHESIS"

Jürgen Siebke

1. The author takes up the discussion of exchange rate determination which has been based on the assumption of continuous asset market equilibrium. Within this portfolio balance approach of particular interest are the possible adjustment processes which move the macroeconomic system from momentary to long-run equilibrium. Henderson presents two adjustment mechanisms: (1) the asset-accumulation process via current account surpluses as formulated by Kouri and (2) the price-adjustment process via a relation between unemployment and the departure from potential output as formulated by Dornbusch. These two different adjustment-processes Henderson calls "extreme views". This is a question of semantics. If one agrees that the main feature of the portfolio balance approach is the assumption of differential adjustment speeds in commodity and asset markets then this characterization seems overemphasized.

If one looks through the highly mathematical paper one realizes that Henderson is mainly concerned with the dynamic responses of the macroeconomic system and its stability properties when exogenous shocks disturb the stationary equilibrium. And I guess the author chooses intervention policy as such an exogenous shock for the purpose of not complicating additionally the technical analysis. A consequence of this simplification is for instance that interest rates are no arguments of the asset demand functions.

In section III and IV the Kouri-model and the Dornbusch-model are reformulated with only some modifications. Therefore, most of what has been said to both models holds also for the versions presented by Henderson.

2. In addition to the original Kouri-model the domestic price level and the rate of exchange do not amount anymore to the same thing. The domestic price level is now an endogenous variable because the model allows for changes in the terms of trade. The outcome of this modification clarifies the discussion about the main feature of the portfolio balance approach. From the Kouri-model the statement has been derived that the asset markets determine the exchange rate. This statement is now not anymore correct. The exchange rate and the domestic price level are simultaneously determined by the asset market equilibrium and the commodity market equilibrium.

3. The modification of the Dornbusch-model is somewhat more significant. Because of integrating only domestic and foreign money real expenditure and the money demand are not dependent on interest rates. By this, the macroeconomic system becomes recursive, at least this effect can only be avoided when using the special price index of equation (1) to deflate the nominal values. This can immediately be derived from the stationary equilibrium conditions. One gets these conditions when imposing restriction (24) on the four equations (23). Now, equation (23c) determines the full employment level which is not affected by intervention policy. Given this income level the equilibrium conditions for the goods market (23a) and for the money market (23b) determine simultaneously the stationary values of the price level ($\bar{P}$) and the exchange rate ($\bar{E}$) in case the deflator is represented by the weighted sum (1) of the output price (P) and the asset price (E). If, as usually is done, the nominal values are deflated by the price of the home good (P) then the money market determines the long-run price level and the goods market the stationary value of the exchange rate. This outcome is quite the opposite to the original Kouri-model. Again one might doubt whether such a strong separation of the determination of the price-level and the exchange rate is correct

or a coherent description of the long-run equilibrium in an open economy.

It seems difficult to interprete the model for the momentary equilibrium consisting of equations (23a-d) as an analysis of a policy measure on the exchange market. This illustrates the foregoing argument that Henderson is more interested in the adjustment process itself and less in an analysis of intervention policy. One can cancel equation (23d) because it gives no information for the explanation of the adjustment process. In the remaining three equations one finds only the money supply Q as a financial stock variable. Now, a variation of Q shall represent an intervention policy measure. But this exogenous shock is identical to a monetary expansion in an economy with a helicopter money supply mechanisms. And now one is even free to give the variable E (exchange rate) another meaning; for instance: E may represent the price of the existing real capital stock. Then one has a model for a closed economy, without even changing the signs of the partial derivatives of the equilibrium conditions.

4. Combining both adjustment mechanisms provides a model representing Henderson's synthesis. This integration clearly complicates the analysis. If one tries to figure out "what makes the model tick" one has to start with the pure price-adjustment process. Given the price level and using again this variable as deflator, equation (28b) determines the output and both variables determine on the goods market (equation 28a) the exchange rate. Therefore Henderson is forced to compare the impact effects with the model of the previous sector and not with the Kouri-model. And here one can explain why the increase in the exchange rate must be less: the wealth-argument reduces the excess money supply, therefore less increase in output is necessary to restore equilibrium on the money market. A lower increase in output requires a smaller increase in the exchange rate to clear the money market. In addition, the wealth effect in the expenditure function dampens the positive impact effect of the exchange rate.

Of course, sketching out the possible time paths of the adjustment process described by the equation system (28) can not be done so easily and heuristically. Statements about the time path must remain ambiguous unless special cases are analysed. Movements of the exchange rate may be cyclical. This might have some political-judgement implications. It is unrealistic to assume that there will ever be a free float. Central banks will continue to intervene in the exchange markets to smooth out so-called erratic swings. But according to Henderson's analysis the outcome of such interventions might be cyclical swings. Then central banks will produce and not prevent useless exchange rates cycles.

5. In a comment to the Kouri-model Alexander Swoboda[1] regrets that the discussion of stability seems somewhat unsatisfactory because no formal analysis had been provided. Henderson's paper fills this gap for a more complex adjustment mechanism.

---

1) Swoboda, A.K., Comment on P.J. Kouri, in: The Scandinavian Journal of Economics, Vol. 78 (1976), S.3o7.

EXCHANGE-MARKET INTERVENTIONS AND OPEN-MARKET OPERATIONS AS INSTRUMENTS OF ACTIVE EMPLOYMENT POLICY UNDER FLEXIBLE EXCHANGE RATES

Harmen Lehment

I. INTRODUCTION

One of the main concerns about a flexible exchange-rate system relates to the possibility that governments or central banks may conduct exchange-market interventions with the aim of improving the economic performance of their countries at the expense of others. One of the most prominent cases of such "beggar-my-neighbour" policies through "dirty floating" is usually stated as follows: A central bank causes a depreciation of the domestic currency by purchasing foreign money. With rigid domestic producer prices, the devaluation improves the competitiveness of domestic factors of production. Employment increases domestically while it falls abroad, i.e., unemployment is "exported".

In order to avoid unfair manipulations of exchange rates the International Monetary Fund has demanded international surveillance over exchange-rate policies. In its "Principles for the Guidance of Members Exchange Rate Policies" and its "Principles of Fund Surveillance over Exchange Rate Policies" the IMF establishes a number of rules which mainly concern intervention policies in the exchange market.[1)]

Economic theory, however, has shown that countries may cause a devaluation of their currency not only by purchasing foreign currencies but also by purchasing domestic or foreign securities

---

1) Cf. IMF (1977), Appendix II., pp.1o7-1o9.

(Mussa (1976, p.239)). A question of interest then is, whether and to what extent the employment effects of exchange-market interventions differ from those of open-market policies. Section II will deal with this question in the framework of a Keynesian two-country model with perfect capital mobility. Particular attention will be paid to the channel through which disturbances are transmitted internationally. Moreover, it will be analysed whether the results of the model are modified by the introduction of preannounced monetary targets which are stated net of currency holdings by non-residents.

In Section III the assumptions of the model will be altered by introducing real-wage rigidity. Recent contributions have drawn attention to the point that with real-wage rigidity the short-run employment effects of a monetary expansion under a regime of flexible exchange rates tend to be smaller for small countries than for large countries, and that short-run employment effects may be larger if the depreciation effect of a monetary expansion is prevented, or at least reduced, by a simultaneous sale of foreign exchange reserves (Giersch, 1977) or a simultaneous monetary expansion abroad (Dornbusch and Krugman, 1976).

Section IV summarizes the main results of the analysis and discusses possible implications for the present controversy about an international coordination of monetary policies.

II. MONETARY POLICIES AND EMPLOYMENT WITH RIGID NOMINAL WAGES

The employment effects of exchange-market interventions and open-market operations will be analysed in a standard two-country model with perfect capital mobility:

(1) $Y = E(Y,Y',i,\tau)$

(2) $Y' = E'(Y,Y',i,\tau)$

(3) $\frac{M}{P} = L(Y,i)$

(4) $\frac{M'}{p'} = L'(Y',i)$

(5) $\tau = \frac{p}{p'e}$

where

$Y(Y')$ = domestic (foreign) real ouput

$E(E')$ = demand for domestic (foreign) real output

i = real interest rate

τ = terms of trade

$M(M')$ = domestic (foreign) money supply

$L(L')$ = demand for domestic (foreign) money

$p\ (p')$ = domestic (foreign) producer price level

e = exchange rate (domestic currency per unit of foreign currency).

The partial derivatives are:

$$1 > E_Y, E'_Y, E_{Y'}, E'_{Y'}, E_Y + E'_Y, E_{Y'} + E'_{Y'} > 0$$[2)]

$$L_Y, L'_{Y'}, E'_\tau > 0$$

$$E_i, E'_i, L_i, L'_i, E_\tau < 0$$

$$E_\tau = -E'_\tau$$

Equations (1), (2), (3), (4) stand for equilibrium in the markets for domestic goods, foreign goods, domestic money and foreign money respectively. The perfectly integrated market for securities being the fifth market in the five-market system is left out because of Walras' law. To simplify the analysis initial values of p, p', e and τ have been set equal to unity.

---

2) $E_Y + E'_Y, (E_{Y'} + E'_{Y'}) > 0$ indicate that the domestic (foreign) marginal propensity to save is positive.

Under Keynesian assumptions p and p' are constant.[3)] Moreover, Keynesian models assume that domestic (foreign) nominal wages w(w') are rigid. Unemployment of labour and technical capacity is due to the fact that either money prices and wages are too high at a given level of nominal demand, or that nominal demand is too low at a given level of wages and prices. A reduction of money prices and wages or a rise in nominal demand by increasing the money supply or the velocity of money will remove unemployment without a change in w/p and w'/p'. A simultaneous increase in nominal demand or a reduction of money prices and wages in both countries, which is neutral in respect to the exchange rate, will raise domestic and foreign employment at constant terms of trade and constant real wages.[4)]

Taking total differentials and writing the system in matrix form one obtains:

$$\begin{bmatrix} -(1-E_y) & E_{y'} & E_i & E_\tau \\ E'_Y & -(1-E'_{Y'}) & E'_i & -E_\tau \\ L_Y & 0 & L_i & 0 \\ 0 & L'_{Y'} & L'_i & 0 \end{bmatrix} \begin{bmatrix} dY \\ dY' \\ di \\ d\tau \end{bmatrix} = \begin{bmatrix} dA_1 \\ dA_2 \\ dA_3 \\ dA_4 \end{bmatrix}$$

where dA_1, dA_2, dA_3, dA_4 stand for autonomous increases in net supply on the respective markets.

An expansionary domestic open-market policy will raise the net supply of domestic money by dA_3. A purchase of foreign exchange by the domestic central bank will also increase the net supply of

---

3) With constant values of p and p' a change in τ is equal to the inverse movement of e.
4) The domestic real wage is w/ [(1-k)p + kp'e], where k is the share of imports in domestic consumption.

domestic money by dA_3 but simultaneously reduce the net supply for foreign money by dA_4; the excess supply of domestic currency must be equal to the excess demand for foreign currency so that $dA_3 = -dA_4$.

The effects of the two policies are stated in Table 1:[5)]

TABLE 1

	Y	Y'	i	τ
open market operation	+	-	-	-
exchange-market intervention	++	--	?	--

As can be seen, both the positive effects on domestic employment and the negative effects on foreign employment are stronger when the domestic money supply is increased through purchases of foreign currency than when it is increased through purchases of foreign or domestic securities.[6)] This result may be illustrated by the

5) For the algebraic results see the Appendix I.

6) It can also be shown that a given increase in Y is connected with smaller negative effects on Y' in the case of purchasing securities than in the case of purchasing foreign currency. The proof is as follows:
Open-market operations and exchange-market interventions have the same effect on Y when

$$(6)\ dY = \frac{\delta Y}{\delta A_3} dA_3 + \frac{\delta Y}{\delta A_4} dA_4 = k \frac{\delta Y}{\delta A_3} dA_3 \mid dA_3 = -dA_4;$$

$k = 1 + \frac{\delta Y}{\delta A_4} / \frac{\delta Y}{\delta A_3}$ is the relation between the increase in M resulting from buying securities and the increase in M resulting from buying foreign exchange. The exchange-market intervention has a stronger effect on Y' if

$$(7)\ \frac{\delta Y'}{\delta A_3} - \frac{\delta Y'}{\delta A_4} < k \cdot \frac{\delta Y'}{\delta A_3}.$$

Using the equations A_2 and A_6 of the Appendix and the information about k, (7) becomes:

$$(8)\ (E_i + E'_i) L_Y + (1 - E_Y - E'_Y) (L_i + L'_i)$$
$$< (1-E_Y-E'_Y) L'_i \{1 + (1-E'_{Y'}-E_{Y'}) L_i / [(E_i+E'_i) L'_{Y'} + (1-E'_{Y'}-E_{Y'}) L'_i]\},$$

and after some operations:

fact that the exchange-market intervention can be regarded as an expansionary domestic open-market policy ($dA_3 > 0$) plus a contractionary foreign open-market policy ($dA_4 < 0$) which amplifies the depressive effect on foreign employment and the stimulating effect on domestic employment.

THE INTERNATIONAL TRANSMISSION OF DISTURBANCES

Why does a domestic monetary expansion have positive effects on domestic output but negative effects on foreign output (and vice versa)? The traditional Keynesian answer to this question is that the increase in the domestic money supply will cause a currency depreciation and a decline in the terms of trade which improves the competitive position of the domestic factors of production as against foreign factors.[7)] Hence, the negative effects on the foreign economy are seen to be transmitted through a change in the terms of trade.

The change in the terms of trade is, however, not a sufficient condition for a decline in foreign output. This can be seen most clearly from the foreign goods market equation (2): the negative effect of a fall in τ on Y' (a substitution effect) may be offset by the positive demand effects that result from the fall in i and from the rise in Y (an income effect), which are also brought about by the domestic monetary expansion. A better way to explain the transmission of monetary disturbances would be to analyse the effects of a domestic monetary expansion on the foreign velocity of money. The reason is that when foreign producer prices are fixed,

---

6) (continued)

(9) $(E_i+E'_i)L'_{Y'}\ [(E_i+E'_i)L_Y+(1-E_Y-E'_Y)L_i]$

$+ (E_i+E'_i)L_Y(1-E'_{Y'}-E_{Y'})L'_i > 0.$

The left hand side is positive. Thus the condition stated in (7) holds true.

7) Cf.e.g. League of Nations (1944), Robinson (1947).

a disturbance originating in the domestic country will affect output abroad through changes in the nominal demand for foreign products. In a flexible exchange-rate system the money supply is exogenous so that these changes in nominal demand have to be brought about through changes in the foreign velocity of money.

In the standard model the demand for money and, hence, velocity are independent from the terms of trade.[8)] Thus, an appreciation of the foreign currency and the corresponding change in the terms of trade which worsens the international competitive position of the foreign country does not imply that the nominal demand for foreign products falls. A domestic monetary expansion, then, has a negative effect on output abroad not because it changes the terms of trade, but because it reduces the foreign velocity of money either directly (through exchange-market interventions) or indirectly by lowering the real rate of interest (through open-market policies).[9)]

---

8) If the terms of trade are included in the demand for money function it is still doubtful whether they have a positive or a negative sign. Recent work in the field of exchange-rate expectations (which have been neglected in this paper) suggests that an appreciation of the exchange rate, which is identical to an increase in the terms of trade when producer prices are constant, may give rise to the expectation of a future depreciation (the case of adaptive expectations discussed by Niehans (1975) and Dornbusch (1976)). The expected depreciation will, then, cause a transitory increase of the interest rate in the country which has appreciated relative to other countries. Thus an increase in the terms of trade may have a positive rather than a negative effect on a country's interest rate and, hence, on its velocity of money.

9) That in the standard model the interest rate is a better indicator for the influence of a domestic disturbance on foreign output than the terms of trade also holds true for fiscal policies. It has been demonstrated by Mundell (1968, Ch. 18) that the effect of a fiscal expansion on the terms of trade is ambiguous, while the rate of interest will certainly increase. If employment abroad depended on the change in the terms of trade one would expect the output effect also to be equivocal. A fiscal expansion, however, will certainly increase employment abroad. This result is indicated by the rise in the interest rate which implies an increase in the foreign velocity of money.

PREANNOUNCED MONETARY TARGETS AND THE EFFECTIVENESS OF EXCHANGE-MARKET INTERVENTIONS

It has been shown that a domestic monetary expansion has larger effects on foreign employment when it results from a purchase of foreign currency than when it results from a purchase of securities. The reason is that in the former case the domestic authorities do not only directly change the supply of domestic money but also the net supply of foreign money. The domestic central bank's ability to "make foreign monetary policy" is, however, automatically reduced when the foreign central bank has announced a money supply target which is stated net of currency holdings by non-residents.[10)]

Assume that the Bank of Japan purchases a certain amount of dollars from U.S. residents. This operation will reduce the U.S. money supply stated on a domestic residents basis below its target value. In order to reach its target the Fed increases the money supply correspondingly by purchasing securities from domestic residents. The attempt of the Japanese central bank to make a restrictive U.S. open-market policy is, then, automatically neutralised by a counteracting open-market operation of the U.S. monetary authorities. In this case the effects of increasing the Japanese money supply by purchasing foreign currency and by purchasing securities are the same.[11)] This result also holds true if the Bank of Japan buys some part of the dollars from non-U.S. residents and if the Fed purchases securities also from non-residents, provided that in both cases the share of non-residents is the same.

A reverse example is the case where the Bank of England sells dollars from its exchange reserves, including borrowed reserves, in order to prevent a decline in the value of the pound against the dollar. The sale of dollars will increase the U.S. money supply above its target value and cause a restrictive open-market operation by the U.S. monetary authorities. Thus, there

---

10) Official monetary targets are usually stated this way.

11) In the model a purchase of foreign currency plus an automatic foreign open-market policy to replace the outflow of foreign money can be written as $[dA_3 - dA_4] + dA_4 = dA_3$, which is identical to a domestic open-market policy.

will be a change in the net supply of pounds but not in the net supply of dollars. This result, however, will also be obtained when the Bank of England sells securities instead of dollars. Under these circumstances a dollar credit to Britain in order to prevent a decline in the value of the pound is of little help. To keep the pound from falling the net supply of pounds must be reduced relative to the net supply of dollars. When the net supply of dollars is fixed by a U.S. monetary target on a domestic resident base, the British monetary authorities can avoid a devaluation of their currency only by reducing the net supply of pounds; but this can be done by a contractionary open-market policy and does not require foreign-exchange reserves or international credits.

III. MONETARY POLICIES AND EMPLOYMENT WITH DOWNWARD RIGIDITY OF REAL WAGES

It has been shown in the previous section that the domestic monetary expansion through open-market operations or exchange-market interventions lowers the domestic terms of trade, when producer prices are rigid. Thus, the real wage falls at home while it rises abroad.

In this section we shall analyse the effects which result from resistance to reductions in domestic real wages. For this purpose we introduce into the model the assumption that a decline in the terms of trade will cause a domestic wage and price push,[12)] represented by an increase in p, which stabilises τ at its initial value.

As can be seen from (1) - (5) a rise in p causes an excess demand for domestic money ($dA_3^* < 0$) and has the same effect as a restrictive open-market policy.

An excess supply of domestic money resulting from an open-market policy which lowers the terms of trade is, then, exactly

12) A symmetric increase in w and p permits to maintain the Keynesian assumption that output is varied at a given ratio w/p.

offset by an excess demand for domestic money resulting from a rise in domestic producer prices which raises the terms of trade to its previous value (i.e. $dA_3 + dA_3^* = 0$). As the initial excess supply of domestic money is completely absorbed by an increase in prices, the effect on domestic and foreign employment is zero. The only change is in the components of the terms of trade: the domestic currency is depreciated by the same rates as the one by which domestic producer prices rise.

If the domestic central bank purchases foreign currency instead of securities the decline in τ will be larger. Subsequently, the increase in p and the price-induced rise in the demand for domestic money will also be larger. Whereas in the previous case the additional demand for money was equal to the amount supplied by the open-market operation ($dA_3 = -dA_3^*$), the exchange-market intervention does not only cause an excess demand for foreign currency but also a price-induced demand for domestic money which exceeds the monetary expansion. Thus, there will be an excess demand for both currencies while the terms of trade remain constant. As we know from fixed exchange-rate models, a monetary contraction in both countries, which leaves the terms of trade unchanged, causes a fall in both domestic and foreign output.[13)]

Therefore, we arrive at the perhaps surprising result that with downward rigidity of real wages a monetary expansion through a purchase of foreign currency (which is not neutralised by the foreign monetary authorities) will not only cause a fall in foreign but also in domestic employment. The effects of open-market operations and exchange-market interventions under downward real-wage rigidity are summarized in Table 2.

TABLE 2

	Y	Y'	i	τ
open-market operation	0	0	0	0
exchange-market intervention	–	–	+	0

13) Cf.e.g. Mundell (1968 ch. 18). An algebraic proof is given in the Appendix II.

The results of Table 2 indicate that in order to increase employment, the domestic monetary authorities have to prevent the decline in the terms of trade resulting from a domestic open market expansion rather than to enlarge it by increasing the demand for foreign currency. The exchange rate and, hence, the terms of trade will be stabilised, if the domestic central bank combines its sale of domestic currency against securities with a sale of foreign currency against securities. In this case the net supply of both currencies can be increased without a change in the exchange rate, and output in the two countries rises.[14)] Again, the positive effects of a monetary expansion on domestic employment are larger when there is an exchange-market intervention. However, while with flexible real wages the domestic employment was additionally raised by a purchase of foreign currency, downward inflexibility of real wages requires a sale of foreign currency in order to raise output.

The ability of the domestic central bank to increase the net supply of foreign currency is, of course, limited by the amount of its foreign liquid reserves. But there are other ways to prevent a decline in the terms of trade which results from a domestic monetary expansion, e.g., a simultaneous expansionary open-market operation of the foreign central bank or a reduction in foreign money wages[15)] and prices which has the same effect on the terms of trade and on employment as a foreign open-market expansion.

---

14) When real wages are rigid downward the system is similar to a system of fixed exchange rates in which the less expansionary country is the reference country, i.e., the country which sets the pace for the international expansion. Just as in a fixed rate system an increase in the money supply through open market policies has no effect on employment, while a purchase of foreign currency reduces the net supply of the reserve currency and, hence, lowers the international level of demand in a similar way as a monetary contraction in the reserve country under fixed rates would do. In this situation a country can only expand when the other country expands as well.

15) A reduction in foreign money wages to stabilise the terms of trade leaves foreign real wages constant.

FULL EMPLOYMENT ABROAD

So far it has been assumed that in both countries unemployment is not the result of excessively high real wages but that it is due to a "liquidity shortage", i.e., real wages are at their full employment level but both money prices and wages are too high at the existing level of nominal demand. Under these circumstances it is possible to raise employment in both countries without a change in the terms of trade and in real wages.

Now we shall regard a situation of full employment abroad and assume that a fall in the nominal demand for foreign goods will still lead to a decline in Y' but not in p', but that a rise in demand will cause an increase in p' at a constant level of Y'. For the domestic economy we retain the previous assumptions. In this case the effects of a domestic monetary expansion through purchasing securities or foreign currency are identical to those listed in Tables 1 and 2. The effect of a simultaneous monetary expansion in the two countries will, however, be different. In the previous case a symmetrical increase in nominal demand was neutral in respect to both e and τ. But under conditions of full employment abroad an increase in the money supplies of both countries, which leaves e unchanged, will cause a rise in p' and, hence, a decline in τ; a monetary expansion abroad, then, cannot offset the reduction in τ which results from the increase in the domestic money supply.

Under these circumstances an increase in domestic employment is not possible without a reduction in domestic real wages.[16)] Thus, the effects of open-market and exchange-market policies on domestic employment depend crucially on the degree to which domestic real wages are reduced. When real wages are completely rigid in the downward direction, the results of Table 2 hold. When real wages are fully flexible so that there is no wage and price push to

---

16) When increases in labour productivity are taken into account the condition is that the rise in real wages must be lower than the increase in labour productivity.

compensate for the change in the terms of trade, the results are those stated in Table 1. In intermediate cases the effects are combinations of these two extremes.

Real wages may be reduced either voluntarily or involuntarily because of "money illusion" or because nominal wages are fixed by wage contracts and cannot be increased until the contracts expire.

Real wages are reduced voluntarily when workers or their organisations

- recognise that a decline in the real wage is required to raise employment, i.e., there must be "economic realism" on the part of the workers (Johnson, 1972, p.1561), and
- are willing to bear the cost (lower real wages) of increasing employment, i.e., unemployment must be above the "natural rate".

An involuntary reduction of real wages resulting from "money illusion" means that workers do not recognise a fall in their real wages due to an increase in prices (here: import prices) and, thus, do not claim for higher nominal wages.[17] As "money illusion" is likely to be a transitory phenomenon, it can be assumed that an increase in M will raise the level of domestic employment only temporarily.[18]

---

17) Cf. Lehment (1978). This concept of "money illusion" has to be distinguished from what may be called "nominal illusion", which means that a reduction of real wages through an increase in the price level is preferred to a reduction through a cut in nominal wages. Some authors (e.g. Vaubel, 1976, Part. II; Giersch, 1976) reserve the term "money illusion" to the case where an increase in domestic producer prices is not recognised, and use the expression "exchange-rate illusion" when an increase in import prices remains unnoticed.

18) There is the possibility of keeping employment at an artificially high level by producing a steady stream of new illusions, e.g. by increasing the money supply at a rate which is always higher than the rate that the public had expected. But this strategy will put the economy on the road to hyperinflation.

The same holds when workers are fully aware of an involuntary reduction in their real wages, but are not able to increase their nominal wages immediately because these are fixed by running wage contracts.[19] In this case the real wage reduction and the positive effects on domestic employment will disappear when the contracts expire.

Two theses have been advanced as to the duration of the involuntary increase in domestic employment (Dornbusch and Krugman, 1976, Giersch, 1977).

First, the increase in employment will last longer if both M and M' rise symmetrically than if only M is expanded. In the latter case, the increase in import prices is brought about through a depreciation of the domestic currency which immediately follows the rise in M. In the former case, the exchange rate remains constant and the increase in import prices results from a rise in p' which takes some time because of the usual lag in the reaction of producer prices to a monetary expansion. This price lag can be ascribed to "money illusion" or to contractual rigidities abroad. Thus it may be said that a coordinated monetary expansion has larger short-run employment effects because in this case the effects of foreign and domestic illusions or contractual rigidities are added, whereas the unilateral domestic expansion has to rely only on domestic illusions or domestic rigidities.

Second, the short-run increase in employment resulting from a rise in M will be stronger the larger the domestic country. One explanation is that a large country has a relatively low share of import goods in consumption. Thus, a rise in import prices may not be recognised as fast as in a small country with a high content of imports. Another explanation may be derived from the fact that

---

19) The role of long-term contracts for the employment effects of monetary policies is analysed in recent articles by Fischer (1977) and by Phelps and Taylor (1977).

a domestic monetary expansion tends to have a depressive effect on the foreign economy. The larger the domestic country and the increase in the money supply, the stronger will be the reduction in foreign output and the more likely is an early monetary expansion abroad to offset the negative effect. As has been shown in the previous paragraph, an increase in M' in addition to the rise in M tends to strengthen the short run employment effects.

Whereas in the short-run the employment effects of open-market operations or exchange-market interventions may differ depending on whether the country is large or small, or on whether there is an additional monetary expansion in other countries as well, in the longer run output will only increase if necessary reductions in real wages are voluntarily accepted. Otherwise the monetary expansion will cause only more inflation but not more employment.

IV. SUMMARY AND IMPLICATIONS FOR THE PRESENT CONTROVERSY ABOUT AN INTERNATIONAL COORDINATION OF MONETARY POLICIES

There is a startling difference in the international reaction to a monetary expansion under nominal-wage rigidity, discussed in Section II, and under real-wage rigidity discussed in Section III. In the first case we have the situation of a classic "beggar-my-neighbour" policy, where non-expansionary countries complain about expansionary countries. The second case represents the "modern" situation, where expansionary countries complain about non-expansionary countries.

Let us first turn to the case of money-price and wage rigidity in both countries. According to the standard model, an increase in the domestic money supply through purchases of securities or foreign currency will raise nominal demand and employment at home, while it reduces nominal demand and employment abroad. The latter effect is not due to a decline in the domestic terms of trade, which improves the competitiveness of domestic relative to foreign factors of production, but results from the fact that a domestic monetary expansion reduces the velocity of money abroad either directly (exchange-market intervention) or indirectly via a fall in the interest rate (open-market policy).

Thus, while an increase in the domestic money supply is a correct policy if unemployment is due to a shortage of nominal demand, as it was in the Great Depression, it will simultaneously increase the demand problem abroad. In this case the appropriate step for the foreign country is not to complain about "exchange dumping"[2o] and to demand a reversal of the domestic monetary policy, but to expand its own money supply as well in order to offset the negative effects of the domestic expansion on the nominal demand for foreign products.

Foreign neutralisation policy has to be larger when the domestic money supply is increased by purchasing foreign exchange than when it is increased by purchasing securities. The reason is that an exchange-market intervention has a stronger negative effect on foreign nominal demand than an open-market operation which raises domestic demand by the same amount. Thus a monetary expansion by purchasing securities is preferable to a purchase of foreign currency as it avoids unnecessarily large compensation policies abroad.

In the case of downward rigidity of real wages, discussed in Section III, an isolated monetary expansion by one country will

---

2o) The expression "exchange dumping" is highly misleading. The aim of a dumping strategy is to drive competitors out of the market by lowering prices and to raise prices later when the competitors have disappared. A real devaluation of the currency, however, will affect the wide spectrum of importable and exportable goods, and it is a rather futile attempt to gain a dominating market position in the whole tradables sector! Moreover, dumping implicitly assumes that the struggle for employment is a zero-sum game. But it has been shown in the paper that with spare capacity of labour and capital equipment in both countries employment may be raised domestically and abroad without a change in the competitive positions.

lower its terms of trade and give rise to a wage and price push which has a negative impact on the effective demand for the country's products. It has been shown that in this case a purchase of securities by the domestic central bank will have no effect on domestic and foreign employment. A purchase of foreign currency will even lower employment in both countries, as the induced increase in money prices and wages more than compensates the effect of expanding the money supply.

When both countries are in a situation, where an increase in the nominal demand for their products increases output at constant producer prices, the decline in the terms of trade and, hence, the wage and price push, which would result from an isolated domestic monetary expansion, can be prevented by a simultaneous monetary expansion abroad which stabilises the terms of trade. In this case, domestic and foreign employment can be increased without a change in real wages. This scenario provides the "ideal" background for the demand for coordinated monetary expansion.

When the diagnosis of a deficiency of effective demand applies domestically but not for the fully employed foreign economy where a monetary expansion will, at least in the longer run, raise prices but not output, a sustained increase in domestic employment is only possible when workers voluntarily accept a reduction in their real wages. An involuntary cut in real wages, resulting from "money illusion" or from contractual rigidities will usually have only short-lived employment effects. A simultaneous monetary expansion abroad may augment the amount of "money illusion" so that for the domestic country the short-run, though not the long-run, Phillips-curve is less steep. But to build a claim for an international monetary expansion on short-run Phillips-curves is highly questionable: in the longer run the increase in the foreign money supply has no positive effects on domestic employment while causing additional inflation abroad.

Moveover, a sale of foreign currency in connection with an expansionary domestic open-market policy in order to bring about an international monetary expansion tends to be either ineffective or unnecessary. It is ineffective when the monetary authorities abroad oppose an increase in foreign nominal demand and absorb the additional foreign liquidity created by the domestic central bank's exchange-market intervention. The sterilisation may take place automatically when the monetary authorities abroad have stated a money supply target net of holdings by non-residents. A sale of foreign exchange to residents of the foreign country will, then, immediately raise the money supply above its target value and cause the required neutralisation policies.

When, on the other hand, the monetary authorities abroad regard an increase in foreign liquidity as desirable they can pursue the expansionary monetary policy themselves so that an exchange-market intervention by the domestic central bank is not necessary.

While a sale of liquid foreign reserves to increase nominal demand abroad is either ineffective or unnecessary, it may cause additional costs connected with foreign sterilisation policies, when the increase in demand is not desired. Thus the negative verdict about purchases of foreign currency as an instrument of active employment policy can be extended to exchange-market interventions in form of selling foreign currency.

Whereas a monetary expansion through open-market operations has been found preferable to exchange-market interventions, we have not yet discussed whether it is better to overcome a deficiency of effective demand by policies, including monetary policies, which raise aggregate nominal demand (or its growth path) or by a lowering of wages and prices (or their growth paths). The answer will mainly depend on the desired rate of inflation. In the Great Depression the situation was clear. Monetary growth rates were negative and prices declined. Price level stability was compatible with a substantial rise in monetary growth rates to increase nominal demand.

Today the policy problem is more difficult. In all countries, except perhaps Switzerland, rates of inflation are too high in respect to the target of price level stability. Growth paths of nominal demand are still well above the level which is required to maintain full employment at stable prices.

Under the aspect of a return to both full employment and price level stability an increase in effective demand by lowering the path of wages and prices is, in this situation, preferable to measures which raise the path of nominal demand. If there is resistence especially against a reduction in the rate of wage increases there may be some scope for incomes policies.[21] Those who argue that even in the present situation of undesirably high rates of inflation an increase in the growth rate of nominal demand to raise employment is preferable because the lower wage and price

---

21) We may distinguish between three types of incomes policies: The first type consists of policies to improve the standard of information in the private sector in order to avoid price and wage-setting decisions which are based on wrong expectations about the future economic development (we may call this "incomes policy 0"). One of the most important measures in this context is a reliable announcement of the course of fiscal and monetary policies. To prevent excessive wage and price increases, it will be especially helpful when the government makes it quite clear that there will be no accommodation by expansionary demand policies. The better the information on which decisions in the private sector are based the better is the quality of the "implicit guidelines" which are contained in these informations.
Apart from raising wages and prices too much (or too little) because of wrong expectations, firms or trade unions may - in an attempt to exploit a monopolistic market position - voluntarily fix prices or wages at levels which are not compatible with full employment.
One possibility, then, is to "tame" the monopoly by what Haberler (1971) has called "incomes policy I": moral suasion, tax-based incomes policies, or wage and price controls. An alternative is to remove the monopolistic position itself by measures to promote competition in goods and labour markets (Haberler's "incomes policy II").

paths are too difficult,[22] will easily find themselves in the position to accomodate, with the same argument, rates of inflation which are much above the present rate.[23]

As to the present controversy about an international co-ordination of monetary policies, the argument for a simultaneous monetary expansion by several countries has been found to be justified only if in each of these countries there is a shortage of effective demand so that a rise in the path of nominal demand leads to a sustained increase in employment. On the other hand it has been argued that in face of the present rates of inflation an expansion of effective demand should be brought about by lowering the path of wages and prices instead of raising the path of nominal demand. Insofar as the diagnosis of a shortage of effective demand applies internationally, the situation, then, calls for a world-wide wage and price restraint, guided and supported, if necessary, by some appropriate incomes policies, rather than for an international monetary "reflation".

---

22) This view replaces Keynes' policy constraint, viz. downward inflexibility of nominal wages, by the downward inflexibility of wage and price paths.

23) For a strong rejection of accommodating high rates of inflation by expansionary fiscal or monetary policies cf. the so-called "McCracken Report" of the OECD (1977), pp. 184-186.

APPENDIX I

The system in matrix form is repeated here for convenience:

$$\begin{bmatrix} -(1-E_Y) & E_{Y'} & E_i & E_\tau \\ E'_Y & -(1-E'_{Y'}) & E'_i & -E_\tau \\ L_Y & 0 & L_i & 0 \\ 0 & L'_{Y'} & L'_i & 0 \end{bmatrix} \begin{bmatrix} dY \\ dY' \\ di \\ d\tau \end{bmatrix} = \begin{bmatrix} d\ A_1 \\ d\ A_2 \\ d\ A_3 \\ d\ A_4 \end{bmatrix}$$

$$D = E_\tau\ [-(E_i+E'_i)L_YL'_{Y'} - (1-E_Y-E'_Y)L_iL'_{Y'}$$
$$- (1-E'_{Y'}-E_{Y'})L'_iL_Y] < 0$$

The effects of a domestic monetary expansion through purchasing securities ($d\ A_3 > 0$) are:

$$(A1)\ dY = \frac{\delta Y}{\delta A_3}\ d\ A_3 = -\frac{E_\tau}{D}\ [(E_i+E'_i)L'_{Y'}+(1-E'_{Y'}-E_{Y'})L'_i]\ dA_3 > 0$$

$$(A2)\ dY' = \frac{Y'}{\delta A_3}\ dA_3 = \frac{E_\tau}{D}\ [(1-E_Y-E'_Y)L'_i]\ d\ A_3 < 0$$

$$(A3)\ di = \frac{\delta i}{\delta A_3}\ d\ A_3 = -\frac{E_\tau}{D}\ [(1-E_Y-E'_Y)L'_{Y'}]\ d\ A_3 < 0$$

$$(A4)\ d\tau = \frac{\delta \tau}{\delta A_3}\ d\ A_3 = -\frac{1}{D}\ [(E'_iE'_Y+E_i(1-E_Y))L'_{Y'}$$
$$+ ((1-E_Y)\ (1-E'_{Y'})-E'_YE_{Y'})L'_i]\ dA_3 < 0$$

The effects of a domestic monetary expansion through purchasing foreign currency ($d\ A_3 = -d\ A_4 > 0$) are:

$$(A5)\ dY = (\frac{\delta Y}{A_3} - \frac{\delta Y}{A_4})\ d\ A_3 = .\ \frac{E_\tau}{D}\ [(E_i+E'_i)L'_{Y'}+(1-E'_{Y'}-E_{Y'})$$
$$(L'_i+L_i)]\ d\ A_3 > 0$$

$$(A6)\quad dY' = \left(\frac{\delta Y'}{\delta A_3} - \frac{\delta Y'}{\delta A_4}\right) d\,A_3 = \frac{E_\tau}{D}\,[(E_i+E'_i)L_Y$$

$$+ (1-E_Y-E'_Y)\;(L_i+L'_i)]\;d\,A_3 < 0$$

$$(A7)\quad di = \left(\frac{\delta i}{\delta A_3} - \frac{\delta i}{\delta A_4}\right) d\,A_3 = -\frac{E_\tau}{D}\,[-(1-E'_{Y'}-E_{Y'})L_Y$$

$$+ (1-E_Y-E'_Y)L'_{Y'}]\;d\,A_3 \gtrless 0$$

$$(A8)\quad d\tau = \left(\frac{\delta \tau}{\delta A_3} - \frac{\delta \tau}{\delta A_4}\right) d\,A_3 = -\frac{1}{D}\,[((E'_iE_{Y'}+E_i\;(1-E'_{Y'}))\;L_Y$$

$$+ (E'_iE'_Y+E_i(1-E_Y))L'_{Y'} + ((1-E_Y)\;(1-E'_{Y'})$$

$$- E'_YE_{Y'})\;(L_i+L_{i'})]\;d\,A_3 < 0$$

APPENDIX II

With real-wage rigidity the terms of trade are fixed and domestic producer prices are variable. The matrix form of the system then becomes:

$$\begin{bmatrix} -(1-E_Y) & E_{YI} & E_i & 0 \\ E'_Y & -(1-E'_{Y'}) & E'_i & 0 \\ L_Y & 0 & L_i & M/p^2 \\ 0 & L'_{Y'} & L'_i & 0 \end{bmatrix} \cdot \begin{bmatrix} dY \\ dY' \\ di \\ dp \end{bmatrix} = \begin{bmatrix} d\,A_1 \\ d\,A_2 \\ d\,A_3 \\ d\,A_4 \end{bmatrix}$$

$$D = M/p^2\;[-L'_iE'_YE_{Y'}] > 0$$

A purchase of securities has no effect on Y,Y' and i. The effects of purchasing foreign currency are:

$$\text{(A9)}\quad dY = \left(\frac{\delta Y}{\delta A_3} - \frac{\delta Y}{\delta A_4}\right) d\,A_3 = \frac{M/p^2}{D}\,[E_{Y'}E'_i + (1-E'_{Y'})E_i]\quad d\,A_3 < 0$$

$$\text{(A1o)}\quad dY' = \left(\frac{\delta Y'}{\delta A_3} - \frac{\delta Y'}{\delta A_4}\right) d\,A_3 = \frac{M/p^2}{D}\,[E'_Y E_i + (1-E_Y)E'_i]\; d\,A_3 < 0$$

$$\text{(A11)}\quad di = \left(\frac{\delta i}{\delta A_3} - \frac{\delta i}{\delta A_4}\right) d\,A_3 = \frac{M/p^2}{D}\,[(1-E_Y)(1-E'_{Y'}) + E'_Y E_{Y'}]\; d\,A_3 > 0$$

REFERENCES

Dornbusch, R., "The Theory of Flexible Exchange Rate Regimes and Macroeconomic Policy". The Scandinavian Journal of Economics, 78 (1976): 255-275.

Dornbusch, R. and Krugman, P., "Flexible Exchange Rates in the Short Run". Brookings Papers on Economic Activity, (1976): 537-575.

Fischer, S., "Long Term Contracts, Rational Expectations, and the Optimum Money Supply Rule". Journal of Political Economy, 85 (1977): 191-2o5.

Giersch, H., IMF Surveillance over Exchange Rates. In: R.A.Mundell and J.J.Polak (Ed.), The New International Monetary System. New York (1977): 53-68.

Haberler, G., Incomes Policies and Inflation. An Analysis of Basic Principles. Washington, D.C. 1971.

International Monetary Fund, Annual Report 1977.

Johnson, H.G., "The Monetary Approach to Balance of Payments Theory". Journal of Financial and Quantitative Analysis, 7 (1972): 1555-1572.

League of Nations, International Currency Experience, 1944.

Lehment, H., "Money Illusion and Balance of Payments Adjustment: A Comment". Journal of Political Economy, 86 (February 1978): 151-154.

Mundell, R.A., International Economics, New York and London

Mussa, M., "The Exchange Rate, the Balance of Payments and Monetary and Fiscal Policy under a Regime of Controlled Floating". The Scandinavian Journal of Economics, 78 (1976): 229-248.

Niehans, J., "Some Doubts about the Efficacy of Monetary Policy under Flexible Exchange Rates". Journal of International Economics, 5 (1975): 275-282.

OECD, Towards Full Employment and Price Stability. A Report to the OECD by a group of independent experts, June 1977.

Phelps, E.S. and Taylor, J.B., "Stabilising Power of Monetary Policy under Rational Price Expectations". Journal of Political Economy, 85 (1977): 163-15o.

Robinson, J., Beggar-My-Neighbour Remedies for Unemployment. Essays in the Theory of Employment, Oxford (1947): 156-17o.

Vaubel, R., "Real Exchange Rate Changes in the European Community: The Empirical Evidence and its Implications for European Currency Unification". Weltwirtschaftliches Archiv, 112 (1976): 429-47o.

COMMENT ON H.LEHMENT, "EXCHANGE-MARKET INTERVENTIONS AND OPEN-MARKET OPERATIONS AS INSTRUMENTS OF ACTIVE EMPLOYMENT POLICY UNDER FLEXIBLE EXCHANGE RATES"

Juergen Schroeder

It is wellknown that the efficiency of national monetary policy is greater in a system of freely floating exchange rates than in a fixed exchange rate regime. Given flexible exchange-rates, there is from the theoretical as well as from the practical point of view another important and interesting question: are there different employment effects at home as well as abroad when the home central bank conducts an expansionary monetary policy either by buying home securities (expansionary open market policy) or by buying foreign exchange (expansionary exchange market intervention)? Lehment's paper can be regarded as a very useful contribution to the contemporary discussion of this issue. Using a Keynesian two country model with perfect capital mobility, the two money markets play a central role in Lehment's investigations. He distinguishes two cases: the case of flexible real wages and the case of constant real wages.

Under the assumption of flexible real wages the exchange market intervention has a larger positive effect on home employment than the open market operation. This is so because in the former case the interest rate decreases less, or even increases. Therefore real output at home has to increase more in order that equilibrium in the money market is maintained (equation (3)). On the other hand an expansionary open market policy or exchange market intervention of the home central bank implies a decrease in real output abroad. This result again is determined in the money market. Equation (4) tells us that with $L_i^! < 0$ a decrease in the interest rate which is brought about by an expansionary open market policy at home must lead to a decrease in real output abroad in order that equilibrium in the foreign money market is maintained. Therefore $|L_i^!| > 0$ is a necessary condition for a decrease in foreign real output as a consequence of an expansionary open market policy at home. It is Lehment's merit to have emphasized very clearly the importance of the money market conditions for the international transmission of business cycles.

When compared with flexible real wages the employment effects of central bank policy under constant real wages are rather different. Moreover, in this case the expansionary open market policy and the expansionary exchange market intervention have a different impact on real output in the two countries. In Lehment's model an expansionary open market policy in the home country has no employment effect at all in both countries.

The economic interpretation of this unexpected and at first surprising result is the following: as real wages are assumed to remain constant, prices of home output and nominal wages increase in proportion to the exchange rate appreciation which is brought about by the expansionary open market policy at home. As in Lehment's model all monetary magnitudes - the money stock, the exchange rate, the prices of home output, and nominal wages - increase in the same proportion, the relative increase in nominal money supply equals the relative increase in nominal money demand for transaction purposes. Consequently there can be no impact on the real magnitudes, i.e. the real interest rate as well as real output and employment in the two countries. Therefore the assumption of constant real wages enables Lehment to reach wellknown classical results from a basicly Keynesian model.

Under the assumption of constant real wages an expansionary exchange market intervention of the home country even leads to a decrease in real output in both countries. This is so because in addition to the money stock increase in the home country there is now a decrease in the money supply in the foreign country. Therefore the depreciation of the home currency is greater than in the case of an expansionary open market policy. So in both countries the real demand for money exceeds the real supply of money: in the home country because prices and wages increase relatively more than the nominal supply of money, in the foreign country because the nominal money stock decreases with constant prices and wages. The money market equations (3) and (4) tell us that in this situation the real interest rate has to increase in order that equilibrium in these two markets is maintained. An increase in the real interest rate implies via absorption a decrease in real output and employment in both countries. This negative employment effect can be avoided and a positive impact can be obtained, if the central bank of the home country combines an expansionary open market policy with a contractionary exchange market intervention, i.e. by selling foreign currency in such a way that the terms of trade remain constant. In this case prices and nominal wages remain constant in both countries. Therefore real supply of money increases in both countries and the real interest rate has to fall in order that equilibrium in the two money markets is maintained. The decrease in the real interest rate induces via an increase in absorption a positive employment effect in both countries.

So Lehment arrives at the interesting results that under the assumption of flexible real wages the expansionary exchange market intervention has a larger positive (negative) effect on employment at home (abroad) than the expansionary open market policy. Under the assumption of constant real wages, however a contractionary exchange market intervention is necessary in combination with an expansionary open market policy to create positive employment effects at home (and abroad).

These results are obtained under some extreme and simplifying assumptions. If for instance the assumption of perfect capital mobility is dropped, we arrive at very different results.

Though capital can be assumed to be highly mobile as long as there are no artificial international barriers, reality shows that even in a system of freely floating exchange rates policy makers hamper international capital movements whenever they tend to endanger national economic policy goals. Another simplifying assumption is the use of just one real interest rate instead of an interest rate structure. An expansionary exchange market intervention usually has an immediate effect on the money market interest rate. When and to what extent the interest rate on the capital market will be affected is a question which may be answered rather satisfactory by the theory of relative prices. It is however the capital market interest rate which has the main impact on absorption. Finally there are from the practical point of view limits to exchange market intervention as a means of active employment policy. Take for instance the case of variable real wages. To get a satisfactory employment effect as a result of an expansionary exchange market intervention the central bank probably has to conduct this policy for quite a time and to quite an extent, i.e. it has to pile up huge amounts of foreign currency as assets. If the central bank reserves figures are published it will become obvious that this country has violated the international rules and conducts an employment policy at the expense of its trading partners. In the case of constant real wages a contractionary exchange market intervention is necessary in order to achieve a positive employment effect. In this case a country will sooner or later run out of international reserves and there exists then from this side a clear constraint. But as Lehment points out correctly, the same positive employment effects which are reached with an expansionary open market policy in combination with a contractionary exchange market intervention in the home country can be achieved by an expansionary open market policy in both countries. So it is obviously better in this situation for the home central bank to persuade the foreign central bank to conduct an expansionary monetary policy as well.

MONETARY AND FISCAL ACTIONS: DID THEIR RELATIVE IMPORTANCE IN THE UNITED STATES CHANGE WITH FLEXIBLE EXCHANGE RATES?*

William G. Dewald

This paper reports an empirical investigation of some of the macroeconomic effects of increased flexibility in foreign exchange rates that commenced after August 15, 1971. On that historic date the United States halted gold sales to official holders of dollars and ushered in an era of floating, though not always freely floating exchange rates.

Our paper is concerned with a small model of the United States. It is based on a common model of Canada, France, Germany, Italy, the United Kingdom, and the United States. Our common model represents a modification of the Federal Reserve of St.Louis "monetarist" model of the United States. But the model that emerges is not monetarist; not only money but also government spending and exports generally affect GNP importantly, particularly for countries other than the United States.

The main objectives of the paper are to discuss how floating affected (1) the multipliers that relate monetary and fiscal policy to aggregate demand and (2) the role of import prices in the formation of inflationary expectations. Two approaches are introduced. The first estimates the effect of floating on the multipliers and on price expectations formation before and after floating. The second extrapolates the endogenous variables of the U.S. model to the floating period based on estimated relationships for the pre-floating period. Before these results are discussed, a summary of

* Financial support under U.S. Department of Labor Contract J9K60029 and the research assistance of Maurice M. Marchon are acknowledged.

our common model is presented.

THE MODEL

Our model[1)] is recursive just as the original St. Louis model. Nominal spending affects price and output determination, but is itself a function of assumed autonomous influences. Estimated for data through the mid-1970s and for five countries in addition to the United States, it yielded some different results from the original St. Louis work based on U.S. data extending only through the 1960s. The main findings are

- Changes in spending depend not only on changes in money (currency and demand deposits held by the public) but also on changes in government spending and exports over a period of about a year to a year and a half.
- Inflationary expectations depend on the histories of not only domestic inflation but also import inflation and demand pressure.
- Inflation depends on inflationary expectations and current demand pressure.
- Changes in real output are defined in terms of changes in spending and inflation.
- Because demand pressure affects inflationary expectations and inflation slowly, real output and unemployment are significantly affected by changes in spending in the short-run.

When the sample was extended to the 1970s, the original St.Louis spending equation held up well with only minor modifications; but

---

1) William G. Dewald and Maurice N. Marchon, "A Modified Federal Reserve of St. Louis Spending Equation for Canada, France, Germany, Italy, the United Kingdom, and the United States," Kredit und Kapital, 11. Jahrgang 1978, Heft 2, pp. 144-212.
__________, "A Common Specification of Price, Output, and Unemployment Rate Responses to Demand Pressure in Canada, France, Germany, Italy, the United Kingdom, and the United States," Weltwirtschaftliches Archiv (forthcoming).

the St. Louis price equation yielded very poor results. The problem is the measure of anticipated inflation. In the original St. Louis model anticipated inflation was simply a weighted average of past inflation rates. The weights were derived from an estimated relationship between long term bond rates and past inflation rates. Unfortunately, anticipated inflation so calculated grossly underestimated actual inflation over the sample period including the 1970s, which can be interpreted as violating rational expectations.

Criticisms of the St. Louis approach have been discussed by various authors.[2)] One alternative is to calculate anticipated inflation on the basis of autonomous influences that could be expected to be considered in formulating expectations. This represents an application of the principle of rational expectations as originally formulated by Muth.[3)] A weak form of this principle and the alternative we applied only requires that the public fully incorporate the relevant information that is available when expectations are formulated. For our model we included the past histories of not only domestic inflation but also demand pressure and import inflation. Our rational expectations price anticipations measure fit the data for the United States much better than the original St. Louis specification and quite well when confronted not only with data for the other five countries but also with data outside the original sample period.

Demand pressure, the theoretical variable that drives price level adjustments in the model, is aggregate demand less supply. As in the original St. Louis model, aggregate demand is defined operationally as $\Delta Y + X_{t-1}$ (ΔY, the change in nominal spending GNP plus X_{t-1}, the lagged level of real GNP). ΔY can be interpreted as

---

2) Edward J. Kane and Burton G. Malkiel, "Autoregressive and Nonautogressive Elements in Cross-Section Forecasts of Inflations," Econometrica (January 1976), 1-16.

3) John F. Muth, "Rational Expectations and the Theory of Price Movements," Econometrica (July 1961), 315-35.

the increase in aggregate demand to be distributed between real output and prices. Aggregate supply is simply the high employment level of output as measured by the Council of Economic Advisers (CEA).

This model is consistent with Milton Friedman's "monetary framework",[4] which is a theory of nominal spending. For the long run he considers real output to be independent of spending, which therefore determines only inflation not output. However, in the short run wide deviations from the long run equilibrium occur. In fact the main function of our model is to provide estimates of short run adjustments to long run disequilibrium positions.

There is a possible distortion in the St. Louis demand pressure variable. On Figure 1, suppose the economy last period was on the demand curve $Y_{t-1} = P_{t-1}\ X_{t-1}$ and the demand curve shifted so that demand was X_t^* at unchanged price level P_{t-1}. If output fully adjusted to keep the economy on the new demand curve, then

$$\Delta Y = Y_t - Y_{t-1} = P_{t-1}X_t^* - P_{t-1}X_{t-1} = P_{t-1}(X_t^* - X_{t-1}).$$

Hence the new demand $X_t^* = \frac{\Delta Y}{P_{t-1}} + X_{t-1}$ and not $\Delta Y + X_{t-1}$ as in the St. Louis formulation. In either case demand pressure would affect both prices and output in the short run (say to P_t and X_t) but only prices in the long run (say to $\overline{P}_t$ with output at its potential XF_t). We have experimented with both demand pressure measures and found slightly larger effects of demand pressure on prices the St. Louis measure. This may be accountable to a number of factors. Since the economy does not stay on the demand curve but rather is generally in long run disequilibrium, it is an open question about how to measure a demand shift in disequilibrium. By using ΔY rather than $\Delta Y/P_{-1}$ as the demand curve shift variable, one implicitly adds to

4) Robert J. Gordon (editor), Milton Friedman's Monetary Framework: A Debate with His Critics. Chicago: The University of Chicago Press, 1974.

FIGURE 1

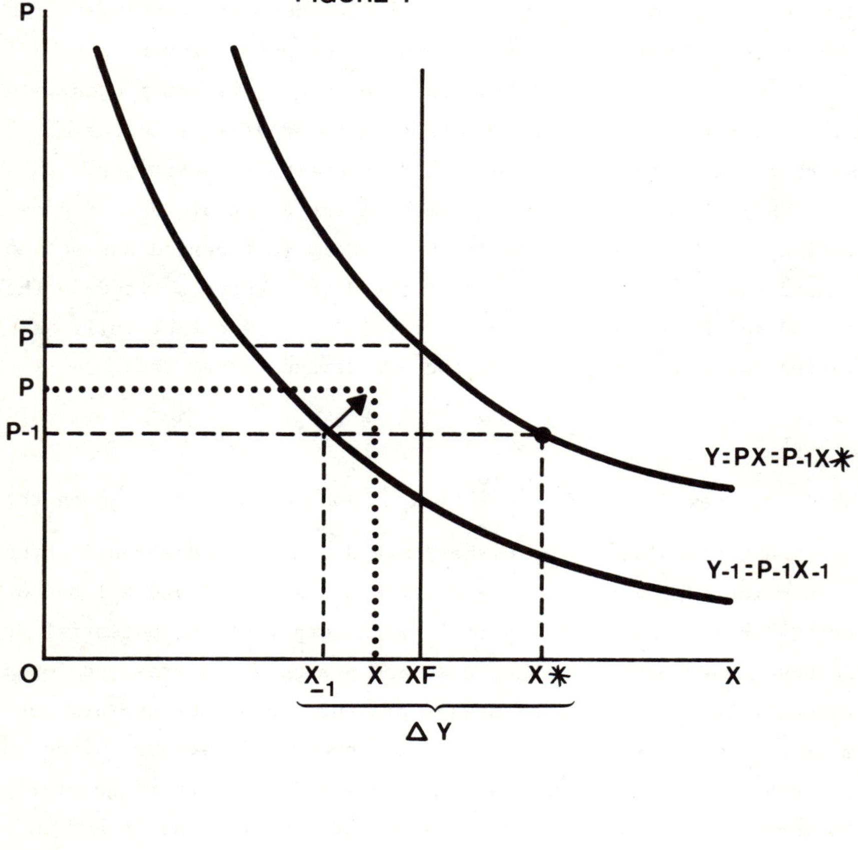

the amplitude of demand variation at higher levels of prices which is at least a theoretical possibility. In any event, the St. Louis demand pressure variable yields a slightly better statistical fit than the alternative which is the reason we used it.

HYPOTHESIZED STRUCTURAL CHANGES DUE TO FLOATING

It seems reasonable to argue that under flexible exchange rates not only the public might be more aware of import price variations but also the policy authorities might be more enabled to validate the domestic price effects of import price inflation. In contrast, under a fixed exchange regime, the balance of payments effects on an autonomous increase in import prices would require the authorities to take restrictive actions to reduce domestic prices (or the equivalent) to prevent a loss of international reserves. Thus, one could expect to find import prices more important in the formation of inflationary expectations under floating than fixed exchange rates.

The advent of flexible exchange rates could also affect the multipliers relating total spending to money and government spending. The assignment problem with respect to monetary and fiscal policy involves both the comparative magnitude and timing of impacts on various goal variables.[5] The issue is the possibility of different comparative advantages of the policies under fixed and floating exchange rates in terms of total effects as well as comparative speeds of adjustment and uncertainty about the multipliers.

The conventional belief is that monetary policy would be more powerful and fiscal policy less powerful in affecting demand under floating. In a world of free capital mobility that fixes real interest rates internationally, money changes would be fully reflected in aggregate demand, prices, and exchange rates. Fiscal policy

5) Egon Sohmen, "The Assignment Problem" and Richard N. Cooper, "Comment" in Robert A. Mundell and Alexander K. Swoboda, Monetary Problems of the International Economy. Chicago: The University of Chicago Press, 1969, 183-197, 235-241.

could only affect the distribution of output between public and private sectors and the distribution of government debt between foreign and domestic holders. Essentially the government would borrow abroad to finance its current deficit which in effect would be spent on foreign goods and services. Interest rates would not be affected.

Even if such a situation could obtain in the long run, it is reasonable to think that shocks originating from monetary or fiscal policy would take a long time to adjust to and might therefore create real disturbances under either fixed or floating exchange rates. In fact, standard macroeconomic analysis - the kind of IS-LM theory that our common model has tended to confirm for six OECD countries - indicates that expansionary fiscal policy not financed by money will at least temporarily raise domestic interest rates and induce a capital inflow which would appreciate the currency. Because exchange rates would be expected to adjust faster than domestic prices and quantities, the appreciated exchange rate would at least temporarily raise the value of exports and lower the value of imports, thereby increasing the balance of trade. Consequently, under flexible exchange rates, an expansionary fiscal policy would be augmented by an increase in net exports until prices and quantities adjusted. In the long run, as mentioned, one would expect a lessened fiscal policy impact.

Thus, under floating one could expect a larger fiscal and a smaller monetary impact on aggregate demand because of the induced (added) effect of increased capital inflows and at least a temporary increase in the value of exports relative to imports. But the reverse would be expected in the long run.

Often "the more things seem to change the more they remain the same". In the present context, adjustable foreign exchange rate pegs and managed floating are not necessarily very different. Furthermore, though the major trading countries have mainly floated, many still have their currencies tied to the U.S. dollar. In fact the dollar in some senses is more of an international reserve currency than ever since there are virtually no gold transactions and there is no need to take extraordinary measures to maintain the international value of the dollar.[6] Consequently, for the United States, it should not be surprising to find little macroeconomic effect of floating.

STRUCTURAL CHANGES IN THE SPENDING EQUATION

Table 1 records estimates of our common spending equation in logarithmic first differences. Over the period 1956 I-1977 II, the money elasticity was estimated at .9, the government spending and export elasticities at .2 and .03 respectively. Table 1 also shows the spending equation estimates for before and after floating.[7] The Chow Test indicates no significant structural change at the 5 percent level of significance. But the money multiplier fell to insignificance after floating. The government spending multipliers were not significantly different in the before and after floating subperiods nor significant.

Looking at the average growth rates before and after floating gives an indication of the modest change in structure. Annual monetary growth averaged 3.4 percent and spending growth 6.1 percent per year in the period 1956 I-1971 II. After floating monetary growth averaged 5.7 percent and spending 9.5 percent, respectively 1.7 and 1.6 times the prefloating rates. Thus, monetary growth would appear to have been of slightly less importance in explaining spending growth after floating. Growth in high employment government spending averaged 7.5 percent annually from 1956 I-1971 II

---

6) Marina v.N. Whitman, "Coordination and Management of the International Economy: A Search for Organizing Principles" in William Fellner (editor), Contemporary Economic Problems. Washington: American Enterprises Association, 1977, 289-345.

7) Symbols and sources are listed in an appendix.

TABLE 1: U.S. Spending Equation[a] (Logarithms)

$$\Delta LnY = Constant + \sum_{i=0}^{4} m_i \Delta LnM_{t-i} + \sum_{i=0}^{3} e_i \Delta LnE_{t-i} + x_0 \Delta LnEX.$$

	1956 I-1971 II	1971 III-1977 II	1956 I-1977 II
Constant	.022 (1.91)	.055 (.81)	.019 (1.91)
m_0	.462 (1.98)	.932 (2.20)	.597 (3.40)
m_1	.032 (.13)	-.143 (-.46)	-.009 (-.06)
m_2	.308 (2.48)	-.074 (-.29)	.217 (2.19)
m_3	.440 (1.84)	.150 (.46)	.400 (2.48)
m_4	-.426 (-1.73)	-.458 (-1.14)	-.337 (-1.88)
Σm_i	.816 (3.43)	.407 (.44)	.867 (4.52)
e_0	-.001 (-.01)	.018 (.17)	.020 (.41)
e_1	.134 (2.01)	.064 (.60)	.112 (2.27)
e_2	.005 (.07)	.013 (.12)	.017 (.34)
e_3	-.003 (-.04)	.040 (.40)	.020 (.41)
Σe_i	.135 (1.19)	.135 (.50)	.170 (1.84)
x_0	.035 (1.33)	.020 (.39)	.032 (1.46)
R^2	.381	.355	.422
F	3.559	.856	6.158
SE	.0349	.0391	.0344
DW	2.072	2.206	1.938
Mean	.0610	.0951	.0705
SD	.0410	.0380	.0428

a The Chow Test F = .41 being less than the 1.97 critical value at the .05 level indicates no significant change in the structure.

and 10.4 percent from 1971 III to 1977 II, up 1.4 times, explaining some part of the slight shortfall of spending growth from monetary growth.

It is interesting to note that the money multiplier at .4 to .9 and the government spending multiplier at .1 to .2 indicate an underlying IS-LM relationship for the United States with comparatively inelastic LM and elastic IS. Though we have not incorporated interest rates directly in the analysis, the consistently larger money multiplier than government spending multiplier suggests that the LM shifts along a comparatively flat IS (or possibly that money shifts both LM and IS - the latter because of real balances). The fact that the government spending multiplier is comparatively low suggests that government spending changes shift the IS along a comparatively inelastic LM. These qualitative results remain unchanged as a consequence of floating.

STRUCTURAL CHANGE IN THE PRICE ANTICIPATIONS EQUATION

Table 2 records estimates of our common price anticipations equation. The Chow Test indicates no significant structural change after floating. Though the estimated effect of lagged import price inflation on actual and anticipated inflation rose relatively after floating, both the estimated effect of demand pressure and the past history of inflation had comparable relative effects before and after floating.

There was a much higher rate of import price inflation after floating. It reflected both the devaluation of the dollar and the rise in the prices of foreign exports. The annual rates of domestic and import price inflation averaged 2.9 and 1.2 percent respectively over the prefloating period but 6.4 and 13.7 over 1971 III-1977 II. That is a very dramatic change; and it was reflected in the regression results.

Since one expects demand pressure to be positively associated with inflation, it is disconcerting that demand pressure as measured averaged a negative 6.2 percent before floating when the inflation rate was

TABLE 2: U.S. Price Anticipations Equation[a] (Logarithms)

$$\Delta LnP = \text{Constant} + \sum_{i=1}^{4} \delta_i LnD_{t-i} + \sum_{i=1}^{15} \pi_i \Delta LnP_{t-i} + \sum_{i=1}^{4} \omega_i \Delta LnW_{t-i} .$$

	1956 I-1971 II		1971 II-1977 II		1956 I-1977 II	
Constant	.0125	(1.61)	-.0556	(-1.30)	.0152	(3.65)
δ_1	.104	(1.78)	.126	(1.41)	.098	(2.59)
δ_2	-.042	(-.46)	-.030	(-.26)	-.098	(-1.74)
δ_3	.023	(.24)	.116	(1.53)	.046	(.84)
δ_4	-.006	(-.09)	.035	(.38)	.012	(.34)
$\Sigma\delta_i$	.079	(2.49)	.246	(2.11)	.058	(3.46)
π_1	-.085	(-.59)	-.205	(-.82)	.091	(.94)
π_2	-.028	(-.31)	.203	(.15)	.068	(1.28)
π_3	.019	(.23)	.166	(1.44)	.052	(1.71)
π_4	.057	(.63)	.240	(2.20)	.041	(1.51)
π_5	.086	(.96)	.259	(2.48)	.036	(1.20)
π_6	.107	(1.35)	.237	(2.51)	.034	(1.17)
π_7	.119	(1.91)	.189	(2.22)	.035	(1.33)
π_8	.125	(2.61)	.128	(1.55)	.037	(1.54)
π_9	.123	(2.69)	.068	(.80)	.039	(1.58)
π_{10}	.114	(2.02)	.025	(.30)	.041	(1.48)
π_{11}	.099	(1.45)	.012	(.18)	.040	(1.39)
π_{12}	.078	(1.08)	.044	(.91)	.037	(1.35)
π_{13}	.052	(.77)	.135	(1.36)	.029	(1.07)
π_{14}	.020	(.32)	.299	(1.32)	.016	(.36)
π_{15}	-.016	(-.16)	.550	(1.33)	-.004	(-.05)
$\Sigma\pi_i$	.869	(3.50)	2.171	(2.01)	.590	(4.19)

TABLE 2 (continued)

	1956 I-1971 II	1971 II-1977 II	1956 I-1977 II
ω_1	.035 (.66)	.019 (.45)	.021 (.85)
ω_2	.062 (1.77)	.063 (1.42)	.095 (3.39)
ω_3	-.021 (-.38)	-.012 (-.22)	.003 (.11)
ω_4	-.060 (-1.09)	.055 (.82)	.020 (.62)
$\Sigma\omega_i$	.017 (.19)	.125 (1.03)	.138 (3.75)
R^2	.648	.902	.820
F	7.512	8.415	27.615
SE	.0112	.0123	.0117
DW	2.000	2.235	2.258
Mean	.0285	.0638	.0384
SD	.0169	.0271	.0256

a The Chow Test F = 1.36 was less than the 1.86 critical value at the .05 level indicating no significant change in the structure.

only 2.9 percent but a negative 9.2 percent when the inflation rate was 6.4 percent (see Figure 2). This may reflect that potential output did not grow as much in the middle 1970s as the CEA had estimated, perhaps because of oil price increases but also because of changes in the work force.[8] Nevertheless, our specification of the price anticipations equation yielded quite plausible results for the full 1956 I-1977 II sample period. Both demand pressure and import prices were estimated to exert a significant influence. But the sum of the weights is unbelievably high over the post-floating sample, presumably partly due to the shortness of the period. Accordingly, a related test is reported in Table 3. It uses the full sample period, hypothesizing that only the constant and the weights on import price inflation changed after floating. The weights on demand pressure and past domestic inflation are hypothesized to remain the same. In this test, one gets the same qualitative finding about the increased importance of import prices in explaining anticipated inflation. Furthermore, the sum of the unconstrained weights is not significantly different from unity; and the sum of the weights on past inflation rates and on past demand pressure are almost identical to those estimated for the pre-floating period. A slightly longer lag specification emerged as the best fit equation for the full sample period than for the pre-floating period which was used for the Chow Test reported in Table 2.

STRUCTURAL CHANGE IN THE PRICE EQUATION

Inflation is estimated as a function of anticipated inflation and current demand pressure. Combined with the autonomous setting of high employment output, this represents an expectations augmented Phillips curve. Anticipated inflation has been formulated

---

8) Robert H. Rasche and John A. Tatom, "Energy Resources and Potential GNP", Federal Reserve Bank of St. Louis Review (June 1977), 10-24.

FIGURE 2

INFLATION RATE AND DEMAND PRESSURE, UNITED STATES, QUARTERLY, 1956 I - 1977 II

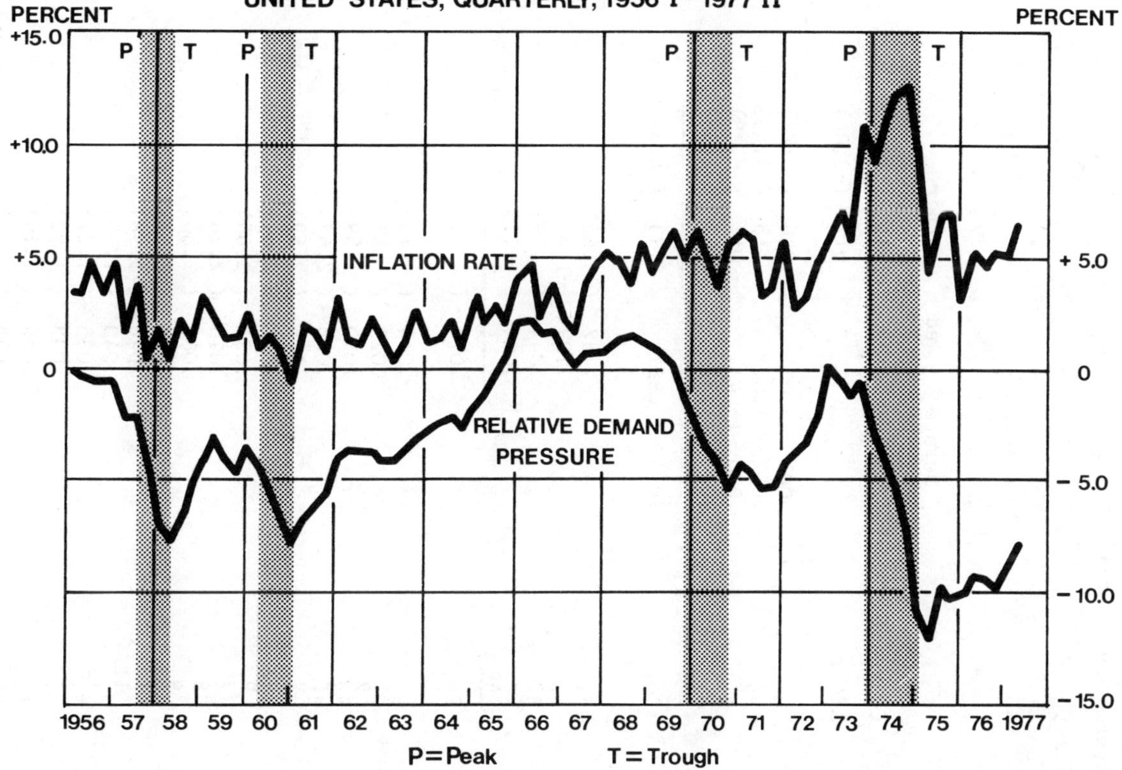

TABLE 3: U.S. Price Anticipations Equation With Before and After Floating Dummy Variables

$$\Delta LnP = \text{Constant} + \beta A + \sum_{i=1}^{4} (\omega_i^b + \omega_i^a)\Delta LnW_{t-i} + \sum_{i=1}^{4} \delta_i LnD_{t-i} + \sum_{i=1}^{17} \pi_i \Delta LnP_{t-i}$$

	Before		and		After			
Constant			.0123	(2.31)				
After					-.0173	(-2.04)		
ω_1	.001	(.02)			.026	(.87)		
ω_2	.052	(1.06)			.118	(3.43)		
ω_3	-.020	(-.42)			-.012	(-.29)		
ω_4	.015	(-.31)			.062	(1.39)		
$\Sigma\omega_i$	.018	(.25)			.193	(4.25)		
δ_1			.138	(3.25)				
δ_2			-.109	(-1.82)				
δ_3			.044	(.79)				
δ_4			.004	(.12)				
$\Sigma\delta_i$			.078	(4.21)				
π_1			-.014	(-.14)				
π_2			.023	(.41)				
π_3			.050	(1.59)				
π_4			.068	(2.67)				
π_5			.078	(2.69)				
π_6			.082	(2.61)				
π_7			.081	(2.65)				
π_8			.075	(2.76)				
π_9			.067	(2.80)				
π_{10}			.058	(2.51)				
π_{11}			.048	(1.98)				
π_{12}			.040	(1.52)				
π_{13}			.035	(1.27)				
π_{14}			.033	(1.22)				
π_{15}			.036	(1.16)				
π_{16}			.046	(.94)			R^2	.842
π_{17}			.063	(.78)			F	21.266
							SE	.0114
$\Sigma\pi_i$			.872	(4.01)			DW	2.235

so as to reflect the observed relationship between import price inflation, demand pressure, and domestic price inflation. Using current information the observed relationship is then projected forward in calculating anticipated inflation for the next quarter as shown in Table 4 which reports the U.S. price equation estimates. Again the Chow Test indicates no significant structural change. Both before and after floating, anticipated inflation almost totally dominates the explanation of the inflation rate. A 1 percent increase in anticipated inflation is linked to almost exactly a 1 percent increase in inflation. Though before and after floating, current demand pressure affected inflation insignificantly, the total effect (current and lagged) was significant but small. An increase in demand pressure of 1 percent was estimated to increase inflation in total by one-tenth to two-tenths of 1 percent. That current demand pressure does not significantly affect the inflation rate means that nearly the full systematic effects of demand pressure on inflation are lagged and presumably incorporated in inflation expectations.

To sum up, the U.S. economy at the macro-level we have explored was not altered much by the advent of more flexible exchange rates in 1971.

. The U.S. spending equation was not significantly changed. Money remained comparatively more important than government spending and exports in affecting demand.

. Though no significant change in the structure of the U.S. price anticipations equation was estimated, import prices were found to play a newly significant role in the generation of inflationary expectations. Past values of demand pressure exerted a small but significant effect on inflationary expectations both before and after floating. There was a long lag in the estimated adjustment of inflationary expectations both before and after floating.

. The U.S. price equation was not significantly altered after floating with inflationary expectations incorporating lagged

TABLE 4: U.S. Price Equation (Logarithms)

$$\Delta LnP = \text{Constant} + \delta_0 \ln D + \gamma \Delta \ln P^e.^{a}$$

	1956 I-1971 II		1971 III-1977 II		1956 I-1977 II	
Constant	.00198	(.40)	-.000585	(-.11)	.000339	(.13)
δ_0	.00818	(.51)	-.0139	(-.24)	.0113	(.29)
γ	.948	(6.81)	1.002	(13.84)	.996	(18.82)
R^2	.649		.902		.820	
F	54.645		96.660		188.614	
SE	.0102		.00886		.0110	
DW	2.008		2.244		2.258	
Mean	.0285		.0638		.0384	
SD	.0169		.0271		.0256	

$$\Delta \ln P^e = \Delta \ln \hat{P}_{t-1}$$

$$\Delta \ln \hat{P} = \text{Constant} + \sum_{i=1}^{4} \delta_i \ln D_{t-i+1} + \sum_{i=1}^{15} \pi_i \Delta \ln P_{t-i+1} + \sum_{i=1}^{4} \omega_i \Delta \ln W_{t-i+1}.$$

a The Chow Test F = 1.44 being less than the 1.70 critical value at the .05 level indicates no significant change in the structure.

demand pressure and import prices closly linked to inflation. Current demand pressure exerted no significant effect on current inflation.

STRUCTURAL CHANGE IN THE OUTPUT EQUATION

Because the model is recursive with percentage changes in spending (ΔLnY) affecting percentage changes in price (ΔLnP) but not the other way around, one obtains output changes definitionally. Real output $X \equiv Y/P$. It follows that $\Delta LnX \equiv \Delta LnY - \Delta LnP$. Needless to say there was no change in the structure. Over 1956 I-1977 II about half of the variation in real output percent changes was accountable to estimated percentage changes in spending and prices. A much tougher test of the model is to extrapolate output changes after floating based on estimates of the model for the before floating period. Of course, one cannot attribute changes in the performance of the model solely to floating.

EXTRAPOLATION OF THE BEFORE FLOATING U.S. MODEL

We estimated our modified St. Louis type model with U.S. data for 1956 I-1971 II and extrapolated the endogenous variables of the model for the period 1971 III-1977 II. The before floating estimates for spending, anticipated inflation, and inflation as recorded in Tables 1, 2, and 3 were used in the extrapolation. Table 5 reports the root mean square errors for the extrapolation period based on this structure and actual values of the autonomous variables (M, E, EX, W, and XF). The before floating unemployment rate equation is reported in Table 5. Figure 3 shows the actual and extrapolated levels of spending (Y), real output (X), price level (P), and unemployment rate (U).

The results are somewhat off base: both spending and inflation were underpredicted. Output was overpredicted; and consequently the unemployment rate was underpredicted. The extrapolated values captured the main movements in these series until about mid-1974.

TABLE 5: Extrapolation 1971 III-1977 II Based on Estimates 1956 I-1971 II

Variables	R^2	Root Mean Square Error	Mean Actual	Mean Extrapolated
Percent change in spending: ΔLnY	.153	.0349[a]	.0951	.0887
Percent change in price level: ΔLnP	.197	.0242[a]	.0638	.0577
Percent change in real output: ΔLnX	.225	.0451	.0313	.0310
Unemployment percent: U^b	.841	.542[a]	6.473	6.064

a The standard errors for the estimation period 1956 I-1971 II where ΔLnY, .0349 (exactly the same as the extrapolation root mean square error); ΔLnP, .0102; and U, .245.

b The unemployment rate equation used in the extrapolations was:

$$U = \underset{(45.14)}{4.236} + \underset{(.42)}{.030}\,\hat{G} + \underset{(3.26)}{.273}\,G_{-1} + \underset{(2.43)}{.091}\,G_{-2}$$

R^2 = .952

F = 372.4

SE = .245

DW = 1.760

ρ = .601 (3 iterations)

Mean = 4.932

SD = 1.081

$$\hat{G} = \frac{XF - \hat{X}}{XF} \cdot 100.$$

Thereafter the errors were substantial during the 1974-1975 recession. But by mid-1977 the extrapolated level of GNP was only 3.8 percent below the actual level, mainly accountable to the difference in the effect of money changes during the extrapolation period from what had been estimated previously. And the extrapolated level of prices fell only 3.6 percent below the actual level by mid-1977, accountable mainly to an increase in the effect of the import inflation rate on anticipated inflation. That errors in spending and inflation extrapolations were largely offsetting translated into only a .2 percent overshooting in the extrapolated level of real output above the actual value and an extrapolated unemployment rate .1 percentage points below the actual rate in 1977 II. But at the 1975 I trough when spending was below and inflation above extrapolated values, real output was 6.3 percent short of its extrapolated value.

The results look quite good as shown in Figure 3. But the 1974-75 recession was not picked up except in the sense of a slowdown in real output growth. The major reason was the failure of the model to forecast how rapidly inflation was actually being generated. The failure of the extrapolation to identify the magnitude of the slowdown in 1974-75 is to some degree a reflection of the magnitude of the real disturbance introduced by oil price increases in 1974-75. Given the actual stance of monetary and fiscal policy, one can make the counterfactual speculation that, if the pre-floating U.S. economic structure had somehow obtained without the effect of import prices there would not have been a recession.

SUMMARY AND CONCLUSIONS

Chow Tests indicate that there was no statistically significant change in the macroeconomic structure of the United States after floating commenced in 1971. But there was a significantly increased importance of import prices in the determination of

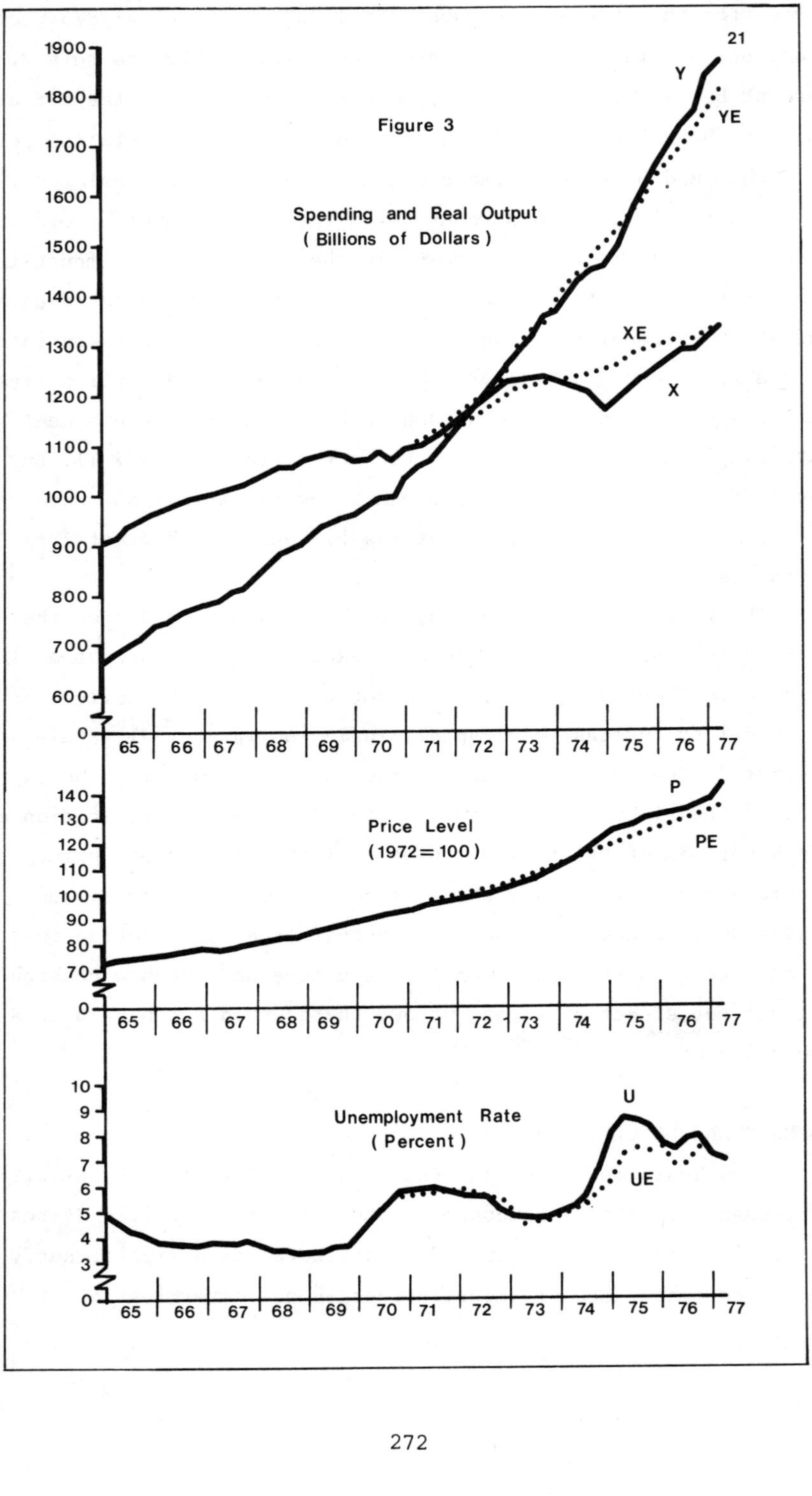
21
Figure 3
Spending and Real Output
(Billions of Dollars)
Y
YE
XE
X
1900
1800
1700
1600
1500
1400
1300
1200
1100
1000
900
800
700
600
0
65
66
67
68
69
70
71
72
73
74
75
76
77
Price Level
(1972 = 100)
P
PE
140
130
120
110
100
90
80
70
0
65
66
67
68
69
70
71
72
73
74
75
76
77
Unemployment Rate
(Percent)
U
UE
10
9
8
7
6
5
4
3
0
65
66
67
68
69
70
71
72
73
74
75
76
77

anticipated inflation. There was no comparable restructuring of the elements of the price or spending equations though by comparison of coefficients estimated before and after floating the effect of money on spending became somewhat muted and the effect of high employment government spending changes comparatively amplified. The sample periods are quite short so one must accept this result with caution. Within the framework of our model, changes in money continued to dominate the determination of total demand after floating. Extrapolations based on the best fit model estimated for the period 1956 I-1971 II fit the actual experience of spending, output, inflation, and the unemployment rate well until the 1974 explosion in oil prices. But then, prediction errors led to extrapolated values undershooting inflation and overshooting real growth. Nevertheless, by mid-1977 the extrapolated values were not far from the actual values. All told, save for the necessity to incorporate import prices in the machinery to determine inflation, our before floating modified St. Louis model captured the main movements in spending, inflationary expectations, inflation, output, and unemployment over the extrapolation period.

It is worth mentioning that both money and government spending policies have been estimated to affect demand within a period of a year to a year and a half - a short lag by conventional monetarist wisdom. Yet this is not much consolation for advocates of discretionary policies because discretionary policies as reflected in the measures we analyzed generally have been the major contributing factor to economic instability. One cannot very sensibly attribute the shock of oil price increases in 1974-1975 to the monetary and fiscal authorities in the United States. But it seems that even in this instance they succeeded in making a bad situation worse by first clamping on the monetary brakes in 1974 and subsequently stepping on the monetary accelerator. The authorities managed to confound interested parties around the world by reigniting inflationary expectations after expectations had cooled in 1974-1975.

The authorities were responsible for successively higher annual rates of monetary growth in 1975, 1976, and 1977; and this was not damped by restrictive fiscal policies.

We do not care to make a fetish out of it, but there is merit in directing the authorities to aim at stabilizing demand growth rather than at moderating inflation or variation in the unemployment rate. Supply variations because of bad crops, oil embargoes, strikes, blizzards, and the like can certainly cause real problems. But year in and year out inflationary and recessionary disturbances have typically come from the demand side. Since our findings suggest that both before and after floating there were powerful policy instruments to influence demand quickly, the policy authorities could contribute to economic stability compared with their past record if they would simply aim at stabilizing demand growth. That is not necessarily all they could do to improve economic performance; but it would be a step in the right direction.

APPENDIX

Glossary and Sources

Symbol	Name	Source
Y	Total Spending (GNP)	U.S. Department of Commerce Survey of Current Business
M	Money (Currency and Demand Deposits)	Federal Reserve Release
E	High Employment Government Spending	Federal Reserve of St. Louis Federal Budget Trends
EX	Exports	Survey of Current Business
P	GNP Deflator	Survey of Current Business
X	Real Output (Y/P)	Calculated
XF	High Employment Output	Federal Reserve of St. Louis Private communication
D	Demand Pressure $(\Delta Y + X_{-1} - XF)$	Calculated
W	Import Deflator	Survey of Current Business
P^e	Anticipated P (see Table 4)	Calculated
U	Unemployment Rate	Survey of Current Business
G	High Employment Output Gap $\left(\frac{XF-X}{XF} \cdot 100\right)$	Calculated
$\hat{}$	Estimated	
Δ	Quarterly First Difference	
Ln	Logarithm	
R^2	Coefficient of Determination	
F	F Statistic	
SE	Standard Error of Estimate	
DW	Durbin Watson Statistic	
ρ	Serial Correlation Coefficient	
SD	Standard Deviation	

A COMMENT ON W.G. DEWALD "MONETARY AND FISCAL ACTIONS: DID THEIR RELATIVE IMPORTANCE IN THE UNITED STATES CHANGE WITH FLEXIBLE EXCHANGE RATES?"

Manfred J.M. Neumann

Dewald and Marchon (D-M) are concerned with the relative importance of monetary and fiscal actions under flexible exchange rates. The authors entertain three conjectures about the probable consequences of the transition from fixed to flexible rates: first, under flexible rates changes in money will have a smaller short- to medium -run effect on total spending; second, changes in government spending, financed by debt, will have a larger effect than before; third, changes in import prices will play a more prominent role in shaping the public's expectations of inflation.

To check on the validity of their conjectures D-M estimate modified versions of the St. Louis spending, price, and price anticipations equations for the period of fixed exchange rates, for the following period of flexible rates, as well as for the total period. From their regression results the authors conclude, first, that indeed changes in import prices nowadays are playing a significant role in the generation of inflation expectations and, second, that money is of somewhat lessened relative importance to government spending in affecting total demand. In the final part of their paper D-M use estimates obtained from the fixed exchange rates period to extrapolate endogenous variables for the flexible exchange rates period. It is not too clear what that exercise is for. Of course, they observe that the extrapolated values for all variables are off base. But that was to be expected anyway, for econometric as well as for theoretical reasons.

ON THE RELATIVE IMPORTANCE OF MONEY AND GOVERNMENT SPENDING UNDER DIFFERENT EXCHANGE RATE REGIMES

D-M's reasoning on the conjectured change in the relative importance of monetary and fiscal policy,[1)] appears to confuse two issues: One issue concerns the short-run versus the long-run effects on income of monetary and fiscal policy under a regime of flexible exchange rates. The other issue concerns the relative importance of monetary and fiscal policy in the shorter run under different exchange rate regimes. While it can be shown that the short-run effect of monetary policy on income - given flexible exchange rates - is smaller than the long-run effect as well as that the short-run effect of fiscal policy is larger than its long-run effect, this argument does say nothing with respect to the question whether the short-run effects of these policies are smaller or larger under flexible rates than under fixed rates.

To make the point let us briefly go back to the Mundell-Fleming analysis. Consider monetary policy first. Given flexible exchange rates and perfect capital mobility, the domestic interest rate cannot deviate from the world interest rate. An expansion of the money supply, therefore, will not result in a fall of the domestic interest rate but in an outflow of capital and thus a depreciation of the currency. The depreciation, in turn, will improve the trade balance and stimulate income and employment. As the interest rate remains unchanged, income will increase in proportion to the expansion of the money supply. This is the long-run case.

In the short run, in contrast, differences between the spot exchange rate and the expected or permanent exchange rate come into

---

1) For brevity I forgo to enumerate the familiar arguments against D-M's identification of changes in the money supply (government expenditure) with monetary (fiscal) actions.

the play. Given a less than unity elasticity of the expected with respect to the spot exchange rate (Niehans, 1975, and Dornbusch, 1976), the domestic interest rate will fall as the spot rate will increase by more than the expected exchange rate. The trade balance may improve (though need not) but by less than later when the expected exchange rate catches on. Consequently nominal income will rise but by less than in the long run because the temporarily lower rate of interest dampens the effect of the monetary expansion through the induced lower income velocity of money.

But will the short-run effects of monetary policy on income be smaller with flexible rates than with fixed rates? The answer is negative. Consider the following expression which can be derived from the Niehans-Dornbusch model described in Table 1:

$$\left.\frac{dy}{d\bar{L}}\right|_{(\text{flex.})} = (1 + a) \left.\frac{dy}{d\bar{L}}\right|_{(\text{fix.})}$$

Provided the Marshall-Lerner conditions holds, $T_e + T_{\bar{e}} > 0$, the short-run effects of monetary policy, given flexible exchange rates, will exceed the short-run effects under fixed exchange rates by a multiplier (1 + a). The multiplier exceeds unity and increases with a rising elasticity of the expected exchange rate with respect to the spot rate.

What can we say about the effects of fiscal policy? In a world of flexible rates the net long-run effect of fiscal policy on income is zero. The explanation is simple: With the domestic interest rate fixed at the world interest rate level the positive income effect of an expansion of government expenditure will be matched exactly by the contractive effects of an exchange rate appreciation. The appreciation of the exchange rate is induced by the upward pressure on interest rates which results from the government's financing of the deficit by issuing additional bonds. With an unchanged money stock and a constant interest rate level, income velocity and, therefore, income will remain unchanged.

TABLE 1: The Niehans-Dornbusch Model

The following model is taken from Dornbusch (1976).

(1) $y = E(i,y,e,\bar{e}) + T(y,e,\bar{e})$, with $E_e = -T_e = -E_{\bar{e}} > 0$

(2) $\bar{L} = L(y,i)$,

(3) $i = i^* + (\bar{e}/e - 1)$,

where y = income, i = domestic rate of interest, i^* = foreign rate of interest, e = spot exchange rate, $\bar{e}$ = expected exchange rate, L = money stock.

The model allows the solutions:

$$\frac{dy}{d\bar{L}}\Big|\ (\text{fix.}) = \frac{E_i}{E_i L_y + (s+m)L_i} > 0,$$ without (perfect) capital mobility

$$\frac{dy}{d\bar{L}}\Big|\ (\text{flex.}) = \frac{E_i - \sigma\theta}{(E_i - \sigma\theta)L_y + (s+m)L_i(1-\sigma)} > 0,$$ with $\theta = E_i + T_e + T_{\bar{e}}$, $\theta > 0$

$$= (1+a)\frac{dy}{d\bar{L}}\Big|\ (\text{fix.})$$

with $a = [-(s+m)L_i\sigma(T_e + T_{\bar{e}})] / \Delta > 0$

$$\Delta = E_i\ [E_i - \sigma\theta)L_y + (s+m)L_i(1-\sigma)]$$

$\frac{da}{d\sigma} > 0$, provided $T_e + T_{\bar{e}} > 0$

Note: σ = elasticity of the expected exchange rate with respect to the spot exchange rate.

In the shorter run, in contrast, the spot exchange rate will appreciate by more than the expected rate. Consequently, the positive income effect of the expansion of government expenditure will only partly be offset by contractive effects induced by exchange rate appreciation. Put it differently, the domestic interest rate will temporarily increase. This allows velocity and, therefore, income to rise.

From this analysis, however, one cannot deduce that the short-run effects of fiscal policy will necessarily be larger under flexible exchange rates than with fixed rates. Without perfect mobility of capital - and this defines the short-run case - the domestic rate of interest will respond to the upward pressure induced by expansionary fiscal policy. Consequently, even with fixed exchange rates velocity will temporarily rise and, therefore, income.

The evidence presented by D-M (see their Table 1) appears to be inconclusive. The Chow-test indicates no significant change in the structure of the spending equation after the transition to floating. The separate estimates for the fixed and the flexible exchange rate periods point to a complete crowding-out. The total elasticity of nominal GNP with respect to government expenditures remains insignificant during both sample periods.[2)] Moreover, none of the individual fiscal terms reaches significance after the transition to floating.

For monetary policy we observe significant positive effects during the fixed exchange rates period. They tend to be distributed over four quarters and sum to 0.82. Under flexible rates, in contrast, monetary policy shows up only in the current quarter though

---

2) Only for the total sample period the impact elasticity of government spending reaches significance. But note that Carlson (1978) found the total elasticity to be insignificant for the period I/1953 - IV/1976.

with an exceptionally large and significant elasticity of 0,93. Given the analysis presented above, this observation rings the bell. It might very well be and fits other observations that the elasticity of the expected exchange rate with respect to the spot rate is much closer to unity already in the very short run than sceptics tend to believe. Of course, we have to acknowledge that D-M's total elasticity of income with respect to money is insignificant and small. But that is probably due to the inclusion of too many lags. D-M choose the same lag structure for the flexible exchange rates period as for the fixed rates period, presumably with regard to the applicability of the Chow-test. What one would like to see, however, is that the authors reestimate the spending equation for the flexible rates sample period with a reduced number of lags for both, the monetary and the fiscal variable.

ON THE ROLE OF IMPORT PRICES

D-M extend the adaptive St. Louis price anticipations equation by adding distributed lags of the demand pressure variable, D, and of changes of import prices, ΔW. While this allows them to obtain a better overall fit, it also introduces collinearity problems which bias the estimated coefficients. Thus we cannot be too sure about the reliability of the estimated structure.

D-M's estimates of the price anticipations equation (see their Tables 2 and 3) uniformly assign a small impact to the demand pressure variable[3] but they do not provide conclusive information on the role of import prices. The estimate presented in Table 2 for the sample period of flexible exchange rates denies any significant effect on price anticipations to import prices.

3) D-M point to a possible distortion in the St. Louis demand pressure variable and present an alternative definition. In estimation they nevertheless use the St. Louis variable on the grounds that it yields "a slightly better statistical fit than the alternative".

The estimate of Table 3, in contrast, uncovers a significant positive impact for the post-floating subperiod when before and after floating dummy variables are included. This result requires explanation.

Why should import prices enter significantly into price expectations under flexible rates but not before? D-M conjecture that flexible rates make the public more aware of the price determining role of import prices. It seems to me that this is a rationalization rather than an explanation. It may be true that the public pays more attention to import prices these days than during the sixties'. I would conjecture, however, that this results from the observation of a much larger variance of the rate of change of import prices since the oil shock rather than from the transition to flexible exchange rates. D-M also suggest that under flexible rates the U.S. authorities might feel free to validate price level effects of import price inflation. If this were the case, however, a "rational price expectations function" would not have to rely on the import price variable. Instead, it would assign a more prominent role to demand pressure or directly to anticipated monetary, fiscal and foreign impulses.[4)]

Finally, let me point to a peculiar feature of the D-M model. The rate of change of import prices enters the price anticipations equation but not the spending equation. This implies that changes of import prices affect (through price anticipations) the domestic price level and real GNP equally, though with opposite signs. The implied numerical equality of the elasticity of the price level with respect to the import price level, $\varepsilon(P,W) > 0$, and of the elasticity of real GNP with respect to import prices, $\varepsilon(X,W) < 0$, constitutes a severe restriction. One would like to learn why the authors believe that this restriction may be justified. According to D-M's estimates changes in import prices have a relatively small effect on anticipated inflation and, therefore, on actual inflation.

---

4) See Dutton (1978).

If true it would mean that the import price shock of the seventies had only a small contractionary impact on real output in the U.S.

REFERENCES

Carlson, K.M 1978, Does the St. Louis Equation Now Believe in Fiscal Policy? Federal Reserve Bank of St. Louis, Review 6o, Nr. 2, 13-19.

Dornbusch, R. 1976, Exchange Rate Expectations and Monetary Policy, Journal of International Economics 6, 231-244.

Dutton, D.S. 1978, The Economics of Inflation and Output Fluctuations in the U.S., 1952 -74, The Problem of Inflation, K. Brunner and A.H. Meltzer (eds.), Carnegie-Rochester Conference Series 8, 2o3-231.

Niehans, J. 1975, Some Doubts About the Efficacy of Monetary Policy Under Flexible Exchange Rates, Journal of International Economics 5, 275-281.

COMMENT ON W.G. DEWALD "MONETARY AND FISCAL ACTIONS: DID THEIR RELATIVE IMPORTANCE IN THE UNITED STATES CHANGE WITH FLEXIBLE EXCHANGE RATES?" *

Robert Solomon

William Dewald and his collaborator, Maurice Marchon, have chosen to explore a topic of considerable importance. Although we have a body of received theory on the implications of different exchange rate regimes for the effectiveness of fiscal and monetary policies (Mundell 1968, Fleming 1971), these results are qualitative rather than quantitative. Empirical testing and measurement are in order. The second objective of the paper - to explore the role of import prices in the formation of inflationary expectations - is also of considerable interest.

Having praised the objectives of the paper under review, I wish that I could be equally laudatory of the outcome. Unfortunately, I find it to be unsatisfactory both in analysis and in interpretation. I shall group my major criticisms under three headings and a conclusion.

THEORETICAL HYPOTHESES

The authors start off with the presumption that the public might be more aware of import price variations under flexible exchange rates than under fixed rates. They argue that, under fixed rates, an increase in import prices would worsen the balance

---

* The views expressed in this statement are the sole responsibility of the author and do not purport to represent those of the Brookings Insitution, its Officers, Trusteers, or other staff members.
I am grateful to my colleague Robert Z. Lawrence for helpful suggestions.

of payments and lead to more restrictive demand management policies that would tend to reduce domestic prices. Under flexible rates, this policy reaction would not occur and therefore import prices would have a bigger role in the formation of inflationary expectations. This result assumes an elasticity of demand for imports of less than unity. If the elasticity is greater than unity, these presumptions are reversed. Under flexible rates, the importing country's currency would tend to appreciate, thereby dampening the impact on domestic prices. Thus the initial theoretical presumption is faulty.

Concerning the impact of fiscal and monetary policies, the authors begin by rejecting for the short run, the now-conventional belief that monetary policy would be more powerful under flexible rates and fiscal policy less powerful. But their argument is based entirely on the temporary J-curve effects of exchange rate changes. A more stimulative fiscal policy with a fixed money supply raises interest rates, which appreciates the currency. Until prices and quantities of tradable goods react, the appreciation increases net exports, thereby augmenting the expansionary effect of the fiscal policy action. As the authors concede, the reverse would be expected once the temporary J-curve effects give way.

THE MODEL

To test their theoretical hypotheses, the authors use a modified St. Louis Model. The spending equation appears to be that of Anderson and Carlson (1972) with an export variable added. Except for exports, the equation contains no variables reflecting private consumer or investment spending or private assets. Changes in nominal GNP are determined by changes in the money stock, with a distributed lag, by changes in high employment Federal expenditures, with a similar lag, and by changes in exports in the current period. This is a world in which there are no autonomous private decisions worthy of consideration. Apart from the omission of variables relating to private behavior, one can quarrel with the fiscal policy variable. High employment Federal expenditures are not an adequate measure of fiscal policy, which can also involve changes in tax rates.

The price equation is a simplified version of Anderson-Carlson with the addition of an import price variable with a distributed lag. Changes in prices depend on changes in excess demand, changes in prices over the past 15 quarters, and changes in import prices over the past 4 quarters. As in the case of the spending equation, it is difficult to relate this model to economic behavior. Neither wages nor productivity appear. Furthermore, one may doubt that price changes over the past 17 quarters, whatever their cause, are an adequate measure of price expectations. Gordon (1972) has criticised this model.

THE STATISTICAL RESULTS

Applying the data to their reduced form equations for nominal GNP, Dewald and Marchon come up with a much higher multiplier for money than for government spending, when the lagged coefficients are summed. But a number of the coefficients are negative, which makes one suspicious. And the sum of the lagged coefficients for the entire period is higher than for either of the sub-periods, 1956 I - 1971 III and 1971 III - 1977 II. My own presumption is that the authors should have found an increase in the money multiplier in the 197o's, a period when velocity increased sharply and given increases in the money stock were associated with larger increases than earlier in nominal GNP. One cannot help believing that the equation is poorly specified.

The price equation shows increased importance for import prices after floating though this is probably not the result of floating but of the shocks of the 197o's. It is plausible - in fact obvious - that the U.S. economy was more influenced by rising import prices in the 197os than earlier. Whether it is plausible that the elasticity of domestic prices rose with respect to import prices is another question.

When they estimate their equations from data through 1971 II and then extrapolate the endogenous variables to the later period, the authors find that the model underpredicts inflation and fails to predict the recession of 1975. Once again, it is not clear whether the apparent increase in the coefficient for import prices is valid or a result of mis-specification. The authors believe that the failure to pick up the recession is attributable to the failure of the model to forecast the rate of inflation adequately. What this seems to mean is that the model predicted nominal income but not the mix between prices and real output. It assumes that nominal income is influenced only by monetary and fiscal policy, leaving no role for the contractionary impact of the increase in oil prices and other autonomous factors, as the authors appear to acknowledge in the latter part of the paper.

CONCLUSION

It is astonishing to find a set of policy recommendations at the end of the paper, considering the rather thin analytical basis for the statistical results. The authors come up with the conventional monetarist prescription: fixed rules rather than discretionary authority. Given the importance of external shocks in the 197os, it is impossible to understand how these conclusions can be justified. Both shocks on the supply side and the reactions of private spending on the demand side seem to justify countercyclical rather than steady fiscal and monetary policies.

In any event, we have to look to future work to throw light on the main question posed in the paper: has the relative effectiveness of fiscal and monetary policies been altered by the advent of floating?

REFERENCES

Anderson, Leonall C. and Carlson, Keith M., "An Econometric Analysis of the Relation of Monetary Variables to the Behavior of Prices and Unemployment," in The Econometrics of Price Determination, Conference October 3o-31, 197o. Washington, D.C. (1972).

Fleming, J. Marcus, Essays in International Economics, Havard University Press, 1971.

Gordon, Robert J., "Discussion", in The Econometrics of Price Determination (1972).

Mundell, Robert A., International Economics, Macmillan, New York, 1968.

A REACTION FUNCTION FOR FOREIGN EXCHANGE INTERVENTION IN THE NETHERLANDS: SOME EMPIRICAL AND METHODOLOGICAL CONSIDERATIONS

M.M.G. Fase and A.P. Huijser

The intervention policy of the monetary authorities is reflected in the code of rules by which the central bank operates in the foreign exchange market and in the forward market. These rules are often restricted by international agreements such as fixed parities or the so-called snake arrangement. Nevertheless, central banks and other intervention agencies usually have considerable scope for manoeuvering, notably since the dollar began to float in 1973.

The interdependence between foreign exchange intervention and domestic monetary policy has always been recognized both by theoreticians and practicians. Of late this interdependence has received considerable attention in the literature through the use of reaction functions for foreign exchange intervention by monetary authorities [see e.g. Artus (1976), De Grauwe (1975), Helliwell (1969) and Hutton (1977)]. One approach followed by Artus, De Grauwe and Helliwell is to complete a structural model of the economy with a reaction function for foreign exchange intervention as one of the structural equations. An important reason for including a reaction function is that estimation biases have to be avoided; this can be achieved by treating policy instruments as truly endogenous. The other approach, applied by Hutton for foreign exchange intervention and by others for monetary policy in a broader sense,[1] extends a structural model with the objective function of the

1) See Fase & Den Butter (1978) for a review of the literature as well as an application to Dutch monetary policy.

monetary authority. Thus, the reaction function results from constrained maximization of this objective function. However, one may argue that in spite of the methodological difference between the two approaches, the choice between them is mainly a question of research strategy. The importance of the reaction function is that it takes explicitly into account the fact that the values of the instrument are generated by the model rather than dictated by the external world. Therefore a reaction function may be viewed as one of the behavioural equations in an econometric model, a point also stressed by De Grauwe (1978) and Minford (1978).

The present paper develops reaction functions for intervention policy in the Netherlands. As we all know, the guilder floats against the dollar but is fixed against the German mark as well as against the other snake currencies. This enables us to study the question put by Lindbeck (1976), whether the effects on politicians, i.e. the behaviour functions of policy makers, differ over the two simultaneous exchange rate regimes.

The paper is organized into four sections. The first section contains a historical record of intervention policy in the Netherlands for the period 1973 - 1977. The second section develops the theoretical framework for the specification of a reaction function. The estimation results, derived from monthly observations over the floating period, are presented in section three. The paper concludes with a summary of the principal findings.

1. INTERVENTION POLICY IN THE NETHERLANDS, 1973 - 1977

The post-war episode of fixed exchange rates came to an end on March 19, 1973. In a deliberate attempt to maintain the informal gold parity after the devaluation of the US dollar on February 12, the central banks of Germany, France, Belgium and the Netherlands had to buy large amounts of dollars at the beginning of March. The Netherlands, for example, made large dollar purchases to the amount of Fl. 2,2 billion (i.e. 1,3 % of GNP in 1973) over a period of only two weeks. As a result, the central banks of the countries adhering to the European intervention scheme (see table 1) withdrew their official rates for the US dollar. This decision seems to form the borderline between the nearly universal fixed exchange rate system and the mixed exchange rate system of floating and fixed parities. This is illustrated in Chart 1, which depicts the effective appreciation of the guilder during the seventies against different trade areas as well as against the member countries of the European currency agreement. The curve denoting the effective appreciation of the guilder against the so-called snake countries also reflects the major events of Dutch intervention policy during the last five years. The dips and tops coincide with major sales and purchases of partner currencies or dollars. Thus, in the period from March 19 to the end of July 1973 the Netherlands Bank had to sell partner currencies, while partner central-banks had to buy guilders to the amount of about Fl 4,8 billion. Effective September 17, 1973 the guilder was revalued by 5 %, resulting in new intervention rates for the snake currencies. The tight money market induced the Bank from September 26 to October 5 to conclude dollar swaps to the considerable amount of Fl. 1,3 billion, while in October intervention amounted to Fl. 1,330 million in partner currencies (mainly French francs) and to Fl. 200 million in dollars.

Because of the strong position of the guilder at the beginning of 1974, the Bank had to buy partner currencies to the amount of Fl. 570 million (mainly French francs). On January 21, the French decided to leave the snake. Following the Herstatt affair most partner central banks had to support the German mark. As a result, the Bank's interventions from July to October 1974 amounted to Fl. 2,3 billion.

In order to stabilize the heavy fluctuations in the dollar rate during 1975 the Bank undertook a large number of small dollar interventions. In the second quarter the Bank had to make purchases to an amount of about Fl. 550 million to support the German mark,

CHART 1: EFFECTIVE APPRECIATION OF THE GUILDER

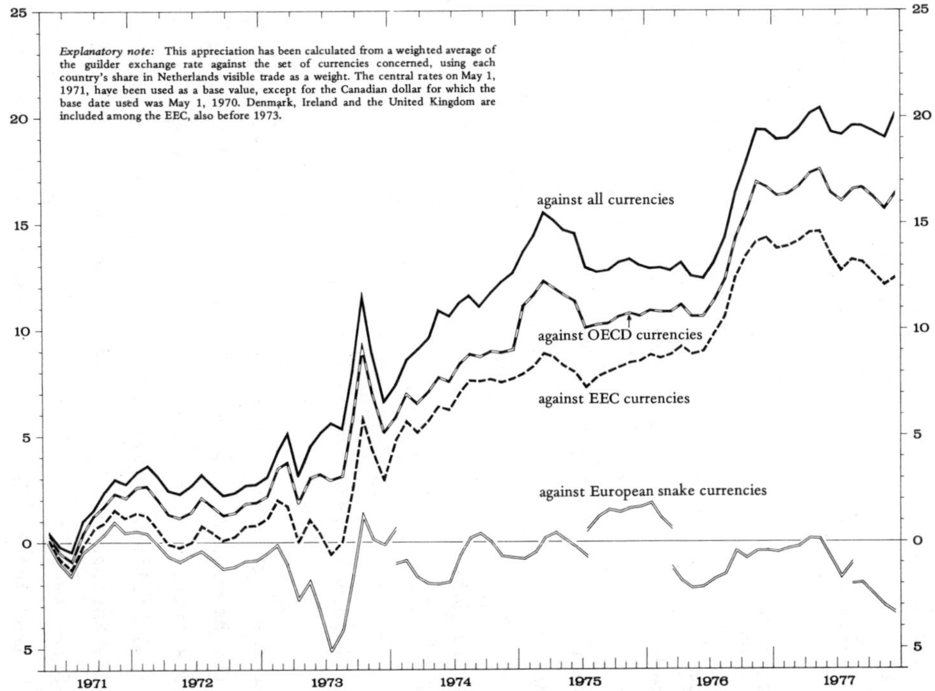

which was then at the bottom of the snake. On July 10 France re-entered the European currency agreement (see table 1). The most dramatic event was the fall of the dollar rate to a low of Fl.2,3375, i.e. a fall of over 6 % on March 3, 1975. The main reason for this was the state of the US economy and the movements of short-term interest rates.

TABLE 1: Member countries of the European currency agreement

Countries	Membership period			
	from	until	from	until
Belgium	1972 : 4			
Denmark	1972 : 5	1972 : 6	1972 : 10	
France	1972 : 4	1974 : 1	1975 : 7	1976 : 3
W.-Germany	1972 : 4			
Ireland	1972 : 5	1972 : 6		
Italy	1972 : 4	1973 : 2		
The Netherlands	1972 : 4			
Norway	1972 : 5			
Sweden	1973 : 3	1977 : 8		
United Kingdom	1972 : 5	1972 : 6		

At the beginning of 1976 substantial interventions took place. Under the Benelux arrangement the Belgian and Dutch central banks undertook intervention in each other's currencies to an amount of over Fl. 1 billion. On March 14, France decided a second time to leave the European exchange rate arrangement, following the heavy loss of reserves to the Banque de France during the preceding days. At the same time the Benelux arrangement - which confined the largest margin of fluctuation between the guilder and the Belgian franc to 2 x 1 1/2 % rather than to 2 x 2 1/4 % - was abandoned.

Throughout the second quarter the guilder remained at the bottom of the snake and had to be supported by the Bank. In May and June the Bank sold $ 950 million to maintain the DM-rate. This resulted in a tight money market with an increase in the rate of interest (from 3 % in March to 8.5 % in June). To relieve the tight money market the Bank concluded one-month dollar swaps to an amount of Fl. 400 million. On August 13, however, a strong demand for German marks in Amsterdam prompted the Bank to sell German marks to a sizable amount, which resulted in particularly heavy borrowing from the Bank by the banking system. After these facilities were restricted, the guilder made a sharp recovery, which enabled the Bank to buy large amounts of dollars and German marks: between August 20 and October 17 total net purchases amounted to $ 580 million and DM 400 million, while at the beginning of October Fl. 640 million one-month dollar swaps were concluded. On October 18, the official rates of the snake countries were adjusted. However, this adjustment hardly affected the market rates of the guilder and the German mark. In view of the money market conditions the Bank bought DM 485 million and $ 150 million during the period from October 18 to the end of November.

After a relatively quiet first quarter, the Bank had to support the German mark to a total of Fl. 1,2 billion during the second quarter of 1977. In addition, it made dollar purchases to an amount of Fl. 550 million. This led to an easy money market, which was reflected by the fall of the rate for one-month interbank deposits from 6 1/4 % in March to 2 1/4 % in mid-May. This corresponded with a strong position of the guilder, making interventions in the foreign exchange market unnecessary. In August 1977 Sweden withdrew from the European currency arrangement. The Norwegian crown and the Danish crown depreciated by 5 %. After that, the guilder dropped to the lower part of the snake, without reaching the bottom however. During the last quarter the Bank had to buy and sell modest amounts of dollars. In December the Bank sold German marks on a small scale at exchange rates somewhat below the upper intervention point. The most remarkable event in 1977 was undoubtedly the sharp decline of the dollar to Fl. 2,28. Contrary to spot interventions, dollar swaps were extensively used to regulate the domestic money market conditions.

A historical account of the major events in the foreign exchange market is of necessity fragmentary. To obtain a more coherent picture, Chart 1 may be helpful as a guideline. The size and frequency of the Bank's intervention activity in the foreign exchange market is also measured by the average size of these transactions and their variations, set out in tables 2 to 4.

There are three ways in which the Netherlands Bank intervenes in the foreign exchange market: snake interventions, dollar interventions and swaps. Snake interventions resemble interventions in a fixed exchange rate system, although the central rate may vary. Table 2 sets out the absolute monthly average of guilder interventions in snake currencies, as well as their variability within the year.

TABLE 2: Foreign exchange intervention by the Netherlands Bank in snake currencies, 1973 - 1977* (millions of guilders)

	Absolute monthly average	Range	Relative variation (%)
1973	1.010	3.660	360
1974	290	1.465	500
1975	50	280	550
1976	310	1.880	610
1977	130	820	630

* To be precise: from April 1973 to October 1977.

Comparison of these figures with data for 1970 - 1972 clearly shows that the decision to maintain fixed exchange rates against the members of the European currency bloc, which was taken when the dollar started to float, has resulted in a considerable increase in intervention activity, which took place at irregular intervals.[2)]

---

2) The absolute monthly averages (and relative variation in %) of total intervention amounted to Fl. 23o mln, Fl. 25o mln and Fl. 35o mln (495 %; 500 % and 490 %) in 1970, 1971 and 1972 respectively.

However, it is also surprising to see that despite the increase in magnitude the relative variability of the amounts involved remained fairly constant, with the exception of 1973.

The Bank's dollar interventions are aimed at smoothing out exchange rate fluctuations or at controlling the position of the guilder in the snake. Although the average size of dollar interventions varied substantially over recent years the relative variation has decreased steadily, as is shown in table 3.

TABLE 3: Dollar intervention by the Netherlands Bank, 1973 - 1977*

(millions of guilders)

	Absolute monthly average	Range	Relative variation (%)
1973	40	360	900
1974	60	380	660
1975	90	390	430
1976	500	2.300	460
1977	140	530	370

* From April 1973 to October 1977.

Although the Bank's swap transactions, set out in table 4, are usually motivated by money market considerations (see Timmerman (1977)), it is obvious that swaps are potentially also an important foreign exchange market instrument. The fact that the range does not differ substantially from year to year reveals the mainly technical character of this intervention instrument.

Intervention in the foreign exchange markets is one of the important channels through which domestic money market conditions are influenced. In view of the monetary authorities' traditional emphasis on orderly conditions, the money market may restrict the capacity of the central bank to control exchange rates provided additional money market instruments are available. The actual relationship between foreign exchange intervention and the easening or tightening of the money market is shown in table 5, indicating the major causes of changes in the ease in the domestic money market during the seventies.

TABLE 4: Swap transactions by the Netherlands Bank, 1973 - 1977*

(millions of guilders)

	Absolute monthly average	Range	Relative variation (%)
1973	280	1.340	470
1974	410	1.480	360
1975	240	1.180	480
1976	190	1.130	580
1977	220	1.020	470

* From April 1973 to October 1977.

TABLE 5: Key indicators of the money market, 1970 - 1977 (averages)

(billions of guilders)

Causes of changes	1970	1971	1972	1973	1974	1975	1976	1977
Treasury	-1.0	-0.9	-1.0	-1.6	-1.7	0.0	1.3	-0.3
Expansion (-) of bank note circulation	-0.4	-0.5	-1.0	-0.8	-0.9	-1.7	-1.3	-1.4
Purchase (+) of foreign exchange	1.6	1.2	2.7	-0.2	4.5	1.2	-0.3	1.3
Money market transactions of the Bank	0.5	0.3	-0.8	2.3	-1.4	0.7	0.3	-0.2
Other influences*	-0.0	0.2	-0.1	-0.4	-0.2	0.0	0.1	0.1
TOTAL	0.6	0.3	-0.2	-0.7	0.3	0.2	0.1	-0.5

* Such as sales (-) of US Treasury paper to banks under repurchase agreements

The first two lines of the table refer to autonomous factors, the next two lines indicate the average magnitude of the compensating money market policy of the Bank. Of course this table does not reveal the pattern behind the figures.

2. AN ANALYTICAL FRAMEWORK FOR FOREIGN EXCHANGE INTERVENTION

2.1 THE REACTION FUNCTION

The central bank's intervention behaviour in the foreign exchange market could be summarized by a policy reaction function in the same way that consumer behaviour in the market for, let us say, cars is described by the demand functions for cars. Following Theil (1964), we view a policy reaction function as the result of the policy maker's attempt to maximize a social utility function (or minimize a loss function) in targets and instruments, taking into account the relevant economic interdependencies. Thus, analytically the derivation of a policy reaction function has been reduced to a constrained optimization process.

Let y_i ($i = 1, 2, \ldots, r$) denote the actual value of the ith policy target and x_j ($j = 1, 2, \ldots, q$) the actual value of the jth policy instrument. The preferences of the policy maker are summarized in his welfare or utility function. We assume that this function $\omega(\vec{x}, \vec{y})$, with $\vec{y}$ and $\vec{x}$ ($r \times 1$) and ($q \times 1$) vectors with the elements y_i and x_j respectively, can be approximated around the desired values $\vec{y}*$ and $\vec{x}*$ by the quadratic loss function

$$\omega(\vec{x}, \vec{y}) = (\vec{x} - \vec{x}*)'P \; (\vec{x} - \vec{x}*) + (\vec{y} - \vec{y}*)'Q \; (\vec{y} - \vec{y}*) \qquad (1)$$

with P and Q diagonal matrices of the order q and r respectively, showing the weight attached to each instrument and target in the utility function. Obviously specification (1) implies some characteristics of the assumed utility function, which make the problem tractable. First, the welfare function is static and the desired target values are assumed to be given for each point in time. Second, specification (1) implies the absence of interaction between instruments and target variables. This means that the policy maker is indifferent as to how the targets are achieved. Third, both instruments and targets enter the loss function, mainly because of the costs involved in using the instruments in the money and foreign exchange markets. Finally, because the arguments of the utility function consist of squared deviations from the desired values of the target variables and policy instruments, the direction of these deviations becomes irrelevant, which may be a rather restrictive hypothesis.

It is assumed that the policy maker attempts to maximize his welfare function over a single period, subject to the constraints of the working of the relevant economic environment. This may be assumed to be given by a linear model with the reduced form

$$\vec{y} = R\vec{x} + S\vec{z} \tag{2}$$

with R and S (r x q) and (r x s) matrices of reduced-form coefficients and $\vec{z}$ a (s x 1) vector of exogenous influences on $\vec{y}$. The effectiveness of instrument k for attaining target j may be measured by $\delta y_j / \delta x_k$. So matrix R in equation (2) contains all information about the effectiveness of the instruments.

The optimal values of the instrument $\vec{x}$ are obtained by maximizing equation (1) subject to constraint (2). This results in

$$\vec{x} = \vec{x}* + P^{-1}R'Q\ (\vec{y}-\vec{y}*) \tag{3}$$

which may be viewed as the theoretical basis for any specification of policy reaction functions. In this framework any x_j equals the corresponding desired value plus a linear combination of weighted deviations of actual from desirable target values. Each weight is the product of the effectiveness of instrument x_j with respect to the particular target and coefficients of the utility function given by (1).

In order to obtain the reduced-form coefficients we need to specify the relevant economic system explicitly.

2.2 THE MONEY AND FOREIGN EXCHANGE MARKETS

In the framework of section 2.1 the policy maker's social utility function has been constrained by a reduced form of the relevant section of the economy. Thus, these equations should reflect the central bank's stylized view on the working of the relevant markets. Of course such a stylized representation ignores a lot of details which are of the utmost importance in the day-to-day operations of the foreign exchange dealers with a central bank (see Timmerman (1977)). In our short-term analysis of intervention behaviour the real sector of the economy is considered to be exogenous. The money market, the foreign exchange market and the forward exchange market are the relevant markets in which the central bank operates. Thus our model, which draws upon previous work by, for example, Artus (1976), consists of three segments and is designed to rationalize the basic structure of the very sector of the economy which constrains the intervention behaviour of the central bank. Therefore we present the model in three distinct segments with the notation explained in Appendix A. An overall schematic view is given in Chart 2.

The first segment describes the working of the money market. It includes a central bank money supply equation and a money market rate equation which are respectively:

$$\Delta L = \Delta NFA + \Delta NDA \tag{4}$$

$$\Delta r^{d} = \alpha_1 \Delta L + \alpha_2 \Delta r^{cb} \tag{5}$$

Equation (4) is a balance sheet equation defining a change in bank liquidity, ΔL, as a net change in the foreign and domestic assets of the central bank, denoted by ΔNFA and ΔNDA respectively. According to equation (5) a change in the domestic money market

CHART 2 FLOW DIAGRAM OF THE MONEY AND FOREIGN EXCHANGE MARKETS MODEL

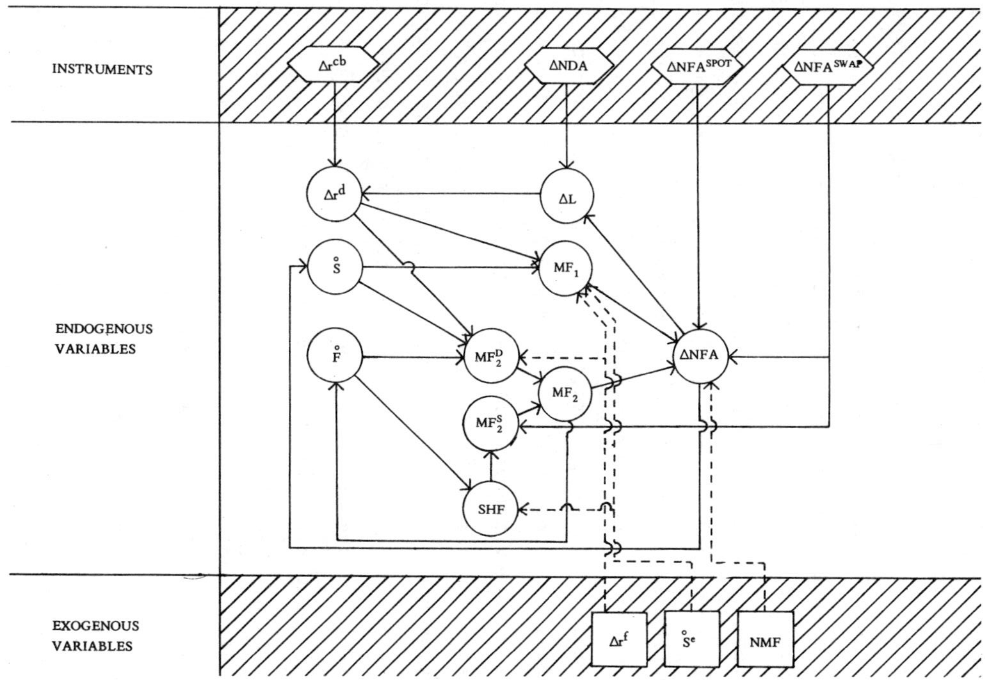

rate, Δr^d, is determined by a change in bank liquidity, ΔL, and a change in the cost of borrowing from the central bank, Δr^{cb}. The signs of the coefficients are $\alpha_1 < 0$, $\alpha_2 > 0$. In this model ΔNDA and Δr^{cb} are exogenously determined: r^{cb} is fixed by the central bank in view of its policy objectives and the development of foreign money market rates;[3)] ΔNDA is also an instrument and is partially determined by autonomous factors as the behaviour of the Treasury's cash balances and the movements of the bank note circulation. The other three variables are endogenous, with ΔNFA being explained in the second segment of our system, which summarizes the working of the foreign exchange market. The spot market is represented by the following four equations:

$$\Delta NFA = \Delta NFA^{SPOT} + \Delta NFA^{SWAP} \tag{6}$$

$$\Delta NFA = MF_1 + MF_2 + NMF \tag{7}$$

$$MF_1 = \beta_0 + \beta_1 \Delta r^d + \beta_2 \Delta r^f + \beta_3 \dot{S}^e + \beta_4 \dot{S} \tag{8}$$

$$MF_2^D = \gamma_0 + \gamma_1 \Delta r^d + \gamma_2 \Delta r^f + \gamma_3 \dot{F} + \gamma_4 \dot{S} \tag{9}$$

Equations (6) and (7) are accounting identities. Equation (6) describes that the supply of foreign exchange takes place via spot or swap transactions. Equation (7) is the balance of payments equation, distinguishing between monetary flows ($MF_1 + MF_2$), and non-monetary flows, NMF, the latter resulting from the basic balance. Equations (8) and (9) are behavioural equations for uncovered, MF_1, and covered, MF_2, short-term capital flows. The two equations are highly simplified versions of relationships derived from a general portfolio model. According to this model the stock of foreign assets is

3) See Fase (1973, 1976) for an empirical analysis of this interdependence.

determined by the level of domestic and foreign interest rates, denoted by r^d and r^f respectively, as well as by the risks and costs involved. In the present case we represent this in equation (8, 9) by the percentage change of the rates, $\dot{F}$, $\dot{S}^e$, and $\dot{S}$. The signs of the coefficients are β_1, γ_1, β_4, $\gamma_4 > 0$; β_2, γ_2, β_3, $\gamma_3 < 0$. In this segment of the model ΔNFA^{SPOT} and ΔNFA^{SWAP} are policy instruments; r^f, $\dot{S}^e$ and NMF are exogenously given and r^d is predetermined. The remaining six variables are endogenous, with MF_2 and $\dot{F}$ being explained in the third segment of our system, which summarizes the working of the forward market. This market is described by the following three equations:[4)]

$$SHF = \delta_1 \dot{F} + \delta_2 \dot{S}^e \qquad (10)$$

$$MF_2^S = SHF + \Delta NFA^{SWAP} \qquad (11)$$

$$(MF_2 \equiv)\ MF_2^D = MF_2^S \qquad (12)$$

Equation (10) describes the supply of forward exchange by speculation, equation (11) defines the total supply of forward exchange, while equation (12) is an equilibrium condition. The signs of the coefficients are $\delta_1 > 0$, $\delta_2 < 0$.

The complete model consists of ten linear equations which determine simultaneously the spot and forward rate of the guilder and the domestic money market rate in Amsterdam. The working of this model is shown in Chart 2, which offers a flow diagram of the model, with the endogenous variables in circles, the instruments in hexagons and the exogenous variables in rectangles.

4) See Tsiang (1959) for a more elaborated version.

2.3 FOREIGN EXCHANGE INTERVENTION

Foreign exchange intervention has two main targets (see Timmerman (1977)). First, it attempts to establish orderly conditions in the domestic money market. In the broader perspective of monetary policy this means that money market conditions should be in accordance with the credit policy of the Bank, which can easily be disturbed by a less appropriate interest rate structure in the money and capital markets. The second main target is the position of the guilder in the foreign exchange market. In our model, a strong guilder (i.e. $\dot{S}^e < 0$) reduces the forward rate in accordance with equation (1o) and encourages (as described in equation (8) and (9)) repatriation of foreign assets. Market equilibrium is reached by a decrease in the foreign exchange rate. Foreign exchange interventions attempt to reduce this upward pressure on the guilder, should it become undesirable. The resulting easening of the domestic money market amplifies the foreign exchange market effect to the interventions. In a small, open economy with a relatively small domestic money market, the impact on the domestic short-term interest rates of events in the foreign exchange market is sometimes very strong.

As mentioned before there are three main instruments through which the Netherlands Bank intervenes in the foreign exchange market: interventions in snake currencies, dollar interventions and swaps. The first two types of transactions are interventions in the spot market. In our analytical model they are indicated by ΔNFA^{SPOT}. Swap transactions, indicated by ΔNFA^{SWAP}, are interventions in the forward market, whereby guilders are exchanged for dollars at a premium or discount for a certain period. This is mainly one month, but sometimes three or six months. Very often the Bank makes use of dollarswaps to reduce excess demand in the money market.

By means of sales and purchases of foreign assets the Bank controls both the domestic money market and the foreign exchange market. To show this in the framework of our model, we have to solve the model by the "price-variables" Δr^d and $\dot{S}$. In doing so we have ignored the forward market for the sake of simplicity and obtain:

$$\begin{bmatrix} \Delta r^d \\ \\ \dot{S} \end{bmatrix} = \begin{bmatrix} \alpha_1 \\ \\ \frac{1-\alpha_1\beta_1}{\beta_4} \end{bmatrix} [\Delta NFA] + \begin{bmatrix} 0 & \alpha_1 & 0 & 0 & 0 & \alpha_2 \\ \\ -\frac{\beta_0}{\beta_4} & -\frac{\alpha_1\beta_1}{\beta_4} & -\frac{1}{\beta_4} & -\frac{\beta_2}{\beta_4} & -\frac{\beta_3}{\beta_4} & -\frac{\alpha_2\beta_1}{\beta_4} \end{bmatrix} \begin{bmatrix} 1 \\ \Delta NDA \\ NMF \\ \Delta r^f \\ \dot{S}^e \\ \Delta r^{cb} \end{bmatrix} \quad (13)$$

With $\Delta NFA = \Delta NFA^{SPOT} + \Delta NFA^{SWAP}$. Obviously the two reduced-form matrices are equivalent to the matrices R and S, used before equation (2). In view of this and the more general expression (3) we can easily derive the following policy reaction function for spot intervention:

$$\Delta NFA^{SPOT} = \Delta NFA^{SPOT^*} - \frac{\alpha_1 q_{11}}{p_{11}}(\Delta r^d - \Delta r^{d^*}) - \frac{1-\beta_1\alpha_1}{\beta_4}\frac{q_{22}}{p_{11}}(\dot{S}-\dot{S}^*) \quad (14)$$

According to our model, spot interventions have a direct impact on bank liquidity, which in turn determines the change in r^d. Thus the coefficient of $(\Delta r^d - \Delta r^{d*})$ is simply equal to α_1, weighted with parameters of the loss function $\omega(\ldots)$. In contrast, the impact of spot interventions on the exchange rate is more indirect, which is reflected by the composed structure of the coefficient of $(\dot{S}-\dot{S}^*)$ in equation (14), before being weighted with q_{22} and p_{11}.

Considering the complete model, which now includes the forward market, the reduced form for the target variables becomes:

$$
\begin{bmatrix} \Delta r^d \\ \dot{S} \end{bmatrix} = \begin{bmatrix} \alpha_1 & \alpha_1 \\ \frac{1-\alpha_1\beta_1-\alpha_1\gamma_1(1+\rho)}{\beta_4+\gamma_4(1+\rho)} & \frac{1-\alpha_1\beta_1-\alpha_1\gamma_1\ (1+\rho)+\rho}{\beta_4+\gamma_4(1+\rho)} \end{bmatrix} \begin{bmatrix} \Delta NFA^{SPOT} \\ \Delta NFA^{SWAP} \end{bmatrix} +
$$

$$
+ \begin{bmatrix} 0 & \alpha_1 & 0 & 0 & 0 & \alpha_2 \\ \frac{-(\beta_0+\gamma_0)}{\tau} & \frac{-\alpha_1\beta_1-\alpha_1\gamma_1(1+\rho)}{\tau} & \frac{-1}{\tau} & \frac{-(\beta_2+\gamma_2)-\gamma_2\rho)}{\tau} & \frac{-\beta_3+\delta_2\rho}{\tau} & \frac{-\alpha_2\beta_1-\alpha_2\gamma_1(1-\rho)}{\tau} \end{bmatrix} \begin{bmatrix} 1 \\ \Delta NDA \\ NMF \\ \Delta r^f \\ \dot{S}^e \\ \Delta r^{cb} \end{bmatrix} \qquad (15)
$$

with $\rho = \gamma_3/(\delta_1-\gamma_3)$ and $\tau = \beta_4 + \gamma_4(1+\rho)$. Again the two reduced-form coefficient matrices correspond to R and S.

Expression (15) shows that the impact of spot interventions on $\dot{S}$ differs from the impact of swap interventions. Assuming $\gamma_3 = 0$, i.e. assuming that short-term capital flows are inelastic with respect to the forward rate, spot and forward interventions have an equal impact on the exchange rate. If we take $\gamma_1 = \gamma_4 = 0$, i.e. assuming that covered capital transactions are independent of r^d and $\dot{S}$, the impact of spot interventions in the complete model is identical to this impact in the truncated model, i.e. without a forward market. The same is true if $\delta_1 = 0$; in this case the impact of ΔNFA^{SWAP} is equal to the impact of ΔNDA.

In conclusion we have derived the two policy reaction functions for spot and swap intervention which are:

$$\Delta NFA^{SPOT} = \Delta NFA^{SPOT^*} - \alpha_1 \frac{q_{11}}{p_{11}} (\Delta r^d - \Delta r^{d^*}) - \frac{1-\alpha_1\beta_1-\alpha_1\gamma_1(1+\rho)}{\beta_4+\gamma_4(1+\rho)} \cdot \frac{q_{22}}{p_{11}} (\dot{S}-\dot{S}^*) \qquad (16)$$

$$\Delta NFA^{SWAP} = \Delta NFA^{SWAP^*} - \alpha_1 \frac{q_{11}}{p_{22}} (\Delta r^d - \Delta r^{d^*}) - \frac{1-\alpha_1\beta_1-\alpha_1\gamma_1(1+\rho)+\rho}{\beta_4+\gamma_4(1+\rho)} \cdot \frac{q_{22}}{p_{22}} (\dot{S}-\dot{S}^*)$$

3. ESTIMATION OF INTERVENTION BEHAVIOUR: 1973 - 1977

Equation (16) in the previous section offers the general framework for our statistical analysis of intervention behaviour, provided that we make additional assumptions as to the desired values of targets and instruments. Although a wide variety of alternatives could be considered, we take $\dot{S}^* = 0$, $\Delta r^{d*} = \Delta r^f$ and $\Delta NFA^{SPOT*} = \Delta NFA^{SWAP*} = 0$. In view of the different exchange rate regimes they represent, we want to consider spot interventions in snake currencies and in dollars separately. Thus we obtain the following specification for our reaction function:

$$\Delta NFA^{i} = a_{i0} + a_{i1}\dot{S}FL + a_{i2}\dot{S}DOL + a_{i3}DR \qquad (17)$$

with $\dot{S}FL$ the relative position of the guilder in the snake;[5)] $\dot{S}DOL$ the US dollar exchange rate; $DR = \Delta r^{d} - \Delta r^{f}$, i.e. the differential between the change in the domestic and foreign money market rates. The domestic money market rate is determined by the interest rate on three-month interbank deposits; the foreign rate by three-month Euro-dollar deposits. As to the dependent variable ΔNFA^{i}, we have used i = FL for spot intervention in snake currencies, i = $ for spot interventions in dollars and i = SWAP for swap transactions. The expected signs of the coefficients are $\alpha_{i1}, \alpha_{i3} > 0$ and $\alpha_{i2} < 0$.

To begin with, we estimated the system of equations (17) with OLS,[6)] employing monthly observations over the period April 1973 - October 1977. Thus our sample period covers 55 months. The basic data are given in Appendix B. The estimation results for equations (17) are shown in table 6. Chart 3 shows the results for the interventions in the snake.

---

5) Computed as an average of the Friday figures of $\dot{S}FL'$, with $\dot{S}FL' = \frac{1/2(\dot{H}+\dot{L})+100}{\dot{F}L + 100} \times 100 - 100$ and $\dot{H}$ the percentage deviation from the parity of the snake currency with the highest appreciation; $\dot{L}$ this percentage deviation of the currency with the lowest appreciation; $\dot{F}L$ the percentage deviation of the guilder.

6) Since the explanatory variables in (17) are the same in each equation, application of Zellner's GLS-SUR technique would not produce any gain in efficiency. See Theil (1971).

TABLE 6: Estimation result for:

$$\Delta NFA^i = a_{i0} + a_{i1}\dot{S}FL + a_{i2}\dot{S}DOL + a_{i3}DR,\ 1973{:}4\text{–}1977{:}10^*$$

dependent variable i	a_{i0}	a_{i1}	a_{i2}	a_{i3}	DW	R^2
ΔNFA^{FL}	-136.1	498.0	26.7	-70.2	1.52	0.47
	(2.0)	(5.4)	(1.1)	(1.5)		
$\Delta NFA^{\$}$	-27.7	158.5	-34.0	-5.4	1.26	0.20
	(0.5)	(2.5)	(2.1)	(0.2)		
ΔNFA^{SWAP}	-34.4	81.8	-3.8	135.6	2.00	0.18
	(0.6)	(1.0)	(0.2)	(3.3)		

* The figures in parentheses are t-statistics.

Although the R^2 of the regressions do not point to a very good fit, the reported estimates show an interesting pattern, which seems to support the view that spot interventions primarily respond to the foreign exchange market, while swaps are mainly determined by the money market. The exchange rates of the guilder and the dollar are significant in the first two equations, but not in the third, while for the interest rate differential the opposite holds. The regression results for the spot interventions suggest some interdependence among snake and dollar intervention. Actually dollar interventions very often coincide with an extreme position of the guilder in the snake. This was particularly true in May and June 1976. To account for this interdependence we have rerun our regressions with a dummy variable which takes the value one for these two months and zero for the other months. The estimation results are shown in table 7. The most important result of the inclusion of the dummy variable is the dramatic decrease of the estimated coefficient of $\dot{S}FL$ in the dollar intervention equation, which also becomes insignificant. This suggests that the hypothesis of interdependence between guilder and dollar interventions is merely a statistical artifact,

Chart 3 Spot interventions in snake currencies

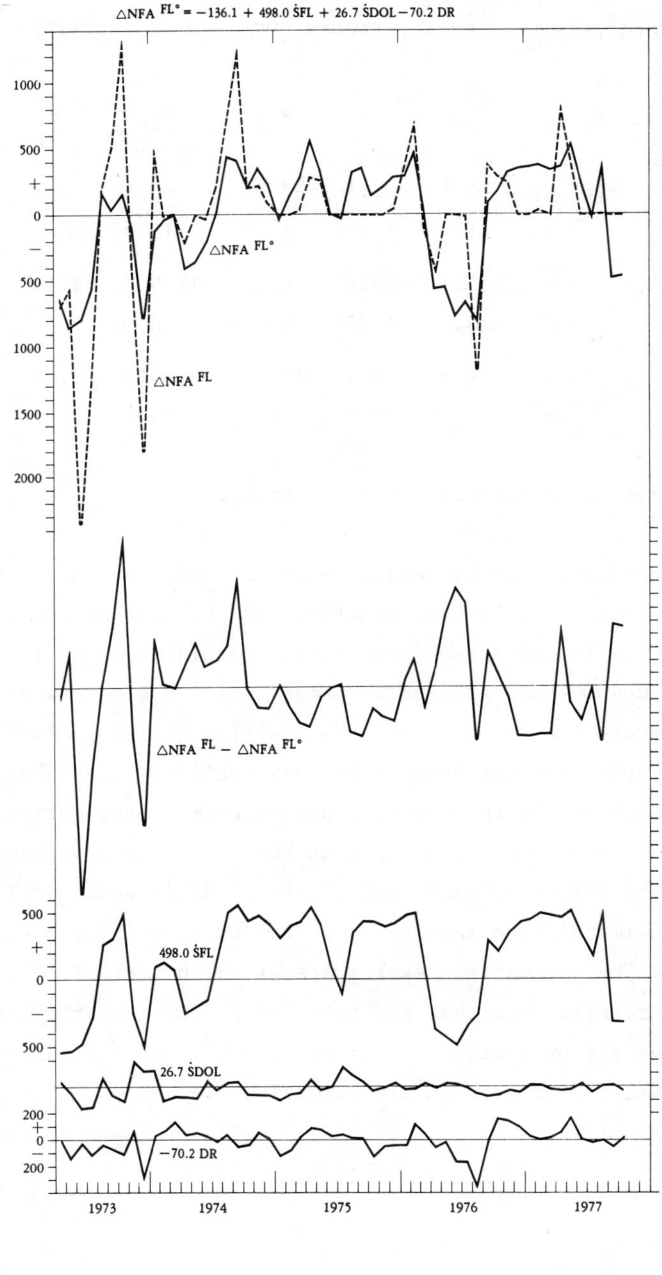

TABLE 7: Estimation results for:

$$\Delta NFA^i = a_{i0}+a_{i1}\dot{S}FL+a_{i2}\dot{S}DOL+a_{i3}DR+a_{i4}d, \quad 1973{:}4-1977{:}10^*$$

dependent variable i	a_{i0}	a_{i1}	a_{i2}	a_{i3}	a_{i4}	DW	R^2
ΔNFA^{FL}	-183.7	559.8	22.4	-75.6	768.4	1.68	0.52
	(2.7)	(6.0)	(1.0)	(1.6)	(2.3)		
$\Delta NFA^{\$}$	54.6	55.6	-26.8	3.5	-1279.3	1.70	0.66
	(1.7)	(1.3)	(2.5)	(0.2)	(8.3)		
ΔNFA^{SWAP}	30.4	76.6	3.4	136.1	-64.3	2.01	0.18
	(0.5)	(0.9)	(0.2)	(3.3)	(0.2)		

* The figures in parentheses are t-statistics.

rather than part of the systematic behaviour of the central bank. We note that in the first two equations the DW-statistic has improved, indicating an absence of serial correlation.

Until now we have assumed a linear relationship between the amount of snake intervention and the position of the guilder within the snake. This does not seem to be very realistic if exchange rates approaching the intervention points evoke interventions to a larger amount than otherwise. To test this hypothesis we have replaced $\dot{S}FL$ by the non-linear term $\dot{S}FL/(1.2^2-\dot{S}FL^2)$ with $\pm$ 1.2 - being approximately the intervention points of $\pm$ 1 1/8 - the asymptotes. The estimation results are given in table 8.

These results show that the non-linear transformation of $\dot{S}FL$ improves the DW statistic, but not the R^2. For a priori reasons the non-linear specification may be preferable.

TABLE 8: Estimation result for:

$$\Delta NFA^i = a_{i0} + a_{i1}\dot{S}FL/(1.2^2-\dot{S}FL^2) + a_{i2}\dot{S}DOL + a_{i3}DR,$$

1973:4-1977:10*

dependent variable i	a_{i0}	a_{i1}	a_{i2}	a_{i3}	DW	R^2
ΔNFA^{FL}	-111.0	191.8	14.4	-94.0	1.76	0.46
	(1.7)	(5.2)	(0.6)	(2.0)		
$\Delta NFA^{\$}$	-8.6	49.0	-37.9	-17.8	1.18	0.17
	(0.2)	(1.9)	(2.3)	(0.6)		
ΔNFA^{SWAP}	-31.7	33.6	-5.8	132.6	1.99	0.18
	(0.6)	(1.1)	(0.3)	(3.3)		

* The figures in parentheses are t-statistics.

The pattern emerging from this table does not differ from the results obtained earlier. Again the equation for $\Delta NFA^{\$}$ suggests some interdependence. Therefore we have re-estimated the equations with a dummy for the dollar interventions in May and June 1976. The results are shown in table 9.

TABLE 9: Estimation result for:

$$\Delta NFA^i = a_{i0} + a_{i1}\dot{S}FL/(1.2^2-\dot{S}FL^2) + a_{i2}\dot{S}DOL + a_{i3}DR + a_{i4}d,$$

1973:4-1977:10*

dependent variable i	a_{i0}	a_{i1}	a_{i2}	a_{i3}	a_{i4}	DW	R^2
ΔNFA^{FL}	141.7	205.2	9.9	-102.2	548.1	1.87	0.49
	(2.1)	(5.6)	(0.4)	(2.2)	(1.7)		
$\Delta NFA^{\$}$	59.7	19.2	-28.0	0.48	-1.299.9	1.67	0.66
	(2.0)	(1.2)	(2.6)	(0.0)	(8.6)		
ΔNFA^{SWAP}	-27.4	31.7	-5.2	133.7	-82.6	1.99	0.18
	(0.5)	(1.0)	(0.3)	(3.3)	(0.3)		

* The figures in parentheses are t-statistics.

These results show that the non-linear transformation of $\dot{SFL}$ improves the DW statistic, but not the R^2. For a priori reasons the non-linear specification may be preferable. The results of table 9 confirm our view that interventions in snake currencies and dollars are not systematically interrelated.

4. CONCLUSIONS

In this paper three reaction functions to describe Dutch intervention policy during the period April 1973 - October 1977, have been estimated with monthly data. We found that the two types of spot interventions were responsive to variations in the guilder exchange rates, but that swap interventions respond mainly to interest rate differentials. Thus our results support the view that spot interventions are mainly reactions to foreign exchange market conditions and that dollar swaps are mainly a money market instrument. Secondly, our results for spot interventions show a slightly different behaviour for snake and dollar interventions: the coefficient of the position of the guilder in the first equation is substantially larger than in the second equation, while the dollar coefficient systematically takes the wrong sign (which, however, is also insignificant) in the snake intervention equation.
This result is particularly interesting because the two reaction functions represent policy behaviour both in a fixed and a floating exchange rate regime. Finally, our findings indicate that foreign exchange intervention is endogenous rather than exogenous, as is implicitly assumed in the traditional treatment of policy instruments in econometric models. This means that actual intervention policy generates data which may lead to biased results if ignored in the estimation of econometric models of the foreign exchange market. The inclusion of a policy reaction function, reflecting the economic behaviour or the policy maker, seems a logical answer to this intellectual dilemma.

APPENDIX A

Notation of variables

Notation	Description
d	dummy, d = 1 for May and June 1976, otherwise d = 0
F	forward exchange rate
L	bank liquidity
MF	private monetary capital flows
MF_1	uncovered private monetary capital flows
MF_2^D	covered private monetary capital flows
MF_2^S	supply of forward exchange
NDA	net domestic assets of the central bank
ΔNFA^{SPOT}	central bank's spot interventions
ΔNFA^{SWAP}	central bank's swap transactions
NMF	basic balance
r^d	interest rate on three-month interbank deposits in Amsterdam
r^{cb}	central bank's discount rate
r^f	gross yield three-month Euro-dollar deposits
S	foreign exchange rate, in guilders
S^e	expected foreign exchange rate
SHF	private supply of forward exchange

APPENDIX B

On the data

Notation	Description
$\Delta NFA^{\$}$	dollar interventions of the Netherlands Bank[1]
ΔNFA^{FL}	guilder interventions in European snake currencies[1]
ΔNFA^{SWAP}	dollar swap transactions of the Netherlands Bank[2]
$\dot{S}FL$	relative position of the guilder exchange rate in the snake[1]
$\dot{S}DOL$	percentage change of the dollar-guilder exchange rate[2]
r^d	interest rate on three-month interbank deposits in Amsterdam[2]
r^f	gross yield Euro-dollar deposits[2]

1) Source: The Netherlands Bank
2) Source: Quarterly Statistics, De Nederlandsche Bank N.V.

TABLE B: Data used

period		(millions of guilders) $\Delta NFA^{\$}$	ΔNFA^{FL}	ΔNFA^{SWAP}	(%) $\dot{SFL}$	$\dot{SDOL}$	r^d	r^f
1973	4	0.0	-692.3	0.0	-1.08	1.612	2.33	8.21
	5	0.0	-552.8	0.0	-1.06	-1.678	4.56	8.51
	6	0.0	-2333.3	0.0	-.95	-5.866	5.25	8.85
	7	0.0	-1280.1	0.0	-.56	-5.466	8.36	10.40
	8	0.0	195.5	0.0	.53	3.015	9.97	11.50
	9	0.0	511.8	58.0	.63	-2.321	10.66	11.17
	10	196.0	1327.1	1164.0	1.02	-3.797	11.09	10.04
	11	0.0	-438.5	-5.0	-.50	7.422	9.79	9.91
	12	-160.0	-1787.9	1335.0	-.97	4.606	14.37	10.63
1974	1	0.0	496.2	-619.0	.19	4.613	12.70	9.41
	2	28.3	-1.0	386.0	.26	-3.732	10.78	8.52
	3	376.8	6.7	-818.0	.14	-2.610	9.57	9.27
	4	0.0	-207.7	-720.6	-.48	-2.807	10.15	10.53
	5	0.0	0.0	-45.3	-.39	-2.937	10.54	11.71
	6	0.0	-31.2	-585.2	-.30	2.006	10.53	12.15
	7	76.9	218.1	-149.9	.33	-.566	12.03	13.53
	8	0.0	769.6	0.0	1.01	1.374	11.53	13.65
	9	0.0	1256.8	499.4	1.13	1.565	11.07	12.47
	10	0.0	208.0	659.9	.89	-2.020	10.10	11.00
	11	136.7	220.8	-79.3	.98	-2.054	8.34	10.16
	12	67.7	83.2	-346.5	.83	-2.159	8.33	10.37
1975	1	156.7	0.0	407.0	.64	-3.534	8.16	8.56
	2	96.4	0.0	-106.0	.82	-1.933	8.03	7.34
	3	49.1	32.5	-593.9	.88	-1.581	7.22	6.93
	4	61.6	284.2	-393.7	1.11	2.210	6.04	7.12
	5	62.4	261.3	-11.7	.83	-.825	4.04	6.27
	6	0.0	0.0	-35.2	.20	.224	3.43	6.16
	7	-51.0	0.0	-134.2	-.18	5.882	3.82	7.18
	8	0.0	0.0	-2.2	.70	3.587	3.69	7.31
	9	-165.6	0.0	-4.4	.88	1.608	3.64	7.49
	10	336.3	0.0	586.5	.87	-1.039	5.03	7.18
	11	95.6	0.0	-419.4	.80	-.056	5.33	6.82
	12	0.0	40.3	227.0	.86	1.242	5.55	6.51

TABLE B: Data used (continued)

period		(millions of guilders)				%		
		$\Delta NFA^{\$}$	ΔNFA^{FL}	ΔNFA^{SWAP}	$\dot{S}FL$	$\dot{S}DOL$	r^d	r^f
1976	1	438.1	352.2	-253.3	.98	-.610	5.13	5.55
	2	231.6	707.9	0.0	1.01	-.351	3.39	5.56
	3	-489.8	-110.7	0.0	.15	1.096	2.99	5.87
	4	-26.9	-406.9	0.0	-.74	-.174	3.26	5.44
	5	-1032.0	0.0	0.0	-.86	1.083	4.00	6.04
	6	-1560.2	0.0	0.0	-.97	.784	6.57	6.28
	7	-180.1	-10.0	0.0	-.69	-.321	8.50	5.84
	8	706.4	-1167.5	438.4	-.52	-1.931	13.21	5.73
	9	776.7	379.1	-438.4	.60	-2.586	12.94	5.56
	1o	384.6	295.2	693.0	.44	-2.267	10.58	5.50
	11	170.1	253.3	427.9	.70	-1.099	8.33	5.34
	12	49.7	0.0	71.4	.86	-1.337	6.56	5.02
1977	1	-37.5	0.0	-793.6	.91	.623	6.24	5.18
	2	45.2	36.9	-305.0	1.01	.451	6.12	5.12
	3	12.5	0.0	227.4	.96	-.641	5.84	5.18
	4	346.0	821.9	-321.1	.94	-.953	4.98	5.19
	5	292.3	432.8	57.5	1.05	-.619	3.13	5.84
	6	-183.4	0.0	-57.5	.68	.907	2.96	5.84
	7	192.8	0.0	0.0	.38	-1.561	3.17	5.84
	8	80.8	3.4	0.0	1.03	.364	3.60	6.35
	9	0.0	0.0	213.9	-.63	.584	4.50	6.61
	1o	226.5	0.0	-213.9	-.64	-1.124	4.75	7.18

REFERENCES

Artus, J.R., 1976, Exchange rate stability and managed floating: the experience of the Federal Republic of Germany, IMF Staff Papers, XXIII, No. 2 (July), p. 312-333.

Fase, M.M.G., 1973, A principal components analysis of market interest rates in the Netherlands, 1962 - 1970, European Economic Review, 4, pp. 107-134.

Fase, M.M.G., 1976, The interdependence of short-term interest rates in the major financial centres of the world: some evidence for 1961 - 1972. Kyklos, 29, Fasc. 1, pp.63-96.

Fase, M.M.G & den Butter, F.A.G., 1978, The endogeneity of monetary policy in the Netherlands: two reaction functions of the central bank, Cahiers économiques et monétaires, (Banque de France) pp. 177-204.

De Grauwe, P., 1975, The interaction of monetary policies in a group of European countries, Journal of International Economics, 5, pp.207-228.

De Grauwe, P., 1978, Monetary policy and the exchange rate, in: Maynard, G. & Szász, A. & De Grauwe, P., Monetary policies in open economies, SUERF Series 19A.

Helliwell, J., 1969, A structural model of the foreign exchange market, Canadian Journal of Economics, II, no. 1 (Feb.), pp.90-105.

Herring, R.J. & Marston, R.C., 1977, National monetary policies and international financial markets, (North-Holland, Amsterdam).

Hutton, J.P., 1977, A model of short-term capital movements, the foreign exchange market and official intervention in the UK, 1963 - 1970, Review of economic studies, XLIV, No. 136 (Feb.), pp.31-41.

Lindbeck, A., 1977, Approaches to exchange rate analysis - an introduction, in: Herin, J., Lindbeck, A. & Myhrman J., Flexible exchange rates and stabilization policy (The Macmillan Press, London) pp.1-13.

Minford, P., 1978, Substitution effects, speculation and exchange rate stability (North Holland, Amsterdam).

Theil, H., 1964, Optimal decision rules for government and industry (North-Holland, Amsterdam).

Theil, H., 1971, Principles of Econometrics (North-Holland, Amsterdam).

Timmerman, P.C. 1977, Het interventiebeleid van de Nederlandsche Bank in de geldmarkt, in: Het functioneren van de Nederlandse geldmarkt, NIBE publicatie No. 3, pp.51-76 (available as: "The intervention policy of the Netherlands Bank in the money market", reprint No.33. De Nederlandsche Bank N.V.).

Tsiang, S.C., 1959, The theory of forward exchange and effects of government intervention on the forward exchange market, IMF Staff Papers, VII, no. 1, pp.75-106.

COMMENT ON M.M.G. FASE AND A.P. HUIJSER, "A REACTION FUNCTION FOR FOREIGN EXCHANGE INTERVENTION IN THE NETHERLANDS"

Frank Münnich

The paper by Fase and Huijser consists of three rather different parts. The first one gives a cursory description of the foreign exchange interventions of the Dutch National Bank during the last years, which I shall not comment upon as it only gives facts on the historical background of the later empirical analysis. Parts two and three are the mainbody of the paper containing a theoretical derivation of reaction functions along the lines of a (static) theory of quantitative economic policy and its application to an analysis of Dutch data respectively.

This approach is certainly a very useful one and especially for the Netherlands which supposedly is more inclined to use quantitative approaches to economic policy going back to Tinbergen than other countries might do and do. On the other hand, any application of this theory has to deal with the thorny problems of assigning plausible target values to the endogenous and instrument variables on the one hand and of estimating the coefficients which express the relative evaluation by the authorities of the losses due to differences between the actual and the intended values of the state variables on the other hand.

The paper gets around these difficulties rather "elegantly" by eliminating them by proper assumptions: the loss which might occur with any variable at any time is perfectly substitutable for any other, the elasticity of substitution being infinite. So the optimization is strictly static, each time period being optimized for its own without any intertemporal interrelations. The objective function - in addition - is completely separable, the matrices expressing the perceived relative losses deriving from deviations of the actual from the target values are supposed to be diagonal. As the objective function is quadratic and the specified structure of the economy strictly linear the derived reaction function of course need not be known in advance in order to allow estimation; they simply are hidden in the estimated coefficients. The assignment of the target values is even simpler: it is done according to plausibility.

These assumptions combined lead to an almost classically simple specification of the reaction functions to be estimated where one would get at without any optimization business at all by simple (plausible) guessing: exchange market interventions depend linearly on changes in exchange rates and international interest rate differentials. Consequently the analytical part has no bearing whatsoever on the empirical one which in turn disproves the assumed diagonality of the evaluation matrices (this being the only real connection between both parts mentioned by the authors).

The empirical part however is no better than the analytical because of fairly poor estimation results. So all published results for the forward exchange market show an R^2 of .18 while the minimum value for rejecting the hypothesis that R^2 would be zero at the 5 percent level would be about .36 to .38 according to the model under estimation. On this evidence I would conclude nothing serious about the tested hypothesis despite the fact that the coefficient of the interest rate differential is significant.

But even when R^2 is significantly above zero it never exceeds .66 and stays at .5 in several cases so that the spot exchange market interventions are poorly explained by the tested hypothesis. At least considering these results one must suspect that other alternative hypotheses might exist the explanatory power of which would be at least as good as that of the tested ones. Looking at the coefficients one easily realizes that quite a few of them are insignificant and of the significant ones there are several which show the wrong sign (the change in the dollar exchange rate shows consistently the wrong sign as the authors have pointed out themselves). Finally it is almost impossible to get an impression how much the explanatory variables contribute to the observed variance of the explained variables.

Looking at the data used in the estimation procedure one gets severe doubts that a technique implying smooth underlying functional relationships was the right thing to use in this case because the endogenous variables show extreme and sharp fluctions (especially compared to the regressors).

On the whole one it surprised at this paper. One is surprised at someone using econometric methods to find out that exchange market interventions like all economic policy are endogenous. After all: all economic policy is a reaction to expectations and experience and therefore endogenous all the time. It is only the analysis of real life situations which might treat economic policy as exogenous. This may certainly point towards as lack of competence on the part of the econometrician in many cases. But on the other hand, in view of the reaction thresholds which all individuals have and especially organizations and in view of the very often rather very abrupt character of political interventions it need not be a foolish research strategy under all circumstances.

One is even more surprised at two insiders using econometric methods on rather raw statistical data. Any econometrician would expect insiders to have much better, more detailed, more differentiated and more accurate knowledge of the motives, the decision processes and the steps finally taken of any policy than you can ever hope to get from an econometric analysis of global data.

AN EMPIRICAL MODEL OF THE SHORT RUN FLUCTUATIONS OF EXCHANGE RATES: THE CASE OF THE DEUTSCHMARK (DM) AND THE SWISS FRANC (SFR)*

Peter Bernholz, Peter Kugler

1. INTRODUCTION

The strong fluctuations of the world's major floating exchange rates are notorious. In the last three years several theoretical models have been developed which are to explain this phenomenon. What are the possible reasons of fluctuations used by some of these models? Let us first turn to a model developed by Rüdiger Dornbusch.[1] The author assumes that an immediate asset adjustment takes place, that trade is always in balance and that perfect foresight is present. From this rather rigorous assumption a first order differential equation results, which does not explain fluctuations endogenously, but leads to an overshooting of the exchange rate as the consequence, say, of a monetary expansion. Moreover, "during the adjustment process, rising prices may be accompanied by an appreciating exchange rate so that the trend behaviour of exchange rates stands potentially in strong contrast with the cyclical behaviour of exchange rates and prices."[2]

Kouri[3] and Calvo and Rodriguez[4] assume, too, in their models

---

* The authors gratefully acknowledge helpful comments from M. Ishaq Nadiri.

1) Rüdiger Dornbusch: Expectations and Exchange Rate Dynamics. Journal of Political Economy, vol. 84(6), December 1976, 1161-76.

2) op.cit., 1162.

3) P.K. Kouri: The Exchange Rate and the Balance of Payments in the Short and the Long Run: A Monetary Approach. Scandinavian Journal of Economics, vol. 78(2), 1976, 28o-3o4.

4) G.A.Calvo and C.A.Rodriguez: A Model of Exchange Rate Determination under Currency Substitution and Rational Expectations, Journal of Political Economy, vol.85(3), June 1977, 617-625.

immediate asset adjustment. The former, moreover, does not really consider trade flows, since these flows adjust passively to the required stock adjustment. It is true that Calvo and Rodriguez extend the analysis by making trade flows dependent on relative prices but they, too, still stick to the assumptions of perfect foresight and instantaneous stock adjustment.

Niehans in a recent paper removes these assumptions and postulates that the adjustment of money assets takes time.[5] The real demands for domestic and foreign moneys are dependent on the ratio of actual and expected exchange rate. Concerning expectations Niehans makes the radical assumption that the expected exchange rate is equal to the equilibrium rate. Even with these rather restrictive assumptions the model is able to generate a rich variety of adjustment paths, since the flow aspects have not been neglected. But Niehans himself is aware of the shortcomings of his simple model:[6] Export and import values react at once to changes in prices and the exchange rate; the formation of expectations is certainly not realistic; interest bearing assets are excluded.

Part of the theoretical and empirical discussion focuses on the question whether the overvaluation or undervaluation of exchange rates is caused by erratic monetary and fiscal policies or by excesses brought about by capital flight, speculation and hedging.[7] The answer to this question is, of course, important because of its political consequences. For it decides whether the public or the private sector is thought to be responsible for the strong fluctuations of foreign exchange rates.

---

5) Jürgen Niehans: Exchange Rate Dynamics with Stock/Flow Interactions, Journal of Political Economy, vol.85(6), December 1977, 1245-1257.
6) op.cit., 1256.
7) Compare Susan Schrader: Sources of Exchange Rate Variability: Theory and Empirical Evidence, International Monetary Fund Staff Papers, vol. XXIV(2), July 1977, 253-296.

As one can see from this sample of models discussed, all of them use only a segment of the rich set of theoretical relations which may be important. In this paper we intend first to formulate an empirically tractable short-run model which tries to incorporate the effects of asset adjustment and trade flows on exchange and interest rates. The term short run is used in the sense that in the time period considered, changes of exchange and interest rates do not affect output and prices. The second aim of this paper is to report the results of an empirical analysis of the dollar/DM and the dollar/SFR exchange rate based on monthly data from 1973 to the summer of 1977.

The contents of this paper can be outlined as follows. In section 2 the model is formulated and briefly discussed. The empirical results for the dollar/DM and the dollar/SFR case are reported in section 3 and 4, respectively. Finally, some conclusions and problems for future research are presented in section 5.

2. THE MODEL

Our model tries to explain the exchange rate between two countries and the ratio of their interest rates, given the exogeneous values of prices, outputs and money supplies of the two countries. In order to make the empirical implementation of the model easier we assume that all variables enter the model as ratios between home and foreign values. Let i_t, m_t, p_t, q_t be the respective ratios of interest rates, money supplies, price levels and output levels at time period t. The exchange rate, defined in units of foreign currency, is given by e_t and its expected value is marked with an asterix.

Under the assumption of immediate asset adjustment the exchange rate is determined by a portfolio equilibrium condition[8)]

8) E.g. $i_{ht} - i_{ft} = (e_t - e_t^*)/e_t$ in the Dornbusch model, where i_{ht} and i_{ft} are the home and foreign interest rates.

which has to be fulfilled at each point in time. If we relax this hypothesis by assuming that asset adjustment takes time, the exchange rate is determined by the balance of payments, i.e. by trade and capital flows.[9] Therefore we have the following structural equation for the exchange rate.

$$(1) \qquad e_t = f(e_t^* - e_t, i_t, p_t, q_t)$$

It is assumed that the capital flows caused by an increase of $(e_t^* - e_t)$ or i_t have a positive effect on e_t and that - given Marshall-Lerner-like conditions - the trade flows brought about by an increase of p_t or q_t depress e_t.

For the ratio of interest rates we postulate the following relationship.

$$(2) \qquad i_t = g(e_t^* - e_t, m_t, p_t, q_t)$$

Adopting the standard money demand hypothesis, we assume that an increase in p_t or q_t has a positive effect, one of m_t a negative effect on i_t. The term $(e_t^* - e_t)$ allows for the possibility that the home and foreign currency are, to a certain extent, substituted; If an increase in the appreciation of the home currency is expected the relative money demand is increased and consequently we have a positive effect of $(e_t^* - e_t)$ on i_t.

To close the model we have to specify an expectation forming process. Since there is little agreement on this problem we adopt a general approach which allows for influences of the observed exchange rate as well as of the fundamental variables determing e_t.[10]

9) For a discussion of this point compare R. Dornbusch and P. Krugman: Flexible exchange rates in the Short Run. Brookings Paper on Economic Activity, vol.3, 1976, 537-575.

1o) The approach is similar to the one used by J.H.Whitaker an M.W. Hudgins: The Floating Pound Sterling of the Nineteen-Thirties. An Econometric Study, Southern Economic Journal, vol.14, 1977, 1478-1485.

(3) $\quad e_t^* = h(e_t, p_t, q_t, m_t)$

The partial derivative of h with respect to e_t is assumed to be greater zero. If the expectations are formed by 'rational' reasoning based on our model, an increase in m_t depresses e_t^*. With reference to a rise in q_t or p_t the model predicts positive effects on e_t if the capital flows induced by the rise in i_t are dominating the trade flows. Negative effects on e_t are to be expected in case of dominating trade flows.

By allowing for adjustment and expectation lags and by inserting (3) in (1) and (2), our linearized stochastic model is given by the following two dynamic equations

$$(4) \quad e_t = -\sum_{j=1}^{k_{11}} b_{11j} e_{t-j} - \sum_{j=0}^{k_{12}} b_{12j} i_{t-j} + \sum_{j=0}^{n_{11}} c_{11j} p_{t-j} + \sum_{j=0}^{n_{12}} c_{12j} q_{t-j} + \sum_{j=0}^{n_{13}} c_{13j} m_{t-j} + \varepsilon_{1t}$$

$$i_t = -\sum_{j=0}^{k_{21}} b_{12j} e_{t-j} + \sum_{j=0}^{n_{21}} c_{21j} p_{t-j} + \sum_{j=0}^{n_{22}} c_{22j} q_{t-j} + \sum_{j=0}^{n_{23}} c_{23j} m_{t-j} + \varepsilon_{2t}$$

ε_{it} = Homoscedastic stochastic disturbances with expectation zero, $i = 1,2$

From a mathematical point of view it is obvious that our model can create a rich variety of adjustment patterns. To give two examples let us consider possible adjustment processes to an increase in m_t and p_t or q_t.

Initially, an increase in m_t depresses i_t. This, in turn, brings about a depreciation of the home currency. Now, if e_t is only slowly adjusted to the new value of e_t, an appreciation of the home currency is expected. If we have a short adjustment lag in the money market, currency substitution will result in a rise in i_t, which has a positive effect on e_t and so on. The feedback between e_t and i_t produces a cyclical adjustment process.

Under the assumption of a short adjustment lag in the money market, an increase in p_t or q_t results in an initial rise in i_t. Now, if capital flows have a higher adjustment speed than trade flows, this leads to an initial appreciation of the home currency. For the sake of simplicity we disregard the possibility of a feedback between e_t and i_t. After some time, the trade flows brought about by the rise in p_t or q_t result in an opposite movement of the exchange rate.

The attempt to estimate the system (4) leads to severe difficulties. The lack of a priori information concerning the lag, distributions and the distributions of the error terms causes an identification problem: Since all exogenous and endogenous variables are included in both equations, the order conditions given by Hatanaka are not met.[11] Therefore, it seems more promising to study the determination of the exchange rate in a final form framework. By introducing the lag operator L, $L^n X_t \equiv X_{t-n}$ for any sequence X_t, we can write (4) as

$$\begin{bmatrix} B_{11}(L) & B_{12}(L) \\ B_{21}(L) & B_{22}(L) \end{bmatrix} \begin{bmatrix} e_t \\ i_t \end{bmatrix} = \begin{bmatrix} C_{11}(L) & C_{12}(L) & C_{13}(L) \\ C_{21}(L) & C_{22}(L) & C_{23}(L) \end{bmatrix} \begin{bmatrix} p_t \\ q_t \\ m_t \end{bmatrix} + \begin{bmatrix} \varepsilon_{1t} \\ \varepsilon_{2t} \end{bmatrix}$$

where the B_{ij} (i,j=1,2) and the $C_{i,k}$ (i=1,2,k=1,2,3) are polynomials in L with parameters b_{ijh} and c_{ijh} respectively.

---

11) This condition is analogous to the classical one (number of excluded exogenous variables $\geq$ number of included endogenous variables), however in- or exclusion of a variable is used with reference to any leading, current or lagged term, M.Hatanaka: On the Global Identification of Dynamic Simultaneous Equations Models with Stationary Disturbances. International Economic Review, vol.16, 1975, 545-554.

The solution of this system of difference equations supplies us the final form of our model,[12)]

$$\begin{bmatrix} e_t \\ i_t \end{bmatrix} = |B(L)|^{-1} \begin{bmatrix} \begin{bmatrix} B_{22}(L) & -B_{12}(L) \\ -B_{21}(L) & B_{11}(L) \end{bmatrix} \begin{bmatrix} C_{11}(L) & C_{12}(L) & C_{13}(L) \\ C_{21}(L) & C_{22}(L) & C_{23}(L) \end{bmatrix} \begin{bmatrix} p_t \\ q_t \\ m_t \end{bmatrix} + \begin{bmatrix} \varepsilon_{1t} \\ \varepsilon_{2t} \end{bmatrix} \end{bmatrix}$$

or

$$(5)\quad |B(L)| \begin{bmatrix} e_t \\ i_t \end{bmatrix} = \begin{bmatrix} B_{22}(L) & -B_{12}(L) \\ -B_{21}(L) & B_{11}(L) \end{bmatrix} \begin{bmatrix} C_{11}(L) & C_{12}(L) & C_{13}(L) \\ C_{21}(L) & C_{22}(L) & C_{23}(L) \end{bmatrix} \begin{bmatrix} p_t \\ q_t \\ m_t \end{bmatrix} + \begin{bmatrix} \eta_{1t} \\ \eta_{2t} \end{bmatrix}$$

where $|B(L)| = B_{11}(L)B_{22}(L) - B_{12}(L)B_{21}(L)$.

From (5) it is seen that e_t and i_t are given as 'rational' distributed lags of p_t, q_t and m_t. It is noteworthy that the denominators of all six rational distributed lags are equal. This property will be lost when the system (4) involves no feedback, e.g. $B_{21}(L)$ is equal zero. In this case the term $B_{11}(L)$ of $|B(L)|$ in the second equation of (5) can be cancelled, i.e. the second equation has an autoregressive part which is of lower order than that of the first equation of (5).[13)]

Furthermore, it can be seen that rather short lags in (4) imply algebraically lags of respectable lenght in (5). However, it is quite probable that the high order lag coefficients of the final equations become too small to be detected statistically.[13)]

12) Compare e.g. K.F. Wallis: Multiple Time Series Analysis and the Final Form of Econometric Models, Econometrica. vol. 45, 1977, 1481-1497.

13) Compare K.F. Wallis: Multiple ...., op.cit., 1484.

In our empirical analysis we have assumed that the maximum lags are relatively small (three or four).[14)]

It can be easily shown that the 'usual' nonautocorrelated stochastic disturbances of the structural equations imply moving average errors in (5). If the structural disturbances are generated by an autoregressive scheme the final form error terms are of the mixed autoregressive moving average type. As a result, in estimating (5) autocorrelated error terms are to be taken into consideration in any case. As an easy to handle assumption we postulate that η_{it} is approximatively generated by a second-order autoregressive process:

(6) $\eta_{it} = \varphi_{1i}\, \eta_{it-1} + \varphi_{2i}\, \eta_{it-2} + \zeta_{it}$ $\qquad i = 1,2.$

3. THE RESULTS FOR THE DM

In this section we report the results of the estimation of the final equation (5) for the DM. The time series used for the current endogenous variables cover the 48 monthly values from June 1973 to May 1977. The interest rates are given as yields on long-term government bonds, the price variables are wholesale price indices, the output variables are proxied by the indices of total industrial production and the money suppley is covered by M1.[15)]
The estimate of the final equation for e_t is given below.[16)]

---

14) Some experiments were also carried out with other lag structures. But the estimation of finite approximations of the distributed lag equations by Almons method brought no satisfactory results.

15) The January 1973 value of the variables i_t, p_t, q_t and m_t is defined as one. Additional information about the data are given in the appendix.

16) The nonlinear least squares problem was solved by a grid search over the values of the two parameters of the error process.

$$
\begin{aligned}
e_t = {} & \underset{(0.141)}{0.791e_{t-1}} + \underset{(0.185)}{0.520e_{t-2}} - \underset{(0.11o)}{0.623e_{t-3}} + \underset{(0.150)}{0.002} \\
& - \underset{(0.158)}{0.046p_t} - \underset{(0.172)}{0.561p_{t-1}} + \underset{(0.176)}{0.187p_{t-2}} + \underset{(0.161)}{0.401p_{t-3}} \\
(7) \quad & + \underset{(0.085)}{0.230q_t} + \underset{(0.087)}{0.070q_{t-1}} - \underset{(0.079)}{0.204q_{t-2}} - \underset{(0.080)}{0.017q_{t-3}} \\
& - \underset{(0.144)}{0.355m_t} + \underset{(0.179)}{0.453m_{t-1}} + \underset{(0.189)}{0.234m_{t-2}} - \underset{(0.153)}{0.287m_{t-3}} \\
& + 0.123\eta_{1t-1} - 0.625\eta_{1t-2} + \zeta_{1t}
\end{aligned}
$$

$$\hat{\sigma}^2_{\zeta 1} = 0.00992 \qquad \chi^2_1 = 7.827$$

The figures in brackets are the standard errors of the coefficient estimates, given the estimated autoregressive parameters of the error process. $\hat{\sigma}^2_{\zeta 1}$ is the estimate of the variance of ζ_{1t} and χ^2_1 is the value of the Box and Pierce Statistic which is asymtotically χ^2 distributed with ten degrees of freedom under the hypothesis of no autocorrelation of ζ_{1t}.[17)]

First we have to note that the difference equation (7) has the roots $\lambda_{1,2} = 0.789 \pm 0.364i$ and $\lambda_3 = -0.808$, i.e. the model shows stable cyclical fluctuations. In view of the graph of the e_t time series given in figures 1 this result is hardly surprising. In order to clarify the pattern of the dynamic influence of p_t, q_t and m_t on e_t, the weights of the lag distributations for lag 0, 1, ..., 14 were calculated and illustrated in figure 2.[18)]

---

17) G.E.P. Box and D.A. Pierce: Distribution of Residual Autocorrelations in Autoregressive Moving Average Time Series Models. Journal of the American Statistical Association, vol. 65, 197o, 15o9-1562.

18) For a discussion of the relationship of the distributed lag weights and the parameters of the autoregressive form see D.W. Jorgenson: Rational Distributed Lag Functions. Econometrica, vol. 32, 1966, 135-149.

Before interpreting these results, we have to present the estimated final equation for i_t:

$$
\begin{aligned}
(8)\quad i_t = {} & 2.160 i_{t-1} - 1.600 i_{t-2} + 0.361 i_{t-3} - 0.309 \\
& (0.182) \qquad (0.341) \qquad (0.211) \qquad (0.278) \\
& + 0.441 p_t - 1.920 p_{t-1} + 1.720 p_{t-2} - 0.133 p_{t-3} \\
& (0.412) \qquad (0.787) \qquad (0.866) \qquad (0.492) \\
& + 0.760 q_t - 0.437 q_{t-1} + 0.045 q_{t-2} + 0.088 q_{t-3} \\
& (0.230) \qquad (0.312) \qquad (0.269) \qquad (0.179) \\
& - 1.060 m_t + 2.530 m_{t-1} - 2.000 m_{t-2} + 0.520 m_{t-3} \\
& (0.389) \qquad (0.726) \qquad (0.712) \qquad (0.337) \\
& - 1.230 \eta_{2t-1} - 0.570 \eta_{2t-2} + \zeta_{2t}
\end{aligned}
$$

$$\hat{\sigma}^2_{\zeta 2} = 0.0354 \qquad \chi^2_1 = 11.36$$

The roots of the difference equation above are $\lambda_{1,2} = 0.879 \pm 0.321i$ and $\lambda_3 = 0.412$.

Since the complex pair $\lambda_{1,2}$ is nearly equal to the one calculated for the exchange rate equation and λ_3 is relatively small we can tentatively conclude with reference to the property of final equations mentioned in section 2 that i_t influences the exchange rate e_t but there seems to be no feedback of e_t on i_t. The weights of the estimated lag distribution of equation (8) were also calculated and illustrated in figure 2. It can be seen that the negative influence of the money supply ratio is almost immediate. This supports the hypothsis of a high adjustment speed of asset markets. Yet, no significant overshooting effect is detected.[19] The explanation of the lag distribution of q_t seems to be offered by different adjustment speeds of goods and assets markets: An output expansion leads to an initial rise of the interest rate and consequently an appreciation of the currency. After some time, the worsening of the trade

---

19) Given the values of the variables of January 1973, we receive an impact elasticity of -1.1.

figure 1: Dollar Value of the DM

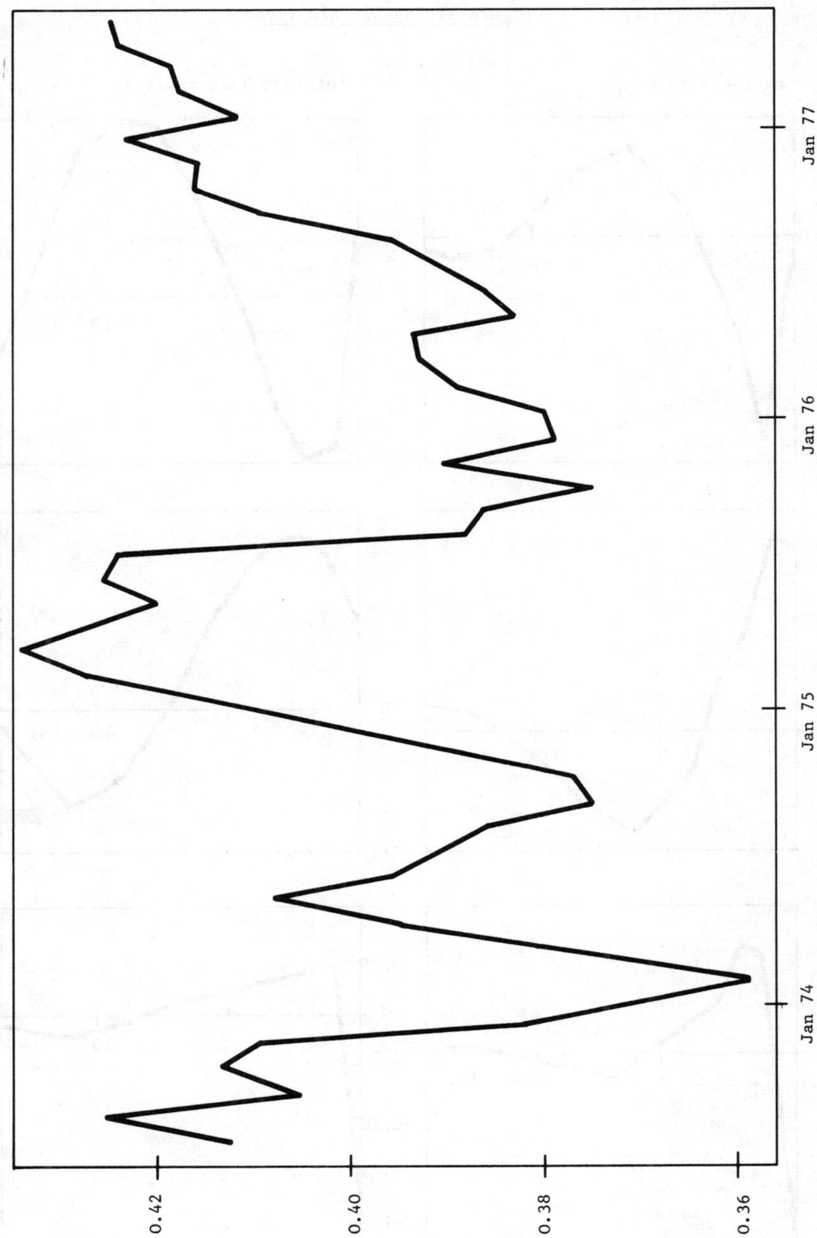

figure 2: Lag Distributions

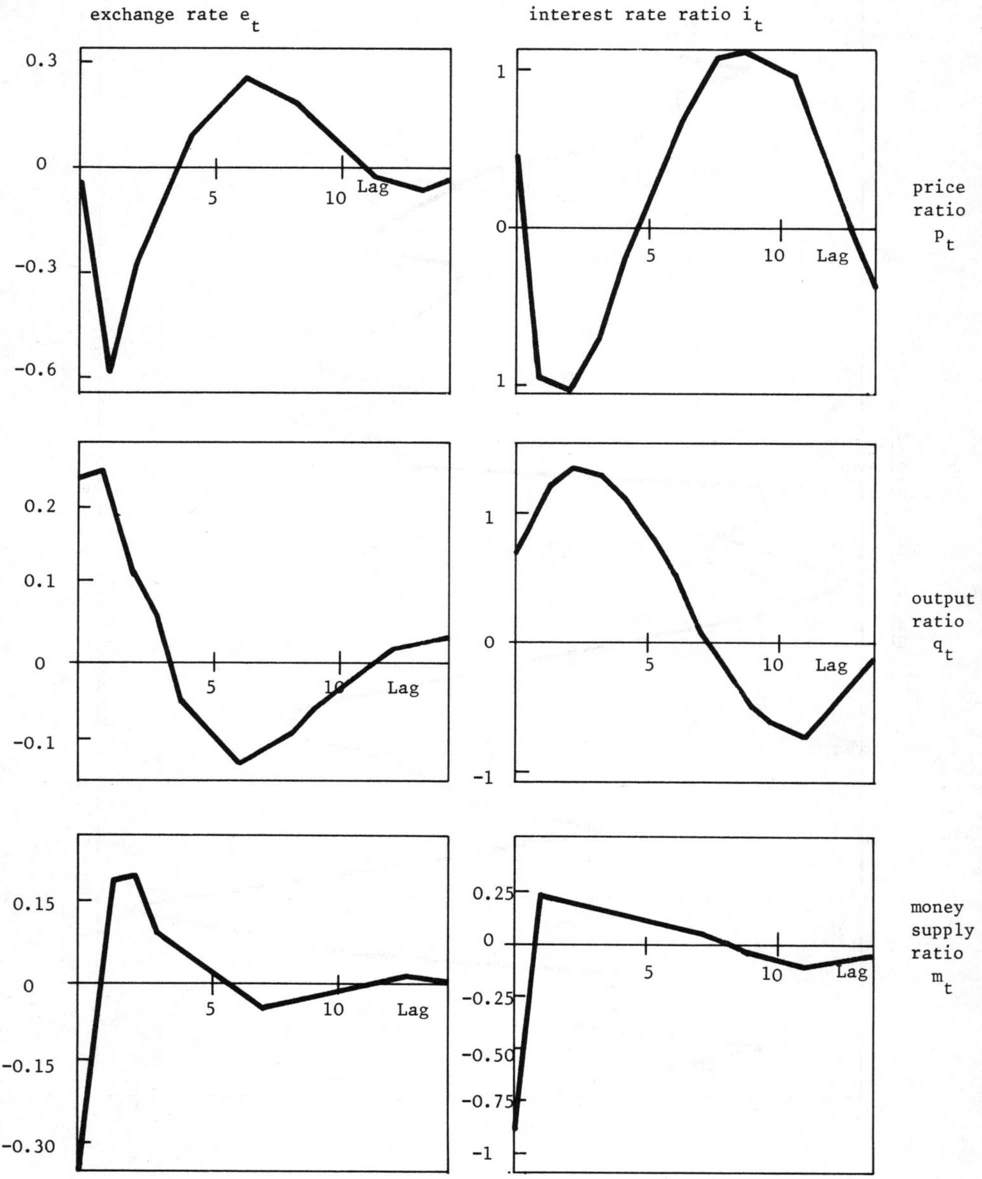

balance results in an opposite movement of the exchange rate. In addition, the lag distributions of the effects of m_t and q_t on i_t outlined in figure 2 are consistent with the explanations given above. However, the distributed lag pattern of the influence of p_t on e_t does not seem to fit into this framework because one would expect a similar one to that of q_t.[2o)] Moreover, e_t reacts highly elastic upon changes of the price ratio: On the basis of the January 1973 values of the variables, a four months elasticity of -3.1 was received. A possible explanation of this fact lies in the hypothesis that the exchange rate expectations are influenced by the price ratio and that they are highly elastic regarding the actual exchange rate.

It is noteworthy that the exchange rate model produces no meaningful long-run results: It can be calculated that the total effect of all three exogenous variables is quite small and insignificant. Apart from the short-run nature of the model and the particular formulation chosen, it seems as if the time period considered is too short to estimate all the effects of the exogenous variables on exchange and interest rates.

Finally, we have to note that the results for the DM are hardly influenced by a respecification of equations (7) and (8): There are only minor changes in the reported findings if we drop the coefficients of the regression equations which are insignificant at a 5 percent level.

4. THE RESULTS FOR THE SFR

The model for the SFR was also estimated with monthly data from summer 1973 to May 1977 for the current endogenous variables. A graphical representation of the dollar value of the SFR for this period is given in figure 3. The variables are equally defined as

---

2o) It is noteworthy that the same 'wrong' lag pattern is given for the influence of p_t on i_t.

in the German case with the exception of q_t. Since there exists no monthly index of total production for Switzerland the output of this country was proxied by the imports of goods (volume index). The two estimated equations are as follows:

$$
\begin{aligned}
e_t = {} & \underset{(0.164)}{0.384e_{t-1}} + \underset{(0.182)}{0.825e_{t-2}} - \underset{(0.198)}{0.441e_{t-3}} - \underset{(0.173)}{0.181e_{t-4}} + \underset{(0.127)}{0.363} \\
& - \underset{(0.153)}{0.188p_t} - \underset{(0.153)}{0.144p_{t-1}} - \underset{(0.132)}{0.146p_{t-2}} + \underset{(0.148)}{0.348p_{t-3}} \\
& + \underset{(0.038)}{0.099p_t} + \underset{(0.031)}{0.112q_{t-1}} - \underset{(0.031)}{0.032q_{t-2}} - \underset{(0.036)}{0.165q_{t-3}} \qquad (9) \\
& + \underset{(0.192)}{0.184m_t} - \underset{(0.222)}{0.233m_{t-1}} + \underset{(0.192)}{0.318m_{t-2}} - \underset{(0.193)}{0.388m_{t-3}} \\
& + 0.450\eta_{1t-1} - 0.850\eta_{1t-2} + \zeta_{1t}
\end{aligned}
$$

$$\hat{\sigma}^2_{\zeta 1} = 0.00934 \qquad \chi^2_1 = 8.45$$

$$
\begin{aligned}
i_t = {} & \underset{(0.268)}{0.006i_{t-1}} + \underset{(0.179)}{0.644i_{t-2}} + \underset{(0.234)}{0.336i_{t-3}} - \underset{(0.212)}{0.259i_{t-4}} + \underset{(0.881)}{0.350} \\
& - \underset{(0.636)}{0.246p_t} - \underset{(0.461)}{0.221p_{t-1}} + \underset{(0.412)}{0.594p_{t-2}} + \underset{(0.660)}{0.735p_{t-3}} \\
& + \underset{(0.122)}{0.085p_t} - \underset{(0.122)}{0.062q_{t-1}} + \underset{(0.123)}{0.324q_{t-2}} + \underset{(0.144)}{0.165q_{t-3}} \qquad (1o) \\
& - \underset{(0.700)}{0.991m_t} - \underset{(0.691)}{0.499m_{t-1}} + \underset{(0.700)}{0.048m_{t-2}} + \underset{(0.718)}{0.992m_{t-3}} \\
& + 0.850\eta_{2t-1} - 0.550\eta_{2t-2} + \zeta_{2t}
\end{aligned}
$$

$$\hat{\sigma}^2_{\zeta 2} = 0.028 \qquad \chi^2_1 = 15.1$$

The results are generally of lower significance than those of the German case. Especially the interest rate equation gives poor results.

figure 3: Dollar Value of the SFR

figure 4: Lag Distributions

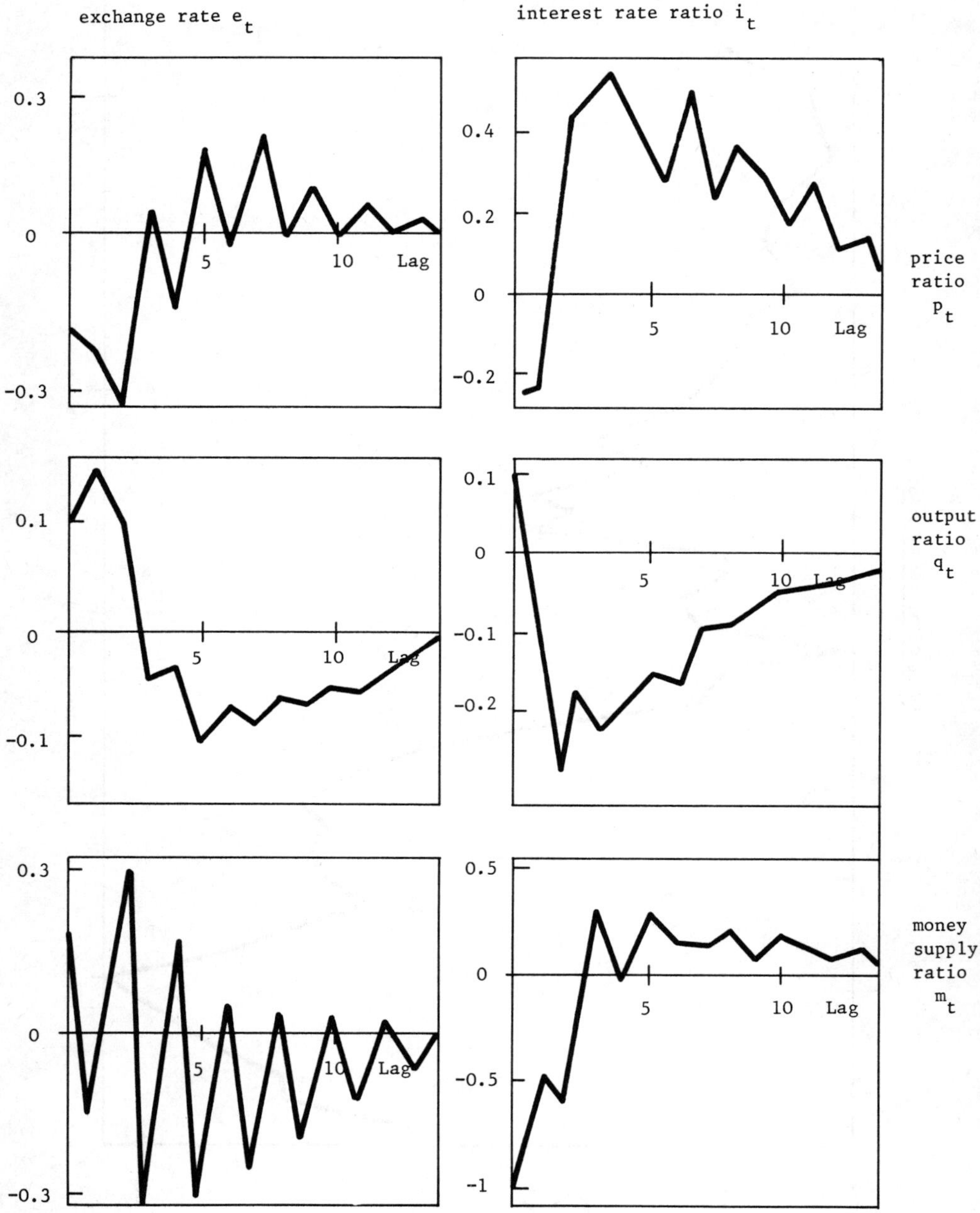

But it is noteworthy that dropping out the coefficients of lowest significance brought only very weak improvements. This led us to the conclusion that the poor results are not attributable to an overparametrisation of the model. Nevertheless, the estimates above indicate that the autoregressive parts of the two equations are identical (there is only some doubt about the equality of the third autoregressive parameters). Therefore, a feedback relationship between e_t and i_t is to be expected. The weights of the lag distributions implied by the equations above are illustrated in figure 4.

The hypothesis of a feedback relation between e_t and i_t offers an explanation for the strong fluctuations of the lag patterns in figure 4: An exogenous increase in the interest rate ratio leads to an initial appreciation of the SFR. Now, if the exchange rate expectations are only partially adjusted, an appreciation of the SFR is expected and consequently currency substitution results in a reduction of the interest rate ratio and so on. This feedback seems to dominate the influence of m_t on e_t. For p_t and q_t, however, we also find the lag pattern already detected for the dollar value of the DM. Moreover, we have again a very high short-run impact of the price ratio on the exchange rate: The four months elasticity on the basis of the January 1973 values is -2.8. The explanation given above is not entirely convincing, since the lag patterns estimated for i_t are not consistent with our hypothesis. Especially the lag distribution of q_t is opposed to the results found for the exchange rate. Nevertheless, the exchange rate equation implies reasonable long-run results: The sums of the distributed lag coefficients are -0.317 for p_t, -0.286 for m_t and 0.034 for q_t.

5. CONCLUSION

An empirical analysis of the DM and SFR exchange rate indicates that their large fluctuations in the recent past are mainly attributable to different adjustment speeds of markets, a high price elasticity of the exchange rates and - in the case of the SFR - to a feedback relation between the exchange rate and the ratio of interest rates. Nevertheless, the highly elastic reaction of the exchange rate to changes of the price ratio, the partly conflicting estimates obtained for the exchange and interest rate equations and the relatively poor results in the Swiss case are problems to be studied further.

Our results are obviously subject to the critics that prices and money supplies are dependent on the exchange and interest rates. In addition, the estimates presented above where derived with the help of 'classical' econometric methods for equations with auto-correlated residuals. However, the application of multiple time series methods should bring more powerfull results.

APPENDIX: Data Sources

There are four data sources:

Main Economic Indicators (OECD)

- DM and SFR exchange rate
- Yields of government bonds (German, Swiss and US)
- Total industrial production (US)
- M1 (Swiss and US)

International Financial Statistics (IMF

- Wholesale prices (German and US)

Monatsberichte der Deutschen Bundesbank

- Total industrial production (German)
- M1 (German)

Die Volkswirtschaft (Eidgenössisches Statistisches Amt)

- Wholesale prices (Swiss)
- Import volume index (Swiss)

COMMENTS ON P.BERNHOLZ AND P.KUGLER, "AN EMPIRICAL MODEL OF THE SHORT-RUN FLUCTUATIONS OF EXCHANGE RATES: THE CASE OF THE DEUTSCHMARK (DM) AND THE SWISS FRANC (SFR)"

M. Ishaq Nadiri

In this paper Professor Bernholz and Kugler discuss an important topic and their analysis could make a significant contribution to our understanding of the short-run fluctuations of exchange and interest rates. The revised version of the paper states the problem and the methodology of their research much more clearly than before. However, it seems to me that some further work is needed to clearly bring out the importance of the authors' contribution: My suggestions are as follows:

1. In the introduction it might be useful to give a simplified mathematical outline of Dornbush's (or Kouri's) model in order to motivate the paper and inform the readers about the structure of their own empirical model. The short-comings of the basic Dornbush/Kouri model and Niehans's modifications can be discussed formally. Then the Kugler/Bernholz model can be stated clearly in the context of this theoretical literature. Such a discussion will provide the needed theoretical background and framework to motivate the empirical analysis of this paper.

2. Some effort should be made to specify the underlying theoretical model of Bernholz and Kugler's model. The discussion on page 4 of the manuscript is not very clear and illuminating. What is the structure and properties of the model the authors have in mind that would provide them with the results stated on the bottom of page 4 and top of page 5 that they expect? Are these results uniquely deducible from their model or are they ad-hoc expectations?

3. The justification for the form of the basic model (1) is not provided. Why should the model include all the specific variables and why should be distributed lag formulation be the way as stated in equation (1) or (2)? What are the potential specification errors that may arise because of the simultaneity of money, prices and output in these equations?

4. It might be helpful to specify clearly what type of expectations process is embedded in the model. The authors make references (for example on page 6) to this phenomenon but why not formulate the exact expectation formulae?!

5. The feedback system underlying the reduced form equation (2) should be discussed in some detail, again explicitly, to show how the structure of the autoregressive part of the equations can tell us something about the feedback between the interest and exchange rates.

6. The empirical results are interesting but several points need to be made

(i) Why the same length of distributed lag is assumed for each explanatory variable? Is there any theoretical or empirical justification for this?

(ii) Why not drop some of the insignificant coefficients? Using convential criterion of t statistics: $t > 2.0$, a large number of the coefficients in each regression equation drops out. How would the results be then interpreted?

(iii) Also, many of the distributed lag coefficients for a given variable have positive and negative signs. What sense the authors make out of this?

(iv) The authors might have considered using the Almons approximation method to estimate their distributed lag model. Then they could have appropriately restricted the form and pattern of the lag structure in (2) according to some a-priori formulation and obtained a more reasonable set of results.

7. There is a strong possibility that a high degree of multi-collinearity pervails among the indepent variables and their lagged values in all the estimated equations. If so the empirical results provided in the paper are highly suspect. The authors should test for presence of multicollinearity and reformulate and estimate their model if necessary.

8. The authors hardly discuss why their model gives contrasting results for Germany and Switzerland: Consider the interest rate equations (5) and (7): In equation (7) the coefficients of money and price variables are hardly significant. While this is not the case for equation (5). What is the economic rationale for this? What is in the two economies that may explain the differences?

9. Finally, it might be desirable for the authors to give more clear interpretation of the economic meaning of whatever empirical results they find. Also it would be good to know whether this empirical analysis leads in any way to modification or confirmation of the Dornbush/Kouri type of theoretical models.

ON THE ROLE OF INTEREST ARBITRAGE, SPECULATION, AND COMMERCIAL HEDGING IN THE DETERMINATION OF THE FORWARD EXCHANGE RATE: THE CASE OF THE FLEXIBLE GERMAN MARK, 1974-1977.

Werner Gaab

I. INTRODUCTION

In recent years a substantial body of literature has developed[1] on the causes of deviations of forward exchange rates from their interest parity rates. The interest rates parity theory (IRPT) states that under certain assumptions[2] forward exchange rates are determined solely by the activities of interest arbitragers, who have a perfectly elastic excess demand for short-term capital and, therefore, for foreign exchange. Thus, the activities of hedging traders and of speculators have no influence in the determination of forward exchange rates. This means that covered interest differentials are zero because existing profit opportunities are eliminated instantaneously by interest arbitrage. Empirically, however, deviations from the parity condition have been observed.

Some authors have tried to explain these deviations from the interest parity line in terms of transaction costs in securities and foreign exchange markets, implying an indifference band around the parity line within which covered arbitrage flows are not profi-

---

1) For a survey see L.H.Officer and T.D. Willet (197o) and H.R. Stoll (1972).

2) It is assumed, that the domestic and foreign securities are identical with respect to maturity and risk and that there are no transaction costs, capital controls and other market imperfections. They differ only in the currency of denomination.

table.[3] These deviations can still be interpreted as equilibrium points in the sense of IRPT.[4] They are not attributed to a less than perfectly elastic covered arbitrage schedule. Further arguments leading to a modification of IRPT without introducing a downward-sloping arbitrage schedule are the existence of capital controls, different tax treatments, the averaging of bid and ask prices and different borrowing and investing rates.[5]

In contrast to these arguments, which only modify the IRPT, the so-called "modern theory of forward exchange" (MT)[6] postulates that the forward exchange rate is determined not only by interest arbitrage but also by expectations of speculators concerning the expected future spot rate. It is assumed that arbitragers' excess demand for foreign exchange is not perfectly elastic.[7] This implies that all variance not explained by the parity forward rate can be explained by speculative expectations.

Empirical studies concerning the influence of interest arbitrage and speculation on the forward exchange rate show very different results. These extend from a relatively strong influence of speculation (see for example J.L.Stein (1965), J.Kesselman (1971), R.D.Haas (1974)) to a small influence (see for example H.Stoll (1968), B.T.McCallum (1977)) and to the assertion that there is no influence of speculation and that the IRPT holds (see for example W.G.Minot

---

3) The estimates of transaction costs differ considerably: J.M. Keynes (1923, p.128) assumed a value of about 0.5 % p.a. to be necessary to induce capital flows, P.Einzig (1967, p.5o) 1/16 % p.a., A.R.Holmes and F.H.Schott (1965, p.55) 0.25 % p.a., W.H. Branson (1969, p.1032) 0.18 % p.a., J.A.Frenkel and R.M.Levich (1975, p.331) 0.15 % p.a. and recently (1977, p.1215) about 1,1 % p.a.

4) J.A.Frenkel and R.M.Levich (1975, pp.326-327).

5) See, e.g. T.Agmon and S.Bronfeld (1975), A.R.Holmes and F.H. Schott (1965), M.F.J.Prachowny (197o).

6) For a broader treatment of MT see e.g., S.C.Tsiang (1959), H.G.Grubel (1963), H.R.Stoll (1968).

7) For a discussion of arguments for a downward-sloping arbitrage schedule see L.H.Officer and T.D.Willett (197o).

(1974), J.A.Frenkel and R.M.Levich (1975), T.Agmon and S.Bronfeld (1975), R.C.Marston (1976), J.A.Frenkel and R.M.Levich (1977).[8)]

This study investigates the rôle of interest arbitrage, speculation and hedging in the determination of forward exchange rates of US Dollar ($), Pound Sterling (£) and Swiss Franc (SFR) vis-à-vis Deutschmark (DM) under "flexible" exchange rates. In order to check if there is any difference compared with a system of "fixed" exchange rates the Deutschmark/Dutch Guilder (HFL) - forward rate has been examined. For the domestic and the foreign interest rate the three month money market rate in Frankfurt (RMON) and the corresponding Eurocurrency market rates in London (REU.) were used, respectively. The same investigations were carried out for the Eurocurrency market using the three month Euro-DM rate in London (REUDM) instead of the money market rate in Frankfurt. We have assumed hereby that deposits in the Eurocurrency market denominated in different currencies are nearly perfect substitutes because they are issued in the same financial center by a small group of large banks and do not differ in their political risk.[9)] It is expected that the assumptions of IRPT are best met in the external Eurocurrency market.[1o)]

II. THEORETICAL FRAMEWORK

According to the modern theory of forward exchange all activities in the forward exchange market can be reduced to three basic

---

8) The results are partly dependent on (i) the underlying time period, (ii) the exchange rate system (fixed or flexible), (iii) the comparability of securities in respect to kind, maturity and risk, (iv) the examined currencies, (v) the modelling of exchange rate expectations and (vi) the estimation techniques applied.

9) R.Z. Aliber (1973).

1o) This has been shown for fixed exchange rate periods by R.Z. Aliber (1973) and R.C. Marston (1976).

activities: (i) pure interest arbitrage, (ii) pure speculation, and (iii) commercial hedging.[11)]

Arbitragers' excess demand for forward exchange is supposed to be an increasing function of the difference between the parity forward rate (F^*) and the market forward rate (F):

$$(1) \qquad x^A(t) = f(F^*(t) - F(t))$$

or as a linear approximation,

$$(2) \qquad x^A(t) = a_1(F^*(t) - F(t)), \qquad a_1 > 0$$

where the parity forward rate is given by the equilibrium condition of traditional IRPT as

$$(3) \qquad F^*(t) = S(t)\,\frac{1+i_D(t)}{1+i_F(t)},$$

with S denoting the spot exchange rate, i_D the domestic interest rate and i_F the foreign interest rate.

In contrast to pure interest arbitragers, who always eliminate the exchange risk by covering in the forward exchange market, speculators hope to profit from fluctuations in the exchange rate by holding open positions in foreign exchange,[12)] which depend on their expectations with respect to the future spot exchange rate. If,

---

11) See, e.g., S.C.Tsiang (1959, p.76), E.Sohmen (1973, pp.84-85). Some authors (for example H.Stoll (1968), J.Kesselman (1971), R.D.Haas (1974)) consider only pure interest arbitrage and pure speculation and subsume the activities of traders to these. J.J.van Belle (1973) has shown that this procedure can lead to a misspecification. For a discussion of this point see also E.R.Canterbery (1975).

12) Spot speculation where speculators buy or sell spot foreign exchange without covering in the forward market, can be considered as a combination of pure interest arbitrage and pure speculation. See, e.g., H.Stoll (1968, p.61), E.Sohmen (1973, p.95).

for instance, the spot rate that speculators expect today to prevail say in three months ($S^e(t)$) is greater than the corresponding three-month forward rate, speculators will demand forward exchange in order to sell it at maturity with profit in the spot exchange market. Thus we can write speculators' excess demand for forward exchange as an increasing function of the difference between the expected spot rate and the corresponding forward rate:

$$(4) \qquad x^S(t) = g(S^e(t) - F(t))$$

or as a linear approximation

$$(5) \qquad x^S(t) = a_2(S^e(t) - F(t)), \qquad a_2 > 0.$$

The third component of supply and demand for forward exchange is commercial hedging. Exporters and importers hedge their receipts and payments contracted for a future time by selling or buying forward exchange. Traders who do not hedge are treated as speculators. The excess demand for forward exchange by traders ceteris paribus can be specified as a decreasing function of the forward exchange rate:[13)]

$$(6) \qquad x^H(t) = h(F(t))$$

or as a linear approximation

$$(7) \qquad x^H(t) = a_o - a_3F(t), \qquad a_o > 0, \quad a_3 > 0.$$

In equilibrium, the excess demands of interest arbitragers, specu-

13) For this assumption see also, e.g. E.Sohmen (1973, p.1o3), B.T.McCallum (1977, p.146).

lators, and commercial hedgers must sum to zero:[14)]

(8) $x^A(t) + x^S(t) + x^H(t) = 0.$

From (1), (5), (7) and (8) follows the MT-solution for the forward rate

(9) $F(t) = a + \alpha F^*(t) + \beta S^e(t)$

with

$$a = \frac{a_o}{a_1+a_2+a_3} ; \quad \alpha = \frac{a_1}{a_1+a_2+a_3} ; \quad \beta = \frac{a_2}{a_1+a_2+a_3} .$$

Because the parameters a_i (i = 0,1,2,3) cannot be identified, only the relative influence of covered interest arbitrage, speculation, and commercial hedging on the forward exchange rate can be estimated from (9). In contrast to the solution of H.Stoll (1968), J.Kesselman (1971), and R.D.Haas (1974) who subsume commercial hedging either to pure interest arbitrage or to pure speculation, the parameters α and β in (9) must not sum to one.

In Figure 1 the modern theory of forward exchange is illustrated graphically. The AA schedule represents excess demand of interest arbitragers, SS that of speculators, and HH the sum of excess demand of speculators and commercial hedgers.

---

14) Temporally, there is another potential participant in the forward market, namely the central bank. According to the assertion of the foreign exchange department, the Bundesbank has carried out only unimportant and sporadic outright interventions in the forward market in the period covered by this study. Owing to past experiences the Bundesbank considers this kind of policy as ineffective. Because data on these activities are neither published nor available on request, we have neglected this component of forward demand.

FIGURE 1

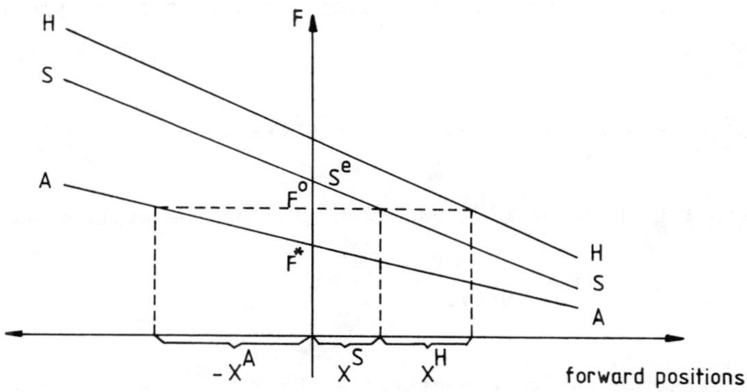

If the AA schedule is perfectly elastic at F^*, interest arbitragers determine the forward rate ($F=F^*$) and both speculators and commercial hedgers determine the quantity of forward commitments and the current capital flow. This is the view of traditional IRPT. According to MT the forward rate is determined at $F^o > F^*$, showing that not only interest arbitragers but also speculators and commercial hedgers play a rôle in the determination of the forward rate. The relative influence of the different activities of participants in the forward exchange market is an empirical question.

III. SPECIFICATION OF EXCHANGE RATE EXPECTATIONS

A difficult problem in incorperating the rôle of speculation in empirical work arises from the lack of an observable variable measuring expectations. In order to make the model described by (9) operational, the unknown expected spot rate ($S^e(t)$) must be replaced by observable variables. In the following some well-known models of the formation of expectations and their implications for the form of (9) are presented.

(i) Adaptive expectations:[15] In modeling adaptive expectations it is generally assumed that expectations are corrected according to the difference between the actual spot rate and the respective expected spot rate. A simple model of this type is given by

$$(10) \quad S^e(t) - S^e(t-1) = (1-\lambda)[S(t) - S^e(t-1)], \quad 0 \leq \lambda < 1.$$

Using the lag-operator L[16] equation (1o) can be written as

$$(11) \quad S^e(t) = \frac{1-\lambda}{1-\lambda L} S(t).$$

(ii) Extrapolative expectations: Extrapolative expectations are formed by adding a constant fraction of the change of the spot rate over the last period to the actual spot rate:

$$(12) \quad S^e(t) = S(t) + \gamma[S(t) - S(t-1)], \quad \gamma > 0$$

or

$$(13) \quad S^e(t) = [1+\gamma(1-L)]\, S(t).$$ [17]

---

15) This kind of formation of expectations for the expected spot rate has been most frequently used. See, e.g., J.L.Stein (1965), J.L.Stein and E.Tower (1967), S.W.Arndt (1968), H.Stoll (1968).

16) The lag-operator is defined as $L^k x(t) = x(t-k)$, $k = \ldots -2,-1,0,1,2\ldots$

17) This model has the disadvantage that it cannot explain movements back to a "normal" or "permanent" exchange rate if any exists.

(iii) Regressive expectations: In regressive expectations models it is assumed that speculators have an expectation on the evolution of the spot exchange rate implying expectations in respect to a "normal" or "permanent" spot rate ($\overline{S}(t)$) to which there exists a tendency for the actual spot rate to return. The formation of regressive expectations can be described by[18)]

$$(14) \quad S^e(t) = S(t) + \delta[\overline{S}(t) - S(t)], \qquad \delta > 0.$$

If it is furhter assumed that revisions of expectations in respect to the normal rate follow an adaptive process[19)]

$$(15) \quad \overline{S}(t) = \frac{1-c}{1-cL} S(t), \qquad 0 \leq c < 1,$$

the equation for the expected spot rate can be written as

$$(16) \quad S^e(t) = \frac{(1-\delta)(1-cL) + \delta(1-c)}{1-cL} S(t).$$

(iv) Combination of regressive and extrapolative expectations: In order to avoid the above mentioned disadvantage of extrapolative expectations, a combination of extrapolative and regressive elements has been proposed and tested by J.Kesselman (1971). Combining (12) and (14) this model can be written as

$$(17) \quad S^e(t) = S(t) + \gamma[S(t) - S(t-1)] + \delta[\overline{S}(t) - S(t)], \quad \gamma, \delta > 0$$

where the "normal" spot rate is described again by the adaptive process (15). Thus we have

$$(18) \quad S^e(t) = \frac{(1+\gamma-\delta c) - [(1+\gamma-\delta)c+\gamma]L+\gamma cL^2}{1-cL} S(t).$$

---

18) J. Kesselman (1971, p.282).
19) See, e.g., J.Kesselman (1971, p.282), J.A.Frenkel (1976, p.56).

(v) Combination of adaptive and extrapolative expectations: Another "dual mechanistic" model incorporating both extrapolative and adaptive elements has been used by R.D. Haas (1974).[2o] It is assumed that revisions of the expected spot rate follow the process:

$$(19) \quad S^e(t) - S^e(t-1) = \gamma[S(t) - S(t-1)] + (1-\lambda)[S(t) - S^e(t-1)]$$

or

$$(2o) \quad S(t) = \frac{1-\lambda+\gamma-\gamma L}{1-\lambda L} \; S(t), \quad \gamma > 0, \; 0 \leq \lambda < 1.$$

(vi) Combination of adaptive and regressive expectations: This type of combination was used by J.A.Frenkel (1975) in modeling inflationary expectations. According to this model the revision of short-run expectations is assumed to depend a) on the difference between the actual and "normal" spot rate and b) on the difference between the actual and the corresponding expected spot rate:

$$(21) \quad S^e(t) - S^e(t-1) = \delta[\overline{S}(t) - S(t)] + (1-\lambda)\,[S(t) - S^e(t-1)], \qquad \delta > 0, \; 0 \leq \lambda < 1.$$

Assuming that expectations about the normal rate follow the adaptive process (15), we have

$$(22) \quad S^e(t) = \frac{(1-\lambda-c\delta)-c(1-\lambda-\delta)L}{1-(c+\lambda)L+c\lambda L^2} \,.$$

2o) In contrast to the model used in this paper the model of R.D. Haas is given by $S^e(t) = S(t)+\gamma[S(t) - S(t-1)]+ (1-c) \sum_{i=0}^{\infty} c^i S(t-i)$. This however, is an incorrect specification, because it implies $S^e(t) = 2\,S(t)$ in the long-run equilibrium.

(vii) Rational expectations: An objection posed to the expectations models described above is that these models, which rely on only autoregressive mechanisms of past spot rates, are essentially ad hoc specifications without any theoretical justification. Therefore the use of the rational expectations hypothesis of J.F.Muth (1961) has been proposed.[21] According to this hypothesis it is assumed "that all participants in the market behave as if they know exactly the parameters of the (linear, dynamic) model that generates market outcomes".[22]

Given information $\phi(t)$ available to market participants in t, the expected spot rate in t+1 can be written as[23]

$$(23) \qquad S^e(t) = E[S(t+i) \mid \phi(t)]$$

where the operator E denotes mathematical expectation and S(t+i) is a random variable with

$$(24) \qquad S(t+i) = E[S(t+i) \mid \phi(t)] + \varepsilon(t),$$

where the stochastic error term ($\varepsilon(t)$) is assumed to be uncorrelated with the variables included in $\phi(t)$, which generate the actual spot rate, and to have zero mean. From (23) and (24) it follows that

$$(25) \qquad S^e(t) = S(t+i) - \varepsilon(t).$$

According to the hypothesis of rational expectations, the conditional mathematical expectation given by (23), and therefore S(t+i)

---

21) For the use of rational expectations in foreign exchange markets see S.W.Black (1973) and B.T.McCallum (1977).
22) S.W.Black (1973, p.22).
23) For the following representation of rational expectations see B.T.McCallum (1977, p.147-148).

can be written as a function of all current and past values of the model generating S(t+i).[24] Therefore, to complete our model in this respect a model for the market of spot exchange must be added. In this paper we adopt the spot market model of B.T.McCallum (1977, pp.150-151) yielding R(t),[25] F(t-i) and $S^e(t)$ as predetermined variables.

By adding a stochastic error term u(t) with E(u(t)) = 0 to the reduced form equation for the forward rate (9), we obtain

$$(26) \qquad F(t) = a + \alpha F^*(t) + \beta S^e(t) + u(t).$$

Substituting equations (11), (13), (16), (18), (20), (22) and (25), which describe different models of speculators' expectations, into equation (26) yields the corresponding regression models presented in table 1. For a comparison of the results of MT with those of IRPT the following equation has been added:

$$(27) \qquad F(t) = a + \alpha F^*(t) + u_1(t).$$

According to IRPT the expected values of parameters in (27) are a = 0 and α = 1.

IV. EMPIRICAL RESULTS

In order to give an impression of the problem, the time series of forward premiums (in % p.a.) of the US-Dollar ($), Pound Sterling (£), Dutch Guilder (HFL), and Swiss Franc (SFR) were plotted in fig. 2-6 against the interest differentials (in % p.a.) between either the German interbank rate (RMON) or the Euromark rate (REUDM) on the one hand and the corresponding Eurocurrency rates on the other.

24) B.T.McCallum (1976, p.44), (1977, p.148).
25) Defined as $(1+i_D(t))/(1+i_F(t))$.

TABLE 1: Regression models for the Interest Parity Theory and the Modern Theory with alternative assumptions concerning the formation of expectations.

Interest rate parity theory (A)	$F(t) = a + \alpha F^*(t) + u_1(t)$
Rational expectations (B)	$F(t) = a + \alpha F^*(t) + \beta S(t+13) + u_2(t)$
Adaptive expectations (C)	$F(t) = a(1-\lambda) + \lambda F(t-1) + \alpha F^*(t) - \alpha\lambda F^*(t-1) + \beta(1-\lambda)S(t) + u_3(t)$
Extrapolative expectations (D)	$F(t) = a + \alpha F^*(t) + \beta(1+\gamma)S(t) - \beta\gamma S(t-1) + u_4(t)$
Regressive expectations (E)	$F(t) = a(1-c) + cF(t-1) + \alpha F^*(t) - \alpha c F^*(t-1) + \beta(1-\delta c)\ S(t) - \beta c(1-\delta)\ S(t-1) + u_5(t)$
Regressive and extrapolative expectations (F)	$F(t) = a(1-c) + cF(t-1) + \alpha F^*(t) - \alpha c F^*(t-1) + \beta(1+\gamma-c\delta)S(t) - \beta[(1+\gamma-\delta)c+\gamma]S(t-1) + \beta\gamma c S(t-2)+u_6(t)$
Adaptive and extrapolative expectations (G)	$F(t) = a(1-\lambda) + \lambda F(t-1) + \alpha F^*(t) - \alpha\lambda F^*(t-1) + \beta(1-\lambda+\gamma)S(t) - \beta\gamma S(t-1) + u_7(t)$
Adaptive and regressive expectations (H)	$F(t) = a(1-c)\ (1-\lambda) + (c+\lambda)\ F(t-1) - c\lambda F(t-2) + \alpha(c+\lambda)F^*(t-1) + \alpha c\lambda F^*(t-2) + \beta(1-\lambda-\delta c)\ S(t) - \beta c(1-\lambda-\delta)S(t-1) + u_8(t)$

FIGURE 2

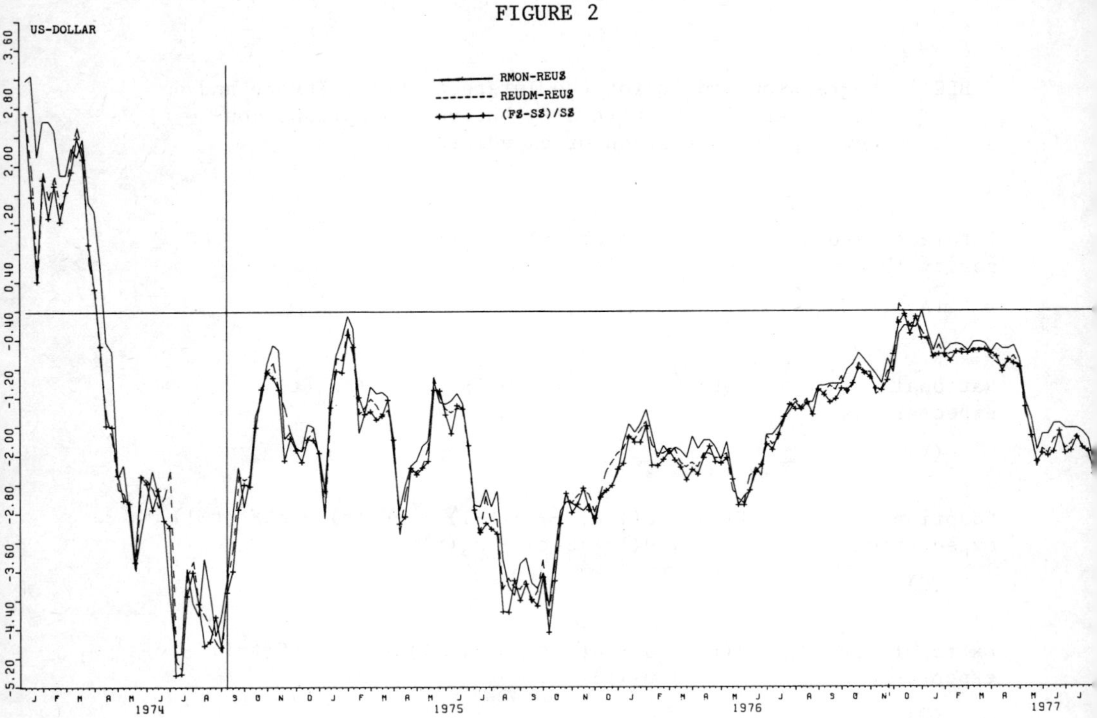

FIGURE 3

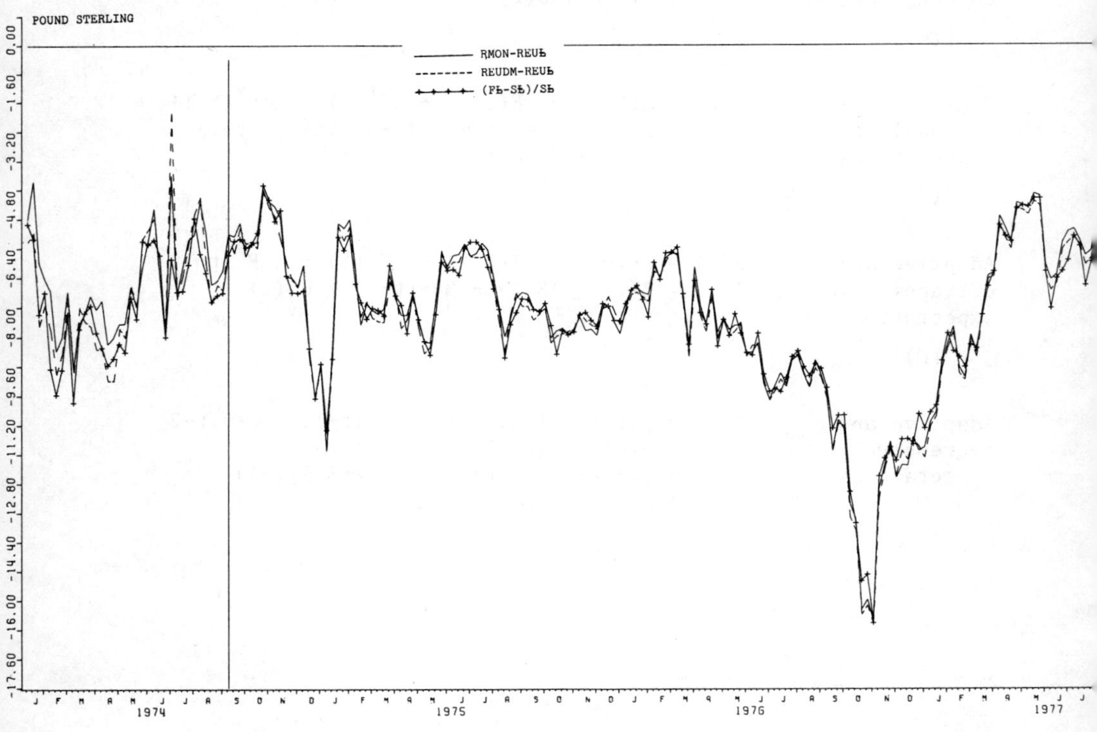

FIGURE 4

DUTCH GUILDER

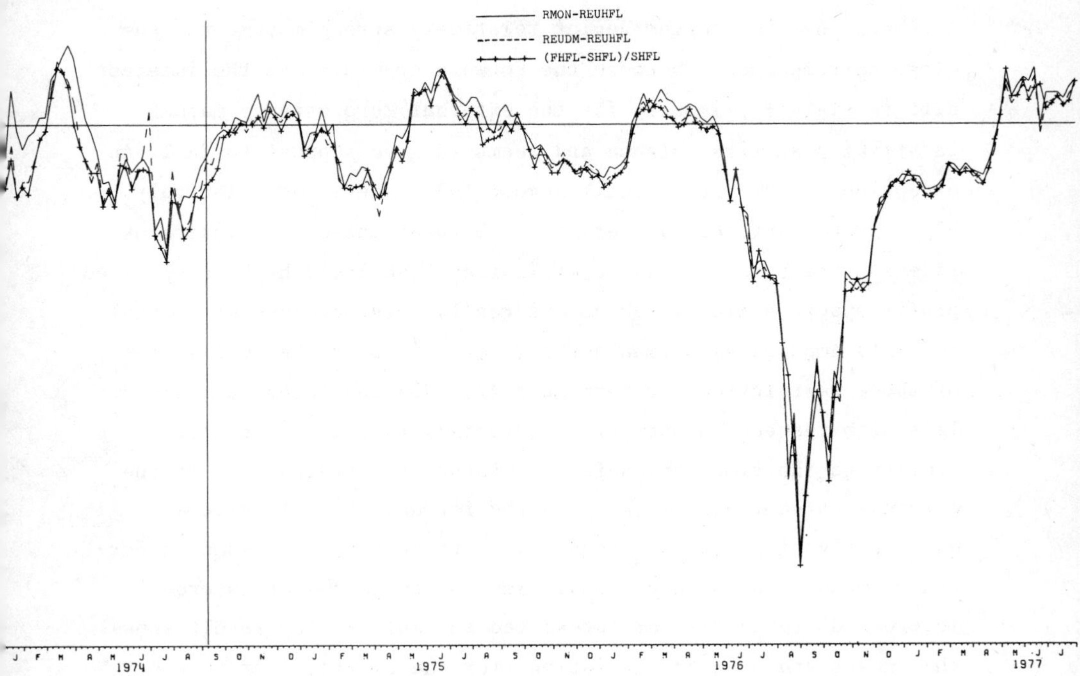

FIGURE 5

SWISS FRANCS

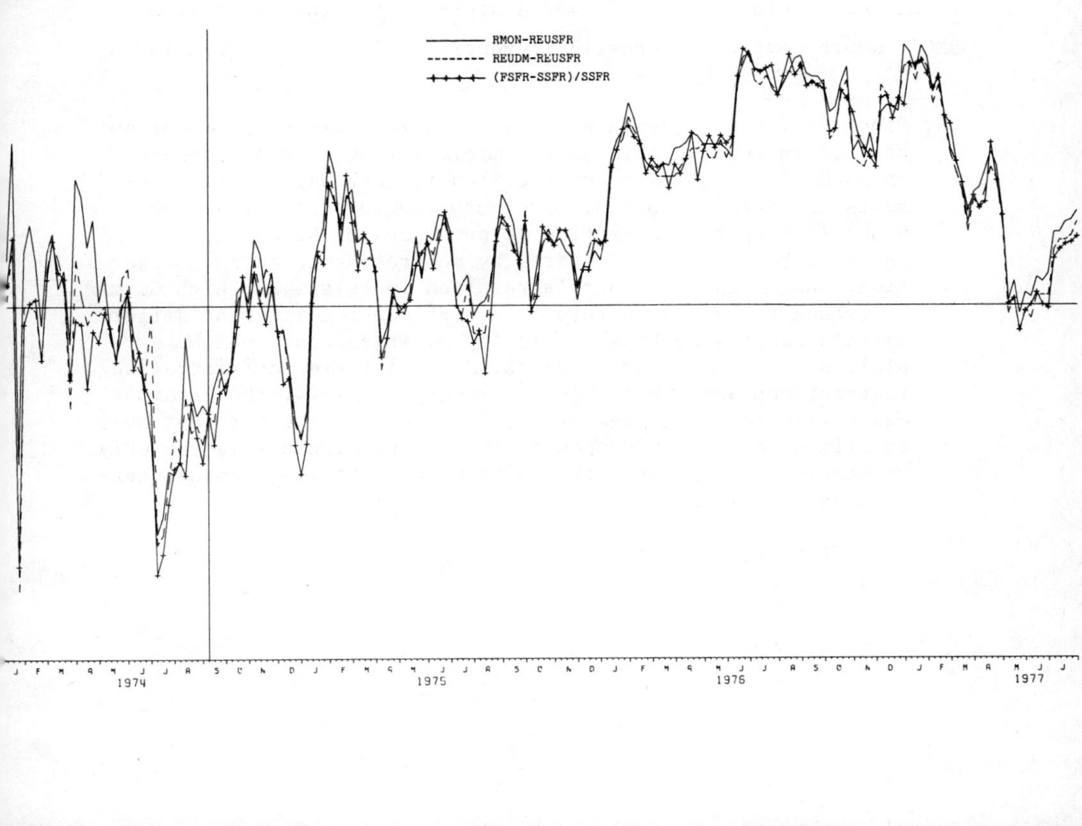

Although the time series depict relatively strong movements, the close correspondence between the forward premiums and the interest differentials - primarily for the external Eurocurrency market - is striking at first glance and seems to give support to IRPT. An exception is the period until August 1974, where the relatively high covered interest differentials between the German interbank rate and the Eurocurrency rates indicate seemingly high unexploited profit opportunities which do not really exist because of capital controls imposed by German authorities.[26)] After the abolishment of these restrictions on September 12, 1974 the interest differentials with respect to the German interbank rate show a picture similar to the time series for the interest differentials of the external Eurocurrency market and the forward rate. To give a quantitative impression, frequency distributions expressed in percents, means, and standard deviations of the means of covered interest differentials are presented in table 2. The result shows that means and standard deviations for the external Eurocurrency market are in part much smaller than when the German interbank rate is used. The distributions presented are not symmetrical about zero. This can be observed especially for the group with RMON, where covered interest differentials lie most frequently in

---

26) Since 1971 the Bundesbank has imposed several restrictions on capital inflows, e.g., special minimum reserve requirements on banks liabilities to non-residents, cash deposit requirements on certain types of foreign borrowings of German non-banks (Bardepot), subjection of purchases of German fixed-interest securities and shares by non-residents to authorization. These capital controls resulted in relatively high German interbank rates and therefore in high covered interest differentials ranging up to about 1o % p.a. which could not be exploited by interest arbitragers. Most of these administrative restrictions were abolished on January 3o, 1974. The Bardepot was eliminated on September 12, 1974. Because we were not able to eliminate the influences of these capital controls properly, we started our investigation with respect to the German interbank rate on September 13, 1974.

the inverval from 0.1 to 0.3 percent[27)] but also to a lesser extent for the external market. An exception is the covered interest differential with respect to SFR, particular for the external market. The positive interest differentials, in most cases in favour of internal and external DM-deposits with respect to $, Ŀ and HFL, may be due to the activities of speculators who speculated on an appreciation of the DM by selling forward these foreign currencies. This behaviour of speculators favouring movement in one direction seems to be not present or present only in a weakened manner for SFR.

TABLE 2: Frequency distributions in percent per annum, means and standard deviations of covered interest differentials.*) (all figures are in percent)

	RMON-REU.-SW.**)				REUDM-REU.-SW.***)			
	$	Ŀ	HFL	SFR	$	Ŀ	HFL	SFR
under -0.9	0.0	0.0	1.9	0.0	0.0	0.0	1.6	0.0
-0.9 to -0.7	0.0	0.0	0.0	0.0	0.5	0.5	0.5	0.5
-0.7 to -0.5	0.0	0.7	0.7	0.7	0.0	1.1	0.0	0.6
-0.5 to -0.3	0.7	0.7	0.7	3.3	0.6	2.1	2.7	4.8
-0.3 to -0.1	6.0	5.3	4.6	14.6	7.5	15.5	10.7	22.5
-0.1 to 0.1	17.2	21.9	27.2	27.8	52.9	27.3	27.8	39.0
0.1 to 0.3	45.7	33.0	28.5	25.8	30.5	20.9	38.5	19.8
0.3 to 0.5	23.8	16.5	23.2	22.5	5.3	14.4	10.7	8.0
0.5 to 0.7	5.3	12.6	6.6	2.6	1.6	10.7	3.7	1.6
0.7 to 0.9	1.3	5.3	4.0	2.0	1.1	4.8	1.6	2.1
above 0.9	0.0	4.0	2.6	0.7	0.0	2.7	2.1	1.1
mean	0.2164	0.2612	0.2074	0.1364	0.0824	0.2046	0.1139	0.0394
standard devation	0.1982	0.2903	0.3844	0.2565	0.1718	0.4450	0.3623	0.2622

*) SW. = (F.-S.)/S.; **) Period: 13.9.74 - 29.7.77 (= 151 weekly observations); ***) Period: 4.1.74 - 29.7.77 (= 187 weekly observations).

27) In the case of the "internal" covered interest differentials this observation may be partly due to the fact that there existed somewhat higher minimum reserves for deposits of non-residents at German banks than for those of residents.

There exist in particular for Ŀ and HFL relatively high positive interest differentials which are hard to explain in terms of transaction costs and random errors.[28] In what follows we examine with the aid of regression analysis whether the observed deviations from interest parity can be attributed to the activities of speculators as is postulated by MT.

Tables 3 - 1o show regression results for the different models presented in table 1.[29] Equations for IRPT (model A) have been estimated by ordinary least squares (OLS). Because the error term $u_2(t) = u(t) - \beta\varepsilon(t)$ in model B, which represents the rational expectations hypothesis, is correlated with the spot rate three months ahead (S(t+13)), OLS-estimates would be inconsistent for this case.[3o] Therefore a two-stage instrumental variable approach has

---

28) Recently J.A.Frenkel and R.M.Levich (1977) have published an article in which they state that in the recent period of managed float (1973-75) transaction costs in the spot and the forward markets have sharply risen to a level of about 1 % p.a. because of higher uncertainty in these markets. They have interpreted the deviations from triangular arbitrage in the spot and the forward markets according to the equation (\$/Ŀ) = (\$/DM)(DM/Ŀ) as transaction costs. This method may be valid when the various exchange rates are quoted at the same moment in time; but this is not the case in the study of Frenkel and Levich. If there is a speculative attack against a currency as has been the case in that period - deviations from interest parity cannot be interpreted as transaction costs anymore. Therefore, we presume that the level of transaction costs computed by Frenkel and Levich are too high.

29) Description of data and sources: All data are Friday quotations (midpoint between bid and ask). When there was no Friday quotation that for Thursday was used. All interest rates on a yearly percent basis were transformed in decimal figures on a three month basis. Eurocurrency rates are quotations of the London market taken from "Financial Times". The values for the German interbank rate are those of the Frankfurt market, published by "Blick durch die Wirtschaft". Foreign exchange rates (spot and forward) are quotations for the Frankfurt foreign exchange market; they are taken from "Statistische Beihefte zu den Monatsberichten der Deutschen Bundesbank, Reihe 5: Die Währungen der Welt", published by the Bundesbank.

3o) For a discussion of this point and the estimation method used, see B.T.McCallum (1977, pp.147-15o).

been employed.[31] The other expectation models imply regression models (C-H) with non-linearities in parameters which are over-identified and subjected to a priori restrictions. Therefore, a non-linear estimation procedure of D.W.Marquardt (1963) has been used to estimate the parameters of these models.[32][33]

Because of lack of space we cannot comment on each equation separately. Therefore, we will concentrate on some main conclusions which can be drawn from regression results. Generally, the results in tables 3 - 1o show that the relative influence of speculators' expectations on forward exchange rates is very small or not significantly different from zero. Exceptions to these findings are the estimates for the Dutch Guilder (see tables 5 and 9) with respect to regressive expectations, the combination of regressive and extrapolative expectations, and the combination of adaptive and extrapolative expectations, where speculation exhibits a relatively strong influence on forward exchange rates. This holds both for the German interbank rate (RMON) and the Euro-DM rate (REUDM). Corresponding estimates for the German interbank rate and the Euro-DM rate do not differ considerably with respect to relative influences of interest arbitrage and speculation. This may be due to the fact

---

31) According to the model for the spot market used by B.T.McCallum (1977, pp.15o-151), the variables S(t-1), S(t-2), F(T-13), R(t), and R(t-1) have been used to generate the fitted values $\hat{S}(t+13)$ with OLS, which can be used in a second stage as an instrumental variable for S(t+13). Resulting estimates are consistent.

32) In order to test for multiple solutions several sets of starting points for the parameters have been used for each equation. Whenever more than one local optimum was found, the regression with smallest standard error of estimate and most plausible estimates for the unknown parameters was chosen for the final version.

33) OLS estimates of the different expectation models without a priori restrictions of parameters yield significant estimates for the relative influence of interest arbitrage - measured by coefficient $\hat{\alpha}$ of F*(t) - which in most cases lie between 0.7 and 0.8. This indicates a relatively strong influence of speculation, which could be found for only one case with the non-linear estimation procedure.

that in the period under examination the German money market and the Eurocurrency market were well-integrated markets and did not differ significantly in terms of their political risk.

In all estimated equations the coefficients α and β sum to one. This means that there is practically no influence of the activities of hedging traders on forward exchange rates and that the restriction $\alpha+\beta=1$ imposed by Stoll, Kesselman and Haas is valid.

Estimates for IRPT are very close to those predicted by this theory, namely $a=0$ and $\alpha=1$. However in almost all equations they do not lie within two standard errors of their theoretical values. Moreover, relatively low values of the Durbin-Watson statistic - especially for the Dutch Guilder (HFL) - suggest a misspecification in some cases. Results for the rational expectation hypothesis do not differ essentially with respect to the influence of interest arbitrage from those of IRPT. Estimates for the coefficient β, which measure the relative influence of speculation, are in all equations either statistically not different from zero or have the wrong sign. With the exception of the equations for the Pound Sterling (Ł), the Durbin-Watson statistic shows extremely low values.[34)]

Regarding statistical significance at a 5 percent level and theoretical plausibility of estimates, adaptive expectations have been found to have an influence only for Swiss Franc, (see tables 6 and 1o), both for the internal and the external DM-money market rate. Values for the adjustment coefficient λ of about 0.28 and 0.26 with respect to RMON and REUDM, respectively exhibit a relatively fast adjustment of speculators, with a mean lag of about

---

34) Equations for IRPT and rational expectations with a low DW-statistic were re-estimated by an interative technique attributed to Cochrane and Orcutt assuming a first-order autoregressive process for the disturbance terms. Because estimates for α and β did not change significantly, we have not reported it in the tables.

0.4 weeks respectively. The values of the DW-statistic show that autocorrelation is not a serious problem.[35)]

Somewhat surprising at first sight is the relatively strong influence of speculation in the models of regressive expectations and in the models combining adaptive and extrapolative expectations with respect to the Dutch Guilder, both for RMON and REUDM (see tables 5 and 9). All coefficients are statistically significant at 5 percent level and have expected signs and orders of magnitude which, moreover, differ very little between both models. This result may be due to the fact that the Dutch Guilder and German Mark are pegged to one another within the so-called European snake, and that, therefore, there is a good reason for supposing that there exists a stronger belief in a "normal" exchange rate in a system of "fixed" exchange rates than in a system of flexible rates, implying a regressive element in the formation of expectations. Moreover, speculators' excess demand for forward exchange will become more and more elastic when the forward rate moves nearer to the official support limits.[36)37)] The estimating equation for the combination of adaptive and extrapolative expectations has almost the same structure as that of regressive expectations, differing primarily

---

35) It must be mentioned that DW-statistic will be biased for models with lagged endogenous variables as independent variables. However, as has been shown by W.Gaab (1974) in a Monte Carlo study, the DW-statistic still can be used with careful interpretation in small samples.

36) For the presumption that under a pegged spot rate speculative excess demand will be more elastic than under a floating rate see, e.g. J.Spraos (1953), p.1o3), E.E.Leamer and R.M.Stern (1976, pp.96-97).

37) H.R.Stoll (1968, pp.69-7o) has found similar results with respect to the relative influence of speculation for both the flexible Canadian Dollar ($\hat{\beta}$=0.035) and the pegged Pound Sterling ($\hat{\beta}$= 0.40)vis-à-vis the US Dollar.

in the interpretation of parameters. For $\dot{c} = \lambda$ and $\gamma = c\ (1-\delta)$ both models are identical. This may explain the similar regression results obtained for both models. With respect to US Dollar, Pound Sterling, and Swiss Francs, estimates for both models show only a small influence of speculation, although in part statistically significant. However, at least one of the other parameter estimates either has a wrong sign or is not significantly different from zero. The latter statements are also valid for the models of extrapolative, extrapolative/regressive, and adaptive/regressive expectations with respect to all foreign exchanges under examination. In some cases high values for standard errors and coefficients may indicate problems of multicollinearity.

IV. CONCLUSIONS

In order to ascertain the relative influence of interest arbitrage, speculation, and commercial hedging on forward exchange rates, a simple model of the forward exchange market according to the so-called "modern theory" has been formulated and tested for the DM/\$-, DM/£-, DM/HFL-, and DM/SFR-rates, relating both the German interbank money market rate in Frankfurt and the external Euro-DM money market rate in London on the one hand to the corresponding Eurocurrency market rates in London on the other. This theory states, that the forward rate can be expressed as a weighted average of the interest-parity forward rate and the expected spot rate. To explain the expected spot rate in terms of observable variables, different models of the formation of expectations have been used.

Our findings can be summarized very briefly as follows: In all cases the estimates of α and β sum approximately to one, which implies that there exists no influence of commercial hedging on forward exchange rates. Therefore, the restriction $\alpha+\beta= 1$ imposed by H.R.Stoll, J.Kesselman, R.D.Haas and others may be valid. In a system of flexible exchange rates speculation plays only a minor rôle in the determination of forward rates, at least in the period covered in this study. Therefore, we can accept the statement of H.R. Stoll (1968, p.78), that "for all practical purposes, we may say that ... the arbitrage demand-supply schedule is perfectly elastic at F*, the forward rate satisfying the interest parity theory (IRPT)". In contrast to this result, which equally applies to the DM/$-, the DM/£-, and the DM/SFR-rates, are the findings for Dutch Guilder to which the Deutsche Mark is pegged. Here we have found a relatively strong influence of speculation, indicating that the speculative schedule may be more elastic in a system of fixed exchange rates than in a system of flexible rates. This may be due to the fact, that "... there will be, in a flexible exchange rate system, considerable uncertainty about the future spot rate, ...",[38] whereas, at least in "normal" periods, speculators have stronger confidence in the maintenance of a pegged rate because of official counterspeculation.[39] These findings apply equally as well to the German money market rate as to the Euro-DM rate. In either case the corresponding parameter estimates do not differ significantly. This may be due to the fact, that in the period covered a high degree of integration has existed between the German money market and the Euro-DM market.

---

38) H.R.Stoll (1968, p.1o3).

39) For a discussion of the policy implications of this point, see, e.g., T.D.Willett (1976, pp.197-199).

TABLE 3: Estimates for the DM/$-forward rate taking RMON and REU$ as interest rates, 13.9.74 - 29.7.77 (= 151 weekly observations).1)

	a	α	β	λ	c	γ	δ	$\bar{R}^2$ DW	SEE (10^{-3})
Interest rate parity theory	0.00439 (1.7)	0.99780 (906.6)						0.9998 1.18	
Rational expectations	0.00244 (0.5)	0.99902 (419.9)	-0.00122 (0.4)					0.9996 o.51	
Adaptive expectations	0.00396 (1.1)	0.97257 (67.0)	0.02517 (1.8)	0.34725 (4.8)				0.9999 1.92	1.1778
Extrapolative expectations	0.00193 (0.5)	1.0055 (23.1)	-0.00682 (0.2)			-0.45458 (0.2)		0.9999 1.34	1.2574
Regressive expectations	0.00529 (1.1)	0.94622 (19.0)	0.05728 (1.0)		0.42093 (4.8)		0.34316 (0.9)	0.9999 2.01	1.1822
Regressive and extra-polative expectations	0.00645 (1.4)	0.91835 (20.2)	0.07815 (1.8)	0.45131 (5.4)		0.19321 (1.1)	0.61177 (1.2)	0.9999 2.03	1.1813
Adaptive and extrapolative expectations	0.00528 (1.4)	0.94786 (43.5)	0.04914 (2.3)	0.3968 (5.1)		0.22428 (1.5)		0.9999 1.97	1.1814
Adaptive and regressive expectations	0.00678 (1.4)	0.90108 (26.1)	0.09521 (2.8)	-0.14792 (2.0)	0.57357 (8.0)		0.38171 (2.5)	0.9999 1.98	1.1783

1) The figures in parantheses indicate t-values; DW is the Durbin-Watson statistic; $\bar{R}^2$ denotes the coefficient of determination corrected for degrees of freedom; SEE is the standard error of estimate.

TABLE 4: Estimates for the DM/£-forward rate taking RMON and REU£ as interest rates, 13.9.74 - 29.7.77 (= 151 weekly observations).

	a	α	β	λ	c	γ	δ	R^2 DW	SEE (10^{-3})
Interest rate parity theory	0.00423 (2.0)	0.99840 (2295.8)						0.9999 1.53	
Rational expectations	0.00195 (0.7)	1.00024 (334.9)	-0.00122 (0.4)					0.9999 1.70	
Adaptive expectations	-0.00106 (0.4)	0.97541 (70.7)	0.02370 (1.7)	0.07054 (0.9)				0.9999 1.95	3.5289
Extrapolative expectations	-0.00126 (0.5)	0.97170 (70.4)	0.02740 (2.0)			0.14681 (0.7)		0.9999 1.77	3.5328
Regressive expectations	-0.00152 (0.6)	0.96889 (66.2)	0.03219 (2.1)		0.11121 (1.4)		-1.3946 (0.7)	0.9999 2.01	3.5229
Regressive and extrapolative expectations	-0.00154 (0.6)	0.96886 (64.2)	0.03025 (2.0)	0.11263 (1.4)		0.33086 (0.2)	1.5215 (0.1)	0.9999 2.01	3.5345
Adaptive and extrapolative expectations	-0.00151 (0.6)	0.96897 (65.1)	0.03014 (2.0)	0.11115 (1.4)		0.26648 (1.3)		0.9999 2.01	3.5229
Adaptive and regressive expectations	-0.00168 (0.6)	0.96887 (60.9)	0.03027 (1.9)	-0.2564 (1.9)	0.34674 (2.8)		0.28644 (0.5)	0.9999 2.00	3.5181

TABLE 5: Estimates for the DM/HFL-forward rate taking RMON and REUHFL as interest rate, 13.9.74 - 29.7.77 (= 151 weekly observations)

	a	α	β	λ	c	γ	δ	$\bar{R}^2$ DW	SEE (10^{-3})
Interest rate parity theory	0.00903 (1.9)	0.98999 (203.8)						0.9963 0.20	
Rational expectations	-0.01563 (0.4)	0.97266 (28.6)	0.03906 (0.6)					0.9330 0.10	
Adaptive expectations	0.00412 (0.8)	1.0110 (83.7)	-0.01580 (1.1)	-0.12367 (1.5)				0.9965 2.02	0.91911
Extrapolative expectations	0.00134 (0.2)	0.99967 (65.7)	-0.00191 (0.1)			18.939 (0.1)		0.9965 2.24	0,92037
Regressive expectations	-0.08858 (2.1)	0.65960 (12.4)	0.43094 (5.3)		0.81582 (17.2)		0.40505 (4.1)	0.9949 2.39	1.0966
Regressive and extrapolative expectations	-0.08810 (2.0)	0.65998 (12.4)	0.43008 (5.3)	0.81754 (16.3)		-0.00975 (0.1)	0.39105 (2.6)	0.9949 2.40	1.1003
Adaptive and extrapolative expectations	-0.08694 (2.2)	0.66297 (12.6)	0.42588 (5.4)	0.81397 (17.1)		0.48415 (5.4)		0.9949 2.40	1.0966
Adaptive and regressive expectations	0.00181 (0.3)	1.0025 (78.3)	-0.00498 (0.3)	-0.06922 (0.0)	0.05293 (0.0)		123.89 (0.0)	0.9964 2.01	0.91986

TABLE 6: Estimates for the DM/SFR-forward rate taking RMON and REUSFR as interest rates, 13.9.74 - 29.7.77 (= 151 weekly observations).

	a	α	β	λ	c	γ	δ	$\bar{R}^2$ DW	SEE (10^{-3})
Interest rate parity theory	-0.00610 (4.6)	1.00562 (741.4)						0.9997 1.27	
Rational expectations	-0.00488 (0.4)	1.00781 (73.1)	0.00 (0.0)					0.9941 0.06	
Adaptive expectations	-0.00778 (3.9)	0.95464 (45.4)	0.05325 (2.4)	0.28291 (4.2)				0.9999 2.05	0.56986
Extrapolative expectations	-0.00520 (3.2)	1.0025 (49.5)	0.00257 (0.1)			-5.3726 (0.1)		0.9998 1.59	0.58073
Regressive expectations	-0.00662 (3.4)	0.97663 (42.8)	0.02998 (1.2)	0.02998	0.22336 (2.8)		0.25556 (1.1)	0.9998 1.98	0.56986
Regressive and extrapolative expectations	-0.00770 (3.5)	0.95664 (31.7)	0.05117 (1.6)	0.22081 (2.7)		1.2332 (1.2)	7.2181 (1.0)	0.9998 1.94	0.5657
Adaptive and extrapolative expectations	-0.00660 (3.0)	0.97706 (32.3)	0.02953	0.22320 (2.8)		-0.35417 (0.6)		0.9998 1.98	0.5699
Adaptive and regressive expectations	-0.91826 (3.4)	0.92771 (25.8)	0.08175 (2.1)	0.48818 (6.1)	-0.24889 (2.6)		0.88059 (1.5)	0.9998 1.96	0.5681

TABLE 7: OLS-estimates for the DM/\$-forward rate taking REUDM and REU\$ as interest rates, 4.1.74 - 29.7.77 (= 187 observations).

	a	α	β	λ	c	γ	δ	$\bar{R}^2$ DW	SEE (10^{-3})
Interest rate parity theory	0.00708 (4.2)	0.99707 (1482.1)						0.9999 1.50	
Rational expectations	0.01978 (2.6)	1.00000 (416.4)	-0.00928 (2.2)					0.9995 0.25	
Adaptive expectations	0.00562 (3.5)	1.0319 (110.9)	-0.03424 (3.7)	0.02665 (0.5)				0.9999 1.95	1.017
Extrapolative expectations	0.00562 (3.6)	1.0322 (136.9)	-0.03451 (4.6)			-0.02132 (0.2)		0.9999 1.90	1.017
Regressive expectations	0.00560 (3.5)	1.0315 (125.9)	-0.03379 (4.1)		0.03561 (0.4)		0.67908 (0.2)	0.9999 1.96	1.020
Regressive and extrapolative expectations	0.00476 (2.7)	1.0140 (79.9)	-0.01602 (1.3)		0.09497 (1.3)	-4.2404 (0.9)	-43.924 (0.6)	0.9999 2.04	1.021
Adaptive and extrapolative expectations	0.00562 (3.5)	1.0324 (141.9)	-0.03468 (4.8)	0.30655 (0.4)		0.00859 (0.1)		0.9999 1.96	1.020
Adaptive and regressive expectations	0.00575 (3.5)	1.0330 (116.4)	-0.03538 (4.0)	0.019214 (0.0)	0.01061 (0.0)		0.36584 (0.0)	0.9999 1.96	1.022

TABLE 8: OLS-estimates for the DM/Ł-forward rate taking REUDM and REUŁ as interest rates, 4.1.74 - 29.7.77 (= 187 observations).

	a	α	β	λ	c	γ	δ	$\bar{R}^2$ DW	SEE (10^{-3})
Interest rate parity theory	0.00935 (3.1)	0.99757 (1699.9)						0.9999 1.89	
Rational expectations	0.00708 (2.2)	0.98853 (200.9)	0.00942 (1.8)					0.9999 1.83	
Adaptive expectations	0.00555 (1.6)	0.94185 (48.2)	0.05547 (2.9)	0.07666 (1.2)				0.9999 1.94	6.125
Extrapolative expectations	0.00598 (1.7)	0.94631 (34.4)	0.05101 (1.9)			0.00194 (0.0)		0.9999 1.79	6.148
Regressive expectations	0.00472 (1.3)	0.92598 (39.0)	0.07123 (3.0)		0.13097 (1.7)		-0.24401 (0.3)	0.9999 1.99	6.127
Regressive and extrapolative expectations	0.00461 (1.2)	0.93020 (38.9)	0.067089 (2.8)		0.12318 (1.6)	1.0216 (0.8)	8.0560 (0.6)	0.9999 1.98	6.127
Adaptive and extrapolative expectations	0.00471 (1.2)	0.92593 (37.7)	0.07129 (2.9)	0.13127 (1.7)		0.16325 (1.1)		0.9999 1.99	6.127
Adaptive and regressive expectations	0.00374 (0.9)	0.91408 (37.3)	0.08310 (3.4)	0.33811 (3.0)	-0.19395 (1.7)		1.9373 (2.0)	0.9999 1.99	6.126

TABLE 9: OLS-estimates for the DM/HFL-forward rate taking REUDM and REUHFL as interest rates, 4.1.74 - 29.7.77 (= 187 observations).

	a	α	β	λ	c	γ	δ	$\bar{R}^2$ DW	SEE (10^{-3})
Interest rate parity theory	0.00171 (0.2)	0.99585 (93.4)						0.9787 0.33	
Rational expectations	0.00391 (0.1)	0.99609 (39.2)	-0.00391 (0.1)					0.9473 0.13	
Adaptive expectations	0.00681 (1.6)	1.0166 (92.9)	-0.02391 (1.9)	-0.10741 (1.5)				0.9966 1.97	0.8629
Extrapolative expectations	0.00407 (0.8)	1.0045 (79.6)	-0.00902 (0.6)			3.3810 (0.5)		0.9967 2.19	0.8594
Regressive expectations	-0.06877 (1.9)	0.69296 (16.9)	0.37733 (5.8)		0.81717 (18.3)		0.32678 (3.6)	0.9955 2.48	0.9942
Regressive and extrapolative expectations	-0.06991 (2.0)	0.69101 (16.9)	0.38045 (5.9)		0.81871 (17.6)	0.00139 (0.0)	0.32964 (2.5)	0.9955 2.48	0.9969
Adaptive and extrapolative expectations	-0.07177 (1.9)	0.68733 (16.8)	0.38607 (5.9)	0.82330 (18.8)		0.55481 (7.0)		0.9955 2.48	0.9942
Adaptive and regressive expectations	-0.11958 (2.2)	0.65841 (16.0)	0.46462 (5.7)	0.86054 (21.2)	0.00214 (0.1)		-251.63 (0.1)	0.9955 2.46	1.0000

TABLE 1o: OLS-estimates for the DM/SFR-forward rate taking REUDM and REUSFR as interest rates, 4.1.74 - 29.7.77 (= 187 observations).

	a	α	β	λ	c	γ	δ	$\bar{R}^2$ DW	SEE (10^{-4})
Interest rate parity theory	-0.00333 (5.0)	1.00342 (1428.3)						0.9999 1.80	
Rational expectations	-0.00366 (0.3)	1.00098 (35.7)	-0.00391 (0.11)					0.98875 0.01	
Adaptive expectations	-0.00506 (4.3)	0.94913 (51.7)	0.05629 (2.9)	0.26224 (4.3)				0.9999 2.15	5.751
Extrapolative expectations	-0.00244 (2.6)	1.0171 (60.9)	-0.01464 (0.8)			0.93997 (0.7)		0.9999 1.86	5.647
Regressive expectations	-0.00286 (2.7)	1.0056 (55.1)	-0.00277 (0.1)		0.07616 (1.0)		-77.522 (0.1)	0.9991 1.98	5.651
Regressive and extrapolative expectations	-0.00489 (3.0)	0.97309 (43.4)	0.03208 (1.3)		0.06053 (0.7)	9.9706 (0.6)	173.14 (0.3)	0.9999 2.05	5.651
Adaptive and extrapolative expectations	-0.00301 (2.7)	1.0018 (48.3)	0.00131 (0.1)	0.08337 (1.1)		-12.457 (0.1)		0.9999 1.98	5.651
Adaptive and regressive expectations	-0.00546 (4.3)	0.93638 (53.1)	0.06958 (3.8)	0.55355 (8.3)	-0.36669 (4.6)		0.50902 (1.5)	0.9999 2.0	5.596

REFERENCES

Agmon, T. and S. Bronfeld (1975), The International Mobility of Short-term Covered Arbitrage Capital, Journal of Business Finance and Accounting, vol. 2, pp.269-278.

Aliber, R.Z. (1973), The Interest Parity Theorem: A Reinterpretation, Journal of Political Economy, vol. 81, pp.1451-1459.

Arndt, S.W. (1968), International Short-term Capital Movements: A Distributed Lag Model of Speculation in Foreign Exchange, Econometrica, vol. 36, pp.59-7o.

Black, S.W. (1972), The Use of Rational Expectations in Models of Speculation, Review of Economics and Statistics, vol. 54, pp.161-165.

Branson, W.H. (1969), The Minimum Covered Interest Differential Needed for International Arbitrage Activity, Journal of Political Economy, pp.1o28-1o35.

Canterbery, R.E. (1975), The Modern Theory of Foreign Exchange and the Net Speculative Residual, Southern Economic Journal, vol. 41, pp.182-187.

Einzig, P. (1967), A Dynamic Theory of Forward Exchange, 2nd ed., London-Melbourne-Toronto.

Frenkel, J.A. (1973), Elasticities and the Interest Parity Theory, Journal of Political Economy, vol. 81, pp.741-747.

Frenkel, J.A. (1975), Inflation and the Formation of Expectations, Journal of Monetary Economics, vol. 1, pp.4o3-421.

Frenkel, J.A. and R.M.Levich (1975), Covered Interest Arbitrage: Unexploited Profits, Journal of Political Economy, vol. 83, pp.325-338.

Frenkel, J.A. (1976), Inflationary Expectations and Some Dynamic Aspects of Welfare Costs, in: M.Parkin and G.Zis (eds.), Inflation in the World Economy, Manchester-Toronto, pp.47-69.

Frenkel, J.A. and R.M.Levich (1977), Transaction Costs and Interest Arbitrage: Tranquil versus Turbulent Periods, Journal of Political Economy, vol. 85, pp.12o9-1226.

Gaab, W. (1974), Schätzung verteilter lags. Eine Monte-Carlo-Untersuchung zur Beurteilung einiger ausgewählter Verfahren, Meisenheim a.Gl.

Grubel, H.G. (1963), A Multicountry Model of Forward Exchange: Theory, Policy, and Empirical Evidence 1955-1961, Yale Economic Essays, vol. 3. pp.1o5-169.

Haas, R.D. (1974), More Evidence on the Role of Speculation in the Canadian Forward Exchange Market, The Canadian Journal of Economics, vol. 7, pp.496-5o1.

Holmes, A.R. and F.H.Schott (1965), The New York Foreign Exchange Market, New York.

Kesselman, J. (1971), The Role of Speculation in Forward-Rate Determination: The Canadian Flexible Dollar 1953-196o, The Canadian Journal of Economics, vol. 4, pp.279-298.

Keynes, J.M. (1923), A Tract on Monetary Reform, London.
Leamer, E.E. and R.M.Stern (197o), Quantitative International Economics, Chicago.
Marquardt, D.W. (1963), An Algorithm for Least-squares Estimation of Nonlinear Parameters, Journal of the Society for Industrial and Applied Mathematics, vol. 11,pp.431-441.
Marston, R.C. (1976), Interest Arbitrage in the Euro-Currency Markets, European Economic Review, vol. 7, pp.1-13.
McCallum, B.T. (1976), Rational Expectations and the Natural Rate Hypothesis: Some Consistent Estimates, Econometrica, vol. 44, pp.43-52.
McCallum, P.T. (1977), The Role of Speculation in the Canadian Forward Exchange Market: Some Estimates Assuming Rational Expectations, Review of Economics and Statistics, vol. 59, pp. 145-151.
Minot, W.G. (1974), Tests of Integration Between Major Western European Capital Markets, Oxford Economic Papers, vol. 26, pp. 424-439.
Muth, J.F. (1961), Rational Expectations and the Theory of Price Movements, Econometrica, vol. 29, pp.315-335.
Officer, L.H. and T.D. Willett (197o), The Covered-Arbitrage Schedule: A Critical Survey of Recent Developments, Journal of Money, Credit, and Banking, vol. 2, pp.247-257.
Prachowny, F.J. (197o), A Note on Interest Parity and the Supply of Arbitrage Funds, Journal of Political Economy, vol. 78, pp.54o-546.
Sohmen, E. (1973), Wechselkurs und Währungsordnung, Tübingen.
Spraos, J. (1953), The Theory of Forward Exchange and Recent Practice, Manchester School of Economics and Social Studies, vol. 21, pp.87-117.
Stein,J.L. (1965), The Forward Rate and the Interest Parity, Review of Economic Studies, Vol. 32, pp.113-126.
Stein, J.L. and E.Tower (1967), The Short-run Stability of the Foreign Exchange Market, Review of Economics and Statistics, vol. 49, pp.173-185.
Stoll, H.R. (1968), An Empirical Study of the Forward Exchange Market under Fixed and Flexible Exchange Rate Systems, The Canadian Journal of Economics, vol. 1, pp.55-78.
Stoll, H.R. (1972), Causes of Deviations from Interest Parity. A Comment, Journal of Money, Credit, and Banking, vol. 4, pp.113-117.
Tsiang, S.C. (1959), The Theory of Forward Exchange and Effects of Government Intervention on the Forward Exchange Market, IMF, Staff Papers, vol. 7, pp.75-1o6.
Van Belle, J.J. (1973), A Neglected Aspect to the Modern Theory of Forward Exchange, Southern Economic Journal, pp.117-119.
Willett, T.D. (1976), The Eurocurrency Market, Exchange Rate Systems, and National Financial Policies, in: C.H.Stem, J.H.Makin, and D.E.Logue (eds.), Eurocurrencies and the International Monetary System, Washington,pp. 193-221.

COMMENT ON W. GAAB, "ON THE ROLE OF INTEREST ARBITRAGE, SPECULATION, AND COMMERCIAL HEDGING IN THE DETERMINATION OF THE FORWARD EXCHANGE RATE: THE CASE OF THE FLEXIBLE GERMAN MARK, 1974 - 1977."

Hans-Jürgen Vosgerau

Being - at least in my own opinion - in the first place a theoretical economist I do not feel obliged to test empirically the assumption underlying the following comment, viz. that the organizers of this conference are quasi-omniscient with respect to the comparative advantages of discussants. From the fact that they allocated Werner Gaab's empirical paper to me I conclude therefore, that they could not have hoped for comments in the field of statistical and econometric techniques. They must have waited for some general, more theoretical discussion, which I propose to deliver under five headings.

(1) The question, which Gaab sets out to answer, is: what determines the forward rate of exchange? This problem is clearly relevant: it is alluded to in several papers presented at this conference, and it crept up in the discussion during the last days. The way, in which the forward rate is determined, is important for the assessment of the exchange rate regimes.

(2) In the literature, there are mainly two answers to the question

a) the forward rate is determined such, that with given interest rates in both countries, interest arbitrage becomes profitless (interest rate parity theory: "IRPT") - going back to Keynes and Einzig.

b) the forward rate is a weighted average of this "no profit forward rate" and the expected spot rate (modern theory: "MT", almost 2o years old by now). Expectations as to the spot rate are formed by speculators, and if they would determine the forward rate by themselves, there would be a third (pure or extreme) answer, but which is adhered to by nobody.

"MT" is certainly the more general solution, but is has no real content, until the weights of the two influences - by interest arbitragers and speculators - are determined. This is mainly an empirical task.

It has been tackled - for the first time, if I see it correctly - by Hans R. Stoll in 1968 for US $, British Ŀ, and Can. $. Gaab's contribution can be viewed as an extension, elaboration and application to DM vis á vis $, Ŀ, sfr, hfl.

(3) As for the empirical analysis of the Case of the Flexible German Mark 1974 - 1977, which has been industriously carried out by Gaab for the first time, there can be no doubt, that this work has its own high merits. In addition there are two generalizations of Stoll's earlier analysis: One (a) is the inclusion of commercial hedging and the other (b) the distinction between different expectation formation hypotheses, each with its own lag specifications.

ad (a) Gaab distinguishes - following well-known authorities in the field, like for instance Sohmen - three groups of agents in the forward market: interest arbitragers, speculators, and commercial hedgers. Stoll on the other hand argues that hedging can be subsumed under speculation and/or arbitrage. This is confirmed by Gaab's empirical results: the influence of hedging gets a weight of practically zero in all cases, which might be an empirical confirmation of the suspicion, that hedging - contrary to Sohmen's classification - is not an important category of its own, at least as far as the determination of the forward rate is concerned.

ad (b) As for the distinction of various hypotheses regarding the formation of expectations, Gaab tackles it very systematically: Adaptive, regressive and extrapolative expectations as well as three different combinations of these are distinguished and their implications empirically tested. In addition to these 6 cases the nowadays fashionable rational expectations hypothesis is included - although I must say that in this respect the paper is rather short.

Together with the old IRPT there are thus 8 cases, which are analyzed, separately for the internal and the external (Euro-) Market, and for 4 pairs of currencies

DM - \$, DM - £, DM - sfr, DM - hfl

the first three of which are floating against each other, while one (hfl) is pegged within the so-called snake.

(4) The empirical results speak for themselves. In addition to what Werner Gaab himself wrote and said it remains only to be emphasized, that for freely floating currencies and well organized markets speculation really seems to play a negligible rôle in determining forward rates of exchange. This means at the same time that it is of no great importance, which expectation formation hypothesis regarding future spot rates is adopted. The old IRPT dominates the field.

Quite different are Gaab's findings for the case of the exchange rate between DM and hfl, the two currencies which are tied together in the European snake. Here it turns out that speculation is indeed important. Especially with regressive expectations and with the two combinations of regressive and extrapolative and adaptive and extrapolative expectations are the relative weights of the future spot rate expected by speculators impressive.

This of course is only one case, and one might wish to verify whether similar cases (ö.S.) produce similar results.

(5) There is one final point I want to raise, which puzzled me when studying Gaab's paper: it is the assumption of equilibrium, always maintained or at least sufficiently quickly restored in the markets under consideration. This assumption underlies the whole approach - finding formal expression in equ (8) (p.-5-).

My last question therefore is: is this procedure legitimate in a world, in which the float has been dirty?

- or put otherwise: what is the influence of official intervention in the exchange market? Could government intervention be incorporated into the analysis, and might this help to solve some of the remaining questions in an otherwise laudable piece of work?

THE EXCHANGE RATE AS AN INTERMEDIATE TARGET OF STABILIZATION POLICY IN AUSTRIA*

Heinz Handler

1. INTRODUCTION

Since the breakdown of the Bretton Woods system, Austria has adhered to an exchange rate policy of adjustably pegging to a basket of currencies. That basket has changed over the years (and at times shrunk to just a single currency - the deutsche mark), as it has been defined according to the respective priorities of overall economic policy. For the same reason, the exchange rate was changed a few times, while the composition of the basket was maintained. With intervention as an instrument of stabilization policy, the exchange rate has served over most of the 1970s as an intermediate goal to approach the short-term target rate of inflation. Balance of payments considerations played a secondary role, at least as long as the recession of the mid-1970s put a veil over underlying balance of payments developments. This has resulted in the so-called "hard currency policy": since 1971, the Austrian schilling has appreciated considerably in terms of a comprehensive trade-weighted basket of foreign currencies.

In this paper it will be attempted to dig for the "philosophy" in the background of the hard currency policy. In the following Section 2, official arguments in favor of the hard currency policy will be presented. They will be organized and analyzed in terms of the "Scandinavian" model of inflation (Section 3), the vicious circle hypothesis (Section 4), and optimum currency area analysis (Section 5).

* The author benefited from stimulating discussion on the subject of this paper with Sven W.Arndt. Helpful comments were also provided by E.Hochreiter and K.W.Rothschild. They are of course not responsible for deficiencies of the paper.

In the final Section 6, a few conclusions will be drawn resulting in a recommendation for actual exchange rate policy.

2. THE CONCEPTUAL FRAMEWORK OF AUSTRIA'S HARD CURRENCY POLICY

As usual in countries whose policymakers incline to keep information scarce for the general public, in Austria no official publication is available manifesting the model which exchange rate policy is based upon. Therefore, one has to rely on such inadequate sources as descriptions of exchange rate measures in the regular publications of the National Bank, oral statements by representatives of the monetary authorities as reproduced in newspapers, and similar information. The general framework extracted from such sources may therefore be biased by personal opinion of the author.

Austrian policymakers have in the past few years produced a series of arguments in favor of the hard currency policy which may be grouped as follows:

1. As a small open economy, Austria is heavily dependent on economic developments abroad. Pegging the schilling to the currency of an important trading-partner country which exhibits a higher degree of internal (price) stability than Austria, will result in "importing stability".

2. Total supply of goods in a particular economy may be disaggregated in one part originating from the internationally competitive sector (C-sector) and another part produced by sheltered industries (S-sector). Since in a small open economy foreign trade prices in international currency are supposed to be given, the hard currency policy will squeeze profits in the C-sector, thus encouraging entrepreneurs to resist excessive wage claims of the unions. This will further reduce inflationary pressures.

3. For a "weak currency policy", i.e., have the home currency purposely "float" downward, in a small economy it would be imperative to adopt supporting measures in order to avoid undesired effects like an increasing inflation rate. Policymakers in Austria are not

confident enough in their ability to effectively introduce such measures that would result in real income losses and perhaps rising unemployment.

4. From empirical evidence on price elasticities and/or absorption criteria it can not be expected that a depreciating schilling would either reduce the share of imports in domestic demand or increase exports. In addition, experiences in other industrial countries with a depreciation policy were not at all encouraging.

5. The hard currency policy is likely to create a climate of monetary stability, thus breaking inflationary expectations fueled by inflation abroad.

6. Via the profit squeeze in the C-sector, an appreciating schilling will induce changes in the production structure such that, on average, productivity will rise; this in turn will improve the long-run competitive position of the C-sector vis-à-vis foreign producers.

7. Since in a small country like Austria the foreign exchange market is necessarily thin, a hard currency policy with official intervention can help avoid short-term disruptive effects caused by speculators.

Most of the points put forward in favor of the hard currency policy can be related to the short-term policy goal of reducing inflation. Although policymakers at times employ long-term arguments, these are not at the heart of the problem. The dominant chain of arguments seems to be based on the theory of optimum currency areas and on the vicious circle hypothesis. According to this hypothesis, attempts to achieve by depreciation any lasting effect on relative prices must fail because of offsetting movements in nominal wage rates and the money supply. The assumptions usually underlying official statements hint at one specific type of macro-model which is supposed to exhibit the vicious circle transmission mechanism: the so-called "Scandinavian model" of inflation.[1] An Austrian version

1) For a recent evaluation of such models and their performance, see Aukrust (1977).

of this model was elaborated and tested by Frisch (1976). Since the Frisch-model seems to have had some impact on Austrian policy-makers in formulating their arguments in favor of the hard currency policy, it will be examined to what extent the Scandinavian model in general is appropriate in the case of Austria and how it can be related to the vicious circle hypothesis.

3. THE SCANDINAVIAN INFLATION MODEL

3.1 The Standard Scandinavian Model

The standard version of the Scandinavian model may be depicted by the following five equations:

(1) $p_c = p_x$

(2) $w_c = p_c + q_c$

(3) $w_s = w_c$

(4) $p_s = w_s - q_s$

(5) $p = (1-\pi)p_c + \pi p_s$

where

p_c inflation rate in the C-sector;

p_x rate of change of export and import prices (expressed in home currency units);

w_c rate of change of nominal wages in the C-sector;

q_c rate of change of labor productivity in the C-sector;

w_s rate of change of nominal wages in the S-sector;

p_s inflation rate in the S-sector;

q_s rate of change of labor productivity in the S-sector;

p overall inflation rate;

π given value share of S-sector output in total production of the economy ($0 < \pi < 1$)

In this (recursive) model, price changes in the C-sector (at fixed exchange rates) are determined by changes in the world price level. The given productivity change in the C-sector together with

p_c determine the growth rate of nominal wages in the C-sector, thus keeping the profit share constant. It is supposed that the C-sector assumes the role of a wage-leader, and that $q_c > q_s$. Market forces and solidarity among trade unions secure that money wages in the S-sector rise at the same speed as in the C-sector. The growth of wages and exogenous productivity in the S-sector together determine the inflation rate in that sector, assuming mark-up pricing which again holds the profit share constant. Given the relative weights of the two sectors, the average rate of inflation of the whole economy can be determined.

There are a few notable results of this model: currency depreciation would result in a rise of nominal wages by an equal percentage; domestic inflation can not be controlled by demand management policies; and the overall domestic inflation rate exceeds the inflation rate in the C-sector and the world inflation rate. The last two statements are obvious, under the above stated assumptions, from the following reduced form equation:

$$(6) \qquad p = p_c + \pi\,(q_c - q_s)$$

Frisch (1976) extended the long-run supply-oriented standard Scandinavian model to incorporate the demand side of the C-sector by means of an expectations augmented Phillips curve:

$$(7) \qquad w_c = A + Bv + Cw_c^*$$

In this equation, v is some indicator of demand pressure in the labor market, and w_c^* the expected growth rate of nominal wages. Frisch approximates w_c^* by the productivity growth rate in nominal terms, i.e., $w_c^* = p_c + q_c$. Inserting this into (7), and defining $V = A + Bv$, yields:

$$(8) \qquad w_c = V + C(p_c + q_c)$$

In the Frisch-version of the Scandinavian model, equation (2) is replaced by equation (8).

For purposes of exchange rate policy in Austria, policymakers seem to rely on an inflation transmission model of the standard Scandinavian type. They argue that in an international upswing the C-sector is pacesetting in wage developments at home: increasing world prices make room for wage increases in that sector, entailing an even higher inflation rate in the S-sector. The hard currency policy, resulting in an effectively appreciating schilling rate, will then be an efficient means to reduce the room for wage increases in the C-sector, which in turn will hold down wage claims in the S-sector. As a result, overall inflation will be lower. For the model to work in this way, wage-leadership of the C-sector as well as accommodating demand and monetary policy must be assumed.

3.2 A Modified Model

For a critical evaluation of this model and its qualification as a basis for Austria's exchange rate policy, the structure of the model as well as the underlying assumptions will have to be examined against the background of behavioral relations in Austria. Several modifications seem to be necessary to make application of the model meaningful in the Austrian context. A slightly modified Scandinavian model is presented below, the modifications being confined to those for which empirical evidence on Austria is already existing.

(9) $p_f = p_w - (1-\alpha)e$

(1o) $p_x = p_f + e$

(11) $p_c = \beta\, p_x$

(8) $w_c = V + C(p_c+q_c)$

(12) $w_s = \gamma\, w_c$

(13) $p_s = \delta\, (w_s-q_s)$

(5) $p = (1-\pi)p_c + \pi p_s$

The reduced form equation for the national inflation rate resulting from the modified model would read:

(14) $p = \varepsilon\ (p_w + \alpha e) + \pi\delta\ (\gamma V + \gamma C q_c - q_s)$

where $\varepsilon = \beta(1 - \pi + \pi\gamma\delta C)$

Newly introduced variables are:

p_f rate of change of export (and import) prices in foreign currency units;

e rate of change of the exchange rate, defined as the price of foreign currency in terms of home currency units;

p_w rate of change of the world price level in foreign currency units.

The modifications suggested serve two major purposes: first, to explicitely introduce the exchange rate; and second, to somewhat adapt the model to be more suitable for the application to short-run problems. Equations (9) and (1o), replacing equation (1) of the standard model, introduce the exchange rate into the model. However, it should be noted that as long as e is treated exogenous, the model will work only in one direction: there is no provision for changes in the national inflation rate, whatever their cause, to have an impact on the exchange rate.

Equation (9) takes care of the possibility that p_f and e are not independent of each other. Although world inflation p_w is not affected by e, a change in the exchange rate may produce a partially compensating move in p_f, meaning that the price change for traded goods in the wake of an exchange rate change will be shared by the market partners. The "pass-through coefficient" α is the fraction of the exchange rate change that is reflected in the home currency price of exported and imported goods. If $\alpha = 1$, then $p_f = p_w$, i.e., the exchange rate change is fully reflected in a change in p_x. If $\alpha = 0$, then $p_f = p_w - e$, i.e., the exchange rate change will completely show up in the foreign currency prices of traded goods while home currency prices will remain unchanged. The size of α will depend on price elasticities of demand and supply and on relative propensities to spend on nontradable goods in the two trading partner countries in question (Dornbusch, 1975, p. 281-2). For a small open economy which by and large is a price taker, α can be expected to be rather high.

Equation (11) removes the implicit assumption of equation (1) that relative price changes, and thereby also relative price levels, of C-sector output and foreign competitive production must not differ: there is evidence that varying price differentiation is a widely used sales strategy (Walterskirchen, 1977, p. 494). Even if there is a tendency to equalize over time the price levels in the various goods markets, adjustment may not be instantaneous. This also implies that inflation rates can differ over protracted periods, the difference being a function of the gap in the price levels.

In equations (2) and (4) it is assumed that profit shares in the C-sector's and the S-sector's total income are constant over time. This strong assumption was removed for the C-sector by introducing equation (8): at given p_c, w_c will now be subject to conditions in the labor market, and the profit rate in the C-sector will have to adjust accordingly. A simple alternative formulation is used in equation (13) to account for slow adjustment of S-sector wage rates to exogenous price shocks; this, too, permits a temporary move in the profit rate.

The wage spill-over hypothesis of equation (3) is based on the assumption that trade unions push for equal percentage increases of nominal wages in both sectors, or that sufficient labor mobility secures actual wage rates to rise at the same speed in both sectors. But even if that relationship holds in the long run, short-term and medium-term deviations should be accounted for. This is possible by introducing the simple equation (12).

The modifications discussed result in the reduced form equation (14), the implications of which for exchange rate policy are quite different from those of equation (6). In the standard model, a devaluation would increase the national inflation rate by an equal percentage. In the modified model, this relationship may be much looser: when $\alpha < 1$, and the values of β, γ, δ and C do not exceed unity, the exchange rate impact will be less than in the standard model. In all other cases the outcome will depend on the combination of parameter values which is a matter of empirical testing.

In spite of the modifications suggested, the model still does not account for various important problems. They shall be quoted here without further investigation, as there is no empirical material at hand to quantify their impacts. The most important deficiency seems to be the model's implication of wage-leadership by the C-sector. In countries like Austria with strong unions, it can be expected that the S-sector may become the wage-leader when in an international downswing total income growth of the C-sector is reduced. In the short run, wage developments in the C-sector may be dominated by those in the S-sector. If Shaw (1973)[2)] is correct that wage-leadership is usually assumed by unions in industries facing income elastic demand for their products, the above stated reasoning would be consistent with the observation of Branson and Myhrman (1976, p.35-38), that, in order to maintain output shares, income elasticity of demand for S-sector output must be large relative to that of C-sector output.

Monetary policy is assumed to be perfectly accommodating. In Austria that would have been an appropriate assumption for an extended period up to 1972; in the period since, credit policy has been employed to restore price stability and external balance.[3)]

---

2) See Van Poeck (1975), p.5o1.
3) For an extension of the Scandinavian model in which prices are supply-determined, but which incorporates money and output, see Argy and Carmichael (1975, p. 17ff).

Another restriction imposed on the model is that of constant terms of trade. In Austria, the terms of trade in 1977 did not differ much from those at the end of the 196os; but from 1969 to 1973, a rise of 5 per cent occurred which has been wiped out since. By introducing exchange rates in the model, and assuming specific price sharing behavior on both sides of the border, their change could result in terms of trade movements. By ignoring these movements, associated real income effects would be neglected.

3.3 Some Empirical Evidence for Austria

Frisch's (1976) application of the Scandinavian model to Austrian data (for the period 196o to 1974) revealed that the inflation rate in the C-sector rises less than the world inflation rate. For the S-sector he found that changes in unit labour costs are only partly passed on to prices and are partly reflected in a change in profit shares. In the C-sector, the Phillips relationship holds, the expectations parameter C being less than unity (i.e., inflation is only partially anticipated). Wage spill-over from the C-sector to the S-sector is weak: just about two thirds of wage inflation in the S-sector can be explained by wage inflation in the C-sector. This results in a reduced form price equation where the coefficient of the world inflation rate is not unity, as implied by the standard Scandinavian model, but only about o.2 to o.4.

In addition to the evidence presented by Frisch, Pollan (1977, p.2o5), dealing only with the manufacturing sector, has shown that changes in wage rates fluctuate widely regardless of the sector, and no simple mechanism of transmitting wage increases from one sector to the other can be detected. Steindl (1977) found that over a ten years period (between 1966 and 1976) the growth of hourly earnings was rather uniform for most of the manufacturing branches. This may indicate that the standard concept of the Scandinavian model may be appropriate for analysing long-term problems; however, it may lead to inadequate conclusions when employed for short-term stabilization purposes. From Schebeck-Suppanz-Tichy (1978) it can be inferred that α is less than unity. In case of import prices, its impact value would be some o.6; after full adjustment it would rise to about o.8. In case of export prices, the size of α would still be lower.

Analysis of the Scandinavian model leads to the conclusion that the standard version, as an essentially long-run model, is not immediately apt to serve as a basis for exchange rate policy decisions. To grasp inflation as it actually is transmitted from abroad, substantial modifications will be required. Empirical evidence on a slightly modified Scandinavian model revealed that in Austria a price increase in the C-sector, e.g., through devaluation, is considerably dampened in its impact on the national inflation rate.

4. THE VICIOUS CIRCLE ARGUMENT

The vicious circle theory as presented, e.g., by Artus and Crockett (1978) and still further developed by Basevi and De Grauwe (1977) can be formulated in a "strong" and in a "weak" version. According to the strong version, an exogenous depreciation will result in an explosive succession of inflation and depreciation. The weak version holds that, following an exogenous depreciation, the vicious economy will suffer a consecutive process of self-reinforcing inflation and depreciation, ending up at a new equilibrium point where prices and exchange rates (expressed in home currency units) are higher than in a non-vicious economy with flexible prices and a continuously controlled money supply. In either case, an inflation transmission mechanism is triggered off by an exogenous exchange rate shock, initially resulting in short-run overshooting of the long-run equilibrium exchange rate. Since prices in the C-sector are a positive function of the exchange rate, the national price level will increase. Because of downward price rigidities and lack of money illusion, exchange rates and prices will not return to their original equilibrium point.

For a vicious circle to be initiated, the following conditions will have to prevail: First, the initial exchange rate change must be exogenous, and causality must run from the exchange rate to the domestic price level.[4)] Second, the import "pass-through effect" must be large. Third, a vicious circle depends on validating monetary policy, at least in the short-run.[5)] Fourth, downward wage and price rigidities (ratchet effects)[6)] must prevail, and no other leakages must occur to an extent that would let the vicious circle crumble after a short period. Fifth, a strong vicious circle can occur only when the economy is dynamically unstable or when extra-economic elements disturb an otherwise stable development.

When downward price and wage rigidities prevail, all or most of the price adjustment to an exchange rate change occurs in the devaluing country by inflating its price level. This could be an argument of not pursuing a depreciation policy. But then, too, no virtuous circle can emerge (Basevi and De Grauwe, 1977, p.294ff) which could serve as an argument justifying an appreciation policy.

Austrian policymakers seem to have in mind some intermediate version of the vicious circle theory. Since, on the one hand, Austrian exchange rate policy in the context of the vicious circle hypothesis has not been based on the notion of an unstable economic setting or on extra-economic disturbances, the strong version will not be suggested further. On the other hand, the emphasis put on the vicious circle hypothesis suggests that it was not seen to feature a short-lived phenomenon; or that price and exchange rate changes resulting from an initial exchange rate shock would in the vicious economy not much differ from those in the non-vicious

---

4) Since it is exchange rate policy that is concerned here, initiation of a vicious circle by other exogenous shocks is not considered.

5) Basevi and De Grauwe (1977) have shown that a weak vicious circle does not necessarily depend on a permanent increase in the money supply.

6) For theoretical arguments on ratchet effects, see Crockett and Goldstein (1976).

economy. Policymakers' predilection to quote as deterrent examples the results of a depreciation policy experienced, say, in Italy and the United Kingdom, also hints at their intermediate interpretation of the vicious circle hypothesis.

As discussed in the previous Section, inflation is regarded to be transmitted according to the Scandinavian model. However, the theoretical and empirical evidence presented revealed that in the short run many leaks moderate the inflation transmission from abroad such that a vicious circle may hardly commence.

Given the balance of payments problem Austria is facing today, wage-earners seem to be prepared to consciously accept a reduction of real wage increases (and perhaps even of real wages) in order to maintain employment. In addition, the recent significant abating of inflation may indicate that C-sector producers accept a reduction in relative prices so as to maintain output and capacity utilization. This indicates the absence of downward rigidities. Although in principle in this situation a virtuous circle would be possible, and therefore the hard currency policy be justifiable, no vicious circle will be initiated. With the hard currency policy Austria seems to have intended exporting its homemade inflation rather than preventing a vicious circle. Exporting inflation means that monetary policy caused inflation which in turn was attempted to be reduced by appreciation. In case of a vicious circle, depreciation would cause inflation which would have to be accommodated by monetary policy. From this the conclusion can be drawn that the hard currency policy in Austria may have had its merits as long as reducing inflation was the primary target of policy actions. However, since the main focus of economic policy has been turned on the balance of payments, there is no ground any more for maintaining the hard currency policy.

Any attempt to reduce the deficit on current account of the balance of payments would have to include either expenditure reducing policies or expenditure switching policies or both. In any case, given a resistance to underutilization, the result would

be a reduction in the growth of real income, either by cutting nominal income growth at constant prices (incomes policy) or by inflating the domestic price level at constant nominal wages (exchange rate depreciation). The decision on the type of policy employed should rest on its relative effectiveness in reducing real income. Artus and Crockett (1978) collected various arguments enhancing the effectiveness of the one or the other type, but finally concluded: "... the case for using the exchange rate to bring about a readjustment in real wage rates rests less on its efficiency in doing so than on the evidence that other available instruments are even less efficient" (p. 23).
Since either type of policy intends to redistribute income in favor of entrepreneurs in the C-sector, it is worth pointing at their different overall consequences for income distribution. With a restrictive incomes policy, redistribution occurs in both the C-sector and the S-sector in favor of entrepreneurs. In contrast, currency depreciation would favor profits primarily in the C-sector. It may be doubted that policymakers in Austria really have in mind to favor all producers at the expense of workers' incomes.

5. THE CURRENCY AREA ARGUMENT

The most recent period of the hard currency policy since mid-1976 came close to forming an informal currency area with Germany, motivated by the "openness-criterion" as elaborated by McKinnon (1963): a considerable portion of Austria's current transactions with abroad concerns trading with Germany. According to this criterion the more open economy will suffer more in terms of price stability when resorting to exchange rate flexibility for curing an external imbalance. As long as inflation was the main economic policy problem in Austria, this argument could be applied to enhance the hard currency policy: employing exchange rates as a vehicle to "import stability" fits the case where a small open economy with relatively low monetary discipline tries to impose on itself monetary restraint. For Austria, though by international comparison it has had a remarkably good inflation record, the German success in keeping price stability was long a desired goal.

However, the conclusion derived from the openness-criterion is completely reverted when the domestic economy is more stable than the foreign economy. Then flexible exchange rates would shield against monetary disturbances from abroad. Austria could be seen to be in such a situation, provided one is prepared to accept a broad interpretation of what "more stable" means: since 1977 or so, policymakers in Austria have become rather uncomfortable by imagining that this country should have to adopt an overall economic strategy similar to the one currently pursued in Germany, with its consequence of high and perhaps rising unemployment. Put in the words of Seidel (1978), it can not be a desirable policy to peg the schilling to the mark, when Germany is pursuing an economic policy which is likely to exert an adverse effect on the German economy itself. The mark may be overvalued which has consequences for investment and employment in Germany. There is no reason for Austria to conduct a policy which would lead to similar results.

Because policymakers believe in downward price and wage rigidities, it may be instructive to confront their attitude with the results of Flanders and Helpman (1978): If a small country, facing downward rigidities and regarding the level of employment as the primary target of economic policy, is pegging its currency to that of a large country, then the large country should be one with relatively rising prices. In Austria the employment level has now become the second most important policy target (besides external balance). Therefore, pegging to the deutsche mark will the more become an inconsistent policy the more that target will further gain importance.

6. CONCLUDING REMARKS

The hard currency policy was originally aimed at fighting inflation. When the international recession spread to Austria and economic growth became the primary target of economic policy, easy fiscal and monetary policies were introduced while the hard currency policy was maintained; external balance was not one of the corners of the "magic polygon", and it was not recognized that such a policy combination could have delayed consequences for the balance of payments. The hard currency policy was still maintained when in 1976 the deficit on current account increased rapidly. Moreover, in this phase exchange rate policy became increasingly inflexible, and eventually the schilling was tied to the deutsche mark. External disequilibrium has in the meantime triggered, on the one hand, an "automatic" tightening of (de facto) monetary policy and, on the other, a slight depreciation since mid-1977 of the schilling vis-à-vis the deutsche mark. However, the mark is still regarded the bell-wether for the schilling rate.

In this paper the main official arguments concerning the hard currency policy have been analyzed. It has been shown that the arguments relating to the vicious circle hypothesis seem to be based on an inflation transmission model of the standard "Scandinavian" type. Analysis of such a model has revealed that it is apt for exchange rate policy decisions only when substantially modified. Empirical evidence on a modified Scandinavian model shows that inflation transmission from abroad is much weaker than inferred by the standard model. There is further evidence that prices and real wages are not as rigid downward as would be required for a vicious circle to be initiated. Some official arguments can be traced to currency area analysis. In this context it has been contended in this paper that the hard currency policy as pursued by Austria may have been meaningful as long as inflation was the primary problem of economic policy. In the current situation of external imbalance and the likelihood of rising unemployment, the deutsche mark may be the wrong currency to peg to.

The main conclusion emerging from this exercise would be that the hard currency policy has been maintained much too long, and that there seems to be a case for a more flexible stance in determining the exchange rate of the schilling. A recommendable way to achieve this would be to abandon the unicurrency peg and to resort again to some composite peg. The composition of the currency basket should be flexible, too,[7)] thereby securing that the "target" rate of exchange could be revised without delay for institutional reasons whenever changing priorities in economic policy are deemed to require changes in exchange rate policy.

---

7) Osunsade (1976) would term such a policy not any more a "composite pegging", but a "managed floating".

REFERENCES

Argy, V. and J.Carmichael, "Models of Imported Inflation for a Small Country - With Particular Reference to Australia", (preliminary) paper presented at the Conference on the Monetary Mechanism in Open Economies, Helsinki, August 1975.

Artus, J.R. and A.D. Crockett, "Floating Exchange Rates and the Need for Surveillance", Princeton University, Essays in International Finance, No. 127, May 1978.

Aukrust, O., "Inflation in the Open Economy: A Norwegian Model", in: L.B.Krause and W.S.Salant (eds.), Worldwide Inflation: Theory and Recent Experience, Washington, D.C. 1977.

Austrian National Bank, "Mitteilungen", various issues.

Basevi, G. and P. De Grauwe, "Vicious and Virtuous Circles: A Theoretical Analysis and a Policy Proposal for Managing Exchange Rates", European Economic Review, December 1977.

Branson, W. and J. Myhrman, "Inflation in Open Economies: Supply-Determined Versus Demand-Determined Models", in H.Frisch (ed.), Inflation in Small Countries, Berlin-Heidelberg-New York 1976.

Crockett, A.D. and M.Goldstein, "Inflation Under Fixed and Flexible Exchange Rates", International Monetary Fund, Staff Papers, November 1976.

Dornbusch, R., "Alternative Price Stabilization Rules and the Effects of Exchange Rate Changes", The Manchester School, September 1975.

Flanders, M.J. and E. Helpman, "On Exchange Rate Policies for a Small Country", The Economic Journal, March 1978.

Frisch, H.,"Eine Verallgemeinerung des skandinavischen Modells der Inflation - Mit einer empirischen Analyse für Österreich", Empirica, 2/1976.

McKinnon, R.I., "Optimum Currency Areas", American Economic Review, September 1963.

Osunsade, F.L., "Generalized Floating and Problems of Policy Response in the Developing Countries", unpublished, International Monetary Fund, January 8, 1976.

Pollan W., "Wage Flexibility and Rigidity in the Austrian Manufacturing Sector", Empirica 2/1977.

Schebeck, F., H. Suppanz and G. Tichy, "The Effect of Exchange Rate Changes on Foreign Trade in Manufactured Goods and on Prices in Small Open Economies - Preliminary Results for Austria", in this volume.

Seidel, H., "Grundzüge einer zahlungsbilanzorientierten Wirtschaftspolitik", unpublished discussion paper presented to "Beirat für Wirtschafts- und Sozialfragen", Vienna, January 1978.

Shaw, G.K., "An Introduction to the Theory of Macroeconomic Policy", London 1973.

Steindl, J., "Lohndrift und Tarifpolitik in den Industriebranchen 1966 bis 1976", Österreichisches Institut für Wirtschaftsforschung, Monatsberichte, 1o/1977.

Van Poeck, A., "The Scandinavian Model of Inflation and the Belgian Economy", Tijdschrift voor Economie en Management, 4/1975.

Walterskirchen, E., "Arbeitskosten im internationalen Vergleich", Österreichisches Institut für Wirtschaftsforschung, Monatsberichte, 1o/1977.

THE EXPERIENCE WITH FLOATING EXCHANGE-RATES IN AUSTRIA

Karl Socher

HISTORY OF FLOATING EXCHANGE RATES

Austria has had a long tradition with floating exchange-rates in the 19th century before joining the gold-standard in 1892.[1)] The Austro-Hungarian Bank developed new techniques of intervention in the forward market during the gold-standard. These techniques of the Austro-Hungarian Bank were mentioned by Keynes and later by Paul Einzig[2)] as a good example for exchange rate policies. During the first World War Austria introduced exchange controls, which have since been used to influence the exchange-rates with the exception of the short time between 1925 and 1931.

During the time of fixed rates under the Bretton Woods agreement Austrian economists (Haberler, Machlup, Sohmen) in their theoretical works helped to spread the idea of flexible rates and Austrian central bankers (Kamitz, Schmitz) were the first ones who had the courage to speak about the possibility of flexible rates and to widen the band of exchange rates.

In practice, however, Austria did not use exchange rate variations from 1953 to 1971. Even when the DM was revalued by almost 1o % in 1969 the Austrian Schilling was kept at the fixed rate to the dollar. Because the Austrian foreign trade and tourism with Germany has a share of 4o % of the total, this fixing to the dollar was equal to an effective devaluation of the Schilling of about 4 %.

---

1) Leland B. Yeager, Fluctuating Exchange Rates in the Nineteenth Century: The Experience of Austria and Russia; in: Monetary Problems of the International Economy, ed. by Robert Mundell and Alexander Swoboda, Chicago 1969.
2) Paul Einzig, A Dynamic Theory of Forward Exchange, London 1967, 2nd edition.

STABILIZATION - THE AIM OF MANAGED FLOATING[3)]

In 1971, after a revaluation of the Schilling in May, the floating since August 15 was managed in a special way. The direction of the intervention was given by the 'indicator'. The target was to keep the exchange-rate stable against a multi-currency basket. As far as I know this was the first example of pegging to a multi-currency basket. The main aim of this policy was to stabilize the effective exchange-rate and to give some security to export industry.

THE POLITICS OF EXCHANGE-RATE POLICIES

The pecularity of Austrian economic policy is the influence of the "social partners" (labor and management) on economic policy. The exchange-rate policy was influenced by the social partners between 1969 and 1973. The divergent interests became apparent since the first meeting. The social partners and the National Bank (partly influenced by the social partners) aimed at the exchange-rate stability - with the aim of protecting employment and export. The government gave a high priority to price level stability because the voters put the responsibility for inflation to the government. The social partners and the Nationalbank are not under the direct pressure of voters decisions. From 1969 to 1973 the social partners and the Nationalbank succeeded in the advisory group. In 1973 inflation reached almost 1o %. The government decided to revalue the Schilling by 2,25 %. Since this decision one part of the 'social partners' - the chamber of commerce - did not agree with the exchange-rate policy any more. Two autonomous revaluations in 1973 by 4,8 % and 1974 by 4,5 % were decided upon by government. In July 1976 the government decided to give up intervention

3) The description is based on: Karl Socher, Österreichische Wechselkurspolitik, in: Beiträge zur Stabilitätspolitik, Dr. Stigleitner Schriftenreihe, Band 13, Wien 1973.

points and to peg the Schilling to a Deutschmark-band (7,o49 - 7,189 Schilling for the DM). The 'indicator' still served as an instrument for the day-to-day exchange-rate policy, but not as a guide for the autonomous decisions since 1973.

THE EFFECTS OF STABILIZATION POLICY

The effects of the exchange-rate policy since 1971 have been a revaluation of the Schilling expressed by the effective exchange-rate. This revaluation effect took place already during the time of the 'indicator' - which aimed at exchange-rate stability - because the indicator included only the main trading partners who in general revalued their currencies against the rest of the trading partners, for instance the US-$.

It is well-known that the measurement of the effective exchange-rate is difficult. There exist some different calculations of the effective exchange-rate. The Austrian Institute for Economic Research and the Deutsche Bundesbank calculate the rate from foreign trade weights without tourism. If tourism would be included, the effective rate would increase less, because the large share of German tourists would increase the share of a country which revalued more. The two measures differed considerably in the last years, the overall increase from 1973 to 1977 is 13 percentage points according to the Institute and 24 percentage points according to the Bundesbank. The effective exchange-rate calculated by the IMF gives about the same values as the Bundesbank.

As there are many inflation theories, there exist many hypotheses about the possibility of exchange rates to influence the price level. In Austria three hypotheses were used in the discussion. The most popular is the theory of the direct impact of import prices on the price level. It is closely connected with the cost-push and the theory of the vicious circle following a devaluation. But it is not conclusive, because it sees the cost-inflation aspect only, neglecting the demand factor. If the import prices decrease and internal nominal demand remains at the same level, the price level

Effective exchange-rate

	Austrian Institute for Economic Research	Deutsche Bundesbank
	196o = 1oo	1973 = 1o7,o
Average 197o	98,3	
Average 1971	99,5	
Average 1972	1o1,3	
Average 1973	1o7,o	1o7,o
Average 1974	111,3	112,3
Average 1975	116,3	116,5
Average 1976	116,7	122,5
Average 1977	12o,5	131,1

Source: Austrian Institute for Economic Research, Deutsche Bundesbank, Monatsberichte, Tabelle IX, 11: Entwicklung des Außenwertes fremder Währungen.
The Bundesbank index starts end of 1972. To compare it with the index of the Institute, the average of the 1973 Bundesbank index was set equal to the average of the Institute index for 1973.
A new index was published by the Institute in August 1978.

can fall, but only because more goods and services from abroad are available, or in other words, because the current balance gets into a deficit. If internal demand is increased, there will be a dampening effect on the price level by the additional net imports, but there is no direct influence of the exchange-rate on the internal demand.

A second theory was based on the cost-push influence of the exchange-rate, not on import prices but on wages. It has been developed in Scandinavia and used for the explanation of the Austrian exchange-rate policy by Frisch.[4] The high exchange-rate for the Schilling hampers the export industry (exposed sector)

4) H. Frisch, Eine Verallgemeinerung des skandinavischen Modells der Inflation - Mit einer empirischen Analyse für Österreich, Empirica, 2, 1976.

to pay higher wages when trade unions demand wage increases beyond the increase of productivity and the foreign price level for the Austrian exports. By the solidarity of the trade unions the increase of wages in the sheltered sector will be held back, so that the total wage-push is reduced.

The Austrian experience has shown that the assumptions of this theory have not been valid. The export industry partly agreed to higher wages so that a profit squeeze developed.[5)] The wage increase in the sheltered sector, for instance for government officials, was not dampened enough to dampen the push. Lastly, the monetary and fiscal policy contributed to an expansion of demand so that the price level was pulled up.

The theory of the direct price and wage effect therefore is not complete. The more realistic theory is the theory of the price dampening effect of a current account deficit. It is based on a demand-pull inflation theory. The demand-pull influence on the price level was dampened by the increase of the supply of the foreign goods and services. This effect could be calculated roughly by comparing the current account deficit with GNP. The current account for Austria was about balanced from the middle of the fifties to the middle of the seventies. In 1976 a large deficit of the current account began to develop which reaches 4 - 5 % of GNP at the moment. One may argue that the price level would be higher by 4 - 5 % if the current account would be balanced. The exchange-rate policy of revaluation had the effect on the current account and only by this influence it influenced the price level.

The effect of the exchange-rate policy aiming at price stability was the mobilisation of the huge foreign exchange reserves of Austria which were accumulated by capital imports - to a large degree by government debts. The cumulative current balance deficit in relation to GNP between 1974 and 1977 was 12 %, the highest

5) OECD, Economic Surveys: Austria, p. 24, Paris 1977.

of 14 OECD-countries with the exception of Norway.[6)]

According to forecasts the deficit of the current account remains at the level of 4 - 5 % of GNP at least in 1978. Then the foreign exchange reserves will be exhausted in one or two years, depending on how the gold reserves are valued. It follows that it is urgently necessary to direct economic policy against the current account deficit.

The question is which role the exchange-rate policy will play in the future.

FREE FLOATING?

Freely floating exchange-rates would stop the deficit immediately, but the exchange-rate would fall considerably at first. Free floating is no alternative for Austria today because of two specialities: Austria always had exchange controls and wants to keep them. The existing exchange controls prevent short-term 'speculative' capital movements which could dampen the fluctuations in exchange-rates. Free floating without short-term capital movements would put all the adaption to the current account which can react only with lags, so that large fluctuations would follow.

Even if short-term capital movements would be freed, any change in the control of long-term movements would lead to an influence of the exchange-rates. The exchange-rate would be influenced by speculation about control policy. Another problem is the large amount of foreign government debt, which does not underlie controls of the Nationalbank. Each change and each forecast of the change in government debt management, switching from internal debt to foreign debt would influence the exchange-rate. Speculation could be destablizing, because it does not speculate on market forces.

---

6) OECD, Austria 1977, p.19.

HOW TO MANAGE FLOATING?

First, some of the arguments against the use of exchange-rate policy should be considered. The main official argument is the vicious circle argument (rising import prices would increase the price level). It was already mentioned that this argument is wrong because the internal price level is not determined from the cost side alone but by demand. If total demand is not expanded too much, a devaluation cannot increase the price level. When this thesis is accepted one can ask: if a restrictive demand policy is necessary to prevent the upward movement of the price level after a devaluation, then why not try the restrictive demand policy without devaluation? The answer is that the restriction of nominal demand has to be stronger without devaluation. For real demand it does not matter, the absorption has to be cut by 4 - 5 % anyway. But it is quite likely that a cut in nominal demand would result in unemployment because wages and prices have been fixed at a high level based on inflationary expectations. In any case - restriction of demand with or without devaluation - the stabilization policy has to do now without the stabilizing effect of a current account deficit.

An important argument against devaluation is the lag of devaluation effects on the current account. In Austria the lag is not estimated to be as long as in other countries, because the tourist traffic reacts quicker than trade. But in a short period it would be that the net improvement of the current balance is small. From the policy aspect it would follow from the existence of lags that more continuity is needed for exchange-rate management.

Another argument for stabilizing the Deutschmark rate is not mentioned in the public but plays a role in the decisions. In public opinion a devaluation is confused with inflation. This confusion induces the politician to avoid a devaluation at least for the time before an election. It is impossible to calculate whether the avoidance will bring more votes than the effects of keeping the rate and revaluing with the Deutschmark will bring fewer votes owing to unemployment, loss of growth potential or more controls.

On the basis of the good old theory of purchasing-power parity it can be calculated how much devaluation Austria would need. The objections against this theory are well known, but the alternative - to calculate the necessary devaluations with elasticities - can be critized too. The author has made a simple calculation with the consumer price indices of 9 main trading countries of Austria and the exchange-rate of their currencies. The weights used are the sum of the import, export, tourist receipts and expenditures, representing about 75 % of the total trade and tourist transactions of Austria.

It was assumed that the rest of 25 % of all trade and tourist transactions shows the same development as the 75 %.

Effective exchange-rate in relation to purchasing-power parity

Purchasing-power parity in 197o = 1oo

197o	1971	1972	1973	1974	1975	1976	1977
100	98,7	99,7	1o3,2	1o6,5	1o7,7	11o,6	113,6

In 1977 the exchange-rate of the Schilling was about 14 % higher than the purchasing-power parity exchange-rate, if the assumption is made that in 197o the purchasing-power parity and the exchange-rate were balanced. This assumption can be made because the current account was about balanced until 1975. The large deficit in the current account occured later than the purchasing-power index indicates. This can be explained by the lags.

A similar calculation was made by the OECD for a diagram: the consumer prices of Austria relative to the consumer prices of 1o major OECD countries measured in US-$ terms as a trade weighted average increased from 197o to 1976 by about 13 to 14 %.[7)]

The conclusion that the Schilling has to be devalued by some 13 or 14 % to bring the current account into equilibrium is not permitted on the grounds of such simple calculations. Many other factors have to be taken into account, for instance the oil price rise, the increasing role of interest payments for the Austrian foreign debt, the development of the capital account and others. But it is a first step to give some rough orders of magnitude.

THE LIMITS OF MANAGED FLOATING

The experience with the aims of exchange-rate policy in Austria has shown that the policy cannot aim at stabilizing the effective exchange-rate and at stabilizing the price level, except in a coordination with other policy measures.

Stabilizing the effective exchange-rate was tried approximately by the indicator. It would have led to an inflation of the same magnitude as the main trading partners. It would have forced to give up stabilization policy by demand management because of the resulting balance of payments surplus.

The use of the exchange-rate as a stabilization instrument was successful only by running into a large current account deficit. It has to be given up when reserves are exhausted. If Austria does not take this step at that point it may be that it will be forced by the IMF when it asks for loans. The stabilization policy with the exchange-rate could have succeeded only, if monetary, fiscal and incomes policy would have been directed at this aim. But they supported more inflation than in Germany. The exchange-rate policy can only temporarily act against this effect as long as there are foreign exchange reserves available.

---

7) OECD: Austria, p. 25. Estimated from the diagram.

The problem can be seen the other way round: for a small country like Austria it is not possible to fix the exchange-rate to a block or a single country like Germany if the internal policy is not directed to keep the exchange-rate stable. It could not persue its own aims. If a small country tries to stabilize the price level by fixing the exchange-rate to a stable country or a block without coordination of monetary, fiscal and incomes policy it is perhaps no exaggeration to say that this will bring a destabilization of the real sector of the economy. The current account deficit and then the measures to stop it will lead to a stop-go-policy for the foreign trade and tourism sector of the economy.

What would be an alternative? If a country wants to follow its own economic aims it can use exchange-rate policy (together with the exchange controls) to balance the current account or the total balance of payments. For Austria, where a free floating does not seem possible, an orientation of the managed floating on the purchasing-power parity could be a workable alternative. The problem of the capital account would not be solved by this 'indicator', but the exchange controls for 'speculative' capital movements could cope with that. However, it may be too much speculation to go into details of this alternative here.

COMMENTS ON K. SOCHER, "THE EXPERIENCE WITH FLOATING EXCHANGE RATES IN AUSTRIA" AND H. HANDLER, "THE EXCHANGE RATE AS AN INTERMEDIATE TARGET OF STABILIZATION POLICY IN AUSTRIA"

Ewald Nowotny

My friend H.Frisch was perhaps somewhat astonished to be credited with the honor to be the ideologue of Austria's exchange rate policy, but I think, Handler is right in pointing out, that the special attraction of the Scandinavian model for Austrian policy makers was the erroneous notion, that a change in the exchange rate would be fully reflected in a corresponding change of the internal price level, whereas balance of trade effects could be more or less neglected. Thus exchange rate manipulations provide a politically rather painless tool for price stabilization. I agree with Handler's view, that the Scandinavian model - besides the problem what really is the exposed sector - is basically a long-run model, where especially the demand side is not adequately represented for purposes of formulating stabilization policies.

But even concerning the long-run effects there is one important element of the official Austrian argumentation, which I would consider even more sceptical than Handler does. This is the idea, that a policy of appreciation forces the export industries to try harder and thus has a positive effect on productivity. This will be true if you consider only the productivity in the industrial and especially in the export sector of an economy, but it need not be true for the economy as a whole. It has to be noted however, that our very substantial system of export subsidies at least partially offsets just these incentive effects of a hard currency policy. But even if this exchange rate stimulus works for the export sector, the main incentive may be to quit this difficult field and to settle down in the more peaceful sector of trading activities, especially importing.

This will be all the more profitable, if the effects of an appreciation are not fully passed over to domestic prices. Such a ratchet effect has been mentioned in general by Handler and will play a special role in Austria, because import prices are not influenced by the "Paritätische Kommission", the Austrian system of price and wages policy. In contrast, the prices of home-produced goods are subject to this price control system, which thus provides a further incentive to switch to importing activities. Such a policy which favors importing activities relative to production and exports may have negative effects especially for new developments and may therefore in Austria be specially damaging for the long-run development of overall productivity. I this would see the main problems of the appreciation policy followed in its long-run effects. Considering short run effects and considering all the qualifications to which especially Handler has pointed in his paper I would agree, that - for short periods! - such a policy can be an effective instrument for price-stabilization in a period of rapid increases in the international price level.

As concerns the evaluation of a hard currency policy in a period of worldwide stagnation I think one has to stress, that the fact, that Austria has balance of payments problems today does not mean, that the policy, that lead us to this was wrong. In the situation of 1973/75 especially for a small country it was a rational strategy not to join a world wide deflationary policy. For a small country enjoys a free-rider position with respect to world market prices and therefore can follow a more expansionist course. This will of course mean, that it looses currency reserves. But it is exactly the reason of holding currency reserves to be able to finance a short run current account deficit. The problem now is, however, what to do, if on the international level a more or less intentional policy of deflation gets out of control.

Here the advice given in the two papers fully reflects the reputation of economics as the dismal science: They both state that all you can do is to choose between using up your currency reserves and get under some form of outside control or reduce demand with the prospect of rising unemployment. A strategy of devaluation in this respect by both authors is not primarily advocated because of its direct foreign trade effect but because it is considered to be an effective instrument to reduce internal demand (thus being in certain contrast to the Tichy-Suppanz-Schebeck-paper). I would agree, that a greater flexibility of the exchange rate, in the sense of returning to a multicurrency basket would offer additional degrees of freedom for a full employment - oriented policy. As I know, Austria since some time has in fact abandoned the exclusive link to the DM and is using again a multi-currency indicator, which however does not include "weak currencies", so that the overall effect up to now has not been very strong.

I am more sceptical as concerns an outright devaluation, about which Sochor is speaking. The example given by him considers only relative price effects and not the effects of different demand situations. I would maintain that the latter influence was the decisive one for the deterioration of our current account position and not the lagged effects of changes in the purchasing power parity. There also remains the problem of destabilizing speculation. Handler's point is only based on conditions, where speculators obviously expect some kind of orderly retreat but does not reflect the situation, when a substantial devaluation would be expected.

Further on there always remains the problem, what lags have to be expected. In this respect also the enlarged Scandinavian model in Handler's paper cannot tell us very much, as it is a basically static concept. There are a lot of further conditions for a successful policy of devaluation, which may be given at this moment but about which we are not definitely sure.

All this would strengthen the argument for policies of cautious change, were expectations have a chance for rational adaptation and economic policy can develop a number of adjusting measures.

COMMENTS ON K. SOCHER, "THE EXPERIENCE WITH FLOATING EXCHANGE RATES IN AUSTRIA" AND H. HANDLER, "THE EXCHANGE RATE AS AN INTERMEDIATE TARGET OF STABILIZATION POLICY IN AUSTRIA"

Kurt Schiltknecht

As central bank economist I am always eager to learn how other central banks are conducting their monetary policy. The papers of Karl Socher and Heinz Handler give a valuable presentation of Austrian exchange rate policy. Since both authors are dealing more or less with the same subjects, many of my remarks will be related to both papers.

The problems raised in the two papers are vital ones. The question as to the role that should be attributed to the exchange rate when pursuing monetary policy in a small open economy leads to the further question whether monetary policy should be orientied directly towards the ultimate targets like output or the price level, or whether there sould be an intermediate target like the exchange-rate, the interest rate ar one of the monetary aggregates.[1)] In the following, I will not enter into the discussion whether a one stage or a two stage procedure of monetary policy is preferable since I believe that most central banks are using explicitly or implicitly a two stage procedure. In my opinion, the more important problem is the choice of the intermediate target. While today more and more large countries are favouring a money stock target, no similar tendencies are discernible for small open economies. Obviously, the Austrian National Bank has chosen the exchange-rate as the intermediate target. As the authors point out quite clearly, the aim of the exchange-rate policy was, at least for

1) On this point see: J. Niehans, The Theory of Money, Baltimore 1978.

the last few years, to stabilize the price level. There is no longer any doubt that price stability should serve as the ultimate objective of monetary policy. However, the question arises whether the pegging of the exchange-rate is the appropriate method to reach this objective. In my opinion, one need not be a strong monetarist to believe that inflation, also in a small open economy, is related to the long term growth in the monetary aggregates. If one accepts this statement, the most obvious solution to fight inflation is to control the long term growth in the monetary aggregates. As an advocate of such policy, I was a bit puzzled to see how much weight is put on the exchange-rate when discussing the inflation problem in Austria and, to say the least, how little importance is attached to the behaviour of the monetary aggregates.

However, as the authors indicate, the Austrian approach to monetary policy apparently rests on the belief that the standard Scandinavian Model is valid for the Austrian economy. I fully agree with the evaluation of this model by Heinz Handler and I share his conclusion that the standard Scandinavian Model is basically a long-run model. Furthermore, it does not describe the inflation transmission mechanism in an appropriate way and does not serve as a useful guide for conducting stabilization policy. But I do not share his conclusion about monetary policy. A shift from the unicurrency to some composite peg must not necessarily imply a major modification of the actual policy. In particular, the question remains when to change the target-rate of exchange and which composition of currencies should be chosen.

To fix an exchange-rate at a certain level has strong implications for the growth of the monetary aggregates and this growth will, in turn, influence the future course of the economy in general and the balance of payments in particular. At least for me, it seems very difficult, if not impossible, to determine the exchange-rate which is consistent with stable prices in the longer run. In my opinion,it would have been worthwhile for the authors to analyze the interaction between exchange rate policy and the growth in the monetary aggregates. Specifically, it might be interesting to compare the domestic component of the money supply with the international component and to check how far an increase in the domestic component was counteracted by a loss of international reserves. This question is even more important in a country with some exchange controls and large official capital inflows because under these conditions an expansion in the money supply, which is not consistent with the chosen exchange rate, need not immediately lead to a loss of international reserves.

In all considered, I do not pretend that Austrian exchange-rate and money supply policies have been inconsistent. I would only like to stress that a careful analysis of this problem would be worthwhile and that such an analysis might give an answer to the question why - despite the fact that the shilling has been pegged to the DM - the inflation rate in Austria is higher than in Germany and why there is a huge deficit in the Austrian current account while the German current account is positive.

For almost the same reason, I do not think the Socher proposal to peg the exchange-rate on the basis of purchasing power parity is operational. In addition, the calculation of purchasing power parity is very sensitive to the price indices used. A further complication stems from the fact that for policy purposes one cannot use the actual purchasing power parity since this is an ex post variable. What one needs is ex ante purchasing power parity.

What can be done instead?

First of all, and this comes hardly as a surprise for those of you who are familiar with the Swiss concept of monetary policy, I believe that controlled floating of the shillings and a flexible money stock policy might be alternatives. Under a flexible money stock policy, the money stock fluctuates around the long term trend that is necessary to keep the inflation rate down. The fluctuations around the trend could be used to dampen exchange-rate fluctuations or to influence aggregate demand. Without any doubt, the costs of such a policy are greater short-run fluctuations of the exchange rate. But how important are such fluctuations for the foreign trade? The existing literature does not offer a conclusive answer to the question whether the observed short-run variability in the exchange-rate is a significant economic phenomenon in the sense that such fluctuations exert a marked disruptive effect on trade flows. I would pretend that, owing to the existence of adjustment costs, importers and exporters do not react strongly to movements in currently observed exchange-rates, as long as such movements are considered to be only temporary.[2)]

From what we could see during the past years in Switzerland the export industry was able to adapt very quickly to heavy exchange rate fluctuations. Personally, I believe that in the long rung it is an advantage if the industry is forced to adapt very quickly to new situations.

In my opinion, international trade is much less threatened by exchange-rate fluctuations than by the worldwide tendencies towards protectionism.

---

2) This argument is made by G. Rich, Short-Run variability of the Exchange-Rate: A Theoretical Analysis, unpublished, Swiss National Bank 1978.

THE EFFECT OF EXCHANGE RATE CHANGES ON FOREIGN TRADE IN MANUFACTURED GOODS AND ON PRICES IN SMALL OPEN ECONOMIES - PRELIMINARY RESULTS FOR AUSTRIA*

Fritz Schebeck - Hannes Suppanz - Gunther Tichy

1. FLEXIBLE EXCHANGE RATES AND EXCHANGE RATE POLICY IN AUSTRIA

Austria is a small, open economy. However, openness in the case of the Austrian economy does not mean trade relations being evenly distributed all over the globe: Austria's foreign trade is heavily concentrated, as two fifths of imports are supplied by Germany, two thirds by EEC-countries and four fifths by OECD-countries. Not surprisingly therefore, Austria's economic policy goals resemble those of Germany, although Austria presses less hard for price stability and more for full employment. As regards policy instruments, Austria puts heavy weight on wage policy and social partnership, less so on monetary policy - due mainly to the considerable foreign influences on the money supply.

Austrian monetary authorities have never refrained from intervening on the foreign exchange market. From mid 1971 to mid 1976, the interventions were guided by an 'indicator'. This intermediate policy target was defined as an export weighted average of 'hard' currencies, 'hard' implying that most of the time the Italian lire, the British pound and the French franc were excluded from the currency basket. Therefore, the DM received an even larger

* The authors are obliged to I.Prucha for his help with the simulations, as well as M.Schultes and to G.Raunicher for preparing the data. The responsibility rests however solely with the authors.

weight than on the basis of transactions; use of the 'indicator' implied a continuous appreciation against all currencies except the DM and the Swiss franc. This policy was chosen with the intention to import stability, i.e. to dampen the rather high rate of inflation by increasing competition from abroad, and thereby avoid discontinuing the full employment policy by means of monetary and fiscal restraint.[1)] The authorities accepted the deterioration of the current account as an involuntary side effect. From mid 1976 to the autumn of 1977 appreciation as an instrument of fighting inflation was even strenghtened by tying the Schilling-rate solely to the appreciating DM.

The unorthodox message of Austria's exchange rate policy is twofold: Firstly, the Schilling is not floating freely but is member of an informal currency union with the snake-currencies and especially the DM. Therefore, it has quasi-fixed exchange rates for two thirds of Austria's foreign transactions of goods and services, and floating rates for one third. Secondly, exchange rate policy in Austria has not been used to control the balance of payments on current account - the text book-case - but to influence wage claims and the rate of inflation, an alternative which up to now has received little theoretical and empirical consideration.

Both peculiarities are closely related to the smallness and the openness of the economy, factors specific not only for Austria: Out of all OECD-countries, two fifths (all of which are small countries) import more than one quarter in terms of GNP, and in only a few of them exchange rates are flexible in the

---

1) Other small countries didn't believe in text book-policy proposal either, as the reader may see from A.Lindbeck: Stabilization Policy in Open Economies With Endogenous Politicians. AER, May 1978, pp.1-19.

textbook-meaning: According to a recent IMF-study only 9 of 72 countries had floating rates, 7 were members of the snake, 15 of the $-zone, 1o of the ffr-zone, 13 pegged their exchange rate to the SDR, 18 to an other indicator.[2)]

Similar evidence is produced by the high amount of official intervention in the exchange markets[3)] and by the fact, found by Williamson,[4)] that changes in foreign reserves (in relation to foreign trade) were larger during the period of floating than in the former period of adjustably pegging. Thus we conclude that the exchange rate regime of every country is a weighted average of the exchange rate regimes of the trading partner countries. A forthcoming study will show that only a small fraction of world trade takes place under flexible rates, the larger one - as earlier - under more or less fixed rates.[5)]

2. THE THEORY OF REVALUATION AND DEVALUATION IN A SMALL OPEN ECONOMY

In recent years, economic theory has not always been of great help for policy decisions, especially in the case of small open economies. Due more to wishful thinking than to facts - as shown above - economists employed the theory of flexible exchange rates, a branch still in its infancy.[6)] The policy institutions

---

2) H.R.Heller: Die Wahl eines Wechselkurssystems. Finanzierung & Entwicklung, June 1977, pp.23.
3) According to estimates of the Federal Reserve Bank of New York, official interventions varied between 2o bill. US $ in 1974 and 75 bill. US $ in 1976. The latter equals approximately one third of the foreign reserves of these countries. The authors are grateful to R.M.Kubarych of the Federal Reserve Bank of New York for providing these figures.
4) J.Williamson: Exchange Rate Flexibility and Reserve Use. In: J.Herin-A.Lindbeck-J.Myhrman: Flexible Exchange Rates and Stabilization Policy. London 1977, pp.195-2o7.
5) G. Tichy: The Gain in Flexibility from Adjustable Peg to the Floating Rate System. Forthcoming.
6) A. Lindbeck: Approaches to Exchange Rate Analysis - An Evaluation. In: Herin-Lindbeck-Myhrman op.cit. pp.1-13.

assumed in theoretical models were those of large countries, notwithstanding the fact that, in order to justify simplifications, the child was given the name "small country assumption"; for a particular country prices and interest rates are given, and its actions are supposed to have no repercussions via world demand or supply. The analysis concentrated on the effects on the balance on current account, disregarding induced price movements which could disturb the first round effect (or, according to the J-curve adjustment process, the second round effect).

Most of the theoretical models studying the effects of exchange rate changes on the balance of payments start either with domestic demand (absorption or its flow of funds-counterpart in the monetary approach) or the usual price elasticity conditions of foreign trade and interest elasticity of international capital flows. More according to tradition than to detailed or convincing analysis, speculation in the standard-model is assumed to be stabilizing rather than destabilizing; changes in the current account or in the balance of payments are assumed to have no effect on the domestic economy, as the money supply is under full control of the monetary authority. This very assumption is a main flaw in these models, as in small open countries foreign reserves are the very counterpart of the money stock;[7] open market operations are negligible in most small open economies; this is due to narrow capital markets which are themselves as much a result of

---

7) This flaw is the more serious, as it contrasts with the normal small country assumption of no repercussion from the rest of the world. If a country is small enough for this assumption to hold, it normally cannot completely sterilize inflows of foreign exchange and therefore has no full control over its money supply. For examples see: H.Kleinewefers: Die außenwirtschaftliche Beeinflussung des monetären Geschehens in der Schweiz. In: A.E.Ott (ed.) Wachstumszyklen. Berlin 1973, pp.233 and: G.Tichy: Bestimmungsgründe und Probleme der österreichischen Geldversorgung. Quartalshefte der Girozentrale 1/1975, pp.23-31.

the lack of trading by the central bank as of the limited number of private traders; in addition, markets are controlled more by credit rationing rather than by interest rate variation.[8)]

However, if the monetary authority has no full control over the money supply, it normally cannot prevent price changes following a change of the exchange rate. Following a devaluation three rounds of effects have therefore to be distinguished: In the first round - according to the now dominating J-curve hypothesis - price effects will deteriorate the current account even if elasticities are favourable; in the second round a net improvement of the current account will occur, as the positive volume effects dominate the negative price effects. The third round starts with the first round increase in import prices, probably not much smaller than the rate of devaluation.[9)] Prices of domestic import-competing goods will follow suit. The higher costs of foreign raw materials as well as the increased export demand in volume terms (higher rate of capacity utilization) will put upward pressure on export prices. If no money illusion prevails the trade unions will compensate the higher cost of living with additional wage claims, thus wiping out another part of the initial devaluation gain in competitiveness.[1o)]

---

8) E.Streissler-G.Tichy: Die Transmission monetärer Impulse über den Kreditmarkt - Zur Bedeutung der Kreditrationierung und ihrer institutionellen Voraussetzung in Europa. W.Ehrlicher-A.Oberhauser, Eds.: Probleme der Geldmengensteuerung, Schriften des Vereins für Socialpolitik 99, Juli 1978.

9) It is not by chance that the so-called Scandinavian model of inflation, implying strong influence on national inflation of foreign price developments, was first applied to small open economies.

1o) Among the better known textbooks only Branson and Kindleberger mention the price effect. Kindleberger emphasizes the possibility of a revaluation to stabilize the price level (p.2o1 of the 3rd edition), Branson mentions the unpopularity of devaluation induced price increases without further analysis of their potential effect on the balance of payments.

It is impossible - a priori - to evalute the relative size of the effects and their net result. Governments of small open economies frequently argue, however, that, if economic policy cannot reduce wage claims to a level consistent with foreign competitiveness, it will hardly succeed in preventing wage increase from neutralizing the income redistribution effects of a devaluation. Furthermore, even if a small country would be able to control its money supply, only the flaw of inadmissible aggregation would allow to disregard price effects. If the consumer price level is not allowed to change, the unavoidable increase in import prices has to be compensated by a reduction of domestic prices. This has no further repercussions if, and only if, the resulting shift in income distribution - profit cuts on the domestic market - is accepted.

In the following paragraphs, a weighting scheme for exchange rates and export prices is introduced together with the respective data which take account of third market effects. With their help it is attempted to evaluate the trade account effect of an exchange rate change as well as the order of magnitude of the compensating price effect. This permits discussion of the question, whether exchange rate policy in small open economies is better suited as a balance of payments policy or as a price policy.

3. DATA ON AUSTRIA'S FOREIGN TRADE IN MANUFACTURED GOODS 1960 - 1976

Price and exchange rate indices as well as values and volumes of Austria's foreign trade in manufactured goods (SITC 5-8) are shown in the following graphs. In calculating export price and exchange rate indices, a method developed by the authors in an earlier paper was applied.[11] The export price and exchange

---

11) F.Schebeck-H.Suppanz-G.Tichy: Preis- und Wechselkursindizes für den Export österreichischer Halb- und Fertigwaren. Empirica 2/1974, pp.2o1-226.

Export Price Indeces for Manufactured Goods Figure 1

1970 = 100

—— Austrian Export Price Index
..... Export Price Index of Competing Countries 1 (B)
•••• Relative Export Price Index 1 (A/B)

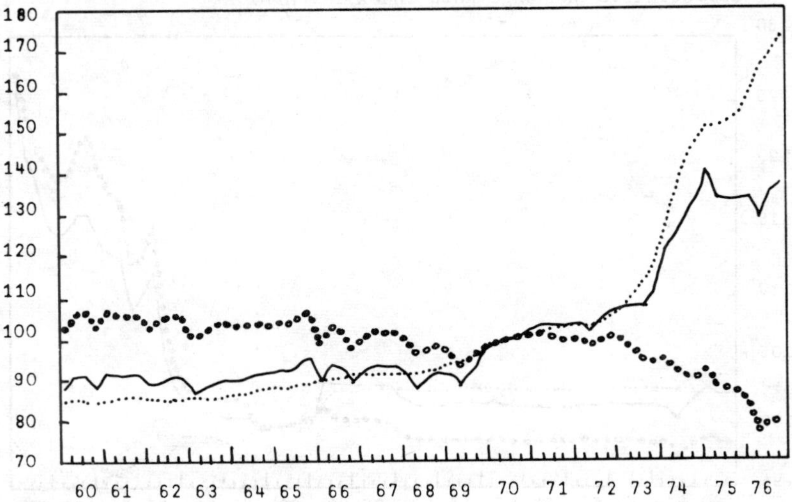

—— Austrian Export Price Index (A)
..... Export Price Index of Competing Countries 2 (B)
••••• Relative Export Price Index 2 (A/B)

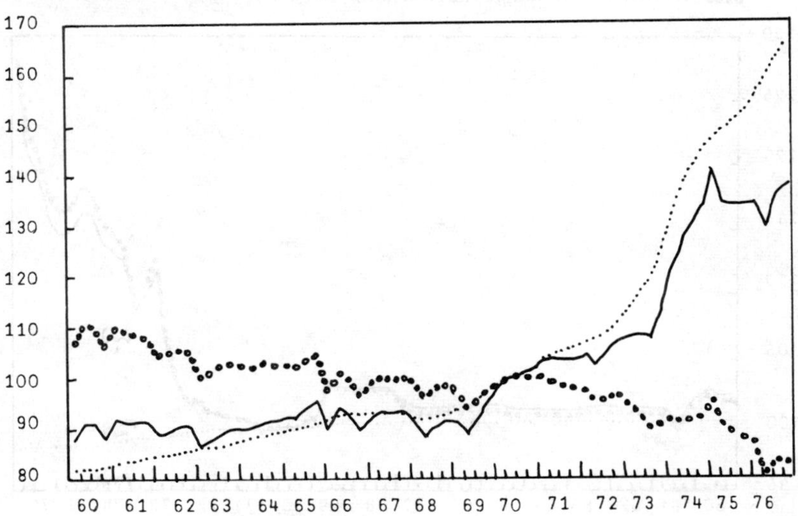

Export Weighted Exchange Rate Indices Figure 2

1970 = 100

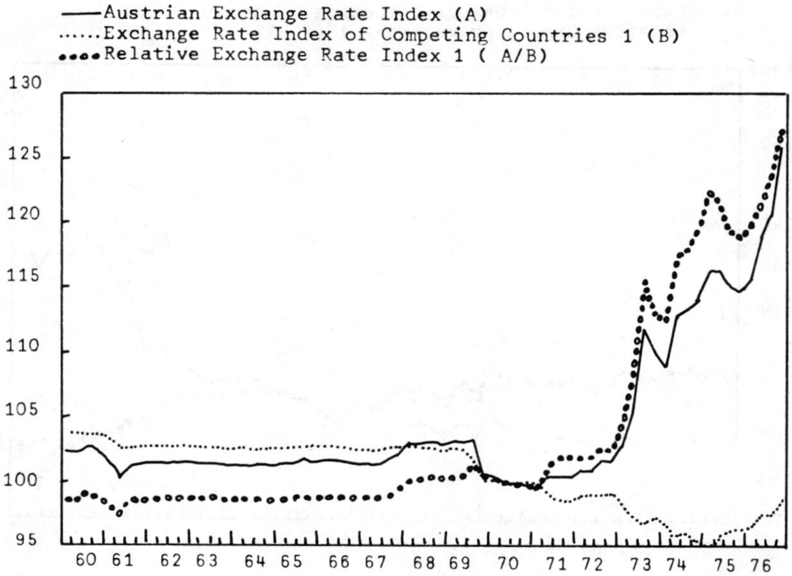

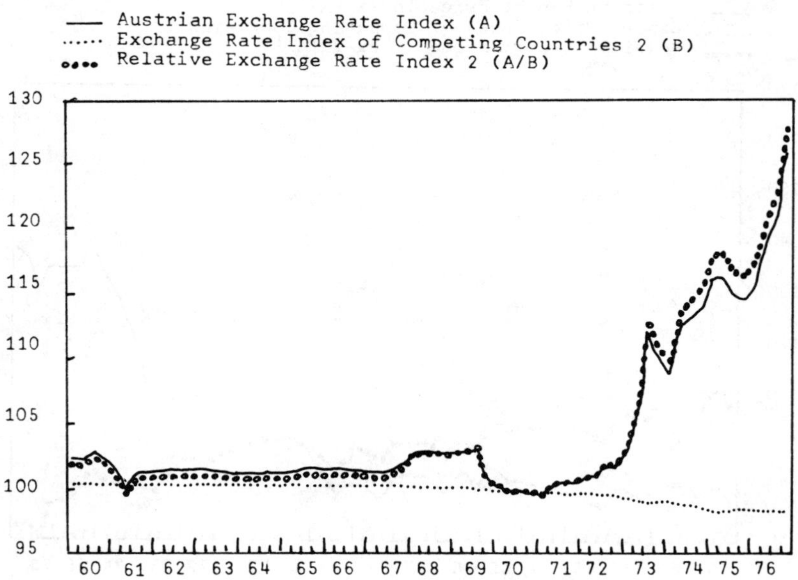

Exchange Rate Adjusted Export Price Indices for Manufactured Goods Figure 3

1970 = 100

—— Exch. Rate Adj. Austrian Export Price Index (A)
······ Exch. Rate Adj. Export Price Index of Competing Countries 1 (B)
▬▬ Exch. Rate Adj. Relative Export Price Index 1 (A/B)

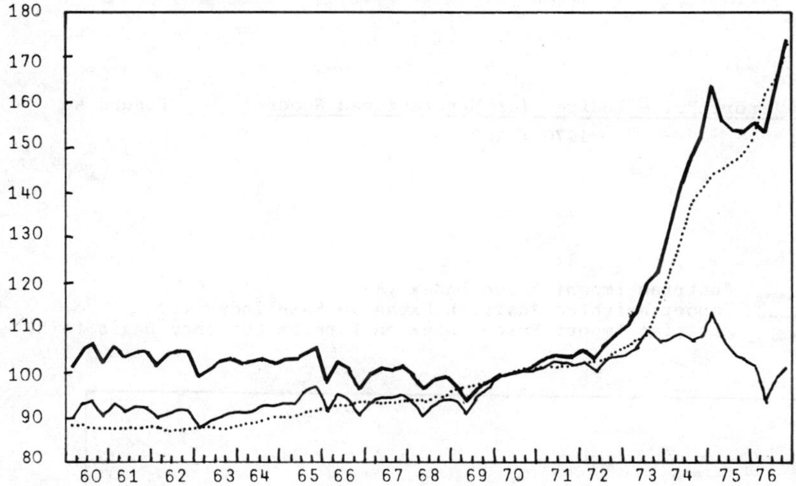

—— Exch. Rate Adj. Austrian Export Price Index (A)
······ Exch. Rate Adj. Export Price Index of Competing Countries 2 (B)
▬▬ Exch. Rate Adj. Relative Export Price Index 2 (A/B)

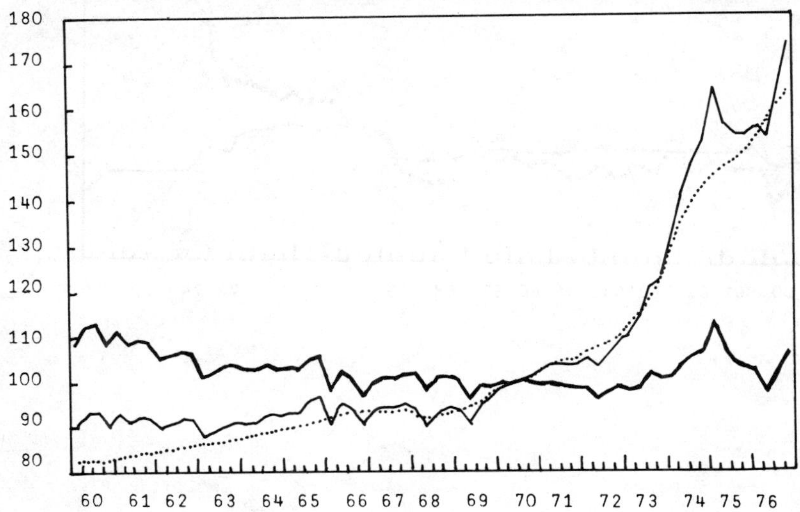

Import Price Indices for Manufactured Goods Figure 4

1970 = 100

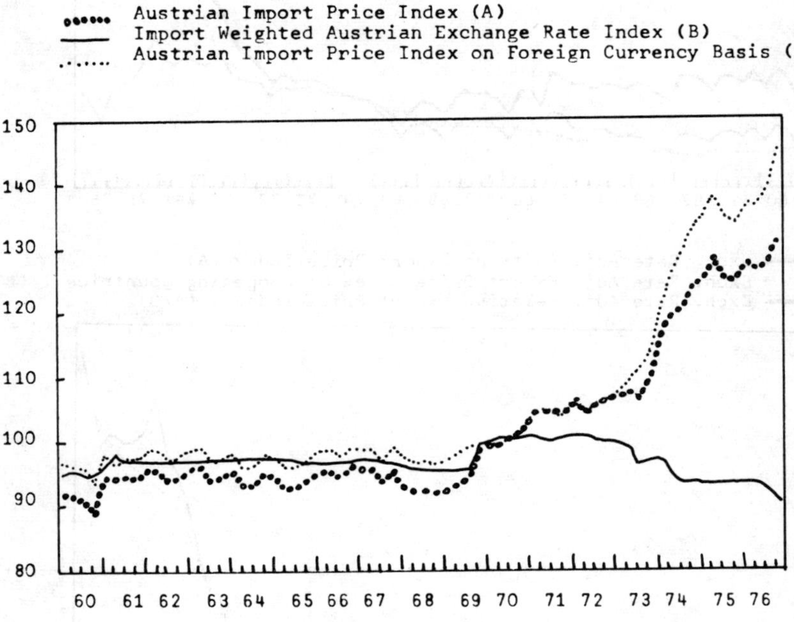

Foreign Trade in Manufactured Goods (SITC 5 - 8) Figure 5

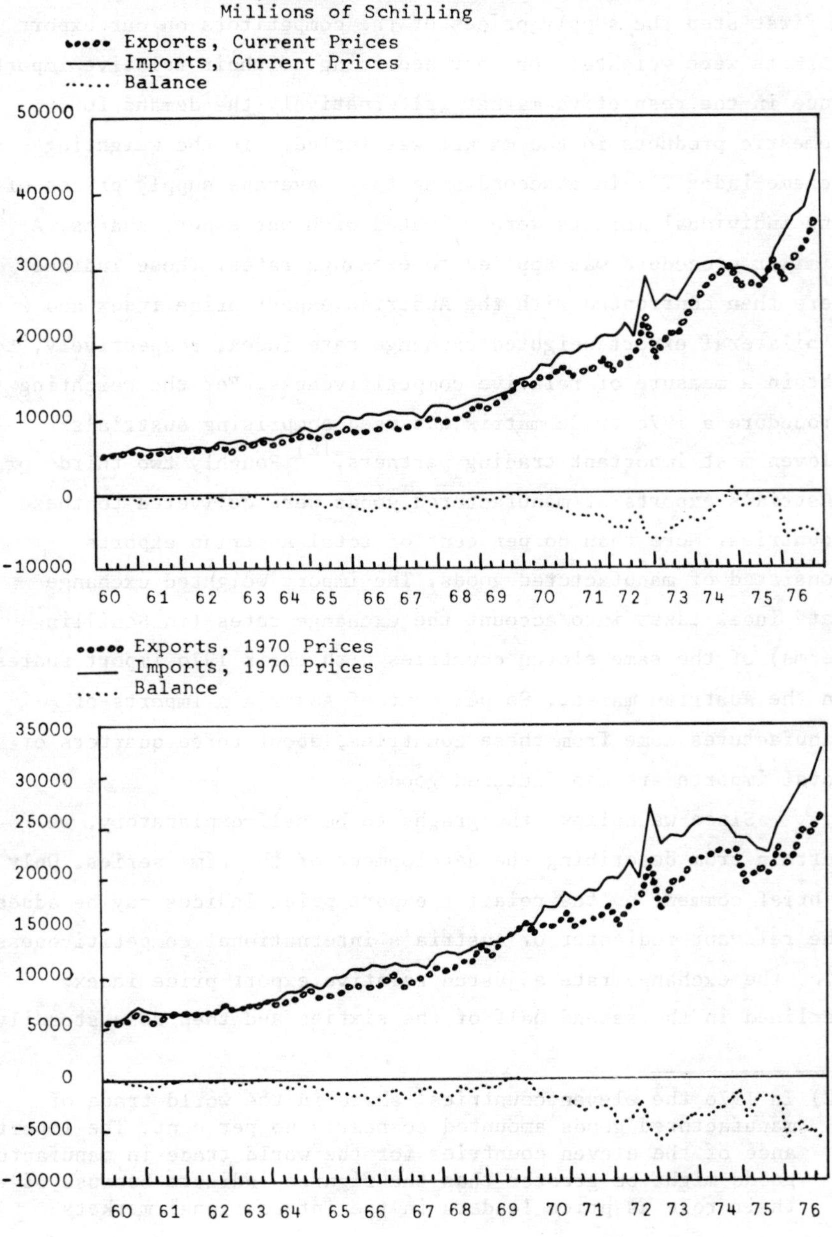

rate indices were calculated by a double weighting procedure: In a first step the supply prices of the competitors on our export markets were weighted together according to their relative importance in the respective market (alternatively the demand for domestic products in the market was included in the weighting scheme-index 2); in a second step these average supply prices of the individual markets were weighted with our export shares. A similar procedure was applied to exchange rates. These indices were then confronted with the Austrian export price index and with a bilateral export weighted exchange rate index, respectively, to obtain a measure of relative competitiveness. For the weighting procedure a 197o trade matrix was used comprising Austria's eleven most important trading partners.[12)] Roughly two thirds of Austria's exports of manufactured goods were delivered to these countries. More than 8o per cent of total Austrian exports consisted of manufactured goods. The import weighted exchange rate index takes into account the exchange rates (in Schilling terms) of the same eleven countries with their 197o import shares in the Austrian market. 9o per cent of Austria's imports of manufactures come from these countries, about three quarters of total imports are manufactured goods.

Since we believe the graphs to be self-explanatory, we refrain from describing the development of the time series. Only a brief comment on the relative export price indices may be added. The relevant indicator of Austria's international competitiveness, i.e. the exchange rate adjusted relative export price index, declined in the second half of the sixties and then rose steadily

---

12) In 197o the eleven countries' share in the world trade of manufactured goods amounted to nearly 6o per cent. The importance of the eleven countries for the world trade in manufactured goods might be greater than the figures indicate because of their role as price leaders in the international markets.

until the beginning of 1975. Therefore, Austria's competitive position improved in the second half of the sixties by 9 to 11 per cent and deteriorated in the period 1972/beginning 1975 by 18 to 2o per cent. From the beginning of 1975 till the middle of 1976 the exchange rate adjusted relative export price index declined considerably. Thereafter it began to rise again, and this between the beginning of 1975 and the end of 1976 resulted in a relative improvement of the Austrian competitive position on export markets by some 6 to 11 per cent. Thus, as a consequence of exchange rate changes there occurred - mainly in the seventies and despite the temporary revised trend in 1975/76 - considerable changes in the price competitiveness of Austrian exports.

4. IMPORT FUNCTIONS, EXPORT FUNCTIONS, AND PRICE FUNCTIONS FOR MANUFACTURES

The new price and exchange rate indices were used to estimate equations for imports, exports, foreign trade prices and domestic prices for manufactures. All equations were estimated by OLS for the period 196o-1976 on the basis of annual and quarterly data transformed in logarithms. The R^2s of the estimated equations are greater than .97 (in most cases greater than .99), the D.W.-values indicate the absence of autocorrelation of the residuals, the t-values of all coefficients are greater than two.

The main determinants of export and import demand are variables of economic activity and relative prices. In the import function, the explanatory variables are real GNP (and alternatively industrial production), an index of capacity utilization, and the relation between import prices and consumer prices for manufactures or between import prices and the GNP-deflator. In addition an indicator for the variation of tariffs was used. Exports were explained by a weighted average of industrial production of the eleven most important trading partners, and by the two types of exchange rate adjusted relative export price indices. As in the import functions, the tariff variable used in addition to the price variable does not only represent price effects of tariff changes but also additional effects of European economic integration. Short-run and long-run elasticities are summarized in table 1.

The estimated long-run income elasticities for Austrian imports of manufactures are - with one exception - smaller than one: they cover the range of .6 to .9. The price elasticities are - again with one exception - smaller than minus one. The results of the quarterly import functions show that in recent years the price elasticities decreased, whereas the tariff elasticities gained importance. In the most cases the adjustment lasts no longer than three quarters.

According to the quarterly functions for exports of manufactures, the long-run income elasticity is in the range of 1.5 to 2.o, for the period 1967/76 it is even higher. With annual data, calculated elasticities are somewhat lower though largely still exceeding unity. The value of the price elasticity is strongly influenced by the introduction of the tariff variable; in that case the price elasticity is reduced from about one to about one third. In any case it seems that export price elasticities have risen in recent years. The adjustment process for exports lasts much longer than for imports: after one year only two thirds of the effect of changes in the explanatory variables becomes reflected in the dependent variable, after two years this figure climbs to roughly 9o per cent.

The import price functions for manufactures reveal elasticities with respect to changes in exchange rates and foreign export prices of .8 and .9 in the quarterly and annual functions, respectively. In addition, variations of tariffs contribute with a small coefficient to the explanation of import prices. Two thirds of the adjustment of import prices to exchange rates, foreign prices and tariffs fall in the current quarter, after one year the adjustment process is completed.

Import prices together with wages (unit labour cost) determine the domestic price level. The elasticity of .3 of consumer

List of Variables

C	Capacity utilization rate (utilization of potential output).
EM	Import weighted Austrian exchange rate index
EX	Export weighted Austrian exchange rate index
M	Imports of manufactured goods at 197o prices
MN	Imports of manufactured goods at current prices
PC	Consumer price index for industrial goods
PM	Austrian import price index for manufactured goods
PQ	Deflator of gross national product
PR	Index of raw material prices
PW	Wholesale price index
PWF	Import weighted wholesale price index of eleven trading partners
PX	Austrian export price index for manufactured goods
PXF	Export price index of eleven trading partners weighted with Austrian import shares
PXFE	Exchange rate adjusted (double) weighted export price index of eleven trading partners (competitors)
PXFS	Export price index of eleven trading partners weighted with Austrian import shares expressed on Schilling basis (via the import weighted Austrian exchange rate index)
PXR1	Exchange rate adjusted relative export price index 1
PXR2	Exchange rate adjusted relative export price index 2
Q	Index of real gross national product
QI	Index of industrial production
QIF	Export weighted industrial production of eleven trading partners
T	Time trend
TA	Index measuring the reduction of tariffs on manufactured goods
ULC	Unit labour costs in industry
W	Average earnings in industry
X	Exports of manufactured goods at 197o prices
XN	Exports of manufactured goods at current prices

TABLE 1: Elasticities in import and export functions

Import Functions

Equation number	Period	Q impact	Q long-run	QI impact	QI long-run	PM/PC impact	PM/PC long-run	PM/PQ impact	PM/PQ long-run	TA impact	TA long-run	C impact	C long-run
1	6o.2-76.4	.49	.83			-1.33	-2.26			-.25	-.42	1.69	2.86
2	6o.2-76.4			.55	.71	-1.o2	-1.31			-.18	-.23	1.38	1.78
3	6o.2-76.4	.51	.72					-1.23	-1.75	-.15	-.21	1.58	2.24
4	6o.2-76.4			.67	.93			- .91	-1.27	-.13	-.18	1.1o	1.53
5	67.1-76.4	.45	.63			-1.23	-1.75			-.36	-.5o	1.86	2.64
6	67.1-76.4			.6o	.75	- .83	-1.o2			-.37	-.45	1.41	1.74
7	67.1-76.4	.49	.63					-1.16	-1.48	-.23	-.29	1.7o	2.16
8	67.1-76.4			.64	.75			- .69	- .81	-.29	-.34	1.2o	1.4o
9	6o -76	1.36				-1.71				-.22		1.56	
1o	6o -76			.74		-1.34				-.2o		1.36	
11	6o -76	.79						-1.76		-.17		2.15	
12	6o -76			.63				-1.7o		-.22		2.3o	

TABLE 1: (continued)

Equation number	Period	Export Functions: QIF impact	QIF long-run	PXR1 impact	PXR1 long-run	PXR2 impact	PXR2 long-run	TA impact	TA long-run
1	60.2-76.4	.77	1.55	-.10	-.20			-.16	-.32
2	60.2-76.4	.40	2.15	-.19	-1.05				
3	60.2-76.4	.76	1.50			-.07	- .14	-.17	-.34
4	60.2-76.4	.33	2.06			-.15	- .94		
5	67.1-76.4	1.62		-.32				-.31	
6	67.1-76.4	.63	2.65	-.38	-1.59				
7	67.1-76.4	1.53				-.21		-.32	
8	67.1-76.4	.55	2.40			-.31	-1.35		
9	61 -76	.62	1.07	-.47	- .80				
10	61 -76	1.16	1.64	-.24	- .34			-.21	-.29
11	61 -76	.49	.76			-.43	- .66		
12	61 -76	1.15	1.56			-.18	- .24	-.23	-.31

prices of manufactures with respect to wages is slightly lower than the elasticity of consumer prices with respect to import prices. The adjustment of domestic consumer prices to wages and import prices lasts more than two years. The estimated function for wholesale prices of finished goods can be regarded superior in terms of theoretical expectations: the coefficients for unit labour costs, import prices for manufactures and raw material prices are .5, .4 and .1, respectively. On the wholesale level, the adjustment process is much shorter. The adjustment period for the GNP-deflator is shorter than for consumer prices, but longer than for wholesale prices.

Export prices are determined by domestic prices, export prices of competitors and exchange rates. The adjustment takes place with a time lag, as only half of the reaction occurs in the current quarter. A one per cent increase of export prices of our competitors and/or of our exchange rate leads to an increase in our export prices which, in most cases, is considerably lower than one per cent. In most functions, the reaction of export prices to changes in the domestic price level is nearly proportional (though in a few cases the coefficient is considerably lower than one). Additional explanation of export price variation is produced by capacity utilization and a tariff variable. The coefficients of the export and import price equations provide the result that, in the short run, a devaluation (revaluation) worsens (improves) the terms of trade as import prices adjust faster to exchange rate changes than export prices (only after a time lag, export prices become affected by the import price induced increase of domestic prices).

5. SIMULATION OF THE EFFECTS OF EXCHANGE RATE CHANGES USING A SMALL MODEL FOR THE AUSTRIAN TRADE IN MANUFACTURES

The equation described in the preceeding section can be employed for quantifying the effects of exchange rate changes on prices and foreign trade. For this purpose we chose annual data

TABLE 2: Price functions *

Import Prices

(Dependent variable: PM)

Equation number	Period	PXF	EM	TA	PWF	PXFS	PM(1)	R^2 D.W.	S.E.
		Explanatory variables							
1	62.1-76.4	.6o9	.567	.o51			.273	.842	.o147
		(7.87)	(4.11)	(2.7o)			(3.o7)	1.721	
2	62.1-76.4		.185	.o7o	.548		.386	.83o	.o154
			(1.35)	(3.29)	(7.13)		(4.61)	1.816	
3	62.1-76.4			.o5o		.612	.271	.842	.o146
				(2.7o)		(7.99)	(3.o8)	1.715	
4	62 -76	.85o	.926	.o74				.9o4	.o113
		(1o.98)	(4.12)	(2.26)				1.2o8	

* The equations were estimated in differences of logarithms

TABLE 2: (continued)

Domestic Prices

Equation number	Period	Dependent variable	W	ULC	PM	PR	Lagged dep. variable	Const.	R^2 D.W.	S.E.
			Explanatory variables							
1	62.1-76.4	PC	.o49		o.59		.837		.939	.oo48
			(3.34)		(2.89)		(2o.62)		1.37o	
2	63.1-76.4	PW		.325	.355	.o76		.o21	.723	.o191
				(6.o2)	(3.92)	(3.oo)		(6.37)	.975	
3	63.1-76.4	PQ		.2o6	.197	.o62		.o36	.528	.o183
				(3.98)	(2.28)	(2.57)		(11.17)	1.681	
4	62 -76	PC	.127		.193		.56o		.879	.oo73
			(2.76)		(2.91)		(4.75)		1.861	
5	63 -76	PQ	.111		.247		.427	.o2o	.769	.o126
			(1.13)		(1.99)		(2.17)	(2.32)	2.361	

TABLE 2: (continued)

Export Prices

(Dependent variable: PX)

Equation number	Period	Explanatory variables PXFE/EX	PQ	PC	C	TA	PX(1)	Const.	R^2 D.W.	S.E.
1	62.1-76.4	.533	.467		.533		.533	-.o2o	.762	.o27o
		(5.86)	(2.5o)		(2.97)		(5.86)	(2.4o)	1.82o	
2	62.1-76.4	.356	.62o		.5o3	.o98	.489	-.o18	.782	.o262
		(3.4o)	(3.21)		(2.89)	(2.2o)	(5.43)	(2.2o)	1.913	
3	62.1-76.4	.313		.766	.584	.o96	.517	-.o12	.759	.o27o
		(2.41)		(2.o2)	(2.86)	(1.94)	(5.4o)	(1.38)	1.93o	
4	62 -76	.634	.993		.4o1	.151		-.o27	.663	.o322
		(5.41)	(4.46)		(1.88)	(2.83)		(2.74)	1.226	
5	62 -76	.672		.895		.236			.724	.o268
		(2.82)		(2.oo)		(2.2o)			1.983	

and formed a small (partial) model using trade functions with relatively low price elasticities.

The model is presented in detail in table 3 and can be summarized as follows: The Austrian import prices for manufactures are determined by foreign export prices, import weighted exchange rates and tariffs. Together with wages, import prices explain domestic prices for industrial goods. The relative development of the endogenous import and domestic prices is a determinant of real imports which are also influenced by real GNP (or industrial production), capacity utilization and tariffs. Imports at current prices are derived from the endogeneous import volumes and import prices. Export prices depend on the ratio of export prices of competitors to the export weighted Austrian exchange rate index; additional explanatory variables are the domestic price level (which is endogenous) and tariffs. The volume of exports is jointly determined by the ratio between exchange rate adjusted Austrian export prices and export prices of our competitors together with foreign demand. Exports at current prices are calculated similarly to imports. Finally the trade balance is obtained.

The simulations are based on the policy assumption that, in order to avoid a direct import of inflation, the import-weighted exchange rate index was kept frozen at the level of 1972. This implies that between 1972 and 1976 the export weighted exchange rate index would have risen by 9 per cent.

In the period 1972/1976 import prices would have increased by about 8 per cent and domestic consumer prices for industrial goods by some 2 1/2 per cent compared with the actual development. The rather modest reaction of consumer prices to exchange rate changes results from, on the one hand, an elasticity of import prices on exchange rate changes slightly lower than one and, on the other, the fraction of imports in the consumer basket of finished goods. Without the revaluation of the Schilling imports of manufactures at constant prices would in 1976 have been 6 1/2 per cent below actual figures. In value terms imports would not

TABLE 3: Simulation Model *)

$$PM = PM(1)*EXP[.85o*LOG(PXF/PXF(1)) + .926*LOG(EM/EM(1)) + \\ + .o74*LOG(TA/TA(1)]$$

$$PC = PC(1)*EXP[.127*LOG(W/W(1)) + .193*LOG(PM/PM(1) + \\ + .56o*LOG(PC(1)/PC(2))]$$

$$M = EXP[.o3o*T + .725*LOG(QI) - 1.36o*LOG(PM/PC*1oo) - \\ - .189*LOG(TA) + 1.374*LOG(C)]$$

$$MN = M*PM/1oo$$

$$PX = PX(1)*EXP[.672*LOG((PXFE/EX)/(PXFE(1)/EX(1))) + \\ + .895*LOG(PC/PC(1)) + .236*LOG(TA/TA(1))]$$

$$X = EXP[1.161*LOG(QIF) - .24o*LOG(PX*EX/PXFE) - .2o8*LOG(TA) + \\ + .292*LOG(X(1))]$$

$$XN = X*PX/1oo$$

---

*) The following functions were used for the simulation model: import price equation no. 4 (table 2), domestic price equation no. 4 (table 2), import equation no. 1o (table 1), export price equation no. 5 (table 2), export equation no. 1o (table 1).

have changed much, as volume and price effects of exchange rate changes cancel out. Compared with realized figures, export prices in 1976 would have been higher by 8 per cent, nominal exports by 9 per cent. For the trade balance, this would have resulted in a reduced deficit, the reduction amounting to 1o billions of Schilling in 1976 and to 26 billions of Schilling in the period 1973/1976.

In the partial model used so far, two important feedback processes are omitted: Firstly, the rise in real exports and the fall in real imports due to constant exchange rates or a smaller revaluation improve the foreign balance and increase GNP and capacity utilization. This in turn leads to higher imports and therefore to a reduction of the foreign balance and so on. Secondly, the partial model does not take into account that exchange rate induced domestic price increases will cause wage movements and additional price rises.

In order to evaluate the magnitude of these effects we tried to quantify the first of the described causal chains. By including its effect, the improvement of the trade balance in 1976 was reduced by at most one quarter; in the previous years the reducing effect was probably smaller. According to the results of a simultaneous wage-price-model,[13] consumer prices (lagged one year) influence the wage level with a coefficient of 2/3. In our price function the long-run wage coefficient amounts to .3. According to our simulation results, the price level in none of the years considered rose by more than one percentage point. The inflationary effects resulting from induced wage claims therefore are modest. The additional rise of the domestic price level increases real imports and reduces real exports; exports at current prices, too. The resulting negative trade balance effect is

13) A. Wörgötter, Lohn- und Preissystem für Österreich. Empirica 2/1977, pp.125-14o.

negligible. This implies that price increases are not anticipated and are reflected in wages only partly and with a time lag - an assumption which should be valid in Austria also in the future. Using this approach, the simulation results are not much biased by the fact that only a partial model was used. But even if we had used an inflation model of the Scandinavian type,[14)] a similar effect on prices and foreign trade would have resulted.

6. THE LIKELY EFFECTS OF A DEVALUATION IN A SMALL OPEN ECONOMY

Previous studies using data for total trade were hardly able to find plausible values for price elasticities which was presumably due to the quality of data. Therefore, we concentrated on manufactured goods and tried to improve the data base. By calculating rather sophisticated relative price indices and relative exchange rate indices we obtained comparatively high price elasticities and therefore considerable balance of payments effects. In the period 1972/76, Austria revalued its import weighted exchange rate by 8 per cent and its export weighted rate by 18 per cent. Under a hypothetical policy of maintaining a constant import-weighted exchange rate - implying a revaluation of the export weighted rate by just 9 per cent - the exchange rate effect alone would have improved the balance of payments by an amount approximately equal to 1o % of exports (or 9 % of imports). Such a relative devaluation would have increased prices as well: import prices by 8 per cent and consumer prices of industrial goods by 2 1/2 per cent. These price effects - to which text books seldom refer - would have reduced the original elasticity effect by approximately one third.

---

14) H. Frisch: Eine Verallgemeinerung des skandinavischen Modells der Inflation - Mit einer empirischen Analyse für Österreich. Empirica 2/1976. See e.g. Modell C, reduced form equation (6) on page 215.

In reality the effects would have been mitigated further by the following facts. The assumed relative devaluation would have increased the quantity of exports and reduced imports, thus giving rise to GNP and capacity utilization (effects not shown by our partial simulation model where GNP is treated exogenous). Higher demand and higher capacity utilization tend to enlarge imports and diminish exports, thus starting a dampened cumulative process. Its order of magnitude may be about one seventh of the original effect. The devaluation induced price increase will have lead to higher wages which in turn will have affected prices. Depending on the type of model this effect may differ in size, the estimation of which will require further work. We can be pretty sure, however, that price effect, capacity effect, and wage feedback reduce the balance of trade effect to almost one half of the original amount.

In summary, our experiments suggest that in a small open economy a devaluation reduces the deficit in the trade balance of manufactures but stimulates price increases. Exchange rate policy may therefore still be better suited as balance of payments policy than as price policy, even if the balance of payments effect is reduced, particularly by the price effect, to less than one half. However, our paper deals with manufactured goods only: in the four years investigated, they contributed less than one third to the deficit of the balance on current account; in the same period, services and transfers achieved a surplus, mainly from tourism. Is it likely that our results hold for the total current account as well? We have not investigated this question yet, we expect however that the answer would be affirmative.

7. SOME CONCLUDING REMARKS

Flexible exchange rates of the text book-variety are used by only a few countries and globally they are of limited importance. Small open economies normally adjust their exchange rate system according to the theory of the optimal currency area, i.e. they peg to countries which are among their major trading partners and which pursue economic goals similar to those of the country in question. This implies that in most cases they actually appreciate or depreciate on a trade weighted basis, and that the weighted effects differ for imports and exports. In the period 1972/76, Austria, e.g., by keeping its DM-exchange rate almost constant, appreciated against its trading partners by 8 per cent when measured by an import weighted index and by 18 per cent when measured by an export weighted index. This has resulted in external disequilibrium.

Generally, elasticities seem to be large enough for a positive balance of payments effect, even if more than half of it is eaten away by price, wage and capacity feedbacks. This implies that exchange rate changes have larger effects on the balance of payments than on the price level even in small open economies. Price effects however are not negligible and policymakers are well advised to use supporting measures to stabilize prices when they resort to devaluation as a means for improving the balance of payments. As the case of Austria reveals, it is not easy to decide on the type of exchange rate policy a small open economy should follow: there seems to be only a choice between holding the competitive position of the country unchanged by stabilizing the export weighted exchange rate, thereby accepting imported inflation; or stabilizing the price level by controlling the import weighted exchange rate which would induce a deterioriation of the current account.[15)]

---

15) The differences are the larger, the smaller the part of the balance on current account one concentrates on. For the total current account the effects will not compensate, however, because of differences in elasticities (for raw materials, manufactures, tourism and so on).

FINANCIAL POLICIES IN THE INDUSTRIALIZED COUNTRIES AND THE VOLATILITY OF EXCHANGE RATES*

Paul De Grauwe

1. INTRODUCTION

The last few years have witnessed a high volatility in the exchange rates of the major developed countries. Some observers have interpreted this as evidence of an inherent instability of a floating exchange rate system. Others have argued that the swings in the exchange rates were quite normal and even necessary given the intensity of the shocks to which the world economy was subjected and the divergent reactions to these shocks by the monetary and fiscal authorities of the industrialized nations.

In this paper an analysis is made of the importance of different intervention rules in the foreign exchange market for the process of exchange rate determination. The instrument of analysis will be a short-term exchange rate model which was estimated and simulated for a group of industrialized countries. The model incorporates recent theoretical findings about the determination of exchange rates,[1)] but adds additional features such as intervention rules in the foreign exchange market.

---

* This study was financed by the Agency for International Development under contract no. AID/OTR-147-77-48 and by the "Fonds Derde Cyclus" of the University of Leuven. Competent research assistance was provided by Carine Holvoet and Michael Steinbeisser. I am also indebted to Giorgio Basevi, Theo Peeters, Danny Leipziger and a number of staff people at the I.M.F., the U.S. Treasury and A.I.D. for comments and discussion. The responsibility for remaining errors is mine.

1) See Dornbusch (1976), Branson (1976).

In section 2 the basic model is presented. Section 3 contains the results of the dynamic simulations. Finally in section 4, the model is simulated for different intervention rules and conclusions are drawn.

2. THE MODEL

2.1 Generalities

The model consists of several national models. These national models have essentially the same structure and the equations, whenever possible, take on the same econometric specification. One purpose of the exercise is to link these different national models. This link is not yet complete, so that in this study only the results of the national models are reported.

The national models are composed of three blocks: first, a monetary block, second, a policy reactions block, third, a price block. The models are essentially short term in nature. They determine, among others, the spot exchange rate, the interest rate, the stock of international reserves. All "real" variables, e.g. the trade balance, national income in real terms, are assumed to be exogenous. The balance of payments is essentially considered a monetary phenomenon, i.e. deficits or surpluses have a counterpart in disequilibria in the money market. In addition since the model is applied to a period of floating exchange rates, the spot rate becomes a key variable in equilibrating the money market. Depending on the degree of intervention in the foreign exchange market the role of the spot rate in equilibrating the money market is reduced. With "complete" intervention (i.e. fixed exchange rates) the spot rate has no equilibrating function. With no intervention (pure flexible exchange rate) disequilibria in the money market are corrected by movements of the spot exchange rate. With limited intervention ("dirty floating" or managed floating) monetary disequilibria are taken care of by movements of both the spot rate and the stock of international reserves.

The domestic interest rates are linked internationally through the Euro-dollar rate. They influence the spot exchange rate directly through the interest parity relationship and indirectly through the demand for money.

Finally there is a feed-back mechanism between the price level and the spot exchange rate. Changes in the price level affect the demand for money and, therefore, the spot exchange rate. Conversely the spot exchange rate influences the domestic price level.

2.2 The equations of the model

2.2.1 The monetary block

This consists of a demand for money equation and a simple money supply mechanism. The money demand equation is a standard log-linear relationship:

$$\ln M_{it}^{d} = a_{1i} + a_2 \ln Y_{it} + a_3 \ln r_{it} + \ln P_{it} \qquad (1)$$

where M_{it}^{d} = the money demand in country i in quarter t

Y_{it} = the real GNP in country i in quarter t

r_{it} = nominal interest rate in country i in quarter t

P_{it} = the price level in country i in quarter t

The money supply equation is a definition:

$$M_{it}^{s} = m_{it} B_{it} \qquad (2)$$

where M_{it}^{s} = the money supply in country i in quarter t

m_{it} = money base multiplier in country i in quarter t

B_{it} = the money base in country i in quarter t

The money base (in changes) is defined as:

$$\Delta B_{it} = \Delta R_{it} + \Delta D_{it} \tag{3}$$

where R_{it} = the foreign component of the money base in country i in period t

D_{it} = the domestic component of the money base in country i in period t

The link between the domestic and the foreign money market is brought about by indroducing the interest parity relationship, i.e.:

$$r_{it} - r_{ET} = x_{it} \tag{4}$$

where r_{Et} = the Euro-dollar interest rate. This interest rate is chosen as the representative foreign interest rate

x_{it} = the percentage forward discount on the domestic currency, i.e.:

$$x_{it} = \left(\frac{F_{it} - S_{it}}{S_{it}}\right)4oo \tag{5}$$

where F_{it} is the forward (three-month) exchange rate and S_{it} is the spot exchange rate.[2)] All exchange rates are defined as prices of the dollar in terms of domestic currency.

Equation (4) cannot be expected to hold exactly. Uncertainty and transaction costs introduce deviations from interest parity. Therefore, for estimation purpose equation (4) was given the following econometric specification:

---

2) It should be noted that equation (4) represents the approximate interest parity relationship. In its exact form this relationship is as follows: $r_{it} - r_{Et} = x_{it} + x_{it}r_{Et}/4oo$. For estimation purposes the last term can be dropped as it is of second order of magnitude.

$$r_{it} = b_1 + b_2 r_{Et} + b_3 x_{it} \quad (6)$$

As the model is applied to European countries some simultaneous equation bias may occur since r_{it} also influences r_{Et}. The existing evidence, however, suggests that this reverse causation between individual European interest rates and the Eurodollar rate is limited. See Marston (1976).

Equilibrium in the money market implies:

$$M^d_{it} = M^s_{it} \quad (7)$$

2.2.2 The policy reaction block

Two equations describe the official intervention rules respectively in the domestic money market and in the foreign exchange market.

2.2.2.1 The domestic reaction function

Here we postulate that the monetary authorities manipulate the domestic component of the money base to achieve particular targets:

$$\Delta D_{it} = c_0 + c_1 \Delta R_{it} + c_2 \Delta Z_{it} \quad (8)$$

where Z_{it} is a vector of target variables specific to every country. It will include such variables as the unemployment rate, the rate of inflation, the rate of capacity utilization.

The coefficient of ΔR_{it}, i.e. c_1, expresses the degree to which the monetary authorities "sterilize" the impact of reserve in - or outflows on the domestic money market. If $c_1 = -1$ there is complete sterilization, if $c_1 = 0$ there is no sterilization. In general $-1 \leq c_i \leq 0$.

2.2.2.2 The foreign exchange market intervention

Major difficulties are encountered when trying to estimate an intervention function in the foreign exchange market. The main reason is that systematic intervention is a very recent phenomenon. Only since the beginning of 1973 have the monetary authorities systematically intervened in the foreign exchange market to guide the exchange rate along a particular target path. As a result the time series that can be used to estimate such an intervention function is too short, at least when using quarterly series. In addition, interventions in the foreign exchange markets have been extremely erratic. For these reasons no foreign exchange market intervention function was estimated. Instead, several alternative intervention rules were postulated. The model was then simulated dynamically, and the results compared.

Some simple intervention rules considered below are the pure floating system, a "leaning against the wind" rule, and a target exchange rate rule. The first one implies absence of intervention in the foreign exchange market, i.e.:

$$\Delta R_{it} = 0 \qquad (9)$$

The "leaning against the wind" type of rule can be specified as follows:

$$\Delta \ln R_{it} = e_1 \Delta \ln S_{it} \qquad (1o)$$

where $e_1 < 0$, implying that when the currency depreciates in the exchange market (S_{it} increases) the authorities of country i sell foreign exchange in order to reduce the rate of depreciation, without however preventing it. This is the kind of intervention rule used by the monetary authorities when these want to smoothen erratic movements of the exchange rate.

The target exchange rate rule takes the following form:

$$\Delta \ln R_{it} = e_2 (\ln S_{it} - \ln S^*_{it}) \tag{11}$$

where S^*_{it} is the target exchange rate of the monetary authorities; $e_2 < 0$, implying that when the market exchange rate exceeds the target exchange rate the monetary authorities sell foreign exchange. The target exchange rate itself will depend generally on one or more variables of the model, e.g. past exchange rates, the interest rate, the price level, etc.

2.2.3 The price block

The price equation used in the model is a nonlinear equation specified as follows:

$$P_{it} = \beta_1 (1-\lambda_1) \sum_{k=0}^{\infty} \lambda_1^k P^m_{it-k} + \beta_2 (1-\lambda_2) \sum_{k=0}^{\infty} \lambda_2^k U_{it-k} \tag{12}$$

and where P^m_{it} is defined as

$$P^m_{it} = P^M_{it} \left(\frac{S_{it}}{S_{i0}}\right) \tag{13}$$

where P^m_{it} = the import price index expressed in domestic currency

P^M_{it} = the import price index expressed in foreign currency

S_{i0} = the spot exchange rate in the base period

U_{it} = the unemployment rate in country i in period t

2.3 The structure of the model

In the following flow chart the interrelationships of the model are represented.

FIGURE 1: Flow chart of the model

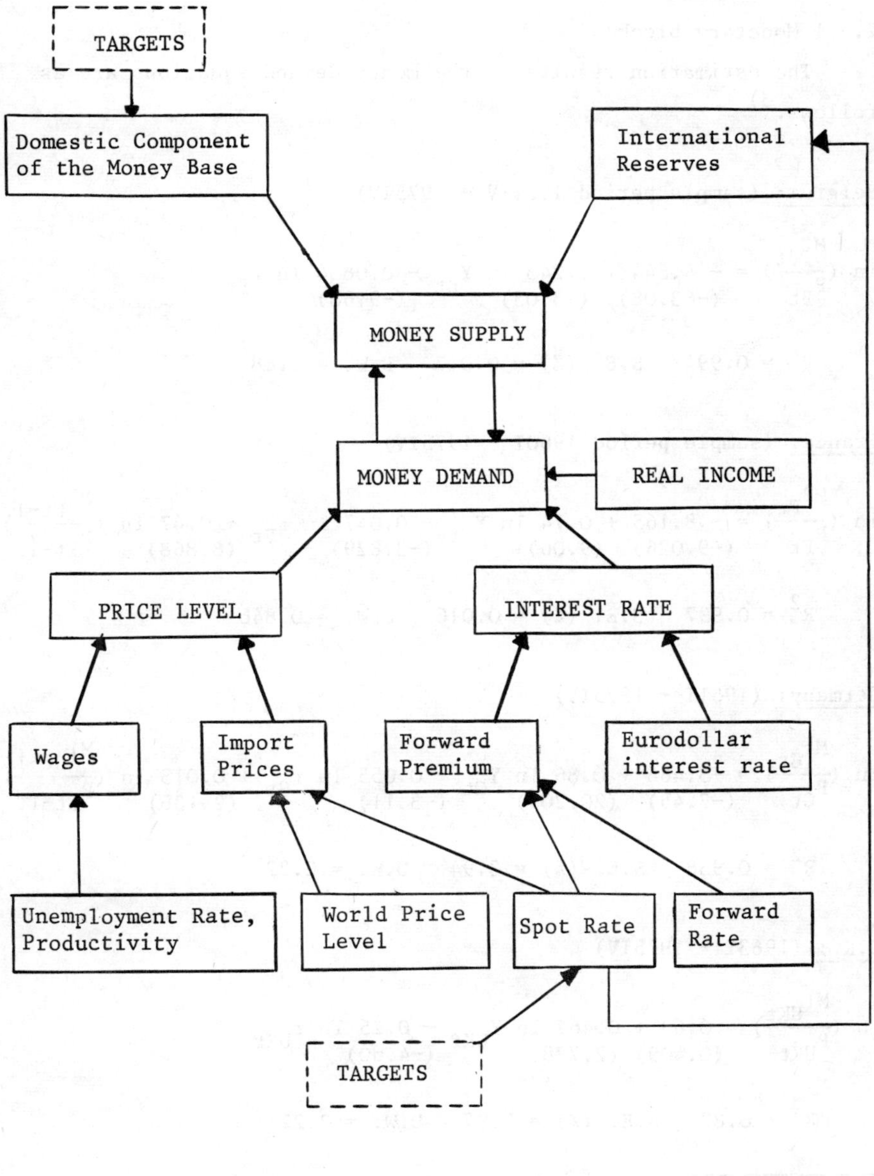

2.4 The estimated equations

In this section the estimated equations are presented. The definitions of the variables are presented in appendix.

2.4.1 Monetary block

The estimation results of the money demand equations are as follows:[3)]

Belgium: (sample period 1961IV - 1975IV)

$$\ln \left(\frac{M2_{Bt}}{P_{Bt}}\right) = \underset{(-63.08)}{-\ 4.644} + \underset{(73.03)}{1.243} \ln Y_{Bt} - \underset{(-9.68)}{0.0854} \ln r_{Bt}$$

$R^2 = 0.994$ S.E. (%) = 0.017 D.W. = 1.68

France: (sample period 1960I - 1975IV)

$$\ln \left(\frac{M2_{Ft}}{P_{Ft}}\right) = \underset{(-9.026)}{-\ 8.165} + \underset{(9.06)}{0.74} \ln Y_{Ft} - \underset{(-3.829)}{0.047} \ln r_{Ft} + \underset{(8.868)}{0.47} \ln \left(\frac{M2_{Ft-1}}{P_{Ft-1}}\right)$$

$R^2 = 0.997$ S.E. (%) = 0.016 D.W. = 0.846

Germany: (1961I - 1975IV)

$$\ln \left(\frac{M1_{Gt}}{P_{Gt}}\right) = \underset{(-7.45)}{-3.466} + \underset{(20.209)}{0.86} \ln Y_{Gt} - \underset{(-3.11)}{0.055} \ln r_{Gt} + \underset{(2.136)}{0.013} \ln \left(\frac{M1_{Gt-1}}{P_{Gt-1}}\right)$$

$R^2 = 0.938$ S.E. (%) = 3.94 D.W. = 2.22

U.K.: (1963I - 1975IV)

$$\ln \left(\frac{M1_{UKt}}{P_{UKt}}\right) = \underset{(0.409)}{0.63} + \underset{(2.738)}{0.467} \ln Y_{UKt} - \underset{(-4.60)}{0.25} \ln r_{UKt}$$

$R^2 = 0.82$ S.E. (%) = 3.94 D.W. = 2.22

---

3) Figures between brackets are t-ratios.

The estimation of the interest parity equations yields the following results:

Belgium: (sample period 1964IV - 1975IV)

$$r_{Bt} = \underset{(2.67)}{2.169} + \underset{(6.1698)}{0.57}\, r_{Et} + \underset{(4.584)}{0.30}\, x_{Bt} + \underset{(0.869)}{0.145}\, SP_{Bt}$$

$R^2 = 0.91$ S.E. = 0.68 D.W. = 1.85 $\rho = 0.767$

France:

$$r_{Ft} = \underset{(-0.75)}{-0.71} + \underset{(8.02)}{1.00}\, r_{Et} + \underset{(2.57)}{0.17}\, x_{Ft} + \underset{(2.01)}{0.97}\, SP_{Ft}$$

$R^2 = 0.64$ S.E. = 1.76 D.W. = 0.63

Germany:

$$r_{Gt} = \underset{(0.31)}{0.46} + \underset{(6.74)}{0.89}\, r_{Et} + \underset{(5.63)}{0.35}\, x_{Gt} - \underset{(-0.187)}{0.33}\, SP_{Gt}$$

$R^2 = 0.91$ S.E. = 0.88 D.W. = 1.36 $\rho = 0.89$

U.K.:

$$r_{UKt} = \underset{(2.71)}{2.503} + \underset{(5.82)}{0.62}\, r_{Et} + \underset{(7.318)}{0.612}\, x_{UKt} - \underset{(-0.214)}{0.040}\, SP_{UKt}$$

$R^2 = 0.91$ S.E. = 0.824 D.W. = 2.20 $\rho = 0.65$

2.4.2 The policy reactions block

Belgium: (1964IV - 1975IV)

$$\Delta D_{Bt} = \underset{(2.759)}{2.827} - \underset{(-0.138)}{0.90}\,\Delta R_{Bt} - \underset{(-1.579)}{1.24}\,\Delta r_{Et} + \underset{(0.89)}{0.135}\,\Delta\%P_{Bt} - \underset{(-7.28)}{10.03}\,s1_t$$
$$+ \underset{(7.81)}{11.23}\,S2_t - \underset{(-6.77)}{10.61}\,S3_t + \underset{(6.77)}{9.41}\,S4_t$$

$R^2 = 0.89$ S.E. = 5.185 D.W. = 2.36

France: (1964IV - 1975IV)

$$\Delta D_{Ft} = \underset{(2.56)}{8.23} - \underset{(-1.99)}{0.40}\,\Delta R_{Ft} - \underset{(-2.11)}{0.73}\,\Delta\%Y_{Ft} - \underset{(-0.53)}{0.15}\,\Delta\%P_{Ft} - \underset{(-0.86)}{0.935}\,S1_t$$
$$- \underset{(-0.85)}{0.935}\,S2_t + 4.13o\,S3_t - \underset{(-2.11)}{2.26}\,S4_t$$

$R^2 = 0.45$ S.E. = 4.17 D.W. = 2.34

Germany: (1960IV - 1975IV)

$$\Delta D_{Gt} = \underset{(0.249)}{0.168} - \underset{(-8.73)}{0.75}\,\Delta R_{Gt} + \underset{(7.10)}{0.45}\,\Delta KAP_G + \underset{(1.43)}{0.23}\,\Delta\%P_{Gt}$$

$R^2 = 0.76$ S.E. = 2.436 D.W. = 2.17

U.K.: (1964IV - 1975IV)

$$\Delta D_{UKt} = \underset{(1.91)}{38.71} - \underset{(-12.42)}{0.94}\,\Delta R_{UKt} - \underset{(-2.57)}{0.13}\,\Delta GF_{UKt} - 0.17\,\Delta\%P_{UKt} + \underset{(0.65)}{54.41}\,S1_t$$
$$- \underset{(-1.69)}{110.92}\,S2_t - 33.11\,S3 + \underset{(3.00)}{89.62}\,S4_t$$

$R^2 = 0.86$ S.E. = 98.15 D.W. = 2.30

2.4.3 The Price block

Belgium: (1959II - 1976IV)

$$P_{Bt} = \underset{(3.23)}{0.19}(1-0.37)(P^{m}_{Bt} - 0.97P^{m}_{Bt-1}) + \underset{(1.07)}{0.007}(1-0.965)(U_{Bt} - 0.37\,U_{Bt-1})$$
$$+ 0.37(0.97)\,P_{Bt-1} - 0.37\,(0.965)\,P_{Bt-2}$$

R^2 0.95 S.E. = 0.0016 D.W. = 2.305 $t_{\lambda 1} = 3.09$ $t_{\lambda 2} = 14.84$

France: (1961III - 1975IV)

$$P_{Ft} = \underset{(3.71)}{0.13}(1-0.49)(P^{m}_{Ft} - 0.96P^{m}_{Ft-1}) + \underset{(1.38)}{0.0037}(1-0.96)(U_{Ft} - 0.49U_{t-1})$$
$$+ (0.49 + 0.96)P_{Ft-1} - 0.0037(0.49)(0.96)P_{Ft-2}$$

R^2 = 0.96 S.E. = 0.0012 D.W. = 1.849 $t_{\lambda 1} = 0.49$ $t_{\lambda 2} = 0.96$

Germany: (1959III - 1975IV)

$$P_{Gt} = \underset{(1.29)}{0.027}(1+0.04)(P^{m}_{Gt} - 1.01P^{m}_{Gt-1}) + \underset{(0.41)}{0.0078}(1-0.1)(U_{Gt} + 0.04U_{Gt-1})$$
$$+ (-0.04 + 1.01)P_{Gt-1} - 0.04(1.01)P_{Gt-2}$$

R^2 = 0.88 S.E. = 0.001 D.W. = 1.57 $t_{\lambda 1} = -0.36$ $t_{\lambda 2} = 32.05$

U.K.: (1961III - 1975IV)

$$P_{UKt} = \underset{(0.26)}{0.01}(1 - 0.36)(P^{m}_{UKt} - 1.03P^{m}_{UKt-1}) - \underset{(-0.0575)}{0.001}(1-1.03)(U_{UKt} - 0.36U_{UKt-1})$$
$$+ (0.36 + 1.03)P_{UKt-1} - 0.36(1.03)P_{UKt-2}$$

R^2 = 0.96 S.E. = 0.0021 D.W. = 1.84 $t_{\lambda 1} = 2.10$ $t_{\lambda 2} = 13.05$

3. DYNAMIC SIMULATION

In this section the dynamic simulations are discussed. The Gauss-Seidel iterative procedure was used to solve the model. The purpose of these dynamic simulations is to provide the control solutions for the policy simulations. Given the lack of reliable estimates of official interventions in the foreign exchange market the dynamic simulations cannot be expected to yield good forecasts of the endogenous variables during the sample period.

As an example, the dynamic simulation of the model using the foreign exchange market intervention rule represented by equation (11) is reported. As the target rate the observed spot rate was selected. In other words it is assumed that the observed spot exchange rate has been the target rate all along. Table 1 contains the test statistics of the dynamic simulation of this model for Belgium, France, Germany and the U.K. As can be seen, despite the simple nature of the intervention rule the model tracks the observed spot exchange rates, money base and money supply relatively well. For the interest rate the absolute RMSE is expressed in percentage points, for the spot exchange rate in amount of domestic currency per dollar, for the money base, international reserves and money supply in billions of the national currency.

The results for the international reserves are less satisfactory. The RMSE are large. It indicates that the assumed foreign exchange market intervention rule is not yet able to capture the complex behavioral pattern of the monetary authorities in the exchange market.

4. POLICY SIMULATIONS

In this section the results of several policy simulations are reported. Three different disturbances will be analyzed, first an exogenous increase in the Eurodollar rate, second, a speculative cycle, third, a domestic monetary expansion. These shocks will be simulated assuming different foreign exchange market intervention rules.

TABLE 1: Dynamic simulation of the model (1972I - 1976IV), using intervention rule (11) ($e_2 = -2$)

	RMSE* absolute	RMSE* in percentage
(1) Domestic interest rate		
Belgium	1.357	22.778
France	0.954	12.260
Germany	1.821	25.609
U.K.	2.049	30.727
(2) Spot exchange rate		
Belgium	0.256	0.881
France	0.752	3.921
Germany	0.026	1.032
U.K.	0.007	1.883
(3) International reserves		
Belgium	52.967	28.427
France	8.151	22.110
Germany	26.147	31.337
U.K.	0.672	31.237
(4) Money base		
Belgium	0.792	0.277
France	1.492	1.143
Germany	0.347	0.453
U.K.	0.057	1.127
(5) Money supply		
Belgium	1.346	0.279
France	12.510	2.553
Germany	2.535	2.073
U.K.	0.149	1.386

* Root mean squared error.

The effects of the exogenous shocks are measured by comparing the endogenous variable of the policy simulation with the value of the same endogenous variable in the control solution. In the following, the impact and total effects will be reported. The former measures the effect during the same period of the exogenous shock. The second measures the effect when all adjustments have taken place.[4] This adjustment time has been set at six quarters in the simulation of the present model.

4.1 The effect of an increase in the Eurodollar interest rate (pure floating)

The effect of a one percentage point increase in the Eurodollar rate on the different endogenous variables of the model crucially depends on the kind of domestic monetary policy rules and of the foreign exchange market rules. In this section we concentrate on the importance of domestic monetary policy and we assume perfectly flexible exchange rates. The same exogenous increase of the Eurodollar rate was simulated under two alternative assumptions concerning the conduct of domestic monetary policy. First it was assumed that the monetary authorities follow a money base rule (model B) and second that they choose for an interest rate rule (model C). The impact and total effects of a one percentage point increase in the Eurodollar rate are given in table 2. The results of table 2 lead to the following observations. First, pure floating does not guarantee complete insulation of the money market from outside monetary shocks. An increase in the Eurodollar rate leads to an increase in the domestic interest rate when the money base is the target and to an increase in the money supply when the interest rate is the target. This increase in the domestic money supply following an increase in the Eurodollar rate may seem surprising. It is, however, a normal result when the interest rate is pegged:

---

4) see Theil (1971).

the Eurodollar induced increase in the domestic interest rate is blocked; this necessitates an increase in the money supply.

Second, when the monetary authorities peg the domestic interest rate the increase in the Eurodollar rate has a stronger impact effect on the exchange rate and on the price level than when the monetary authorities follow a money base rule. The exception is the U.K. where the choice of the target does not affect the result. This result must be interpreted as follows. With flexible exchange rates an increase in the Eurodollar rate has an expansionary effect on the domestic money supply. As a result the exchange rate has to increase more than under a money base rule in order to equilibrate the exchange market.

The results of table 2 also shed some light on the issue of the "overshooting"[5]. The results indicate that the impact effect of an increase in the Eurodollar rate on the exchange rate is higher than on the price level. In other words, in the short run the exchange rate has to deviate from purchasing power parity relationships (assuming PPP holds initially) in order to maintain equilibrium in the money market. The degree of overshooting is the highest for France and for Germany and the lowest for Belgium. This corresponds to a-priori expectations: overshooting is likely to be lower for small open economies than for larger less open economies. In small open economies currency depreciations are transmitted faster to the price index than in less open economies, and, therefore, reduce the possibility of overshooting.

The Eurodollar interest rate is dominated by the U.S. interest rate and, therefore, ultimately heavily influenced by the U.S.

---

5) This issue has been popularized by the writings of Dornbusch. See e.g. Dornbusch (1976). Note, that the term overshooting is not used here in the sense as used by Dornbusch, i.e. that the currency first depreciates and later appreciates. The present model provides no evidence for the latter phenomenon.

TABLE 2: Effect of a one percentage point increase in the Eurodollar rate

Country	Endogenous variable	Impact effect		Effects after 6 quarters	
		Model B	Model C	Model B	Model C
Belgium	dom. interest rate	0.042		0.044	
	spot exchange rate (in %)	0.425	0.503	0.483	0.488
	price level (in %)	0.110	0.164	0.180	0.160
	money supply in %		0.166		0.159
France	dom. interest rate	0.019		0.011	
	spot exchange rate (in %)	1.449	1.515	1.495	1.532
	price level (in %)	0.089	0.102	0.091	0.093
	money supply in %		0.105		0.105
Germany	dom. interest rate	0.007		0.006	
	spot exchange rate (in %)	0.599	0.653	0.648	0.599
	price level (in %)	0.017	0.018	0.017	0.016
	money supply in %		0.018		0.014
U.K.	dom. interest rate	0.002		0.0	
	spot exchange rate (in %)	0.263	0.259	0.256	0.255
	price level (in %)	0.015	0.017	0.016	0.016
	money supply in %		0.017		0.016

monetary policy.[6)] The previous results then suggest that while the U.S. monetary policy has a strong influence on the European exchange rates, the quantitative impact of a given U.S. monetary policy will depend to a certain extent on the kind of domestic monetary policy rules applied by the European monetary authorities. In general, when the latter follow policies of interest rate pegging a U.S. monetary policy action results in a stronger impact on

6) Marston (1974) provides strong evidence of this.

the European exchange rate than when European monetary authorities pursue a money base target.

4.2 The effects of a domestic monetary expansion (pure floating)

The previous simulations related to shocks originating outside the countries studied. We now concentrate on shocks originating inside those economies. Using model B, it was assumed that the target money base increases by a given amount, during six quarters. The results of the simulations are presented in table 3. They confirm the results on the overshooting issue arrived at in the previous section. Overshooting is more a problem for France, Germany and the U.K. than for Belgium (a small country). This can be seen from a comparison of the impact effects[7)] on the exchange rate and on the price level. In Belgium the monetary expansion leads to an immediate depreciation of the currency which is about 3 times as high as the increase of the price level, whereas in France, Germany and the U.K. the impact effect of a monetary expansion on the exchange rate is substaintially higher than the impact effect on the price level. The reason again is that for a very open economy the feedback effect of the exchange rate on the price level is stronger than in a more closed economy.

4.3 The effect of a speculative cycle (pure floating)

The question of how speculative movements affect the monetary systems of different countries has recently become of significant importance. The present model allows to analyse some aspects of this question.

The model was simulated assuming that an exogenous speculative cycle occurs. This cycle was assumed to take the form of a depreciation of the currency in the forward market followed by a return

---

7) Here we concentrate on the impact effects only. The long-run effects of a monetary expansion on the price level are not yet worked out satisfactorily in the present model.

TABLE 3: Effect of a 1o percent increase in the target money base

Country	Endogenous variable	Impact effect
Belgium	dom. interest rate	-2.491
	spot exchange rate (in %)	+2.028
	price level (in %)	+0.559
France	dom. interest rate	-1.805
	spot exchange rate (in %)	+2.675
	price level (in %)	+0.171
Germany	dom. interest rate	-2.130
	spot exchange rate (in %)	+1.482
	price level (in %)	+0.037
U.K.	dom. interest rate	-0.299
	spot exchange rate (in %)	+0.263
	price level (in %)	+0.006

to the initial level (-1 % in the first quarter, -2 % in the second quarter, -3 % in the third quarter, -2 % in the fourth quarter, -1 % in the fifth quarter). The effects on the spot exchange rate, the interest rate, the price level and the money supply were then computed. The results are presented in tables 4 and 5. Table 4 contains the results of simulating model B, i.e. the model in which the monetary authorities follow a money base target. In table 5 one finds the results for model C, i.e. the model with interest rate pegging.

As in the previous simulations we find that the impact of a same speculative cycle on the spot exchange rate and on the price level is different depending on whether a money base or an interest rate rule is followed.[8] In the former case a speculative movement has a smaller impact on those variables. In the case of

8) Again, the exception is the U.K.

an interest rate rule speculation has a more pronounced effect. This is especially the case in Belgium and France, but less in Germany.

A final point is that as in the case of an increase in the Eurodollar rate, perfect flexibility of the exchange rate does not allow a country to completely insulate its money market from outside monetary shocks. This is especially the case for Belgium where the interest rate and the price level are significantly affected by the speculative movement. It is less so for France, Germany, and the U.K. although with the interest rate policy we do find that speculation leads to a significant increase in the money supply.

From the preceding it can also be deduced that the relationship between the exchange rate, the money supply and the interest rate is far from clear-cut, at least in the short run. A depreciation of the currency may be accompanied by an increase in the money supply, or an unchanged money supply. It is conceivable that a depreciation goes together with a decline in the money supply, e.g. if the monetary authorities react to a speculative movement by monetary restriction. The same applies to the relationship between the exchange rate and the interest rate. This feature makes the use of simple reduced form regressions between exchange rates and monetary aggregates (or interest rates) uninteresting. In addition, it explains the sometimes bewildering movements of the exchange rates, the interest rates and the money supplies which have been observed in the recent past.

4.4 Simulation of the model under managed floating

In the previous sections we assumed a system of perfect flexibility of the exchange rate. In this and the following sections it will be assumed that the monetary authorities follow a simple intervention rule in the exchange market. The rule which is used is given by equation (11). The value of the parameter e_2 was set at -2. This implies that when the market exchange rate deviates

TABLE 4: Effect of a speculative cycle (model B : money base target)

Country	endogeneous variable	1972I	1972II	1972III	1972IV	1973I
Belgium	dom. interest rate	0.104	0.157	0.308	0.195	0.105
	spot exchange rate (in %)	0.891	1.862	2.729	1.830	0.912
	price level (in %)	0.273	0.658	0.946	0.616	0.300
France	dom. interest rate	0.013	0.021	0.027	0.014	0.005
	spot exchange rate (in %)	0.983	1.969	2.955	1.956	0.990
	price level (in %)	0.063	0.124	0.176	0.115	0.060
Germany	dom. interest rate	0.010	0.014	0.019	0.016	0.007
	spot exchange rate (in %)	0.978	1.994	2.921	2.015	1.002
	price level (in %)	0.027	0.056	0.081	0.056	0.027
U.K.	dom. interest rate	0.009	0.011	0.013	-0.001	-0.008
	spot exchange rate (in %)	1.052	2.067	2.955	2.137	0.990
	price level (in %)	0.072	0.145	0.204	0.142	0.066

TABLE 5: Effect of a speculative cycle (model C : interest rate target)

Country	endogenous variable	1972I	1972II	1972III	1972IV	1973I
Belgium	money supply (in %)	0.381	0.712	1.052	0.697	0.334
	spot exchange rate (in %)	1.035	2.008	3.006	2.007	1.006
	price level (in %)	0.368	0.711	1.052	0.686	0.334
France	money supply (in %)	0.077	0.136	0.196	0.131	0.067
	spot exchange rate (in %)	1.015	2.000	2.992	2.007	0.999
	price level (in %)	0.072	0.129	0.189	0.124	0.060
Germany	money supply (in %)	0.029	0.056	0.080	0.051	0.023
	spot exchange rate (in %)	0.995	2.038	2.968	2.006	1.019
	price level (in %)	0.028	0.057	0.082	0.054	0.027
U.K.	money supply (in %)	0.074	0.145	0.202	0.145	0.066
	spot exchange rate (in %)	1.036	2.046	2.948	2.127	0.990
	price level (in %)	0.076	0.147	0.206	0.145	0.065

from the target rate by 1 percent, the monetary authorities vary their stock of international reserves by 2 percent. Admittedly this is a crude intervention rule. Further research should make it possible to determine the sensitivity of the results to different intervention rules.

With managed floating the sterilization operation of the monetary authorities become important again. Therefore, exogenous shocks will be simulated under two alternative assumptions concerning sterilization. First, we use the sterilization coefficient as estimated in section 2.4.2. Second, we set this sterilization coefficient equal to zero, which means that the monetary authorities abstain completely from sterilization policies.

The model was simulated for a speculative cycle. The results are given in table 6. They highlight again the importance of domestic monetary policies, in casu sterilization policies, in the transmission process of exogenous disturbance. The most important results of table 6 can be summarized as follows. First, when the monetary authorities sterilize outflows of reserves, the impact of a given speculative cycle on the spot exchange rate will be substantially higher than when they abstain from sterilization policies. At the hight of the speculative cycle, the spot exchange rate depreciates about 5o per cent more with than without sterilization policies.

Second, as could be expected, when there is no sterilization of reserve outflows the domestic interest rate is much more affected by the speculative movement than when the authorities sterilize reserve outflows. The difference, of course, will depend on the size of the sterilization coefficient. Our simulation results suggest that, assuming sterilization coefficients as estimated previously, the impact of a speculative cycle on the domestic interest rate is reduced substantially in comparison with a situation of absence of sterilization policies.

Third, the same speculative cycle leads to a substantially higher reserve outflow when the authorities use sterilization

TABLE 6: Effect of a speculative cycle (model A: managed floating)

Country	endogenous variable	with sterilization					without sterilization				
		1972I	1972II	1972III	1972IV	1973I	1972I	1972II	1972III	1972IV	1973I
<u>Belgium</u>	dom. interest rate	0.157	0.232	0.499	0.423	0.375	0.302	0.667	1.494	1.558	1.436
	spot exchange rate (%)	0.873	1.804	2.569	1.645	0.686	0.699	1.415	1.689	0.691	-0.221
	price level (%)	0.315	0.637	0.890	0.555	0.226	0.202	0.503	0.567	0.246	-0.085
	inter. reserves (in %)	-1.735	-5.184	-9.872	-12.762	-13.947	-1.304	-4.044	-7.170	-8.461	-8.035
<u>France</u>	dom. interest rate	0.023	0.046	0.070	0.071	0.068	0.080	0.187	0.309	0.379	0.351
	spot exchange rate (%)	0.967	1.931	2.890	1.895	1.009	0.884	1.725	2.544	1.452	-0.462
	price level (%)	0.062	0.122	0.180	0.116	0.054	0.058	0.110	0.160	0.092	-0.027
	inter. reserves (in %)	-1.909	-5.594	-10.826	-14.111	-15.623	-1.749	-5.064	-9.723	-12.314	-13.106
<u>Germany</u>	dom. interest rate	0.059	0.126	0.221	0.296	0.264	0.412	0.806	1.403	1.642	1.374
	spot exchange rate (%)	0.979	1.932	2.826	1.795	0.534	0.759	1.457	1.934	0.785	0.067
	price level (%)	0.028	0.054	0.078	0.050	0.021	0.024	0.042	0.055	0.019	0.006
	inter. reserves (in %)	-1.911	-5.569	-10.655	-13.800	-15.168	-1.548	-4.355	-7.943	-9.314	-9.559
<u>U.K.</u>	dom. interest rate	0.019	0.033	0.047	0.024	0.025	0.089	0.174	0.276	0.230	0.248
	spot exchange rate (%)	1.052	2.067	2.955	2.137	0.990	1.052	2.067	2.955	1.895	0.740
	price level (%)	0.074	0.145	0.203	0.145	0.065	0.071	0.141	0.197	0.138	0.059
	inter. reserves (in %)	-2.035	-5.900	-11.143	-14.772	-16.401	-1.962	-5.726	-10.819	-14.306	-15.791

policies than when they do not.

The various results have the following interpretation: When the monetary authorities intervene in the foreign exchange market to guide the exchange rate in a particular direction, these interventions have monetary effects and will influence the domestic interest rate and the money base. The authorities can offset these effects with the use of sterilization policies. As a result the impact of a given exogenous shock, such as a speculative movement, on the domestic interest rate will be mitigated. However, sterilization policies under these circumstances also imply that domestic monetary policy is at cross purpose with the intervention policy. In other words, the authorities buy domestic currency to limit the depreciation of the currency following a speculative cycle, but at the same time they sell domestic currency in the money market (against bonds, or commercial bills). This policy maintains disequilibrium in the money market and, therefore, necessitates a larger adjustment in the exchange rate.

Our results, therefore, indicate that even in a managed floating system there is a trade-off between control over domestic monetary aggregates and control over the exchange rate. Too much emphasis on controlling domestic monetary aggregates will make it difficult for the monetary authorities to maintain a particular rule of intervention in the foreign exchange market.

The previous results also have some relevance when interpreting recent exchange rate developments. Since early 1973 one observes large swings in the exchange rates of major currencies, despite attempts at managing those exchange rates.[9)] At the same time the monetary authorities of most industrialized countries have continued

---

9) Studies by Brown (1976), Williamson (1976) and Suss (1976) indicate that intervention in the foreign exchange market has been higher during the recent period of managed floating than during the period of fixed exchange rates, for many currencies.

the old practice of sterilizing reserve flows. The latter policy may explain why the management of exchange rates by major industrialized countries has been relatively unsuccesful.

It is also evident that absence of management of the exchange rate, i.e. pure floating, would not necessarily have produced larger swings than those that occurred in practice.

5. CONCLUSION

The short term variability of exchange rates is an inevitable outcome of a pure floating exchange rate system. This variability is the result of the overshooting of the exchange rate following monetary disturbances. The simulations of the model for some industrialized countries confirms this feature of exchange rate adjustments. In addition, it was shown that this overshooting of the exchange rate is more pronounced for larger and less open economies than for smaller and more open countries.

The fact that some degree of volatility in the exchange rates is inherent in a pure floating exchange rate system does not imply that the monetary authorities cannot implement policies aimed at reducing this volatility of the exchange rates.

First of all, the monetary authorities can manage the exchange rate, i.e. intervene in the exchange market so as to reduce the short-term variations in the exchange rate. In fact, management of the exchange rate has been practiced, by most monetary authorities since 1973.

The results of the simulations suggest that managing the exchange rate is not sufficient to reduce the volatility of exchange rates. When monetary authorities offset their foreign exchange market interventions by opposite interventions in the domestic money market (sterilization policies) the former become ineffective. This kind of inconsistent monetary behavior has occurred frequently since 1973 and helps to explains why exchange rates have continued to behave erratically despite attempts at managing them.

Second, the volatility of exchange rates also depends on the kind of domestic targets the monetary authorities set for themselves. If monetary policies are conducted in terms of money base targets, speculative movements will have a lower impact on the spot exchange rates, than when policies are conducted in terms of interest rate targets. Although some industrialized countries recently have shifted to monetary aggregate targets, many still maintain policies aimed at interest rate targets. A stronger use of monetary targets may help to reduce the volatility of the exchange rates. The counterpart of this, however, is that the monetary authorities would have to accept a larger volatility of the domestic interest rates.

APPENDIX

Definition and source of variables

Variable name	Definition	Source
I. BELGIUM		
r_B	interest rate on "acceptations bancaires non visées"	I.R.E.S.
r_E	Euro-dollar three-month deposit rate	B.I.S.
Y_B	gross national product, billion BF	D.U.L.B.E.A.
$M1_B$	money stock (currency + demand deposits + time deposits up to 1 month)	National Bank of Belgium
x_B	three month forward discount	National Bank of Belgium
SP_B	dummy accounting for discrete parity changes (1971V, 1973I)	
D_B	domestic component of the money base	National Bank of Belgium
R_B	foreign component of the money base	National Bank of Belgium
P_B	consumer price index (197o = 1oo)	National Bank of Belgium
S1,S2,S3,S4	seasonal dummies	
P_B^M	import price index	I.M.F., International Financial Statistics
U_B	number of unemployed	Office National de l'Emploi

Variable name	Definition	Source
II. FRANCE		
r_B	"Taux de base bancaire" quarterly average	Banque de France
Y_F	Gross domestic product, billion FF	I.N.S.E.E.
$M2_F$	Masse monétaire SIE Raccordés, end of period, in billion FF	Banque de France
x_F	three-month forward discount	O.E.C.D. Economic Outlook
SP_F	dummy accounting for discrete parity changes (1969III, 1971IV, 1973I)	
D_F	domestic component of the money base	computed from Banque de France
R_F	foreign component of the money base	computed from Banque de France
P_F	consumer price index (197o = 1oo)	O.E.C.D., Main Economic Indicators
S1,S2,S3,S4	seasonal dummies	
P_F^M	import price index (197o = 1oo)	I.M.F. : I.F.S.
U_F	registered unemployed	O.E.C.D., M.E.I.

Variable name	Definition	Source
III. GERMANY		
r_G	Money market rate on three-month loans in Frankfurt	Deutsche Bundesbank, Monthly Report (D.B.M.R.)
Y_G	Gross National Product, in bill. D.M.	Deutsches Institut für Wirtschaftsforschung
M_G	money stock (MI) in bill. D.M.	D.B.M.R.
x_G	three-month forward discount	D.B.M.R.
SP_G	dummy accounting for discrete parity changes (1961I, 1969IV, 1971IV, 1973I, 1973II)	
D_G	domestic component of the money base	Computed from D.B.M.R.
R_G	foreign component of the money base	Computed from D.B.M.R.
KAP_G	index of capacity utilization in industry	Deutsches Institut für Wirtschaftsforschung
P_G	consumer price index	I.M.F. : I.F.S.
P_G^M	import price index	I.M.F. : I.F.S.
U_G	unemployment rate	Bundesanstalt für Arbeit

Variable name	Definition	Source
IV. <u>U.K.</u>		
r_{UK}	interest rate on three-month deposits with local authorities	Bank of England Quarterly Bulletin (B.E.Q.B.)
Y_{UK}	Total final expenditures at current prices, in millions of Ŀ	Central Statistical Office
M_{UK}	notes and coines in circulation + UK private sector sterling sight deposits, millions of Ŀ	Bank of England
x_{UK}	three-month forward discount	B.E.Q.B.
SP_{UK}	dummy accounting for discrete parity changes (1967IV, 1971IV)	
D_{UK}	domestic component of the money base	computed from B.E.Q.B.
R_{UK}	foreign component of the money base	computed from B.E.Q.B.
P_{UK}	consumer price index	O.E.C.D., M.E.I.
P^{M}_{UK}	import price index	I.M.F., I.F.S.
U_{UK}	total unemployed	Department of Employment

REFERENCES

Arndt, S., and Pigott, C., The Influence of Monetary Aggregates on Exchange Rates under the Current Float: Some Empirical Results, mimeo, 1976.

Branson, W.H., "Asset markets and relative prices in exchange rate determination", Institute for International Economic Studies (Stockholm), seminar paper no. 66 (Dec. 1976).

Brown, W., "World Afloat: National Policies Ruling the Waves", Princeton Essays in International Finance, no. 116, May 1976.

Dornbusch, R., The Theory of Flexible Exchange Rate Regimes and Macroeconomic Policy, Scandinavian Journal of Economics, 1976, no. 2.

Marston, R., American Monetary Policy and the Structure of the Eurodollar Market, Princeton Studies, no. 34, 1974.

Suss, E.C., "A Note on Reserve Use Under Alternative Exchange Rate Regimes", International Monetary Fund, Staff Papers, July 1976 (vol. 23, no. 2).

Theil, H., Principles of Econometrics, Wiley, 1971.

Williamson, J., "Exchange Rate Flexibility and Reserves Use", Scandinavian Journal of Economics (May 1976, vol. 78, nr. 2).

INTERNATIONAL ECONOMICS RESEARCH PAPERS

1. De Grauwe P., Conditions for Monetary Integration. A geometric interpretation, 1975, p.14.
2. De Grauwe P., A Model of European Monetary Interdependence under alternative exchange rates regimes, 1976, p. 46.
3. Denton G. and Peeters T., The Foreign Economic Policy of the European Community, 1976, p. 32.
4. De Grauwe P., A simple dynamic monetarist model for an open economy, 1876, p.16.
5. Kennes W., Activity analysis models as a tool for agricultural planning, 1976, p. 28.
6. De Grauwe P. and Holvoet C., On devaluation, terms of trade and wage indexing, 1977, p. 25.
7. Kennes W., Some further thoughts on the labor content of Belgian exports, 1977, p. 17.
8. Boll F., Monetary Policy and Dual Exchange Rates in Belgium, 1977, p. 32.
9. Peeters Th., Fiscal Stabilisation Policy in the Community and Monetary and Exchange Rate Policies, 1977, p. 18.
1o. Basevi G. and De Grauwe P., Vicious and virtuous circles. A Theoretical Analysis and a Policy Proposal for Managing Exchange Rates, 1977, p. 37.
11. Boll F., Capital Movements, Capital Controls, and the Exchange-Rate Regime, 1977, p. 33.
12. De Grauwe P., Kennes W., Peeters T. and Van Straelen R., Trade Liberalization with the Less Developed Countries. A Case Study of Belgium, 1977, p. 17.
13. Peeters Th., Problems of Monetary Policy in Open Economies, 1977, p. 18.
14. De Grauwe P., Floating Exchange Rates. Current Experiences and Policies of LDC's, 1978. p. 52.
15. De Grauwe P., Financial Policies in the Industrialized Countries and the Volatility of Exchange Rates, 1978, p. 31.
16. De Grauwe P., Steinherr A., Basevi G., The Dynamics of Intervention in Foreign Exchange Markets according to the Optica Rule, 1978, p. 26.

COMMENT ON P.DE GRAUWE, "FINANCIAL POLICIES IN THE INDUSTRIALIZED COUNTRIES AND THE VOLATILITY OF EXCHANGE RATES"

Sven W. Arndt

Among the questions which have occupied theoreticians and policymakers since the onset of generalized floating, one concerns the role of economic structure on exchange rate dynamics, the other the influence of policy on the behavior of exchange rates. Paul de Grauwe addresses himself mainly to the latter issue.

The insights he offers are derived with the aid of a model of the financial sector consisting of a money market, an interest-parity condition, a price equation, a reaction function governing the domestic behavior of the monetary authority, and several rules governing its exchange market intervention. The model is of the stock-adjustment type, with no flow responses permitted; the trade balance, for example, is strictly exogenous, implying that asset stocks can be altered only by official action. After equations resembling those of the theoretical model are estimated, the effects of a variety of exogenous shocks are simulated.

Recent empirical work has underlined the difficulties involved in tracking exchange rate behavior by means of single-equation regression models. de Grauwe's effort to enlarge the estimating model is thus a welcome step in the right direction. That step, however, should not be arbitrary and the direction of enlargement should be considered carefully. The choice of a reaction function is plausible, though such functions are difficult to model and unlikely to be stable over long periods of time. de Grauwe, who fits a single function over a period covering both fixed and floating rates, does not explain the selection of variables included in the reaction function nor the results obtained by estimation. Yet in the Belgian reaction function, for example, only the constant term and the seasonal dummies are significant, while in both Belgium and Germany an increase in the price index prompts the authorities to expand the monetary base.

In addition to the reaction function, de Grauwe has chosen to augment his model by fitting a price equation. While there are several ways of motivating this approach and of specifying such an equation, the author offers no explanations. Yet the price equation plays a central role in producing a phenomenon which de Grauwe calls "overshooting" and which he views as a major policy problem. "Overshooting" is, however, merely the necessary consequence of the specification of this equation in which import prices have a direct impact on the general price level, while the domestic sector is exogenous and thus does not. Moreover, the usefulness of the equation is compromised by the estimation results in which the price index rises when unemployment rises or falls moderately, and falls only when unemployment falls sharply. As a description of the estimation period in its entirety this version of stagflation is highly improbable.

The simulation results themselves offer no surprises and are, on the whole, consistent with recent theoretical developments and empirical findings. They suggest, for example, that the exchange rate changes resulting from various shocks are larger when the monetary authority pursues an interest-rate rather than a money-stock target. Further, the exchange rate change is proportionately larger than the associated change in the domestic price index, with the differential widening as the openness of the economy declines.

de Grauwe makes much of this phenomenon of "overshooting". This is surprising since the result follows directly from the model and depends simply on the relative weight of import prices in the overall price index. To take a simple example, suppose that in two countries, more or less identical except for the degree of openness, the price level must rise by a given proportion in order to equilibrate the money market. Suppose further that exchange rate changes are the only means of changing the price level. Then it is clear that in both economies the exchange rate will change proportionately more than the price index so long as the weight on imports is less than unity, and that the exchange rate in the less open economy will have to work harder and change by more in order to bring about the needed change in the price index. In the present model this outcome is guaranteed by the assumption that the domestic determinants of the price index are unaffected by any of the shocks.

de Grauwe is concerned that the exchange rate "deviates from purchasing power parity", although he has not indicated where and why purchasing power parity is relevant in his model and with respect to what price or price index it is defined. In the context of this model, this concern is thus extraneous and the drawing of policy conclusions unwarranted. More important, there is an implicit suggestion here that the exchange rate should not move more than the "fundamental" variables of the system. In the debate over the efficacy of floating exchange rates, this "fundamentals" argument has appeared in various guises with many commentators suggesting that the system performs poorly whenever exchange rates are more volatile than the fundamentals.

The argument is, however, fallacious when applied to economic systems in which different markets adjust at different speeds to a given disturbance. In economies in which labor and commodity markets respond more sluggishly than asset and foreign exchange markets, the opposite is more nearly correct: exchange rates and asset prices will initially vary more than such fundamentals as employment and output, wage rates and commodity prices, etc. By absorbing the initial impact of a shock, the exchange rate is doing its job and in doing it providing other variables with the extra time needed to adjust. To argue that the exchange rate should have changed by no more than the observed change in fundamentals is to misunderstand its function; to use the observed volatility or lack thereof in other variables as an indicator of the efficacy of a system of floating rates is to apply an inappropriate standard.

With respect to another popular issue, de Grauwe concludes that flexible exchange rates do not "guarantee complete insulation of the money market from outside monetary shocks". This is correct, but somewhat off the mark. The traditional concern has been over the extent to which floating rates provide autonomy with respect to the money supply rather than the money market. No one would expect floating rates to insulate the entire money market in a world of substitutable assets and interrelated financial markets.

de Grauwe points out correctly that the relationships among interest rates, exchange rates and money supplies are "far from clearcut". This is a point worth making and repeating. It follows from the fact that in most situations interest rates and exchange rates are endogenous and not related in a simple causal sense, and that money supply represents only one side of the money market. The author is on the mark when he warns against the use of "simple" reduced form regression analysis, but he must recognize the limitations of his own results which are obtained in the context of rather special experiments.

One such experiment involves a "speculative cycle" which appears and disappears without cause or motivation and without being related to any other variable in the system; it is in fact an exogenous change in the forward rate. This ad hoc treatment of expectations is unfortunate in light of substantial recent evidence suggesting that expectations and the manner in which they are formed play a crucial role in determining the short-run behavior of exchange rates. A preferred alternative is for expectations to be endogenized and to reflect anticipations not only about exchange rates but about other related variables such as commodity prices.

In another simulation experiment, the "target" exchange rate determining official intervention is assumed to be the observed spot rate. Since in that case $(\ln S_{it} - \ln S^*_{it}) = 0$ and thus $\Delta \ln R_{it} = 0$, the distinction between this rule (equation 11) and the one for pure floating (equation 9) is blurred and statistically intractable, which may explain the poor root-mean-squared-errors for international reserves reported in Table 1.

These experiments were clearly selected for their simplicity. Their virtue is that they hold the number of endogenous variables to a minimum; their defect is that they suppress important elements in the adjustment mechanism. (In this respect, the present model represents a step backward from recent single-equation studies in which (rational) expectations are modeled explicitly.)

In sum, de Grauwe is to be commended for attempting to enlarge on the single-equation model and particularly for his efforts to bring the monetary authorities to stage-center. A great deal of work remains, however, both in terms of model specification and the design of simulation experiments before the more interesting questions about exchange rate dynamics can be answered.

COMMENT ON P.DE GRAUWE, "FINANCIAL POLICIES IN THE INDUSTRIALIZED COUNTRIES AND THE VOLATILITY OF EXCHANGE RESERVES"

Alfred Steinherr

This paper is a very timely empirical contribution to the current discussion on flexible exchange rates and official intervention in exchange markets. The simulation results help to understand better the various effects of monetary policies, exchange rate intervention, and external shocks. They are therefore extremely helpful for policy discussion.

My comments can be regrouped under three headings: first, they concern the theoretical model; second, the estimation results; and third, the interpretation of the results.

1. THE MODEL

The model is centered on the money market. Money supply is defined as money base times a money multiplier. The latter is computed so as to maintain the definition while the two components of monetary base, domestic credits and international reserves, are endogenized through reaction functions. But only the reaction function for domestic credit creation is estimated. Several reaction functions for foreign exchange intervention are postulated for simulation purposes. Money demand is being estimated and equality between supply and demand for money determines the exchange rate. Of the three arguments of the money demand function one, real income, is exogenous whereas the other two are endogenized: Nominal interest rates via the interest rate parity relation and prices through their dependence on the exchange rate (and endogenous demand pressure as well as lags). Perhaps surprising is the fact that in this kind of model the forward rate is left exogenous. Fluctuations in the spot rate, or in interest rates, produce no effects on forward rates, nor, of course, on expected future rates that are not included into the model. Endogenous speculation is thus assumed away.

The flow chart is a little bit misleading about the structure of the model. For example, it indicates that the spot rate is exclusively determined by the forward rate. But, as explained above, it is determined by money market equilibrium conditions.

One of the most interesting aspects of the model is that it is applied to a set of highly interdependent economies. Asymmetries in structure, differences in policy behavior or effectiveness, and effects of being interlocked can be analyzed. So far the individual country models are not yet tied together but this is the objective for future research.

2. ESTIMATION

Equations are estimated by OLS. This raises, of course, the question of how serious the simultaneity bias is. As shown by the flow chart the structure of each national model is highly interdependent. My own experiments have shown that the estimated parameters take on significantly different values when the model is estimated with two-stage least squares. In addition there is an interdependence among the country models so that, eventually, the whole model should be estimated simultaneously.

All equations are estimated for roughly the period 1961 to 1975 on the basis of quarterly data. This spans three different exchange rate regimes: the fixed rate system, the intermediate stage from 197o to 1973, and finally the floating rate system. One may wonder whether the behavioral functions have been stable for the entire time period. Reaction functions of policy makers certainly were different under different regimes. But even the money demand function or the interest rate parity relation look different. I have estimated these functions for the periods 1961 to 197o, 1961 to 1971, 1961 to 1977, 1961 to 1976 and obtained for each observation period substantially different results.

Let us now turn to the estimation of individual equations.

DEMAND FOR MONEY

The income elasticity ranges from o.467 for the UK to 1.243 for Belgium and is statistically significantly different from one for the UK. For France and W-Germany the lagged dependent variable is highly significant, for Belgium and the UK not! The question now is whether these results really reflect differences in behavior and structure or whether the equations are not properly specified for all countries. I would rather lean towards the second alternative. A priori there are no good reasons why adjustment in the French money market should take twice as long as in the Belgian market. The D.W.-statistic also suggests misspecification of the equation for France.

INTEREST RATE PARITY

Autocorrelation of the error terms is a general problem here. What is puzzling is that the coefficients of r_{Et} and X_{Bt} are very different from each other and from 1, the value to be expected a priori.

DOMESTIC CREDIT CREATION

The estimation results are not entirely satisfactory. A major reason is probably the non-constancy of the reaction function over the estimation period.

PRICE EQUATIONS

Unemployment is never significant so that domestic prices are exclusively explained by their own past values and current and past import prices. More information on how this non-linear equation was estimated would be desirable.

3. SIMULATION RESULTS

Not all simulation experiments can be discussed here so I will concentrate on one: the effect of an increase in the Euro-dollar interest rate. The results indicate several important features. First, the importance of the kind of monetary policy pursued. Second, pure floating cannot guarantee complete insulation of the money market from outside monetary shocks. Third, the model generates "overshooting".

I would like to focus more particularly on the exogeneity of the forward rate and the absence of speculation in the pure floating model with an interest rate rule (model C).

With domestic interest rates fixed in the money market and the forward exchange rate given, the interest arbitrage condition alone determines the spot exchange rate. Hence, neither relative prices nor speculation enter here into the determination of the spot exchange rate. The simulation results are, of course, conditioned by these features.

If the rate of interest on Euro-dollars increases the spot price of domestic currency must depreciate: with the forward rate and domestic interest rates fixed, demand for dollars increases, the price for domestic currency falls until the forward premium compensates for the interest differential. Depreciation of the exchange rate tends to affect domestic prices but only with lags. The outcome is therefore necessarily overshooting. Moreover, the exchange rate remains permanently at a depreciated level independently of how prices react. The possibility of a vicious circle, where higher domestic prices feedback the exchange rate is thereby excluded.

However, as argued before, I find it more realistic to assume that forward rates also start moving and take on part of the adjustment. Overshooting may then still exist but it would not be a necessary outcome anymore. One possibility is that with an increased demand for dollars, the spot and forward rates depreciate and overshooting would be even stronger. I find this case possible, but unlikely. With covered arbitrage operations the future demand for domestic currency increases and the forward rate should appreciate; this would reduce the necessary depreciation of the spot rate. However, the case I find most convincing is the following. If interest rates on Euro-dollar deposits increase permanently this is likely to reflect an inflation differential. Hence, if purchasing-power-parity reflects the long-run exchange rate an appreciation of the domestic currency should be expected. In this case interest rate parity can be maintained by a movement of the forward rate without overshooting of the spot rate. It seems therefore that necessary overshooting is the result of the particular assumptions of the model where the interest-rate-parity condition alone determines the spot rate and where, since expectations are constant, one does not allow prices to have any influence on the spot rate.

To conclude, I would like to congratulate the author for his very clever and most stimulating work and I would like to express my hope that exchange rate expectations will be introduced into this highly interesting model and that the model will be made truly simultaneous.

LIST OF EDITORS AND CONTRIBUTORS

Aoki, Masano, Dr., Prof., School of Engineering an Applied Science, University of California, Los Angeles

Arndt, Sven W., Dr., Prof., Department of Economics, University of California, Santa Cruz

Basevi, Giorgio, Dr., Prof., Department of Economics, University of Bologna

Bender, Dieter, Dr., Prof., Department of Economics, University of Essen

Bernholz, Peter, Dr., Prof., Institute of Social Research, University of Basel

Bronfenbrenner, Martin, Dr., Prof., Department of Economics, Duke University, Durham

Claasen, Emil, Dr., Prof., Université de Paris-Dauphine

Cohen, Benjamin J., Dr., Prof., Fletcher School of Law and Diplomacy, Tufts University, Medford, Mass.

Dewald, William G., Dr., Prof., Department of Economics, University Ohio State, Columbus

Fase, Martin M. G., Dr., De Nederlandsche Bank, Amsterdam

Frenkel, Jakob A., Dr., Prof., Department of Economics, University of Chicago

Frisch, Helmut, DDr., Prof., Department of Economics, Technical University of Vienna

Gaab, Werner, Dr., Prof., Department of Economics, University of Mannheim

De Grauwe, Paul, Dr., Prof., Centrum of Economic Studies, University Leuven

Handler, Heinz, Dr., Austrian Institute of Economic Research, Vienna

Henderson, Dale W., Dr., Assistant Officer, Federal Reserve System, Washington, D. C.

Huijser, A. P., Dr., De Nederlandsche Bank, Amsterdam

Kugler, Peter, Dr., Doz., Department of Statistics, University of Basel

Lehment, Harmen, Dipl.-Volksw., Dr., Institute of World Economics, University of Kiel

Muennich, Frank E., Dr., Prof., Institute of Economic Theory, University of Innsbruck

Nadiri, Isaq M., Dr., Prof., Graduate School of Arts and Science, University New York

Neumann, Manfred J. M., Dr., Prof., Department of Economics, Free University of Berlin

Nowotny, Ewald, Dr., Prof., Institute of Public Finance, University of Linz

Salant, Walter S., Dr., The Brookings Institution, Washington, D. C.

Schebeck, Fritz, Dr., Austrian Institute of Economic Research, Vienna

Schelbert, Heidi, Dr., Prof., Institute for Empirical Research in Economics, University of Zürich

Schiltknecht, Kurt, Dr., Priv. Doz., Swiss National Bank, Zürich

Schröder, Jürgen, Dr., Prof., Department of Economics and Statistics, University of Mannheim

Schwödiauer, Gerhard, Dr., Prof., Department of Economics, University of Bielefeld

Siebke, Jürgen, Dr., Prof., Department of Macroeconomic Theory, University of Essen

Socher, Karl, Dr., Prof., Institute of Economic Theory and Policy, University of Innsbruck

Solomon, Robert, Dr., The Brookings Institution, Washington, D. C.

Steinherr, Alfred, Dr., Prof., Université Catholique de Louvin, Belgium

Suppanz, Hannes, Dr., Institute for Advanced Studies, Vienna

Tichy, Gunther, Dr., Prof., Department of Economics, University of Graz

Viotti, Staffan, Dr., Prof., Institute of International Economic Studies, University of Stockholm

Vosgerau, Hans-Jürgen, Dr., Prof., Department of Economics and Statistics, University of Konstanz

Printed by Printforce, the Netherlands